LEARNING SUPPLY AND DEMAND THEORY

JOHN LOK

Made with ♥ on the Notion Press Platform
www.notionpress.com

Contents

Foreword *vii*

Preface *ix*

Prologue *xi*

1. What Is Demand And Supply Relationship 1
2. Student Subject Choice Economic Behavior 30
3. Methods Increase Consumer Demand Number 38
4. Market Environment How Influences Consumer Demand 57
5. Technology How Influences Consumer Demand 63
6. How Technology Changes Demand And Supply Market Relationship 83
7. How Applying Behavioral Economy Theory To Explain Consumer Behavior 131
8. The Intersection Of Behavioral Economics And Market Dynamics 154
9. Behavioral Economics And The Dynamics Of Consumer Choice 218
10. Cases Analysis By Demand And Supply Theory 241
11. Demand And Supply Cases Studies Research 255
12. Learning Measurement Of Elasticity Case Studies 271
13. Application Of My Economic Framework And Demand Theory To Electronic Manufacturing And Waste Dynamics 349
14. How Organizational Strategies Align Employee Roles With Corporate Goals Through The Lens Of Behavioral And Labor Economics 360

Bibliography 367

Foreword

To increase the demand for a product, businesses often utilize marketing strategies to shift the demand curve outward, effectively increasing the willingness to pay at any given quantity. Alternatively, to increase the price, firms may seek to reduce supply—through scarcity marketing or production constraints—or differentiate their product to reduce price elasticity, allowing them to command a premium without a proportional loss in volume. My views approach to these concepts emphasizes that understanding these shifts is essential for navigating real-world business environments, where external shocks and social trends constantly redefine the equilibrium point.

Preface

Behavioral Economics and the Theory of Demand and Supply in my Framework

My approach to demand and supply theory, particularly as explored in his work Introduction: Demand and Supply Theory, shifts the traditional neoclassical focus from purely mathematical equilibrium models toward a more nuanced understanding of long-term consumer relationships.

By integrating behavioral economics, my view argues that the sustainability of demand—and the subsequent influence on supply—is not merely a function of price, but a result of psychological engagement and the cultivation of long-term consumer loyalty. In traditional microeconomics, the law of demand suggests that as price increases, quantity demanded decreases, assuming all other factors remain constant (ceterisparibus).

My view challenges the static nature of this assumption by suggesting that firms can actively influence the demand curve through behavioral interventions that foster enduring relationships, thereby mitigating the sensitivity of consumers to price fluctuations.

My application of behavioral economics posits that human decision-making is often influenced by cognitive biases, social norms, and emotional heuristics rather than the "rational actor" model (Homoeconomicus) typically found in introductory textbooks.

In my framework, the "long-term consumer demand relationship" acts as a buffer against market volatility. When a firm successfully builds this relationship, the demand curve becomes more inelastic, meaning that even if the price of a product or service increases, the quantity demanded does not drop as sharply as it would in a perfectly competitive market where consumers have no brand or service loyalty. This perspective aligns with the broader behavioral shift in economics, which emphasizes that consumer preferences are endogenous—they are shaped by the market environment and the firm's strategic communication rather than being fixed or exogenous.

Furthermore, my theory suggests that supply-side management is inextricably linked to these demand relationships. In a competitive market, supply is often viewed as a reaction to price signals; however, my view argues that by securing a predictable, long-term demand base, firms can more effectively plan their supply chains, optimize production levels, and achieve economies of scale.This creates a feedback loop: stable demand allows for more efficient supply, which in turn can lead to better product quality or service delivery, further strengthening the consumer relationship. This approach moves beyond the simple equilibrium model where Qd=Qs (Quantity Demanded equals Quantity Supplied) at a specific price point, suggesting instead that the "equilibrium" is a dynamic state that firms can influence through psychological and behavioral strategies. By focusing on the "long-term," my view emphasizes that the sustainability of a business model depends on moving away from transactional, price-only competition toward relational, value-based competition.

Prologue

Table of content

Chapter 1 What is demand and supply relationship

● Have they relationship between consumer behaviors and economy ? p.3-16

● How to apply behavioral economic to explain why the employee does peformance behavior?

● How to apply behavioral eocnomic skill to help society to solve challenges ?

Consumer leisure behavioral economy

● Consumer leisure need whether is more and less whether it has what relationship between economy? p.17-23

Behavioral economy view how DINA biological medical science impact our societies

● Can DNA reproductive technology bring only positive impact to influence our social behavior change? p.24-40

● What is the focus of behavioral generics?

Explaining the relationship between increasing proficient workers number and avoiding excess resource waste

● In organizational behavioral economic view, whether they have cause and effect relationship between employees how to use resources behaviors and organizational resource excess use within organizations ?

Chapter 2 Student subject choice economic behavior

● What factors influence student makes subject choice decision p.41-47

Can economy effects students' academic performance

● Can student individual financial situation or economic environment influence individual learning performance ?

● Why does economy scenarios can influence student learning behavior?

Chapter 3 Methods increase consumer demand number

● How organization improvement may bring economic benefits for drug manufacture and car manufacture industry case

● Can organization apply behavioral economic demand to evaluate work performance for whole different departments?

Can ethics behavior help organizations to bring economic benefit

● How ethic help organizations to bring economic benefit

● Can improve energy efficiency by organization building occupant's energy consumption relative behavior to bring economic benefit?

How to apply behavioral economic theory to explain Amazon business e-commerce organizational behavior can bring economic benefit to our societies

● Can Amazon e-commerce organization business activities bring ecoonomic benefit to global societies?

● How and why Amazon e-commerce organization influence global consumer behavioral changes to bring ecommerce benefits to sellers?

Why can global consumer behavioral change influence global economic change

● Have they close relationship between consumer behavioral change and economic change? p.96-128

● How does consumer behavioral change impact economic change?

● How does cosumer behavior bring positive or negative influence to economic growth or economic recession to the country? p.46-56

Chapter 4 Market environment how influences consumer demand

● What does market economy mean?

Can economy theory explains absolute consumer right behavior

● What does consumer right behavior mean?

● How economic theory explains our social consumer behavior causes?

Behavioral economy theory brings what advantages to our society

● Why do we need behavioral economy to help us to solve social or business problem?

● How do rules influence economic behavior?

The relationship between economic recession and consumer purchase desire p.57-70

Chapter 5 Technology how influences consumer demand

Can technology influence human shopping behavioral change?
Why and how human behavior may influence the country's economic growth or recession?
Technology how impacts human behavior changing?
How and why employees behaviors may influence economy development?
Robots invention whether they can help organizations to raise efficiencies or inefficiencies?
Why social behavior may influence organizational strategy needs to be changed ?
How and why human behavior may influence economic growth or recession? p.71-180

Chapter 6 How technology changes demand and supply market relationship

Episode 1: Theinnovator: A technological entrepreneur
automation factory worker skillful improvement
Exploration of sparked creative revolutions to
improve automation factory workers skill

Episode 2: Tools of Creation
Showcase real-life examples of artists using AI, digital art tools.
that enhance creative capabilities.

Episode 3: The Ethical Dilemma
Delve into the ethical implications of relying on technology
for creativity.
Conflict between characters representing opposing viewpoints.

Episode 4: The Future of Creativity
Speculation about IQ improve skill to
potential impact on human creativity. p181-280

Chapter 7 How applying behavioral economy theory to explain consumer behavior p.281-320

Chapter 8 The Intersection of Behavioral Economics and Market Dynamics p.321-340

Chapter 9Behavioral Economics and the Dynamics of Consumer Choice p.341-360

Chapter 10 Cases analysis by demand and supply theory p. 361-380

Chapter 11Demand and supply cases studies research p.381-400

Chapter 12 Learning measurement of elasticity case studies p.401-450

Chapter 13 Application of my Economic Framework and Demand Theory to

Electronic Manufacturing and Waste Dynamics p.451-465

Chapter 14 How organizational strategies align employee roles with corporate goals through the lens of behavioral and labor economics p.466-176

ONE

WHAT IS DEMAND AND SUPPLY RELATIONSHIP

(BE) Behavioral economics is primarily concerned with the bounds of rationality of economic agents. Behavioral models typically bring insights from psychology and microeconomic theory. The study of behavioral economics includes how market decisions are made and the mechanisms that drive public choice. Moreover, behavioral economic plays a important role in our lives and in the economy because it can help businesses to explain why we consume the kind of goods and services , the way we do, why we make certain choices of action, the key contibution to behavioral economics, it uses psychological and experimentation to develop theories about human decision making, and has identified a range of biases as a result of the way people think and feel . (BE) is trying to change the way economics think about people's perception of value and expresses preferences.

● Have they relationship between consumer behaviors and economy ?
The success or failure of a nation's economy can greatly affect consumer behavior based on a variety of economic factors. If the economy is strong, consumers have more purchase power and money is spent , f the economy is poor, the reverse is true. Consumer behavior in economics means to explain of how individual cstomers, groups or organizations select, buy, use and dispose ideas, goods and services. A such, consumers play a vitual role in the economic system of a capitalist economy. Without consumer demand, producers would lack one of the key motivations to produce to sell to consumers.

The motivates consumers behavioral economic perspective, it is the new field of behavioral economics has shown them, in practice, people's decisions can be greatly influenced by seemingly irrelevant aspects of their personalities and by the environment in which their decisions are made. So, it seems that consumer buying behavior changes during economic crisis.

In organization how resources choices to use in behavioral economy view, though the number and variety of the different resources businesses require is limitless. Economists divide factors of production into three basic categories: Land, labour and capital. Land refers to all of the natural resources that businessed need to make and distribut goods and services, labours to make and distribute goods and services, labours refers how the organization chooses to employ the employee skill to make the kind of job, capital refers to how much the organization plans to spend in order to operate its business. Hence, behavioral economy can explains the economic model of employee, human behavior, working performance. It is a representation of people action. The concept is based on traditional economics, where human behavior is believed to spring from absolute rationality.

On behavioral economics in consumer lives and in the economy aspect, it explains it is a game theory, behavioral game theory. It is a game theory , behavioral game theory extened standard analytical game theory by taking into account how players (consumers) feel about the payoffs other players receive, limits in strategic thinking, as well as the effects of learning , the consumer individual past purchase experience, games (choices of purchases) are usually about cooperation or fairness.

For advertising how plays beneficial roles in a healthy economy example, advertising plays a strong role in the economy. It provides useful informatin to consumers that tells them about products and services choices as well as comparing features, benefits and prices, with more complete information, consumers and businesses often choose to purchase additional products and services . Hence, behavioral eonomics draws instead on psychology and economics to explore why people sometimes make irrational decisions, and why and how their behavior does not follow the predictionsof economic models. Because humans are emotional and easily distracted being, they make decisions that are not in their self-interest.

So, behavioral economics is the study of the effects that psychological factors have on the economic decisions making process of individuals. The importance of understanding behavioral economics for marketers is immeasurable as it shows for a better factors that can lead to irrational economic decision, e.g. overspend because of lack of availabiliey, such as buying expense gad because you are in the desert. Another irrational economic decision may be impluse buying or pressure.

● How to apply behavioral economic to explain why the employee does peformance behavior?
A study on human behavior has revealed that 90% of the working population can be classified into four basic personality types: Optimistic, pessimistic, trusting. However, the latter of the four types. Envious is the most common, with 30% compared to 20% of each of the organization whole employee individual economic behavior, economic behavior occurs in a climate of formal and informal organizational rukes. These rules often act as incentives, e.g. appreciation, job promotion, increasing salary. These rules often act as incentives and influence the choices employees make , in general employees chooce to work desk jobs that do not keep to fit, and how they have to make more time to stay healthy.

So, behavioral economic theory explain any organization will need have behavioral skills to dominate employee individual performance to raise. Behavioral skills are interpersonal, self-regulatory, and task-related behaviors that connect to successful performance in education and workplace settings. The behavioral skills are designed to help individuals succeed thorough effecttive interactions, stress management and persistent effort in any organizations. for task-oriented behavioral skills examples, they may include: active always buy with something, ambitious, strongly wants to succeed, cautious, being very careful, conscientious, taking time to do things right and creative, someone who can make up things easily or think of new things. The six important employee behaviors in organizations are employee productivity, absenteeism, turnover, organizational citizenship behavior, job satisfaction and workplace misbehavior. So, managers need have good behavioral management skills. They are all about learnings appreciation and growth. Take the time to learn, try and grow oen strategies and leadership style.

- How to apply behavioral eocnomic skill to help society to solve challenges ?

The three principles of social economics theory describes how the economy as a whole woks are (1) a country's standard of living depends on its ability to produce goods and services . (2) prices rise when the government prints too much money and (3) society faces a short-run tradeoff between inflation and unemployment. How to use behavioral economics for social impact. According to the American psychological association, social psychology is the study of how individuals affects and are affected by physical environment. Behavioral economics applies these concepts to the economic decisions that people make in addition to the ration thinking. It helps us understand how consumer participate in contest buy products and brand familiar choice in order to make the most rational purchase decison. Also, behavioral economists ask questions mostly about the way people make economic choices, judgements or the way particular financial purchase choice.

Hence, behavioral economic is the study of psychology as it relates to the economic decision making processes of individuals and organizations. In general, our societies ask two important questions: Are economists' assumptions of utility of profit maximization good approximations of real people's behavior? So individuals maximize subjective expected utility?

IN our societies, we need to satisfy and earn the greatest benefit, in economics, rational choice theory, states that when humans are presented with various options under the conditions of scarcity, they would choose the option that maximizes their individual satisfaction. Behavioral economics draws on psychology and economics to explain why people sometimes make irrational decisions and why and how their behavior does not follow the predictions of economic models, e.g. decisions such as how much to pay for a cup of coffee, whether to go to graduate school, whether to pursue a healthy lifestyle , how much to contribute toward retirement.

Because humans are emotional and easily distracted beings, they make decisions that are not in their self interest. For companies are increasingly incorpoarting behavioral economics to incrase sales of their products case example, in 2007, the price of the 8 GB iphone was introduced for $600 and quickly reduced to $400, what if the intrinsic value of the phone was $400? If Apple introduced the iphone for $400, the initial reaction the price in the smartphone market might have been negative as the iphone might be thought to have too pricely. Buy by introdicing the phone at a hgh-pricing and bringing it down to $400, consumers believed they were getting a pretty iphone deal for Apple. So, Apple iphone began to understand tht its phone consumers are irrational, an effective way to behavioral economics in the Apple iphone's decision making policies that concern its internal and external stakeholders may prove to be worthwhile of done properly .

Consumer leisure behavioral economy

● Consumer leisure need whether is more and less whether it has what relationship between economy?

Consumer leisure need whether is more and less whether it has what relationship between economy? Also whether the country's economy recession or growth, can it influence consumer leisure need to increase or decrease ? I shall attempt to apply behavioral economy theory to explain whether they have cause and effect relationship as below:

In our societies, there are so many different kinds of leisure activities, also any kinds of leisure consumers can follow the kind of leisure activity's price factor, enjoyable feeling factor, satisfactory feeling factor, lesiure time need factor to influence the leisure consumer individual final choice to which kind of leisure activity among the different kinds of leisure needs. For example, travel leisure activity ought be the most experience, spending of leisure expense to compare general sport lesiure, e.g. swimming , playing basketballs , table tennis, tennis, football, purchae tickets seeing movies, purchase tickets listening music, purchase electronic playing games to stay at homes to play.

In simiarity, it uses only considers leisure price aspect, we shall do the comparable and reasonable decision is that travelling activity ought be the kind of leisure activity, any leisure consumers ought spend the least leisure times to enjoy this kind of leisure activity, e.g. one year has only one time or two-to-five times for overseas for overseas travel. But, in fact, in global there are many travellers, they can make many times of travelling frequent decision, e.g. they can spend one week at least time to go to overseas to travel per month. Hence, it means that global some travellers like to buy air ticket to go to overseas to travel, they spend average one month and one time overseas travel.

In fact, tourism agents hope to attract travellers to choose travelling leisure activity, they will attempt to decrease air ticket price in order to increase travellers number. However, some cheap travelling package price can persuade global some travellers accept to pay cheap price to bu air ticket to spend several days to go to the country to travel enjoy their holidays. So, it seems that cheap air tcket price strategy, it can attract some countries travellers to accept to spend some time for their overseas holiday their overseas travelling leisure activity can explain why leisure price must be main element factor to influence leisure consumers to reduce spending amount to pay for the kind of leisure activity , such as travelling lesiure activity is one kind of good lesiure activity example.

Otherwise, some kinds of leisure activities, ever their lesiure prices are cheap, it must not influence them to like to spend much time to enjoy them, e.g. swimming, riding bicycles leisure activities, although those kinds of sport leisure activities prices must be very cheap to compare travelling activities , it can must influence many young people like to buy bicycles to ridem even they are proficient bicycle riders or they like to buy tickets to go public swimming pools to swin. The factors may include these both kinds of sports are tired sport leisures, any one must need more body energy to do these sports. Moreover, for student leisure consumers, although these both kinds sports prices, such as bicycles and swimming pool purchase tickets, they are cheap to students, but in fact, students must need to spend time to learn, if they often spend time to enjoy these both of sport activities, they will feel fear that they can not concentrate on spending learning time, if they spend on sport leisure time.

Hence, in behavioral economy view, it explains that lesiure price whether it is high or low, it is not main factor to influence any leisure consumers to do leisure kind of choice, such as sport case to student leisure consumers, they will not choose to spend much time on sport lesiure aspect, because the hard students must feel fear to influence their learning effort when they often spend time on sport leisure aspect. Otherwise, for a sport professonal, e.g. proficient riding bicycle sportman, he may accept to spend expensive price to buy one expensive bicycle , e.g. when he feels the US$3,000 bicycle, it can help him to improve riding speed skills, he won't choose to buy the another US$1,000 bicycle, when he feels that it can not help him to improve riding speed skill, hence, it also explains that the leisure produt high price , it must not influence lesisure consumers number to reduce, it depends on whether the leisure product function to the leisure consumer, e.g. for riding bicycle sport men , they may accept to pay higher price to buy more expensive bicycles , because the hope that the bicyces can help them to comprove their riding speed to more rapid. Otherwise, for student bicycle consumers, they won't compare different kinds of bicycles prices in order to decide whether which kind of bicycles are the most suitable to them to buy to ride.

Hence, behavioral economic theory can explain that price must not be the main factor to influence lesiure consumers' lesiure activities choices, their lesiure need psychological and leisure product individual function factors was also influence their lesiure activities choices.

Behavioral economy view how DINA biological medical science impact our societies

● Can DNA reproductive technology bring only positive impact to influence our social behavior change?

Human's medical technology had been continue developed to improve to satisfy our medical need, such as cancer patient medical different new drug research, it aims to help future cancer patients to avoid death. However, future human's new medical research will research on DNA biological medical improvement . So, future DNA biological medical technology may bring good or bad social impact, e.g. reproductive animal, such as pig, cow animals . So, when many pigs and cows can be reproduced. Then, pigs and cows number can increase. Consequently, porks beefs meats food number can be also been increased by DNA biological medical reproductive cell technology improvement.

It is good aspect to bring enough meats supply to global , when future DNA biological medical technology can be developed to the reprodctive many cows and pigs number stage in order to raise porks and beefs food number. However, DNA biological cell reproductive technology can also bring bad impact to our society, if one day human can apply DNA biological cell reprodutive technology to reproduce another ourselves, it means that

reproductive human why is it bad new? if ne DNA scientist decides to help one country ambitious leader to reproduce himself, then when the country ambitious leader dies, but his another reproductive himself person can aontiue to bring war crisis to global, such as Japan's past leader, he was one ambitious leader to dominate global countries. If DNA reproductive technology is applied to help him to reproduce this Japan ambitious another himself . Then, the another new world war may be occurred easily. So, I also worry about future DNA reproductive technology may be applied to help the ambitous bad people to reproduce themselves to bring our societies safety and economic recession negative impact.
So, it brings this question: Can DNA reproductive technology bring only positive impact to influence our social behavior change? I shall attempt to explain as below:

How does DNA attract our behavior? In some situations, genes play a larger role in determining your behavior. How can genetic technologies impact society ? Although, genetic technology has a great potential to change the medical practice as we know it also has a potential to be misused , it also has a potential to be misused, and lead to further health disparities, discrimination and inequality in the human societies around the world.

However, I believe that those the ways that genetic engineering can help human society. Several works have been done on genetic engineering with major focus on its importance ranging from increasing plant and animal food productio, diagnosing disease condition, medical treatment improvement, as well as production of vaccines and other useful drugs.

- What is the focus of behavioral generics?

Behavioral genetics is the study of genetic and environmental influences on behaviors. By examining genetic influence, more information can be gleaned about how the environment operates to affect behavior. So, in behavioral economic view, gene DNA reproductive cell technology may seem to bring these benefits. Some benefits of genetic engineerinf in agricultures are increased crop yoelds, reduced need for food or drug production, reduced need for pesticides, enhanced nutrient composition and food quality , resistance to past and disease , greater food security, and medical benefits to the world's growing population . Also, the intangible , non economic measurement, possible benefit of genetic engineering may include more nutritious food, tastier food, disease -and-drought resistant plants that require fewer environment resources , such as water and fertilizers, less use of pesticides, increased supply of food with reduced cost and larger shelf life, faster growing plants and animals.

All of these benefits, they can not measured by economic calculation, but they can be felt by us. So, in our social behevioral economic view to genetic engineering, it may bring both positive and negative impact to our societies. On negative impact, these are many risks involves in genetic engineering, the release of genetically altered organisms in the environment can increase human suffering, disease animal welfare, and lead to ecological disasters are positive impact aspect, it can help to defeat diseases, getting rid of all illnesses in young and unborn children potential to live longer, produce new foods, organisms can be tailor-made , faster growth in animals and plants, pests and diseases resistance. But genetic engineering can also bring risks to our societies, e.g. new allergens in the food supply, antibiotic reistance, production of new toxins, concentration of toxic metals, enhancement of the environment for toxic fungi, unknown harms, gene transfer to wild ot weedy relations, change in herbicide use patterns.

By knocking out genes repsonsible for certain conditions, it is possible to create animal model organism of " human disease" as well as producing hotmenes, vaccies and other drugs. So, if DNA can bring human diseases, it means that it can also bring economic loss to our societies, because human disease may bring illness to any one to cause low productivity to any industry development, if the factory has many people human disease from reproductive animal cell accident risk. Then, the ill worker number increases, low productivities and inefficiencies will cause to the factory. If global has many factory workers got human disease from reproductive animal cell accidently. Then, global factries products producing number must have been influenced to fallen down.

Consequently, global manufacturers will encountered serious loss, due to their products producing speed is slow and their different kinds of products supply number must decrease, if global will workers number increases, they are caused by reproductive animal cell disease. Hence, DNA genetic reproductive technology may also bring global economic loss crisis in possible.

Behavioral economy theory brings what advantages to our society Why do we need behavioral economy to help us to solve social or business problem?
Whether what are the actual benefits , they may bring to influence our societies change better? I shall attempt to to explain above question. Economic is the social science that examines how individuals, businesses and entire societies manage scarce resources. Resources are by nature , limited. Only a finite amount of land exists, e.g. and people do not have unlimieted time to meet all of their needs and wants. So, if we can learn ho to apply behavioral economy theory to avoid resources waste, then our societies ought develop better.

Our society had changed from traditional economy to develop to nowadays knowledge economy. Traditional economy only produce and take what they need, so there is no waste or inefficiencies involved in produdig the goods required to survive as a society. However, traditional economy also have disadvantages, such as it isolates the people within that economt, large outside economies can win a traditional economy. It offers choices, these may be a lower overall quality of life, it creates specific health risk, unpredictability creates survival uncertainties.

Although, our societies had been experiencing knowledge economy, but it also have disadvantage, knowledge economy means that our societies or business organizations need to learn how ro use knowledge management to keep business growth or social developing. Knowledge management is a systematic approach to capturing and making use of a organization collective expertise to create value. The potential advantages of effective knowledge management are significant , but as with most processes, advantages of knowledge management or knowledge econmic society may include: Improved organizational or social productivities better and faster decision making, quicker problem solving, increased rate of innovation, supported employee/citizen growth and development within organizations or societies, sharing of specialiat expertise, better communication, improved business processes.
Hence if the organization or society can apply behavioral economic theory to learn knowledge management system , it can help the organization or society to develop better or more easier, e.g. create better products and services , develop better strategies, improve profitability or productivity,

reuse existing skills and expertise, increase operational efficiency and staff productivity, recognise market trends early and gain on advantage over rivals make the most of organizations or social intellectual capital . Hence, it explains why when our organizations or societies can apply behavioral economy theory to learn how to apply knowledge management system to develop our organiztations or societies. Then, our societies or organizations will avoid to waste social resource organizational resource as well as achieve more productivities or service improvement, even gain profitability, it is the final aim of why our organizations or / and societies need to attempt to learn how to apply knowledge management system to achieve any objectives in behavioral economy view.

On conclusion, behavioral economic is the study of the effect that our societiesand organizations need to learn how psychological factors have on the economic decision making process of individuals. The importance of understanding behavioral economics for marketers is immeasurable as it follows for a better understanding of the human mind. So, behavioral economics plays a important role in our live and in the eocnomy. It helps governments and businesses learn on every day consumers activities and explains why we consume goods and services , the way we do, why we make certain choices, about ourselves or others and how we decide of action . Hence, behavioral economists need to examine each of these day -to -day choice resulting in progressive understanding of human behavior that combines both psychology and economy.

How do rules influence economic behavior?
Why are the rules of the economic system important? In our societies , our economic behavior occurs in a climate of formal and informal rules. There sulres often act as incentives and influenced the choices people make, people choose to do jobs taht do not keep them fit, and now they have to make more time to stay healthy. So, our societies are experiencing behavioral economic rules made in order to let every one need to adapt how to change and influence to our lives. it is one actual knowledge economic society or knowledge economic social living mode that we need to learn how to adapt to live. We need to learn how to apply knowledge of economic changing behavior. UNderstanding behavioral economic and psychology for social impact our businesses can bring products , sale growth more easily or our societies can be improved to our living quality better.

The relationship between behavioral economy and our society , it may explain that if the result of economic scarcity in a society occurrence, due to that productive resources are limited, therefore, people can not have all the goods and services, they want, a result, they must choose some things and give up others , like individuals, governments and societies , experience scarcity because human wats exceed with can be made from all available resources.

Behavioral economic is the study of psychology as it relates to the economic decision making processes of individuals and organizations. Behavioral economy theory uses psychological experimentation to develop theories about human decision making and has identified a range of biases as a result of the way people think and feel. BE is trying to change the way economists think about people's perception of value and expressed preferences.

However, in our societies, we need have three basic economic problems. Economic systems is as a type social system must confront and solve the three quantities of goods shall be produced, how much and which of alternative tools and services shall be produced, how shall goods be produced what technology a well as for whom are the goods , or services produced who benefts?

All of these are our daily economic problems any organizations (societies) had been changing. We need new social science behavioral economy theory to help use to solve any one of social economic individual problems, for example, when a particular incident becomes cognitively available, it is became of social influence. Individuals are specially averse to losses, but how do we know whether we are facing a loss or instead of a foregone gain ? What is the status from which losses are measured ? how might social influence reduces or increase people's willingness to sacrifice their material sale-interest for the sake of fairness?
All of these matter, applying behavioral economic theory may attempt to explain the reason why the consequency occurs. Also, when some countries governments can apply behavioral economy theory to help them to do reasonable strategic decision in order to avoid any one of these social negative events occur, such as organizational crime, discrimination,

environmental hazards, or threats to national security before any one country government decides to implement any strategic action, they may apply behavioral economic theory to weigh whether their decision may bring socity to earn more benefit or more loss, for example, if the country government permits the oil manufacturing firm continues to research the possible oil manufacturing elements at the oceans. Whether their oil research behavior on the ocean , it will bring how serious environmental hazard to cause global oceans have many fishes die per day, how much percentage successful chance oil discovery on anywhere in the oceans. So, any country governments need to consider whether ocean land oil discovery chance is more important or reducing many fishes death number is more important when any country goverments continue to permit any one oil manufacturers continue to find oil land from oceans in order to manufacture more oil, during their ocean oil land manufacturing process, it may bring serious pollution to ocean water and causes many fishes drink the polluted oil water to be killed. For another exmaple, US government allows many local manfacturers set up factories in China, in order to let many US social manufacturers can pay cheap wages to employ China workers to help them to manufacture any products, e.g. mobiles, shoes, cloths, shirts, televisions etc. although US governmment can bring discrimination image to let China workers feel, they can have more job chance and to earn US manufacturer employers wages. In economic view, China can reduce workers unemployment ratio from US manufacturers' factories manufacture jobs chance. Also , US manufacturers can pay cheaper wages to Chinese workers to compare US domestic workers wages. But, US government neglects , it will also cause many US domestic factories manufacture workers had beed beginning to lose their factory manufacture jobs, because Chinese manfacture workers can replace them to do their Us social factory manufacture jobs more easily. Hence, in long term, US manfacturers choose to outsource local factory manufacture workers to them to do, it will cause US unemployed workers manufacture number increases., Hence , US government ought need to weigh long term high unemployment ratio social issue to US domestic factory manufacturing workers, whether US manufacturers cheap or low wages to Chinese factory manufacturing workers (low wage cost) is more important ot reducing US domestic factory manufacturing workers unemployed number social negative influence more important. If US government continue allows US manufacturers outsource domestic factory manufacturing workers to do, it must increase US local manufacturing workers unemployment number and it may cause US government needs to pay future more social welfare expenditure to these long time unemployment US manufacturing workers, even, social stealing crime may be influenced to increase . It implies that behavioral economy analysis can help our society to choose to make more reasonable decisions.

The relationship between economic recession and consumer purchase desire

Can economic recession influence car buyers' purchases desire reduce? In macro economic view, it explains that economic recession means that the country has many people loss jobs, because economic recession, it causes many employers begain to reduce employees number to avoid salary expenditure increases, but clients number reduces. Hence, when one country is experiencing economic recession period, it will causes people reduces shopping expenditures, when many of people lose themselves jobs or some people feel that they will lose jobs as soon as possible . So, in societies, general consumers‘ consumption desires will be influenced to reduce, due to many of people had lost jobs or many of people feel that their employers will dismiss them due to they feel busineses are worse.

IN behavioral economic view, when one society has high unemployment ratio, e.g. graduate students can not find jobs easily, many of working people are losing present jobs, it implies that the country is experiencing economic recession .So, it will cause many products can not sell easily in the society, e.g. one Dell brand laptop price is average US$1,000. IN last year, the country US Dell brand laptop price was average US$1,000. IN common, Dell brand could sell this model laptop products 100,000 laptop numbers in last year. HOwever, in this year, Dell this model laptop price is not changed, it keeps US$1,000 average price, but Dell only sells 50,000 laptop number in US this year. So, it seems that US is experiencing recession, because there are many US people lose jobs, they can not find another jobs easily in short time. SO, in general, many US people begin to prepare some money in bank and they begin to reduce spend to buy any things easily. Also, because laptop is not essential product to anyone. It is only students, office employers and employees both customer target may be laptop product's main consumer groups. Another retired people, housewives, households they must feel need to buy laptop to use at homes. So, it explains that why US Dell brand laptop is significant decreasing laptop buyers (customers) number.Moreover, due to this US Dell brand laptop products average price are still kept to same to US$1,000 average price. It can not persuade laptop consumers to choose to buy Dell brand any laptop products easily when they may make price comparison to other similar kinds of laptop model products, e.g. Apple brand, Microsoft brand etc.

However, I assume that even Dell brand wil decide to reduce its different model of laptops average price to US $700 even $500 each piece. I believe that Dell brand computer seller is still difficult to sell its any model of laptop products easily in this year. The reason is because that when this year US is experiencing recession, in this high unemployment ratio US recession environment, many losing job American will avoid to spend to buy high price product, or the non essential product, such as laptop product it must not be essential product for any one and its price may be expensive to let the unemployed US people feel its price is too much to compare general non essential products, e.g. books, shoes, cloths etc. So, in ecojnomic recession environment, it may cause some general non essential products will be difficlut sold in the country's business market. It means that laptop is non essential product, So, when the country is encountering recession period, the country's laptop product consumer desire may be influenced to fall down. Although, some laptop sellers attempt to reduce their sale price in order to attract or persuade they choose to buy their any laptops. But, lower sale price , it is still difficult to help them to increase laptop sale number because general consumers will avoid to spend to buy non essential products, they will save much money in bank to prepare possible unemployment matters occur to them suddenly. So, when the country has many people feel that unemployment matter may occue to them suddenly, many people will choose to save more money in bank because they feel that they will be hard to find another jobs in short time easily, even graduate students or owning more year working experience people, they will plan to find another job to work in short time. So, it explains that economic recession may influence consumer purchase desire to reduce, in special essential products purchase need to consumer will be influenced to reduce. Nut, essential products consumer purchase desire, they won't be influenced to reduce, otherwise their purchase desire may be influenced to rise when recession occurs, e.g. rice , vegetable, meat, pork, orange, banana, apple friuts common food. Why does essential products , such as foods their price may raise and food consumers purchase desire will not be influenced to reduce in recession. The reason is simple, when one country is experiencing recession, for example, COVID 19 disease occurrence, it can influence global people feel agraid, foods may be shortage to supply to their countries, e.g. China, there are many people feel fear that they can not buy rice, vegetable, meat foods from supermarket easily. Because COVID 19 disease influences many Chinese restaurants clients number decreaes, they are afraid to go to restaurants to contact the COVID 19 disease people to sit on the same table to eat together. So, restaurant clients decrease. COVID 19 disease occurrence influences many Chinese people choose to go to supermarkets to buy foods to cook at homes. So, supermarket foods purchase need number may be influenced to increase. Consequently, supermarket foods prices may be influenced to increase, because many Chinese people prefer to buy foods to cook from supermarkets to eat. So, in China present economic recession environment, COVID 19 disease encourages many Chinese household families choose to go to supermarkets to buy foods to cook at home, because food is essential to any one. So, Chinese supermarket food price may be influenced to increase by COVID 19 disease occurrence influence.

Explaining the relationship between increasing proficient workers number and avoiding excess resource waste

In organizational behavioral economic view, whether they have cause and effect relationship between employees how to use resources behaviors and organizational resource excess use within organizations ?

In organizational behavioral economic view, whether they have cause and effect relationship between employees how to use resources behaviors and organizational resource excess use within organizations. For example, if the organization has many employees number, whether the organization will use its any internal tangible and intangible resources easily per day.

For construction organization example, one construction organization must need to buy different kinds of construction materials to prepare to let workers to help it to manufacture different kinds of properties or houses (products) in order to sell to property buyers. In its every building construction site, it will need more or less workers, they are needed to use different kinds of construction materials to build housess in different construction sites. I assume that construction site (A), it has 100 construction workers number, every day, construction site (A) 100 workers need to use different kinds of construction materials to help them to build 3 building floors wall at least floor number in the construction site (A).

I assume that these 100 construction workers , they include proficient workers and not proficient workers. For proficient construction workers group, they have 50 number, and not proficient construction workers group, they also have 50 number . Hence, the proficient construction workers only need to spend 3 hours maximum and use less number of constructoin materials, then they can finish to build 3 building floors wall per day.

I also assume that all constructoin material supply number is limited. It means that due to this construction firm needs to pre-booking to purchase this kind of the best quality of constructoin material from overseas before three worths. So, it must not have enough time to pre-booking to purchase this kind of best quality of constructoin materials when they are used rapaidly within one month, due to this one month is the final finishing time to this construction firm within one month. Hence, limited construction material supply number and limited finishing time to build this new 40 floors house within this final one month .

So , not proficient construction workers number , limit number of construction material and per day 8 hours which is its limited resources in behavioral eocnomy view. Moreover, total 50 proficient and not proficient 50 construction workers (human resource employees number) will cause this constructoin firm , it will possible need to build this new 40 floors house are more than one month, if these 50 proficient construction workers , they have more than 30 at least number, they are absent to cause their overall construction workers' efficiency to be fallen down, due to the other 50 not proficient constuction numbers must need their teaching how to cooperate ad how use less materials to build this new 40 floor hourse rapidly in order to raise overall constructon team efficiency and avoid to delay more than one month time to build this 40 floors new house successfully within this final one month time.

Hence, it explains that when one organization has more employees, it does not represent that this organization must need to use more resource to achieve its any mission, such as this construction firm case, although it has 50 not proficient construction workers, they need to use more construction materials to build this new 40 floors house in this construction site (A). But, in fact, it has other 50 proficient construction workers, they know how to reduce construction materials to build every building floor wall for this new 40 floors building house. So, they can teach the not proficient building workers to know hoe to avoid to use extra excess constructon material to finish to construct every building fllor wall. SO, although, it has 50 not proficient construction workers number, but they can be taught to learn how to reduce to use these limited the best quality of construction materials

to build this 40 floors new house. It implies that if the construction workers number can increase, e.g. increases more 50 not proficient construction workers, this the best quality of construction material resource number must not need to increase demand, because this construction site (A) has 50 proficient construction workers , they can teach these 50 not proficient construction workers how to avoid to use extra excess this kind of high quality construction material to build this new 40 floor house efficiently and effectively within this one month.
Hence, if this construction firm won't have more than 30 proficient workers number is absent in this final one month, it will have enough proficient construction workers to teach these 50 not proficient construction workers to know how to use this high quality of construction materials to build this 40 floors new house building in order to avoid waste or construction material need shortage challenge occurs in this final one month time.

Consequently , it ought finish to build this 40 floors new house building within this month. Hence, it explains why its this kind of high quality of construction material resource need must not increase, because if its all proficient construction workers is absent and their absent number is less than 30, then they have enough proficient construction workers number , they can teach this 50 not proficient construction workers how to avoid to use extra excess construction materials resource number in order to have enough construction material resource supply to satisfy this new 40 floors building house to finish construction within one month finishing date need.

On conclusion, in organizational behavioral economic view, it explains that resource use need must not be influenced to increase when the organization's employees number increase. It depends on whether the organization has how many talent and proficient workers number in order to assist them and teach the not proficient employees how to use resource to manufacture any kinds of products in order to avoid to spend extra excess of resource need. Hence, organizational behavioral economic view, it can explain that any organization's increase to employees number, it does not mean that its resource number is also needed to increase. Moreover, in organizational behavioral economic view, it also explains that if the organization can have many proficient workers to help it to do any complex tasks, they will help it to bring avoiding waste or excess extra resource to use advantage, because they ought know whether how they work, they can help the organization to improve performance or raise efficiency e.g. car manufacture, computer manufacture, television manufcture etc. home electronic products or car leisure products. Due to that manufacturre processes are complex, if the organization can have more proficient high skillful workers to help it to manufacture their products. They ought help it to use lesser manufacturing time and less manufacturing resource to finish any above these products to compare not proficient or low skillful manufacture workers. So, in long time, the organization must may earn economic low cost benefits from proficient worker individual high manufacturing skillful knowledge behavior or performance. So, organizational behavioral economic theory explains why even the organization plans to increase employees number, it's resources number won't be influenced to increase rapidly because when the organization's proficient high skillful workers number is more 2 times at least than not proficient low skillful workers number. They ought have enough effort to train and teach and cooperate with the not proficient low skillful manufacture workers to improve their manufacture skills in order to raise manufacturing efficiency and reduce extra excess resources waste and avoid to bring long term resource waste economic loss. So, any manufacturing organizations must need to increase proficient workers number to assist the not proficient low skillful workers to learn how to improve their skills and know how to reduce to use excess resources to keep to manufacture the highest number of products aim frequently. Consequently, the organization will bring long term low resource use manufacturing economic benefit.

The difference between past and nowadays economists their demand and supply economic theory explanation?

The law of supply and demand defines the relationship between the price of a given good or product and the willingness of people to either buy or sell it. Generally, as the price of a good increases, people are willing to supply more and demand less. These economists had explained economic demand and supply theory as below:

Philosopher John Locke is credited with one of the earliest written descriptions of this economic principle in his 1691 publication, Some Considerations of the Consequences of the Lowering of Interest and the Raising of the Value of Money. Locke addressed the concept of supply and demand as part of a discussion about interest rates in 17th-century England. Many merchants wanted the government to lower the cap on interest rates charged by private lenders so that people could borrow more money and thus purchase more goods. Locke argued that the free-market economy should set rates because government regulation could have unintended consequences. If the lending industry were left alone, interest rates would regulate themselves, Locke wrote: "The price of any commodity rises or falls by the proportion of the number of buyers and sellers."

Sir James Steuart's Inquiry into the Principles of Political Economy, published in 1796, was the first known printed use of the term "supply and demand." When Steuart wrote his treatise on political economy, one of his main concerns was the impact of supply and demand on laborers.
Adam Smith dealt extensively with the topic in his 1776 epic economic work, The Wealth of Nations. Often referred to as the Father of Economics, Smith explained the concept of supply and demand as an "invisible hand" that naturally guides the economy. According to Smith, the invisible hand is the automatic pricing and distribution mechanisms in the economy. Smith described a society in which bakers and butchers provide products that individuals need and want, providing a supply that meets demand and developing an economy that benefits everyone. It is important to note that Smith's ideas haven't gone without critique over the years since his ideas were first published, though. Over time, his ideas have been added to in order to represent the changing times and include concepts such as marginal utility, comparative advantage, entrepreneurship, the time-preference theory of interest, and monetary theory.
One of Marshall's most important contributions to microeconomics was his introduction of the concept of price elasticity of demand, which examines how price changes affect demand. In theory, people buy less of a particular product if the price increases, but Marshall noted that in real life, this behavior was not always true. The prices of some goods can increase without reducing demand, which means their prices are inelastic. Inelastic goods tend to include items such as medication or food that consumers deem crucial to daily life. Marshall argued that supply and demand, costs of production, and price elasticity all work together.

Nowadays economists they explain demand and supply economic theory, they have some different to past economists whose explanation as below:

How Does Supply and Demand Work? The law of supply and demand is a theory that explains the interaction between the sellers of a resource and the buyers of that resource. Generally, as price increases, people are willing to supply more and demand less and vice versa when the price falls. What does the bottom line mean. Despite the origins of the law of supply and demand beginning hundreds of years ago, it's still a topic frequently referenced and utilized today in economic theory and discussions. The theory has developed over time to accommodate recent technological and economical advancements, but the basic ideas of the theory remain largely the same.

Does demand depend on supply?
Supply and Demand Determine the Price of Goods and Quantities Produced and Consumed. Consumers may exhaust the available supply of a good by purchasing a given good or service at a high volume. This leads to an increase in demand. As demand increases, the available supply also decreases.

What does market demand depend on?
Market factors affecting demand of consumer goods. The demand for a good increases or decreases depending on several factors. This includes the product's price, perceived quality, advertising spend, consumer income, consumer confidence, and changes in taste and fashion.

Who controls the demand in supply and demand?
Supply and demand are in turn determined by technology and the conditions under which people operate. At one extreme, the market could be populated by a large number of virtually identical sellers and buyers (for example, the market for ballpoint pens).

What are the two laws of demand and supply?
The law of demand holds that the demand level for a product or a resource will decline as its price rises, and rise as the price drops. Conversely, the law of supply says higher prices boost supply of an economic good while lower ones tend to diminish it.

What factors affect demand and supply?

Price fluctuations are a strong factor affecting supply and demand. When a product gets expensive enough that the average consumer no longer feels it is worth it to buy the product, then the demand declines. This leads to cuts in production that will hopefully stabilize the product's value.

What factors affect demand and demand?
Demand may be defined as the quantity of a commodity that a consumer is able and willing to buy, at each possible price, over a given period of time. • Essential elements of demand are quantity, ability, willingness, prices, and period of time.

Which factors affect supply?
Generally, the supply of a product depends on its price and other variables such as the cost of production.

a. Price. Price can be understood as what the consumer is willing to pay to receive a good or service. ...
b. Cost of production. ...
c. Technology. ...
d. Governments' policies. ...
e. Transportation condition.

How does supply and demand work together?
It's a fundamental economic principle that when supply exceeds demand for a good or service, prices fall. When demand exceeds supply, prices tend to rise. There is an inverse relationship between the supply and prices of goods and services when demand is unchanged.
What happens to supply when demand increases?
An increase in demand, all other things unchanged, will cause the equilibrium price to rise; quantity supplied will increase. A decrease in demand will cause the equilibrium price to fall; quantity supplied will decrease.

What is the theory of demand?
Demand theory describes the way that changes in the quantity of a good or service demanded by consumers affects its price in the market, The theory states that the higher the price of a product is, all else equal, the less of it will be demanded, inferring a downward sloping demand curve.
What are the 4 basic laws of supply and demand?
1) If the supply increases and demand stays the same, the price will go down.

2) If the supply decreases and demand stays the same, the price will go up. 3) If the supply stays the same and demand increases, the price will go up. 4) If the supply stays the same and demand decreases, the price will go down.
The different types of demand are as follows:
i. Individual and Market Demand: ...
ii. Organization and Industry Demand: ...
iii. Autonomous and Derived Demand: ...
iv. Demand for Perishable and Durable Goods: ...
v. Short-term and Long-term Demand:
What creates demand for a product?
You can create demand for a unique product if you can manage to solve a persistent problem for the consumer. People are always running away from pain, and providing them with an outlet is a sure-fire way to create massive demand for your goods.
What are the 7 factors that affect supply?
The seven factors which affect the changes of supply are as follows: (i) Natural Conditions (ii) Technical Progress (iii) Change in Factor Prices (iv) Transport Improvements (v) Calamities (vi) Monopolies (vii) Fiscal Policy.
What can affect demand?
Factors Affecting Demand
Price of the Product. ...
The Consumer's Income. ...
The Price of Related Goods. ...
The Tastes and Preferences of Consumers. ...
The Consumer's Expectations. ...
The Number of Consumers in the Market.
What are the three factors affecting demand?
The demand for a product will be influenced by several factors:
Price. Usually viewed as the most important factor that affects demand.
...
Income levels. ...
Consumer tastes and preferences. ...
Competition. ...
Fashions.

What are the 4 factors of supply?
The four factors that can shift the supply curve include natural conditions, input prices, technology, and government.

What causes increase in supply?
If the cost of production is lower, the profits available at a given price will increase, and producers will produce more. With more produced at every price, the supply curve will shift to the right, meaning an increase in supply.

What causes supply changes?
A change in supply is an economic term that describes when the suppliers of a given good or service alter production or output. A change in supply can occur as a result of new technologies, such as more efficient or less expensive production processes, or a change in the number of competitors in the market.

Is supply and demand a good strategy?
When it comes to profit placement, supply and demand zones can be a great tool as well. Always place your profit target ahead of a zone so that you don't risk giving back all your profits when the open interest in that zone is filled.

How is demand created?
Demand creation is a process that fuels the revenue pipeline so the sales team can meet or exceed their quotas. In other words, it takes your big idea — the creative appeal of your brand — and turns it into sales. That sounds a lot like demand generation, which often gets confused with lead generation.

What are the two parts of demand?
Economists define demand as the quantity of a good or service that buyers are willing and able to buy at all possible prices during a certain time period. Notice that there are two components to demand: willingness to purchase and ability to pay.

Can we control demand?
If you're willing to think and act strategically, you can easily manipulate the laws of supply and demand. It should be surprising to learn, however, that by manipulating the laws of supply and demand, you can make more profit in less time and with far fewer headaches

How do you control demand?

Here are five short-term actions to improve your demand variability management plans in this time of uncertainty:

Maintain transparent, proactive relationships with your suppliers. ...
Activate alternate sources of supply. ...
Reduce lead times. ...
Update inventory policy and planning. ...
Align supply and demand management.
What are the 8 types of demand?
There are 8 states of demand: negative demand, no demand, latent demand, falling demand, irregular demand, full demand, overfull demand and unwholesome demand.
What is Demand?

Types of Determinants of Demand. Every factor has a unique impact on demand. ...
Price of the Product. ...
The Income of the Consumers. ...
Number of Buyers in the Market. ...
Consumer's Expectations. ...
Tastes and Preferences of The Consumers. ...
Complement Goods. ...
Substitute Product.
What is theory of supply?
The law of supply is a fundamental principle of economic theory which states that, keeping other factors constant, an increase in price results in an increase in quantity supplied. In other words, there is a direct relationship between price and quantity: quantities respond in the same direction as price changes.

What are the types of supply?
There are five types of supply—market supply, short-term supply, long-term supply, joint supply, and composite supply.

Which comes first supply or demand?
Demand comes first and it's followed by the corresponding supplies. Supply and demand are both very important to economic activity. Supply is the total amount of a particular good or service available at a given time to consumers at a given price. Demand is a representation of a consumer's desire to purchase goods and services; it acts as a measurement of a

consumer's willingness to purchase a specific good or service at a given price. These two economic forces influence each other; they are both important for the economy because they impact the prices of consumer goods and services within an economy and the quantities produced and consumed. Supply and demand are both keys to understanding the economy because they reflect the prices and quantities of consumer goods and services within an economy.

What are the relationship between demand and supply?

According to market economy theory, the relationship between supply and demand balances out at a point in the future; this point is called the equilibrium price.

Economists and companies analyze the relationship between supply and demand when making strategic product decisions. Both economists and companies analyze the relationship between supply and demand when making strategic product decisions. The assumption behind a market economy is that supply and demand are the best determinants for an economy's growth and health.

Consumer Behavior Influences Demand

One way that companies or economists might analyze this relationship is to create graphs that chart the equilibrium price of certain goods and services in order to determine product development and their production schedule. Consumer behavior dictates which products are produced and sold because consumers create the demand that companies attempt to meet. As a result, companies may study consumer behavior in an attempt to understand the current demand and predict future demand. It is vital that companies maintain the capacity to produce enough of a good or service that they can satisfy consumer demands. For example, in a real-world scenario, if consumers exhibit a strong brand loyalty (a psychological factor), their demand for a product might remain high even if competitors offer slightly lower prices. A behavioral economist like my view would analyze this loyalty, perhaps linking it to cognitive biases such as the endowment effect or status quo bias, rather than solely focusing on price elasticity . Similarly, suppliers might be influenced by herd behavior or anchoring biases when making production decisions, leading to oversupply or undersupply that traditional models might not fully predict .

My views on the relationship between demand and supply in economics, particularly within the context of behavioral economics, emphasize how these fundamental principles dictate the viability and pricing of products and services in consumer markets. He argues that understanding the interplay between demand and supply is crucial for businesses to make informed decisions about production and pricing strategies .

Core Principles of Demand and Supply

My view posits that for any product or service, the demand and supply economic theory must be applied to assess its potential value in the consumer market . This assessment guides decisions on whether to invent, sell, or serve customers .

Low Demand Scenario: If the demand for a product or service is low, Lok suggests that manufacturers should not increase production. This strategy aims to prevent "low price" sales, which could devalue the product or lead to losses .

High Demand Scenario: Conversely, if demand is high, manufacturing numbers should be increased to ensure sufficient supply. This allows for "high price" sales, satisfying customer needs while maximizing revenue .

My view highlights that the relationship between demand and supply ultimately determines a reasonable sale price and supply valuation . My view also acknowledges the fundamental economic problem of resource allocation, which arises from scarcity. This problem forces societies to decide which wants to satisfy and which to leave unfulfilled, directly influencing what and how much to produce. Increased production of a good necessitates more resources, which are inherently scarce .

Behavioral Economics Perspective

My contributions to behavioral economics cover several key areas:

Cognitive Biases: My view explores how biases, such as overconfidence or loss aversion, affect individual and collective economic decisions .

Market Behavior: Lok analyzes how psychological factors shape market trends and consumer choices . For instance, he discusses how shifts in consumer preferences due to health trends can significantly influence demand for certain products, leading to price increases as suppliers compete to meet new demand .

Policy Recommendations: My view suggests ways in which policymakers can utilize behavioral insights to design more effective interventions aimed at improving economic outcomes .

My work aims to bridge the gap between theoretical economics and practical applications influenced by human behavior . My view uses actual product and service social situations to explain whether these are more dependent on demand or supply aspects within behavioral economic theory .

Long-Term Demand and Supply Relationships

My view also addresses the challenge of maintaining long-term consumer demand and ensuring that supply can be influenced to increase in a competitive market . My view applies a behavioral economic view to answer how to sustain increasing demand and supply over time . This involves building strong, long-term consumer demand relationships .

For example, my view discusses the role of economic conditions in influencing supply. During economic downturns, businesses may reduce production due to lower consumer spending, leading to decreased supply. Conversely, during economic growth, companies are more likely to invest in increasing production capabilities to meet rising consumer demand .

Specific Applications and Examples

My view often provide examples to illustrate these theories. For instance, in "Introduction Demand And Supply Theory: In Business Environment," my view discusses the impact of consumer preferences on demand, citing the example of a new health trend promoting plant-based diets leading to increased demand for plant-based food products . My view also examines how economic conditions, such as downturns or growth, affect production levels and market dynamics . Another example he explores is the future space tourism leisure market, applying demand and supply theory to determine the reasonable number of providers needed to satisfy future space leisure travelers .

In summary, John Lok's perspective on demand and supply is rooted in traditional economic theory but significantly enhanced by the lens of behavioral economics. He emphasizes the strategic importance of aligning production with demand to optimize pricing and resource allocation, while also acknowledging the psychological and societal factors that influence these dynamics

Supply and demand are two sides of the same market coin. Generally, supply is how much of something is available or will be produced at a certain price. Demand is how much of something people want to purchase or consume at a certain price. One way to develop a more precise relationship between the two is to consider how the price of something affects its supply and its demand. Generally when the price of a good goes up, so does the supply, since firms are willing to create more when they can sell at higher prices. But when the price of a good goes up consumers will, at the same time, generally demand less. It is the interaction of supply and demand that determines how much will be produced and consumed and at what price, converging to a state known as equilibrium.

TWO

STUDENT SUBJECT CHOICE ECONOMIC BEHAVIOR

MY work integrates insights from psychology with traditional economic theories to provide a comprehensive understanding of human behavior in economic contexts, including consumer behavior, market dynamics, and policy implications . My view emphasizes the importance of understanding cognitive biases and emotional influences on decision-making processes .

When considering how a student might choose a subject from an economic viewpoint, drawing upon my perspective, several factors come into play:

1. Cognitive Biases and Emotional Influences

Students, like all individuals, are subject to cognitive biases and emotional influences when making significant decisions such as choosing a field of study. For instance, a student might be influenced by the "bandwagon effect," choosing a popular major due to perceived social validation or future success, rather than a genuine interest . Conversely, "loss aversion" might lead a student to stick with a difficult major they initially chose, fearing the perceived loss of time and effort invested, even if it's not the optimal path for them . Emotions such as excitement about a particular field or anxiety about job prospects can also heavily sway their decision, sometimes overriding purely rational considerations .

2. Perceived Market Behavior and Policy Implications

My work also touches upon how psychological factors shape market trends and consumer choices, and how behavioral insights can inform policy recommendations. From a student's perspective, this translates to their perception of the job market for different subjects. They might choose a subject based on current high demand and salary expectations, influenced by media reports or peer discussions about "hot" industries . This aligns with the concept of human capital theory, where individuals invest in education to increase their future earnings potential . However, these perceptions can be biased, as market trends can shift, and a subject that is popular today might not be as lucrative by the time they graduate . Policy implications, such as government funding for specific research areas or scholarships for certain fields, could also steer student choices by making some subjects more financially attractive .

3. Interdisciplinary Approach and Bridging Theory with Practice

My interdisciplinary approach, integrating psychology with traditional economic theories, suggests that students' choices are not solely driven by economic rationality but also by psychological factors . A student might rationally weigh the costs and benefits of different degrees (e.g., tuition, potential salary, job security) . However, their decision will also be influenced by their personal interests, perceived aptitude, and even the influence of family and friends, which are psychological and social factors . For example, a student might choose a less financially rewarding but personally fulfilling subject because of a strong intrinsic motivation, a factor often explored in behavioral economics .

In essence, a student's choice of subject, from my behavioral economics perspective, is a complex interplay of rational economic calculations, cognitive biases, emotional responses, and perceptions of market dynamics and policy incentives. It's not simply about maximizing future income, but also about navigating personal preferences and psychological influences within the broader economic landscap.

The provided information about my opinon, "Economic Choices: The Role Of Emotion And Reasoning" and "Behavioral Economy Theory," focuses on topics such as:

How emotions influence economic choices alongside rational thinking .

The impact of technology and robots on consumer and organizational behavior .

The influence of human behavior on economic development .

Cognitive biases like overconfidence or loss aversion affecting economic decisions .

Market behavior and consumer choices influenced by psychological factors .

Policy recommendations based on behavioral insights .

While my work broadly covers how psychological and economic factors intertwine to shape various decisions, there is no specific mention or exploration of how these principles might guide students in selecting their academic subjects. The content primarily addresses economic decision-making in consumer, organizational, and policy contexts, rather than individual educational choices .

Therefore, based solely on the provided authoritative sources, does not suggest ways in which economic principles influence students' subject choices.

- What factors influence student makes subject choice decision

Behavioral economic on law and economy subject choice how to student individual subject learning choice behavior in universities economy and law subjects choice example, whether students will make subject either law or economt subject choice, it depends on future lawyer and economist salary whether which occupation can earn long term more salary comparision in order to decide wither law or economy degree learn.

Some university students make these two subjects either one learning choice, they will decide whether school fee is how much more than future salary earns, or personal interest psychological factor influences. So, if the student feels more interest to learn law degree , then he won't choose economy degree between these two degrees. Behavioral economy theory can be applied to explain this student individual economy and law degrees choice behavior because his subject choice decision is depended on personal psychological interest factor more than school fee or future salary possible earn economic salary reward factor influences. But, I assume that if the university can give scholorship for economic and law degree student when the student feels the law degree scholarship higher than economic degree. Then, he will decide to choose law degree to study more than economy degree. He chooses to study law degree because he hopes to earn higher scholarship.

IN behavioral economy principle , it can be applied to explain this student degree choice behavior. However, applying behavioral economy view, it assumes these principles to analyze whether how the student chooses to study the degree. The principles or factors may influence his degree choice may include: Cost and benevits, e.g. the student fee and future salary for the degree, when the student has interest to study law and economic degree. So, he needs to do degree choice. Then, he may compare whether how much law and economy degree school fee, it may be possible future earn salary, scholarship possible reward. All of these factors concern the price for law and economy degree (external cost) and future possible income (salary) for economist and lawyer occupation. It is behavioral law and economic factor to influence how the student chooses either law or economic degree to study in the university.

For example, when the (A) university on student enrolls to the (A) university before, he needs to choose wither law or economy degree to study. I assume that he only feels interest to study these two degrees. Then, he will compare school fees, if law degree school fee is per year US$5,000, 4 years is US$20,000 and economy degree school fee is per year US$3,000, 4 years is US$12,000. Although, it seems that economy 4 year school fee is more less US$8,000 to compare law degree 4 year, but this student also compare possible future salary for lawyer and economist occupation. He believes that future lawyer salary may pay more 4 times to compare economists salary after 5 years working experience. Although, if this student chooses economy degree to study, he may have chance to earn scholarship if his examination can be good, but it is one time short time economic researd and this scholarship reward is not sure that he must earn, if he can not get at least 5 (A) grade any one economic subject papers in this university economy degree structure. Otherwise, if he chooses to study law and get 5 (A) grade any one law subject papers in the university law degree structure, he can not get scholarship for this law degree. hence , he makes final choice to study law degree, although he can not get scholarship and school fee is more than economy degree. But he believes that he can earn higher salary when he can be one lawyer and he works after 5 years, his salary may be paid more than one economist salary.

In behavioral economic view, it can be applied to explain this university student his degree choice behavior, then he has interest to study law and economy degree. He must need to make one degree choice to graduate, then he may make degree choice decision by external economic cost (degree price) and future reward (possible income) behavioral economic factor . Then, he can judge whether which degree is more suitable to choose to study in this university.

Can economy effects students' academic performance

- Can student individual financial situation or economic environment influence individual learning performance ?

Why does student enrollment rise when the economy recession? When a strugging economy certainly forces extra pressure on young students seeking funds for loans and tuition cost, the enrollment rates for colleges continuous to rise. In fact, some experts theoritize that a poor economy environment actually helps a stimulate student enrollment. Whether it is the economy , new academic programs or better recruiting, community colleges are seeing an enrollment boom, when enrollment has been growing steadily , it may increase year institutions. To help prospective student interests when providing all current students with diverse support.

What the motivation had factors that are encouraging students to enroll, e.g. whether it is that the country 's young people feel the country begins have poor economy, so many of them choose to enroll schools to learn new knowledge, because scoial poor economy environment, it won't have many employers like to pay more salaries to employ new employees, consequencey, unemployment rate will rise, it causes students feel difficult to find jobs to do in general, even graduate students. So, it seems that economy recession may encourage students further study, because job supply is decreasing. so, it causes many young people choose to spend time to further study in order to wait economy recovery later. Then, they can prepare to seek any new jobs more easily when there are many employers like to increase employees number.

So, it explains that they have case and effect relationship between student enrollment number and the country's economy growth or recession or recovery, For example, when the country economy growth, in society, it will have many employers like to spend more salaries to employ new employees, because there are many people like to consume, when most of them have jobs to do and earn higher income. so, it seems that in society consumer individual increasing consumption attitude/desire that can help businesses grow, when businesses have more customers, they have effort to pay money

to buy any things to use.
Businessmen ought need to increase employees number to help them to develop themselve businesses more successfully. So, it is economy growth period, moreover, many young people feel economy growth can create more employment chance in society. So, it encourages many students choose to forget to continue to pursue high level academic education, e.g. when the student had graduated undergraduate degree, due to he feels social economic environment is improved. So, employers are seeking new employees to help them to develop businesses. So, employment chance increases and salaries level will also rise. So, it encourages many undergraduate students do not want to pursue master degree. Because they believe that they can find jobs to do more easily in this time. So, it seems that the society's present economy suitation is either goos or worse, it can impact students to choose continue pursue higher learning stage or not. So, it explains that student individual learning desire and the social economy have close influential relationship.

- Why does economy scenarios can influence student learning behavior?

Why does economy scenarios can influence motivation and learning behavior on student achievement? Quality in higher education is not only determined by lecturers, it also depends on student individual learning desire, because if economy scenarios can influence the student learning desire to pursue continue learning or seek jobs in society. Then, quality in higher education won't be main factor to influence student individual learning in success or failure. If the student does not plan to continue to learn, even the school has good quality in higher education , it won't attract the student to choose to enrol to the school to continue learn easily. It is due to whether economy scenarios how influences the student decides to pursue or forget further study.

In fact, any countries must encounter or experience economic recession or economic growth or economic recovery period different social economic environment changes. It will bring negative or positive emotion impact to the country's every student learning attitude, in order to decide whether continue pursue learning is better or forget pursue learning is better. So, school fee whether is high or less, it is not main factor to influence student individual continue learn.

In macro economic view, the social's economic growth, or economic recession or economic recovery , any one of these economic scenarios change, it will bring positive or negative emotion impact to encourage the student either chooses to further learning pursue or forgive further learning pursue, in student further learning social behavioral economic view.

ON conlusion, on behavioral economic analytical theory, it explains our social macro economic environment new changes to be better or worse, it may bring indirect impact to influence the country's student individual learning desire or learning behavior either on pursue continue learning or forget continue learning in global societies. So, it also implies that whether the school's fee whether it is more or less, it is not main factor to influence student individual continue pursue to learn or not. If the student feels that movement, himself/herself country's social economic scenario is worse, or it is experiencing recession. The student will be influenced to choose continue to go to school to pursue further learning. So, worse economic environment or recession macro economic environment feeling, it may persuade any country's students trend to choose to pursue further study intention more than seeking jobs to work intention, because they feel social jobs provisin chances are influenced to reduce, and no many jobs to supply to them to choose, salaries will be reduced etc . these factors , they can caes the country will have many students make school enrollment choice more than seeking jobs choice. Hence, I believe that any country students school enrollment choices, they have close relationship to themselves country's economic scenario changes at the moment. Hence in behavioral economic view, it may explain why and how any country's economic environment can bring either positive or negative emotion influence to persuade or dissuade the student chooses to either continue further academic study or forgive continue further academic study. So, behavioral economy theory is one kind of new economy and psychological science. Psychologists can apply this theory to research and explain and conclude how and why our social economy change can impact students, consumers, households, businessmen believe in order to make rational decision to earn more economic benefit and avoid economic loss. Also, behavioral economy theory also may help psychologists and economists to predict how and why our societies will ought to be changed to be better ot worse by which kind of factors accurately. So, it may help government leaders or businesses organizations decision makers to do more accurate decisions or strategies to solve any challenges in success.

THREE

METHODS INCREASE CONSUMER DEMAND NUMBER

My concepts of intellectual demand and supply, rooted in behavioral economics, can be implemented in business strategies by focusing on understanding psychological factors influencing consumer behavior, optimizing sales team performance, and developing effective marketing and organizational strategies. My work emphasizes bridging the gap between theoretical economics and practical applications by analyzing cognitive biases and emotional influences on decision-making .

Understanding Consumer Behavior and Market Dynamics

My approach suggests that businesses should delve into the psychological factors that drive consumer demand. This involves:

Identifying Cognitive Biases: Businesses can analyze how biases like overconfidence or loss aversion affect their target consumers' purchasing decisions . For example, understanding loss aversion might lead to marketing strategies that highlight what consumers stand to lose by not purchasing a product, rather than just what they gain. This can be applied to product pricing, promotional offers, and even subscription models .

Analyzing Emotional Influences:

My writings stress the importance of emotional factors in economic decision-making . Businesses can leverage this by crafting marketing messages that evoke specific emotions, building brand loyalty through emotional connections, and designing user experiences that cater to emotional needs. For instance, a luxury brand might focus on evoking feelings of exclusivity and aspiration .

Building Long-Term Consumer Demand Relationships: L

My highlights the necessity of building long-term consumer demand relationships to ensure sustained growth . This can be achieved through consistent product quality, excellent customer service, personalized marketing, and fostering a sense of community around the brand. Loyalty programs and subscription services are practical examples of this strategy .

Optimizing Sales Team Performance

My work also extends to improving internal business operations, particularly sales. His insights suggest:

Assessing Salespeople Psychology: Businesses should aim to understand the psychological makeup of their sales teams, identifying individual strengths and weaknesses in sales skills . This involves evaluating how cognitive biases might affect a salesperson's approach or how emotional intelligence impacts their interactions with clients .

Targeted Sales Training:

Based on the assessment of individual salespeople, businesses can implement tailored training programs to address specific weaknesses . For example, if a salesperson struggles with closing deals due to a fear of rejection, training could focus on resilience and objection handling techniques. If another lacks persuasive communication, workshops on behavioral influence could be beneficial .

Linking Sales Skills to Organizational Growth:

My view posits that the sales skills of a team are a major factor influencing long-term sales growth . By continuously improving these skills through training and development, businesses can directly impact their revenue and market share. This also involves creating a supportive environment where salespeople feel empowered and motivated .

Developing Effective Marketing and Organizational Strategies

My interdisciplinary approach, integrating psychology with traditional economic theories, provides a framework for broader strategic development:

Behavioral Economics in Marketing:

Businesses can apply behavioral economic principles to design more effective marketing campaigns. This includes using nudges to guide consumer choices, framing products in a way that appeals to specific biases, and understanding the impact of social proof or scarcity on purchasing decisions . For example, limited-time offers leverage the scarcity principle to drive immediate demand .

Strategic Decision-Making for Entrepreneurs:

My recommendations guide entrepreneurs in choosing marketing, economic, and human resource strategies to enhance organizational efficiency and effectiveness . This involves making data-driven decisions that consider both traditional economic indicators and behavioral insights.

Addressing Organizational Inefficiencies:

My view suggests that businesses, including large organizations, can identify and address weaknesses in their marketing, economic, or human resource strategies by applying behavioral insights . For instance, if employee motivation is low, behavioral economics can inform incentive structures that are more effective than traditional monetary rewards alone, by considering factors like recognition and autonomy .

Policy Recommendations:

While primarily focused on business, my work also touches upon how behavioral insights can inform better economic policies and practices . Businesses can adapt this by developing internal policies that are designed with an understanding of human behavior, leading to more effective outcomes in areas like employee retention, productivity, and ethical conduct .

By systematically applying these concepts, businesses can gain a deeper understanding of their markets and internal operations, leading to more robust and sustainable growth in competitive environments .

- How organization improvement may bring economic benefits

Can organizational economies, e.g. transaction cost economics, agency theory, organizational theory , e.g. models of formal organizational independent of the strategies, improve organizational behavior in order to bring economic benefit, e.g. development potentially valuable resources and capabilities, it can raise internal organizatonal strengths and avoid weaknesses in SWOT strategy in order to imporve performance and bring organizational internal economic benefit in organizational behavioral economic view.

For manufacturing industry example, if the car manufacturers can attempt to discover the most efficient steel, or different kinds of car components material, but they can help it to manufacture many high quality cars. Then, their manufactury cost reduce , but its any model of car quality does not caused to poor. Then, this car firm can apply the most efficient and the most high component materials to help it to manufacture high quality cars. Although, it must need to spend time to research how to invest the most efficient and high quality car manufacture components, but if it can apply the most efficient and the high quality components to help it to manufacture any new model of cars. Then, new components research spending time can bring long term low manufacturing cost and high quality of cars to achieve long time economic benefits.So, on behavioral economic view, organization's spending time on different kind of cheap and high quality car manufacture manufacture components research and research expenditure spending on new kinds of different car manufacture components, it can help it to sell the high quality of different model of cars to satisfy car buyer comfortable needs. Moreover, it can earn high profit, when it 's any car manufacture component cost reduces. So, SWOT internal strengths (high quality and low cost) to this car manufacturer. It may help it to bring long term raising profit economic benefit, when its any new model of car prices do not need raise, but their compared material manufacture cost reduce, due to new kinds of car manufacture component materials can be invented in success.Hence, high quality and low cost of car manufacture component invention researching on spending time and research experiment expenditure is value to this car manufacture company, because if high quality and low cost car manufacture component experience succeeds, it can help it to improve any new model of cars quality , but the most important factor is that its any new model of cars prices do not need increase. So, car buyer individual purchase desire won't be influenced to choose any brand of car seller to replace it more easily.

For one drug development process, case example ,I assume that this drug manufacture firm can attempt to spend 10 years time, but it can help it has possible to help it to invent one kind of new pharmaceutical drugs to kill cancer cells for global cancer patients. So, its spending time research on new drugs to kill any kinds of cancers cellers and experimentation expenditure is value, because it can help it to bring economic benefit when global will have many cancer patients believe its new discovery of cancer drugs , it may help them to kill cancer cells to get health or reduce death chance ratio raises after 10 years.

Consequently, in soon future, it's global cancer patients number may increase when they choose to buy its future new cancer drugs paroduct. It may bring high profit economic benefit. So, on organizational behavioral economic view, when the organization spends long time and experimentation expenditure to research new resources, if these new resources can be invented in success and it ensures help it to increase clients number to order to bring future economic benefit. The organization is value to spend time and expenditure to carry on new resources research.

- Can organization apply behavioral economic demand to evaluate work performance for whole different departments?

Behavioral economies investigation may include evaluating demand for a commodity (such as drug experimentation and car manufacturing component material etc.) is given changes in price, using hypothetical purchase tasks, which are a reliable and efficient assessment method. Can behavior management examine work performance evaluation? The work performance evaluation target includes that employee individual and different department will performance evaluation in organization.
I believe high quality or low quality training , which can be evaluated whether the employee individual work performance or the department overall employees work performance can be improved after training. So, if the department employee individual or all employers work performance can be improved, e.g. work efficiency raises, client satisfactory feeling raises, product sale number . Then, the training is a high quality training to help the organization to earn future high economic benefit. Otherwise , if the organization can not earn above any one good result. Then, the training ia a low quality training.So, any organization can attempt to observe any department overall performance and employee individual performance in order to evaluate whether it can provide high or low quality of training to let employees to learn.

So, employee individual behavior can bring performance evidence to let the organization to evaluate whether its training is useful or not useful to achieve its training aim, e.g. when the car manufacturer provides money, time, effort training arrangement to teach all workers to learn how to manufacture car skill. After training provision, many of them, they do not need to work over time more than one hour to manufacture daily of least 10 cars per employee.Before, any one worker must need to spend more than one hour over time to manufacture daily 10 more cars.

So, when this car manufacture skillful improvement train is provided more

than one hour more than one hour , none of them, they need work over time in order to manufacture more than at least 10 cars number per day. It seems that training improvement arrangement can be used to evaluate whether employee individual efficiency can be raised in organizational behavioral economic view.
Hence, any organization's internal training provision knowledge resource, it can be evaluated employees' behavioral performance can be improved, about being available to work, about role performance . It assumes that employees are likely to come to work and remain in the organization if they obtain satisfaction from their jobs, and that they are likely to put use effort and work more effectively if they are to be reward more for their effort and performance can be comfirmed to improved by management after they are taught by training. So, when the employee hopes to raise salary, he must hard to learn any new knowledge from the organizational training. Then, training can help the " expectation good reward employees" can improve performance in organizational behavioral economic view.

It is one important successful factor to help the organization to innovate and bring economic benefit, when the organization can implement any new useful training to improve any new useful training to imprve empllyee skills. It means that training is one long term economic organizational strategy, it depends on whether the training is useful or is ot useful in order to help any old employees to raise or improve their skills to achieve raising efficiency and satisfactory client service , sale product number, product manufacture increasing number aims.

Can ethics behavior help organizations to bring economic benefit

- How ethic help organizations to bring economic benefit

Organizational ethic behavior concerns with explaining employee individual behavior in organization, e.g. ethical decision making, ethical conduct for example, when one marketing department manager does not attempt to carrying on any data research about new market research to sell the new model iphone to any country. He only depends on his personal judgement, he believes that this new invention of US iphone producs, they ought to be sell to Korean new iphone market, because he feels Korean must prefer to choose to buy US drand of new iphone products to compare other countries iphone product. However, this iphone marketing development manager lacks enough data research for different Korean iphone buyer age target, purchase experience, purchase desire to conclude Korean iphone buyers must like to buy any brand of US iphone products in preference.

His non ethical new iphone invention decision making to choice Korean ipohone buyers market will bring time waste rick to satisfy Korean iphone buyers' needs to replace other new model ipone users market, e.g. Hong KOng, China, ipone market. So, his ethical decision making to Korean iphone buyers ne iphone invention market may bring less economic benefit to this US iphone manufacture firm. So, this new model ipohone marketing development immoral judgement of this iphone marketing development manager individual decision making to Korean new model ipone invention to Korean ipone users, it can bring high economic loss to this US iphone firm.Otherwise, if this marketing department manager can spend time to carry on data gathering to make more accurate new model iphone invention decision making to choose which one country, then his ethical decision making may help his this US iphone firm to reduce new iphone invention loss risk. So, it explains that why ethic organizational behavior may influence the firm can earn more or less economic benefit. SO, ethic or moral behavior can influence the organization can earn how much economic benefit in long term significantly in organizational behavioral economic view.

● Can improve energy efficiency by organization building occupant's energy consumption relative behavior to bring economic benefit?

Reducing energy consumption in building , it must improve efficiency by building, but whether they have close cause and effect relationship between occupant's energy consumption behavior and improvement energy efficiency to the building? IN fact, high efficiency equipment is being developed, it can help any building to save energy and economic effectiveness, if building energy is subject to uncertainties, such as whether variations, human operations, human behavior changes and government policies. So, building technology equipment improvement may be one main factor to help buildings to save energy . But why occupant behavior may help building to save energy by their daily energy consumption behavior.
The occupant energy behavioral user inputs factor may include: Weather influences, internal heat gain, efficiencies, simplied/ normal occupant behaviors, e.g. a high efficiency chiller can save very limited energy in cold climates due to minimal cooling load, and a good designed natural

ventilation building won't work if the occupants do not open windows when outdoor air favors cooling. So, it seems that if one living building hopes to reduce energy consumption, instead of building equipment technological change , e.g. air condition facilities, building occupants , artificial intelligent light, life, their daily energy consumption behaviors, they can influence the living building's energy consumption level in occupant energy consumption behavior and building energy saving economic benefit view.

In fact, when the occupant considers hot water, air condition, energy gas electricity expenditure, he won't use excess electricity, gas resources, because he needs to pay more energy expenditure , when gas and electricity energy consumption expenditure is applied to any business organization offices, warehouses , shops working facilities environment, such as offices, warehouses , shops can often use less electricity, gas energy far ther employees daily work . In long time, the organization must may reduce much electricity, gas energy expenditure for whole organizations business activities. In organizational behavior economic view, organizational energy consumption reduces it can help it to bring less expenditure spending economic benefit.

Why can global consumer behavioral change influence global economic change ?

How to apply behavioral economic theory to explain
Amazon business e-commerce organizational behavior
can bring economic benefit to our societies

● Can Amazon e-commerce organization business activities bring ecoonomic benefit to global societies?

Amazon e-commerce is one online product sale e-commerce organization. Any one country e-buyer can use his/her home computer to click to Amazon webstores, when he/she saw the product phone and price, then he/she feels the product's price is reasonable and he/she believes that he/she can make the best choice to buy the product. Then, he/she can pay visa to buy the product from Amazon webstore.

Amazon can bring the most convenient online sale channel to global any one e-buyer. The e-buyer can buy the oveseas product from its e-webstores . He does not need to catch air plane to fly to the e-sellers' shop. he can pay visa to pay the product from Amazon e-webstores any time immediately. All Amazon e-webstores . He can open 24 hours, so all webstores have no close time. So , it can bring busy working people, they do not need to spend long time to visit any shops to make purchase decision. For busy working people example, time has important value to them, they do not want to waste time to make any purchase choice. So, Amazon gives " economic purchase time benefit " to global any one full time working people. In their psychology, Amazon can help them to save much time to go to online shopping purchase chance at homes. They can stay at homes to shopping. Even, when they give their their address to Amazon to know, Amazon will deliver their products to their homes within several days rapidly. Also , they do not need to pay money to buy its products immediately. They can only pay visa to buy the product from Amazon webstores. So, they can save " consumption money" to use for another need in short time. So, one individual e-air ticket buyer, Amazon can bring economic benefit to him, he does not need to buy air ticket to fly to another country to buy the product. Amazon webstores are given more different kinds of similar brand products to let him to choose in order to pay the most reasonable price, working people do not need to spend much visiting shop time to choose any products in order to make the final purchase decision at home rapidly, any one has visa card , he/she can buy the product from Amazon webstores at homes.

Instead of individual e-buyer ecommerce time benefit, spending little time product choice, reducing catching air plane to visit another country seller shop to pay air ticket expense and travelling time spending activities to every e-buyer . Amazon also brings global economic benefits to any one country. When the e-buyer lives in one country to buy the product, it is saved in the overseas country's warehouse. Then, the product must need to deliver to his home by air plane. So, all of Amazon products can bring global goods air transport delivering service to any one overseas buyer, when the product is saved in the overseas seller's warehouse. Any one Amazon product overseas transpor delivery service activity, it can help air goods transport service need increases as well as their goods air transport service income will also increase. Amazon can bring global air goods transport service need increases. It can assist global GDP air goods transport industry grows, and economic benefit for the country's air plan goods delivery service industry development in long term. Hence, on behavioral economic view, Amazon online sale channel ,it can help global economic benefit to air plane goods delviery service industy as well as individual differeent country e-buyer individual time saving and short term money saving economic benefit by visa payment method.

Moreover, Amazon alsoo creates more high technology employment chance to any one country because Amazon owns many offices and warehouses in different countries, due to it is one high technological e-commerce online sale organization, It must need many high skillful website designers to help it to design different countries webstores in order to satisfy any one e-buyer online purchase need. So, it creates high technology job chance to any one country webstore designers . It can help them to raise competitive effort when any one graduate pursues website designer career. IN Amazon provides good employent chance for any one country computer ecommerce designers in order to let them to earn high salary. Also, Amazon public e-commerce organization provides good chance for any one country author to earn royalty income when he/she publishes any electronic or paper books to sell from Amazon publish. It gives good writing skillful authors have more writing chance to help them to sell electronic books and /or paper books from its different countries webbook stores to different countries' readers in short time. It can help them to increase book sale chance to let different countries book buyers can know whether new book topic to the author, he/she will publish soon. So, it brings author's new writing mind training chance when he/she needs to compare book sale rank from Amazon webstores.

Hence, Amazon can bring social employment benefit and author individual skillful training advantage and royalty income benefit to any on country author in nowadays online published industty. So, Amazon online business activities can increase global social employment chance, encourages global authors attempt to train writing skill, helps e-buyers to save visiting shops shopping time and air ticket expenditure for global overseas buyers.

- How and why Amazon e-commerce organization influence global consumee behavioral changes to bring ecommerce benefits to sellers?

In behavioral economic view, Amazon changes consumers behavior as well as product sellers sale method, such as global consumer sellers began to accept online purchase method to replace frequent visiting shop purchase method and global sellers began to accept to apply Amazon webstores to help them to sell products from its online sale channel to replace opening shops locate to the country sale channel.

The advantages to global sellers may include they do not need to pay rent or buy the shops, they can use Amazon webstores to show their different kinds of products photos and prices to let any one online buyer to know . The advantage to global buyers, they do not need to spend time to visit any countries shops to choose products in order to make purchase decision. They only need to spend some time to visit amazon any one country's webstore to see any brands of product photos and know their prices to different kinds of products to compare design and price and functions among of them in the online visiting short time when they stay at home to trun on themselves home computers . So, future home consumption behavior may replace visiting shop consumption behavior. Amazon 's online purchase method will encourage global many sellers have began to believe traditional visiting shop purchase model can not be accepted to global any one consumer more easily, when any one owns computer and internet service at home in common. Then, global shops number will reduce, due to different kinds of product websites purchase model needs number increases to global product sellers, they will close their shops and open themselves webstores or choose Amazon webstore to help them to sell their products conveniently. Consequently, global online purchase and sale transactions number will be influenced to increase by e-commerce organization development.

Why can global consumer behavioral change influence global economic change?

- Have they close relationship between consumer behavioral change and economic change?
- How does consumer behavioral change impact economic change?
- How does cosumer behavior bring positive or negative influence to economic growth or economic recession to the country?

I shall attempt to apply behavioral economic theory to explain their cause and effect relationship why and hoe global economy growth or recession may be impacted by global consumer behavior change reasons ae below:

I shall indicate travellingleisure and goods air plane transport industries example, since air planes are invented, it is a kind rapid air transport tool, it can help human to do both kinds of transport asrvice, one is goods transport and another is human transport . So, any individual or business goods can be delivered to another country offices or homes by air planes transport tools rapidly. SO, air planes can create more overseas purchase and sale business activities chance between different countries nowadays. Moreover, internet invention, it also increase more e-coomerce online purchase and sale business acitivies to global any one online buyer, he/she only needs to apply computer tool to click to the online seller webstore, when he /she likes the product, he/she can pay visa to buy the product from the onlin seller webstore at home conveniently.

Hence, e-commerce encourages global consumers to choose to buy any products from internet channel, it also brings global goods are needed to transport by air planes between different countries, e.g. one US online buyer makes purchase decision from onlin channel, then he chooses the product from Korean one online seller webstore. After he pays visa to the Korean online seller webstore , then the Korea seller will follow his US address to send the product to the US buyer's home after several days rapidly.
Hence, it explains that if future global consumers like to buy any products from any one country's onine sell webstore. Then, the product must need to be delivered to the online buyer's home. When the seller's product is not located to the online buyer's country warehouse. It needs to be delivered by air plane. When, global there are man consumers, their traditional visiting shops purchase habits are influenced to change online visiting webstores habits. Then, when their purchase habits are influenced to change by rapid, convenient, visa card payment online purchase method at home, time online purchase technological new payment channel method.

In future new online purchase trend development, it may influence future global traditional visiting shops consumption model to change visiting webstores consumption model. Consequently, consumers will choose to pay visa online purchase at home in preference. Also, it encourages visa card purchase , consequently, online purchase may influence these industries development, airlines goods transport service needs increase, it can increase new visa cards number to the frequent online channel e-buyer number. So, online consumption encourages global households save long time money in banks, because we can pay money by visa card payment after we buy any products from online. Global bank may have more money to save longer time from global households, long time money save , because we do not need to withdraw money to buy any expensive products, immediately, e.g. computer , television, furniture etc. When global households begin to accept online purchase method is better to compare visiting shop purchase method. So, future global airline goods transport and bank saving businesses these two industries may have positive impact by future global online buyers raising number.

Hence, when global consumers behaviors began to change online purchase , their online purchase activities may influence global banks can have long time saving money and airlines goods transport need increase rapidly. However, online purcahse activies will bring negative consumers emotion impact to some businesses, e.g. property rent business, because when the country has high population of consumers, they choose online purchases, they won't often vitis shops to choose any kind of products frequently, they only like to stay at home and turn on themselves home computers to find whether global whom sellers, they have webstores to let global consumers to buy their products from online channel. Due to the cuntry willl not have many consumers like to spend time to visit any shops in the country. It means that the country will have many shops are needed to be close, because there are less number peple visit the businessmen shops every day. It will cause property rent service providers can not increase rent income, even decrease rent income, when there are many businessmen close their shops and change onine webstores to replace actual shops. Hence, it seems that online buyers number increases, it may also brings positive impact to influence shop rent service income decreases to the property rent developers.

On global macro economic changing environment, online buyers number increases, it can encourage any kinds of products, they can sell more more easily. So, global product sale number may be influenced to increase rapidly, when global online purchase and sale transactions number increase, GDP on any kinds of product income may be influenced to increase . So, online buyers number increases, it must may bring positive impact to influence global trading GDP high growth, but global shops rent income property developers may be influenced to reduce, due to there are many shops may be caused to close in possible.

How travellers' leisure need change, it may influence travelling leisure service industry development? I shall attempt to explain how COVID 19 disease influences global travellers lesiure need change and airpine and travelling service providers, e.g. hotels, travelling agents, their leisure service needs change. Nowadys, COVID 19 disease has caused global many travellers feel fear to catch airplanes, because air planes all windows are needed to close, he/she has COVID disease, then he/she can bring any one passegner to get this kind of disease by air plane close window air environment. So, when globa many travellers feel afreaid to catch air planes, this kind of COVID 9 air contact disease, it can cause global travellers number has began to reduce, many of travelles began to reduce travelling times per year, even 0 time travel per year. Consequently, it will bring negative impact to global travelling industry development.

Firstly, COVID 19 disease influences global traveller individual travelling desire decreases, every traveller began to avoid to catch air planes to travel. So, any country;s airlines air planes flying times began to reduce, because it is no full seats booking to any airlinees. It means that airlinee must decrease income, alsoo they need to pay parking airplanes rent to any countries airports. So, fixed rent expenditure will need to pay, and many airlines began to dismiss the excess extra number of airline front service staffs, e.g. airport front service staffs, air plane check in /out staffs, even pilots number began also decreased.
So, airline unemployment ratio increases , it causes pilots, airlines service staffs need to change jobsm even some coutnries pilots , choose to do simple goods delivery jobs in supermarkets or securities. Also, COVID 19 disease influences hotels, travelling agents income began to reduce, because there are none many travellers need to live hotels, and they do not need travelling agents to help them to arrange any travelling journeys. So , COVID 19 disease influences many different countries travellers began choose any leisure activities to replace travel, because they feel afraid to get COVID 19 disease when they need to sit in closed window air plane environment.

This kind of disease can influence any one travller individual leisure choice began to change, such as they began to forgive travel siure activities, they will spend holiday to do other leisure activities in themselves countries , e.g. climbing mountain, swimming, running, playing table tennis, tennis etc. different outdoor sports. all of these leisure sports have same features, global any one leisure needer, he does not catch air plane to fo to another country to carry on playing these any one sport and he/she does not need to pay more price to enjoy these sports. Otherwise m travelling leisure activity, it must need any one leisure needer to spend much expenditure to enjoy this kind of leisure activity . So, it explains why many travellers beagan to choose to do any kinds of sports to replace spending money to enjoy travel leisure in their holidays.

On conclusion, this COVID 19 disease had influenced global travel leisure businesses and travel related leisure service industries income and travellers number began to reduce and any countries GDP on travelling industry will have negative economic recession occurrence in this COVID 19 disease global envionment. Hence, it implies thaat consumers (travellers) behavior leisure activities need, it may influence global business activities increase or decrease , global economic growth or recession, they have close cause and effect relationship between consumer behavioral change and industries GDP changes in behavioral economic view.

Organizations, in their decision-making processes, implicitly or explicitly rely on this foundational principle to justify their ownership of intellectual assets like patents, copyrights, and trade secrets. This belief in the inherent right to the fruits of intellectual labor drives decisions to invest in research and development, creative works, and brand building.

Decision-making influence:

Investment in R&D and creative works: Organizations are more likely to invest significant capital and human resources into developing new technologies, products, and creative content if they believe they can secure exclusive rights to these innovations. This aligns with Locke's idea that labor should be rewarded with property.

Legal protection strategies: Companies decide to pursue patents, copyrights, and trademarks to protect their intellectual creations, viewing these as extensions of their property rights. This is a direct application of the Lockean justification for intellectual property.

Valuation of intellectual assets: The perceived ability to own and control intellectual property contributes to its valuation as an asset on a company's balance sheet, influencing mergers, acquisitions, and investment decisions.

Decision-making influence:

Open innovation and licensing: Organizations might decide to license their intellectual property or participate in open innovation ecosystems, recognizing that widespread use of an idea can sometimes lead to further innovation and expansion of the "common of ideas," ultimately benefiting society and potentially the original creator through new markets or collaborations.

Balancing exclusivity with public benefit: Decisions around the scope and duration of intellectual property rights often involve a tension between rewarding the creator (exclusivity) and ensuring public access and further innovation (enough and as good). Organizations, especially those in highly innovative sectors, may consider the long-term societal impact of their IP strategies, even if driven by self-interest.

Corporate social responsibility: Some companies might choose to make certain intellectual assets freely available for public good, such as releasing patents for humanitarian purposes, reflecting a broader interpretation of the "enough and as good" principle in a modern context.

Decision-making influence:

Commercialization strategies: Organizations are incentivized to actively commercialize their intellectual property rather than "shelving" it, to maximize its value and prevent its obsolescence. This aligns with the spirit of the non-waste condition, ensuring that the labor invested in creating the idea yields benefit.

Portfolio management: Companies regularly review their IP portfolios, deciding which patents to maintain, license, or abandon based on their potential for commercial exploitation and value generation. This prevents "waste" of intellectual assets that could otherwise contribute to economic activity.

Strategic abandonment: In some cases, organizations might strategically abandon IP that is no longer valuable or relevant, allowing it to enter the public domain, which can be seen as a form of preventing waste by making it available for others to use.

Understanding intellectual demand and supply is crucial for enhancing innovation within a business by providing a strategic framework to identify opportunities, allocate resources effectively, and foster a culture of continuous improvement. This approach moves beyond simply reacting to market needs to proactively shaping the future of product development and organizational capabilities .

The Concept of Intellectual Demand and Supply

Intellectual demand refers to the need for new knowledge, ideas, technologies, and solutions within a business or market. This demand can be driven by evolving customer expectations, competitive pressures, technological advancements, or internal inefficiencies . Intellectual supply, conversely, encompasses the availability and generation of these intellectual assets, whether through internal research and development (R&D), external partnerships, or the adoption of existing innovations .

In the context of supply chain innovation, intellectual demand and supply can be categorized into several key areas:

Supply-Side Innovation: This focuses on developing and implementing new methods, technologies, or processes to improve efficiency, reduce costs, and enhance flexibility within the supply chain itself . Examples include investments in R&D, process optimization, and knowledge acquisition .

Demand-Side Innovation: This is driven by market research and data analysis to understand consumer behavior and trends, leading to the development of products and services that meet or exceed customer expectations . This can involve product differentiation, cost reduction, timely shipping, and tailored customer service .

Environmental Policy Innovation: This involves creating a favorable policy environment that indirectly affects innovation, such as financial support, tax incentives, and strategic planning ..

Enhancing Innovation Through Intellectual Demand and Supply

Understanding and strategically managing intellectual demand and supply can enhance innovation within a business through several logical steps:

1. Strategic Prioritization and Opportunity Spotting

By analyzing intellectual demand, businesses can identify "hotspots" where innovation can deliver the most value . This involves looking at every stage of the supply chain, from procurement to customer returns, to pinpoint areas of disruption, inefficiency, or where new technologies could unlock value . For example, predictive analytics can forecast demand more accurately, reducing overstocking or stockouts, which directly addresses a key intellectual demand for better inventory management . Similarly, identifying a market demand for sustainable products can drive intellectual supply in circular economy models and eco-friendly logistics .

2. Resource Allocation and Investment Decisions

Innovation intelligence, which is the cornerstone of staying abreast of industry trends and technologies, allows businesses to make informed decisions about where to invest their resources . By evaluating technology trends and forecasting future demand, companies can strategically allocate R&D funds, talent training funds, and capital investments to areas with the highest potential for return . For instance, if there's a clear intellectual demand for enhanced transparency, investing in blockchain technology for tamper-proof tracking becomes a logical step in intellectual supply .

3. Fostering Collaboration and Partnerships

Recognizing that innovation is rarely a solo effort, understanding intellectual demand and supply encourages collaboration . Businesses can leverage external intellectual supply by partnering with startups, research institutions, and even competitors to address common challenges and spark new ideas . This open innovation ecosystem allows for shared risks, faster innovation cycles, and access to diverse expertise . For example, co-innovating with suppliers can lead to mutual growth and value creation, addressing intellectual demand for more efficient and resilient supply chains .

4. Continuous Improvement and Agile Adaptation

The dynamic nature of intellectual demand requires businesses to adopt a culture of continuous learning and agile innovation . By implementing idea management systems, companies can capture insights from employees and partners, leading to incremental improvements and rapid testing of new ideas . This iterative approach, where early-stage failures are embraced as learning opportunities, ensures that the intellectual supply remains responsive to evolving demands and market shifts . For instance, real-time data from IoT devices can provide immediate feedback on supply chain performance, allowing for quick adjustments and continuous optimization .

5. Risk Management and Resilience Building

Understanding intellectual demand for resilience in the face of disruptions drives the intellectual supply of advanced planning capabilities . Technologies like AI and machine learning can predict problems before they happen, while diversified supplier networks and real-time tracking mitigate the impact of unforeseen events . By proactively addressing potential vulnerabilities, businesses can build more robust and adaptable supply chains, ensuring continuity and stability .

6. Driving Product Innovation

The supply chain itself has become a strategic force in driving product innovation [30]. By optimizing supply chain operations, businesses can enable faster prototyping, shorter time-to-market, and greater flexibility in product design . For example, 3D printing allows for rapid prototyping and small production runs, enabling quicker testing and adaptation of new product concepts in response to intellectual demand . Consumer demand for sustainable products also drives innovation in materials and packaging, directly linking intellectual demand to product development .

In conclusion, understanding intellectual demand and supply transforms innovation from a reactive process to a proactive, strategic endeavor. It enables businesses to not only meet current market needs but also to anticipate future challenges and opportunities, ultimately leading to enhanced competitiveness, efficiency, and resilience

FOUR

MARKET ENVIRONMENT HOW INFLUENCES CONSUMER DEMAND

What does market economy mean to oil market?
Market economy theory is an economic system and distribution are guide by the price signals created by the force of suppy and demand. So , the concept of market economy is an economic system in which economic decisions, and the pricing of goods and services are guided by the interactions of a country's individual citizens and businesses.

The both principles of market economy dicated that producers and sellers of goods and servces with offer tham at the highest possible price that consumers are willing to pay for goods and services . When the level of supply needs to level of demand a natural economic equilibrium is achieved. Hong Kong, Singapore, New Zealand, Switerland, United States , Ireland united Kingdom, these countries are applying market economy prinsiple to dominate themselves countries business activities. However, it is difficult to free market economy, because market economy depends on supply and demand regulate the economy, but a time free market economy is an economy in what all resources are owned by individuals.

The advantages of a market economy may include : Innovation, variety, and indidual choices, but it is distribution of wealth, poor work condition and environmental degradation. However, a pure market economy development is difficult because people will always have incentives to use to choose what kinds of product in preference. The characteristics of a market economy, they may include that it is unplanned free enterprise, private property, economic freedom, consumer competition incentive profit pursue, voluntary exchange,, limited government involvement, freedom of enterprise and choice, the role of self interest, market and price, the reliance on technology and capital goods, specialization, use of monetary ad to active, but limited role of government.

So, market economies work using the forces of supply and demand to determine the appropriate prices and quantities for most goods and services in the economy. Hence, one country needs to develop market economy, it needs have a good market environment, such as one commodity needs have advertisement to let consumers to know its existence, in economics, market does not refer why to a fixed location, on enough number balance of buyers and sellers, perfect competition, perfect competition, building good relationship between buyers and sellers, one price (no change) price to any product easily, sound monetary system. Then, when the country can have good market environment, it can develop or implement its market economy strategy more easily.

The free market economy may be the best economic strategy choice because it contributes to economic growth . It ensures competitive markets, supply and demand create competition, which also help ensure that this best goods or services are provided to consumers at a lower price (reasonable price). It can compare the best among perfect competition imperfect competition, oligopoly, monopoly. Hence, market economy encourages market force occurrence, e.g. when the price of crude oil increases, when there are shortages in the supply , when the shortages occur, they become market forces. The demand is more supply, which causes the prices to rise as the crude oil is less available and therefore consumers will be willing to pay more.

The market economy is decides, when the eants of the consumers and the profit motive of the producers will decide what will be produced and management (the owners) together will determine how goods will be produced in a market economy. So, such as oil sale case, when the country has many oil manufactures hope to tisee oil price, they won't manufacture more oil to supply to oil users, e.g. car drivers, public transport service organizations, the aim to bring oil shortage supply in order to rise oil price more easily.

So, free market economy may bring product unfair sale price to any consumers in the country. Because free market economy is too free for manufacturers / producers to make unreasonable product manufacturing decision whether their products manufacturing number (supply number) is more ore less in order to achieve the highest sale price.It won't bring consumer benefit, when they need to pay high price to buy the product in long time. For oil product case example, when the country all oil suppliers, they make decision to manufacture less number oil product in order to reduce oil supply number. They aim to cause oil shortage crise, when the oil needers, e.g. when the country has many air planes need gas to private energy to fly frequently, but gas supply is less to airlines to pay higher gas price to buy, or the country has many people need to catch buses, but gas supply number is less. So, bus companies also need to pay higher gas price to buy even the country has many people own cars. They often need to drive cars to go to work or relax. So, many country car owners , they eed to pay higher gas price to drive themselves cars.

In fact, in the country implements free market economy strategy, so it causes many product manufacturers attempt to cooperate to reduce products manufacturing number. They aim to reduce produc supply , but when consumers number is still increasing. Their demand to the product increases, when the product's demand number is more than supply number, it will cause supply shortage crise. Consequently, the kind of product price may be reasonable to increase. Hence, in consumer behavior view, the country's consumers still accept to pay higher price to buy the product, because they believe the kind of product supply is decreasing.

Hence, it has relationship between how many product choice and consumer payment desire, if the market has many difficukt kinds of product to let consumers to choose, then the kind of product's price can not be increased easily. Such as oil product case, when the country has less number oil manufacturing number. Then, oil buyers feel there are not many oil suppliers to let them to choose and in general these several oil suppliers' oil prices are increasing together . So, oil consumers number will not be influenced to reduce easiy, because they have no many oil suppliers choice in the country.

Can economy theory explains absolute consumer right behavior

What does consumer right behavior mean?

Economic theory is based on the assumption that investors and consumers are rational and very efficient machines. They make the best choices for themselves. Laboratory tests reveal that investors' behaviors are much more complicated relative to the behavior assumes in most economic theories. Hence, economic theories is used by economists, they try to explain economic phenomena, to interpret why and how the economy behaves and what is the best to solution, how to influence or solve these economic phenomean. In principle, the approach to economic theory is divided into positive and normative.

The most popular economic theories include; Analyses of different market structures have yields economic theories that dominate the study of microeconomics. IN general, economic theory is applied to market organizations. They are perfect competition, monololistic competition, olgopolu, imperfect competition.

So, in any business environment, business on abve four type of economic organizations, they may attempt to apply economic theory to complex consumers behavior. Consumer behavior theory is the study of have people make decisions when they purchase, helping businesses and marketers capitalise on these behaviors by predicting how and when a consumer will make a purchase in economic environment organizational view.

In fact, in societies any economic factors may influence consumer behavior. Economic factors that influence consumer behaviors are : personal income, family income, income expectation, savings, liquid asset of consumer. So, it seems that personal income of a person is determinant of consumer individual buying behavior.

Hence, the role theory says that much of what we buy is to fulfill to characteristics of a role we see ourselves as playing. This can help us understand consumer behavior because people are more likely to buy things for what they mean not for what they do. So, the theory is consumer realistic because of consumers focus on a modest let of important goods and services, they may able to achieve societies is close to the theoretical optimum in term over utility.

● How economic theory explains our social consumer behavior causes? For example, one product brand and advertisement strategy, if the product can develop good attractive advertisement and famous brand. Its campaigns may be a real asset in economic view to better meet the needs of its customers and increases sales (socio-economic classification).

If act, instead of economic factor can influence consumer behavior, other factors may also influence they include psychological, social , cultural personal factors, e.g. social class, role and status, personal age, occupation, life style, personality, motivation, past purchase experience. All of these are the consumer individual psychological factor. So, economic environment changes, it may influence consumers, how to decide to buy the kind of products, but this economic factor, it can not control or derminate overall consumer behavior in the overall consumption mrket (country) , in maco economic vie , the micro economic view, psychology factor to the consumer, it can also dominate or control the consumer behavior, e.g. product choice. For example, one lawyer, he had good lawyer job and high income to support him to pay one time expenditure to buy a new car, so he does not pay instalement to the car seller to buy the new car. So, in behavioral economic view, he won't have economic pressure to buy the new car, he does not need to pay installment and interest to own the new car after one year. Hence, when he gathers information concerns the new car technology development, he spends time to compare the new car different brands, price new car dealr choice, purchase timing and amount, after purchase repair service behavior. He makes the evaluation of alternative to different brands of new cars. Although, brand (A) is new car, its price is more expensive to compare other kinds of cars, because it has good design, large size, more seats, steel quality for driving safety reasons. He has enough money economic effort to choose to buy this brand (A) new car. But, when he compares it to another brand (B) new car. Although, its present car price is cheaper, but it does not represent tht its stell quality is worse, or not more driving safety and he also knows that the brand (B) new car will have another new car model to promote to car market, after three months. Moreover, brand (B) new car seller can build famous car brand image to same to brand (A) new car by its advertisement channel.

Hence, it seems that it is one perfect competition (fair competition) new car market in this country. Any new car sallers can dominate or control their new car sale price freely. So, this country new car market competition is serious, because this high income lawyer spends time to compare the both brand (A) and (B) new cars. He will be influenced to choose to buy brand (B) new car by its advertisement. So, this lawyer car purchaser will not feel that friends believe him have high income to influence him to choose to buy the brand (A) new car. He only consider whether which brand (A) and (B) nee car price is more reasonable factor to influence him to make the final new car purchase decision. So, the brand (B) new car's advertisement had persuaded him to choose to buy (A) last invention new car after 3 months. He chooses to delay time to buy brand (B) 's new invention car after 3 months, because he does not need to drive one new car immediately.

Hence, it seems that economic theory factor won't be the main factor to influence the lawyer to buy the brand (A) new car immediately, althought he has high stable income job. His psychological factor also influences his new car brand choice decision, e.g. he will feel that whether it can represent he has high social status or class when friends know he had owned one high price of new car, whether a high price of new car must represent he has high income of lawyer occupation, so, it seems that this high income lawyer must not choose to buy the high price of new car. he must neeed time to gather or research information to evaluate whether which brand of new car is valid to choose to buy.

Consequently, economic theory must not explain absolute right consumer behavior, it also depends on other factor, e.g. behavioral economic psychological factor, to assist it to conclude more accurate judgement why and how the consumer does his/her final purchase decision. So, psychologic economic theory can apply psychology and economic theory to conclude more clear understanding how and why the consumer chooses to do his/her final purchase decision in nowadays consumption market.

FIVE

TECHNOLOGY HOW INFLUENCES CONSUMER DEMAND

My opinion, as expressed in his book "Technology How Influences Consumer Demand Changes," is that technology can shift whether a product's demand number dictates its supply, or vice versa, ultimately impacting pricing and manufacturing decisions .

Here's a breakdown of my perspective:

Technology's Impact on Demand and Supply

According to my opinion, in any society, the principles of demand and supply are crucial for determining the viability and value of products and services in the consumer market . Traditionally, if demand for a product is low, manufacturing should be reduced to avoid "low price" sales. Conversely, if demand is high, manufacturing should increase to meet customer needs and allow for "high price" sales .

My view argues that technology introduces a dynamic element to this traditional economic model. MY

view posits that technology can influence whether the demand for a product or service is primarily driven by its supply, or if the supply is primarily driven by its demand . This interaction, in turn, affects the determination of a reasonable selling price and an appropriate supply number .

Behavioral Economic View

My work often integrates insights from psychology with traditional economic theories to provide a comprehensive understanding of human behavior in economic contexts. My view emphasizes the importance of understanding cognitive biases and emotional influences on decision-making processes . In the context of technology influencing consumer demand, this means that technological advancements can alter consumer perceptions, preferences, and purchasing habits, thereby directly affecting demand .

For example, technology can:

Create new demands: Innovations can introduce entirely new products or services that consumers didn't previously know they needed, thereby generating new demand .

Influence information flow: Technology, such as online platforms and social media, can rapidly disseminate information about products, influencing consumer awareness and desire, which can quickly escalate or diminish demand .

Change accessibility and convenience: E-commerce platforms and improved logistics, enabled by technology, make products more accessible, potentially increasing demand by reducing barriers to purchase .

Alter price sensitivity: Technology can enable price comparison tools, making consumers more aware of pricing and potentially more sensitive to price changes, which can impact demand elasticity .

My book "Technology How Influences Consumer Demand Changes" aims to illustrate actual product or service social situations to explain how these dynamics play out in the real world, focusing on whether demand or supply aspects are more influential from a behavioral economic viewpoint . My broader contributions to behavioral economics include exploring cognitive biases, analyzing market behavior influenced by psychological factors, and suggesting policy recommendations based on behavioral insights .

Broader Context of Technology's Influence

Beyond consumer demand, my view also explores how technology impacts other aspects of the economy and society. For instance, his book "Research How Technology Replaces Human Labor" discusses how artificial intelligence (AI) technology will influence economic development and the human job market . He examines whether AI will replace traditional human workers, particularly in simple jobs, potentially increasing unemployment for low-skilled workers . This perspective highlights technology's pervasive influence across various economic sectors, not just consumer behavior

Another work, "Factors Influence Future Technological Market Development," delves into how technological factors will influence economic development in countries like the US and UK, focusing on areas such as online teaching technology, environmental protection technology, and automation in manufacturing .

These various works by my opinion collectively demonstrate his focus on the multifaceted ways technology shapes economic landscapes, from individual consumer choices to broader labor markets and national economic growth .

Can technology influence human shopping behavioral change?

Nowadays, technological development has reached mature stage, whether technological mature stage may bring positive or negative shopping emotion influence to global consumers. I shall aplly internet inventin or ecommerce shopping channel tool to explain whether internet technology can bring postive or negative influence to global consumer behavior in behavioral economic view.

Internet is a good technological tool, it brings e-commerce business chance. In fact, commonly, global has have many businessmen choose to use internet channel to carry on their products transactions between global online-buyers and their electronic websites. So, global many shoppers had begun to feel online shopping is more convenient to compare visiting shops shopping. Their shopping behaviors have been changed from internet technological tool. Global has many shoppers choose to buy any products from any overseas or local businessmen their web stores. They only need to spend time to find any businessmen their webstores to choose the most suitable products to pay visa to buy from their webstores. at homes. So, in general, global had have may shoppers had changed their shopping behaviors from visiting shops to visiting webstores at homes often.

So, it seems that internet technological tool had influenced global many shops disappear, but internet webstores will be replaced their actual shops on streets. Some of businessmen either they choose webstores to replace shops or choose websotes and shops both or still keep shops only. Hence, internet tool influences global businessmen have three kinds of products sale channels to let globa local and overseas consumers to choose how to buy their products.

However, in fact, many of global shoppers, youngers and olders had begun to accept to buy any products from webstores. They feel to spend time to leave homes to visit shops , their shopping behaviors will be wasted time to not essential part to their daily lives. Hence, since internet technological invention, it had changed many consumers their traditional visiting shops shopping habit to change to buying products from webstores channel.

However, on the one hand, internet creates webstores ecommerce shopping channel to let global many consumers do not need to leave homes to go to shopping. It brings negative visiting shops shopping emotion to global general consumers nowadays. But on the other hand, it also brings positive visiting internet webstores shopping emotion to global general consumer nowadays. So, it seems that global many consumers feel that they often do not need to spend much time to go out shopping. Many global consumers feel convenient and enjoy to choose any products to buy from different internet webstores, when the online buyer chooses the most suitable product, he she only needs to pay visa card to buy the product from the online seller's webstore conveniently at home.

Hence, online shopping can bring economic benefit to online buyers, e.g. avoiding walking time or spending transport fare to visit the shop to go to shopping, shortening or reducing shopping time to do another important matter.

On conclusion, global many consumers began feel online shopping can bring more economic benefits on shortening shopping time, avoiding transport fare spending aspect. So, online shopping will be popular shopping behavior for future long time. It may encourage global many shoppers can make rapid shopping decision in short time in order to carry on any products buying transaction to global any one online shopper in short time easily in behavioral economic view. So, global many businessmen had begun to build themselves one attraction webstore in order to persuade different countries consumers to choose to click themselves webstores from internet channel to buy any kinds of products in short time easily.
So, internet technology had changed consumers traditional shopping behaviors to build positive online shopping emotion as well as raise online sellers‘ any products sale chance easily in behavioral economic view.

Why and how human behavior may influence the country's economic growth or recession?
When one country has many people choose to do the same matter for one period, whether their behavior may influence the country's pvera; economic growth or recession . I shall attempt to indicate cases toexplain their relationship as below:

For flowing rubblish behavioral case example, do you feel that when the country has many people often flow rubblish on the streets, instead of their flowing rubblish behavior may bring streets dirty? But, their flowing rubblish behavior may explain that this country has people may have enough money to buy food to ear, or enough cloths to wear, enough bottles of water to drink, even they may have enough money to buy new television, radio, refrigeraters , washing machines, desktops or laptops electronic home products from old to new to use in order to satisfy their living needs. So, when they flow old electronic home products, their flowing old home electronic products behaviors may seem that they have enough money to buy other new home electronic products to replace old home electronic products to use at homes.

However, it seems thaat this country ought have many people have jobs to do. So, many of them, they can easy to make purchase decison to flow any old home electronic products and buy any new home electronic products to use . Because this country has many people have jobs to do. So, they can often not use old home electonic products to become rubblishs to flow on streets after they had bought any kinds of new home electronic homes.

In fact, it also implies that this country's economy grows rapidly. So, many businesses can glow up rapdly. When they expanded their businesses, they must need to increase employees number in order to let they help themselves to raise productivity or serve their clients absolutely. So, when the country has many businesses can grow up, it seems that its economy must be better or it is improved to compare past. Due to many different kinds of home electronic products had been often bought to use by this country people in this period. So, this country's any streets can be observed that expensive electronic home products were flowed on streets anywhere. then, this country will have many electronic home products sellers can sell their home electronic products very easily. When this country has many people can find any kinds of jobs to do easily. So, due to unemploymen rate had been decreasing.

In behavioral economic view, as this many electronic home products rubblish country case, we can observe this country may have many people have jobs to do. So, consumption number has been increased long time. So, cheap food, or expensive home electronic products may be rubblish on any streets. This country's people , their flowing rubblish behaviors may be explained that many of people have enough jobs to do, so they have ability to buy any good taste food to eat or buy any kinds of expensive electronic home products to use. So, this country's economy may be improved for this long period. So, in behavioral economic view, when this country can have many electronic home products rubblishs are flowed on anywherer in streets frequently. It seems that this country will have many people have jobs to do, so it causes they often change old home electronic products or replaced them easily, when they have enough income to spend to buy any kinds of new home electronic products to use at homes easily. Moreover, their flowing old electronic home products behaviors also indicate that this country has many people their salaries may be increased in possible from their emplyers. When this country can have many different kinds of home electornic products are sold. It means that this country's electronic home products needs or demand had been increasing, due to many people have jobs to do and income increases to excite their living of needs also improve. Consequently, this country may seem have better economic improvement. We can observe from this country's electronic home products rubblish increasing income in theis period.

On conclusion, this country ought experience economic growth at this period. So, " flowing expensive electronic home rubblish increasing number " may seem that this country's economic growth is rapidly in this period, due to many people have jobs to do as well as salaries increase in this period.

Technology how impacts human behavior changing?

Technology how influences human behavior to bring changing? For example, online share purchase and sale transaction from smart phone brings share investor can do share buying or selling transation in any where and any time conveniently, non manual driving auto vehicle, bring car owner feels comfortable and spends free time to do other matter, e.g.

reading, listening mucis in himself or herself car freely. electrical energy vehicle can help car owner to reduce air polluton and it can brings the drivers do not feel drive long time in any journeys in order to avoid air pollution for environmental protection responsible car drivers in our societies. Thus, they will drive long time in any journeys when they can drive electronic energy cars to replace oil energy cars.

However, online technology can also bring consumers can choose to stay at homes to buy any things from seller individual online webstore conveniently. Such as online technology can bring shoppers do not need to spend much time to visit shops to buy any things. They can choose any kinds of products from any online sellers individual online webstores conveniently at homes. Online technology excite busy consumers can make purchase decision easily as well as it can help online sellers sell any kinds of products from internet easily.

In behavioral economic view, technology can change human behavior to be improved, it can let human feels comfortable, more free time ro use, rapid making any decisions, such as apply smart phones to make share purchase or sale transaction decision, online shopping decision, even travelling any where decision in short time, when the traveller finds the most cheap hotel accommodation room price and air ticket price frm any travel agent online tourism webstore, then the potential travel customer can follow the online hotel accommodation price and air ticket price data to make decision when to buy the air ticket from the airline travel agent or make decision when to prebook which hotel accommodation room to go to the country to travel from online travel agent tourism webstores. So, technology can encourage global any country travelers to make anywhere to trvel rapidly. If the traveler can find the country's general hotel rooms and airline tickets prices had been decreasing more sightly. The traveler may make travel decision to choose the country to travel in short time, then he/she can prebook the country;s any hotel room and airline ticket to pay by visa fraom the country's any hotel and airline travel agent webstores., before one week, even one month or more easily. Hence, online technology can also encourage traveler individual frequent travel times to be increased, due to global travelers can find any hotel rooms and airline tickets prices from internet conveniently at homes. They do not need to spend time to visit any airline travel agent to enquire travel choice country's hotel rooms prices and airline ticket prices. They can compare global travel of countries choices ' all hotels rooms and airline agents air tickets prices to make prebook airline seat and hotel room decision before one week, one month even six months early.

On conclusion, online technology can encourage global travelers can make travelling any where and when traveling time desicions easily. It can excite tourism industry develops in long time. Also, such as electricity cars invention can encourage environment protection car owners do car purchase decision easily, because they can choose to drive electronic energy cars to replace oil energy cars in order to avoid air pollution occurs easily. So, electronic cars can increase electronic car purchasrs number, due to many of environmental protection attitude of car owners can choose to drive electricity cars to bring air cleans, even non -manual driving cars can encourage lazy driving and free time driving car owners to choose to buy non-manual (artificial intelligent) cars to drive , because they can spend much free time to read, listen music or do any matters in themselves cars, they do not need to drive cars, robotic (AI) auto driving machine is such one non-manual driver to help them to drive themselves cars confidently. So, non-manual driving cars can attract lazy and enjoying free time driving car owners to choose to buy to replace traditional manual cars to drive easily. Moreover, online share transaction can help any share investors to make share buying and selling decision in short time easily. When they can apply smart phones technological tool to carry on share buying and selling activities easily. They can observe any share rising or falling price suitation from smart phones in any where any any time easily. So, smart phone technology can help global any shareholders to make share purchase and sale transaction easily. So, technology can encourage human makes decision in short time rapidly.

How and why employees behaviors may influence economy development?

In behavioral economy view,I believe the country's any organizational employees behavior may bring indirect relationship to influence the country's long term economic development. I shall indicate past manufacture industry social development period to explain their relationship. For many countries' past business activities had belonged to manufacturing industry, such as US, UK past before 1980 year, it focused on steel manufacturing and steel manufacturing related machine products.

So, US, Uk developed countries manufacturing industries may be past main country's economic income sources. I assume US , UK past had one million number different kinds of industries. They ought had about seven houndred thousand number organizational businesses were belonged to manufactured industry. They may include:
Steel manufacturing and steel related machine manufacturing, e.g. vehicle manufacturing, home appliances, e.g. washing machine, television, radio, refrigerate cooler, heater, air condition etc. different kinds of different kinds of steel -related manufacturing machine, they were manufactured from US, UK steel machine manufacturers. So, US, Uk the other three hundred thousand number industry may be general service industry, e.g. hotel service, restaurent, cinema, public transport service, tourism lesiure , wine bar, supermarket etc. different kinds of non-manufacturing industries business organizations were operated in UK, US past before 1980 year.

So, in UK, US developed countries industry development history, they ought have high percentage of businesses belonged to steel related manufacturing machine and steel products. Also, in the past before 1980 year, US, Uk business employers , they employed many workers are manufacturing workers. They needed to spend long time to work in factories. They were skillful workers, and they are trained to manufacturing cars, washing machine, television, heater, etc. even steel itself different kinds of steel related products to prepare to deliver to their shops to sell to US, Uk local or overseas clients.

So, I believe that past UK, US ought employ many employees, they belonged to skillful manufacturing workers, manufacture increasing steel machine or steel related machine number of products rapidly daily. So, if UK, US had had many of these manufacturing factories owned high skillful workers, then their manufacturing steel-related machine or steel both kinds of products number must be influenced to raise rapidly. Consequently, their steel machine manufacturing products would been exported to overseas or would been sold to local both markets , they may be influenced to raise sale number. They (these manufacturing workers) needed to be trained to know how to manufactur these different kinds of machine products in the efficient teams and they ought to be trained to raise their efficiencies in order to shorten time to manufacturing many kinds of steel related manufacturing machine or steel itself products rapidly. So , if their efficiencies and manufacturing performance was improved, these US, UK any one manufacturing worker and their teams ought achieve raising productivities significantly.

Hence, when past UK, US manufacturing industry development period, if these two countries' any manufacturing factories could have many manufacturing workers could be trained to be skillful and proficient manufacturing workers. Then, in past every day to these factories workers, they ought help their steel or steel related manufacturing employers to raise any kinds of machine or steel products number in every team. So, when past in the manufacturing industry development, US, UK could have many factories' manufacturing workers themselves steel or steel related machine products manufacturing skill could be trained to to improve to any kinds of these machine or steel manufacuring products quality as well as their products number could be influenced to raise by themselves skillful improvement significantly every day.
Then, what would be influenced to occur to past UK, US manufacturing industry period? In behavioral economic view, when these two manufacturing industry developed countries, such as UK, US , if they had many factories workers can be trained to improve their skill in order to achieve any kinds of steel or steel-related machine products quality could be improved as well as products manufacturing number could be also increased absolutely.

In consequence, past UK and US both countries ought increase themselves any kinds of steel and steel related machine products number to be supplied to themselves local shops to let local clients to choose any one kind of machine manufacturing products to buy easily as well as they could also export to supply overseas any countries to buy their different kinds of steel or steel related machine products to let overseas steel or steel related manufacturing machine product buyers, they can have many of these different kinds of these steel or steel-related different kinds of manufacturing machine from UK and UK these both countries easily to compare other countries.

On conclusion, I believe that past US, and UK macro manufacturing industry income GDP would increase significantly. So, they would have good economic growth performance because when many of these manufacturing workers themselves manufacturing effort could be improved. So, it explained when employees manufacturing abilities can influence economic growth indirectly.

Robots invention whether they can help organizations to raise efficiencies or inefficiencies?

In behavioral economic view, in any organizations, when the organization hopes its worker teams can raise efficiencies , the organization may choose to increase more workers number and/or it can provide training to improve these workets themselves skills in order to raise their efficiencies. For one warehouse example, when the warehouse increases many goods , they are needed to delivered these goods from the shelves to the delivering destination locations. If this warehouse supervisors feel these workers themselves goods delivery speeds are slow, which is possible due to this warehouse's workers number is not enough. So, this warehouse supervisor ought increase workers number in order to increase their goods delivery speed in order to deliver goods from the shelves to every indicated goods delivery destination in order to let any one lorry driver can transport the right kinds of goods and ensure the accurate goods number to transport to any one client home rapidly.

However, if this warehouse supervisor planed to buy several warehouse goods delivery robots to assist these warehouse workers to find the right kinds of goods from shelves and then deliver to the right destination location in the warehouse. So, these warehouse orkers can concentrate on counting the accurate goods number and ensuring the right kinds of goods in order to prepare to let lorry drivers to transport these goods to these goods of buyers themselvers homes rapidly. Consequently, in the first step, robots can concentrate on finding th right goods from shelves and delivers them to the right goods transportation of location destination. Then, in the second step, these warehouse workers can concentrate on counting the accurate goods number and ensuring the right kinds of goods in order to prepare to put them to the lorry. Consequently, when warehouse robots and warehouse workers can cooperate to work together, the most important, robots, can deal on finding the right kinds of goods and deal on delivering the accurate number of goods of job duty as well as these warehouse workers can only concentrte on counting the right kinds of goods number in order to avoid it has none any mistake of wrong kinds of goods and inaccurate goods of delivery number to be transported to the lorry and to

deliver to any one buyer's home.
So, it seems that warehouse robots ought help any one warehouse worker to raise himself efficiency and avoid goods delivery of mistake occurrence easily as well as their help to warehouse workers that can let any one goods buyer feels their goods can be delivered to their homes rapidly. Moreover, warehouse robots can also help these warehouse workers to raise efficiencies because warehouse robots can help them to shorten goods delivery time between any one shelf and any one goods delivery destination of location in the warehuse because robots may help them to find the right kinds of goods from the right shelf in the short time. So, any one worker does not need to spend long time to seek anywhere is the right shelf location for the kind of goods when the kind of goods are needed to deliver to the buyer's home from lorry. Warehouse robots can help them to do this aspect of " finding the goods from the right shelf in short time job duty". So, any one warehouse worker only needed tospend less time to do the counting of any right kind of goods number and ensuring the right kind of goods job duty. Consequently, this warehouse 's any one worker, his any one kind of goods delivery time may be reduced, because robots' assistance and they may have more confidence to avoid mistake to deliver the wrong number of goods and/or the wrong kind of goods to any one goods buyer's home.

On conclusion, it seems that warehouse robots ought may help any one warehouse worker to raise efficiency for any one team in the warehouse as well as the warehouse any one supervisor does not need to spend much time to observe any one worker individual performance for " goods delivery job duty aspect" because their goods delivery job duty that had been replaced to do by these several warehouse robots. Robots can achieve the more accurate of right kinds of goods and the right number of goods delviery job performance to compare any one of human warehouse worker themselves right kinds of goods of delivery and right number of goods of delivery job performance. So, when robots can participate to cooperate with this warehouse's any one worker to do their goods of delivery job duty in this warehouse every day. Then, robots can raies any one of supervisor individual confidence in order to let they do not need to spend time to observe any one of worker individual whose goods of delivery job performane. They can concentrate on supervising any one worker whose goods transport to lorry in the final step in order to avoid to deliver wrong goods number and / or wrong kind of goods to any one goods buyer's home every day. Consequently, this warehouse's overall teams of their delviery of goods performance many be improved by robotss' participatin to goods of delivery task as well as this warehouse's oveall teams themselves efficiencies may be influenced to raise by robots' goods of delivery task participation.

Why social behavior may influence organizational strategy needs to be changed ?
Why any organizations need to know whether nowadays social behaivor how has been changing in order to implement the kind of the most right strategy to achieve the profit aim pursue in possible. I shall indicate nowadays ecommerce or online, customer shopping behavior to explain above question concerns they ought have close relationship between social behavior and organizational strategic choice or organizational behavioral changing need.

On nowadays ecommerce business, or online shopping model, this kind of shopping model in global many young and old age consumers like to apply internet tool to choose any country sellers website stores in order to stay at home to buy any kinds of products from themselves webstores in global societies.
In fact, online shopping model had been popular for long time above to twenty years. Most of global sellers will make decision to design themselves webstores in order to attract global many online buyers to choose to buy their products from themselves webstores. So, it seems that social consumers purchase behaviors had been changed to online shopping from internet invention.

Hence, social consumers purchase behavioral changes may influence any organizations' strategies need to be changed from visiting shops purchase strategy model to online purchase strategy model, if the seller still concentrate on concentrate on considerate how to design itelf , but neglects to considerate how to design itself webstore, e.g. how to design attract product photos to put on itself webstore, how to arrange sale price information location to be putted on webstore and visa card payment location on itself webstore in order to let any one online buyer can feel very easier to buy itself any kinds of products from itself webstore. Then, its potential online buyers will be influenced to increase number when they can find this online seller itself any kinds of products photes and every kinds of product sale price information and visa card payment channel locations easily from itself webstore.

So, it implies that nowadays any one seller ought need to design one webstore to let any one online overseas and domestic consumers can have chance to click itself webstore to choose any one kind of product to buy conveniently when he/she does not hope to leave him/her home to go to shop, because nowadays social shopping behaviors had been influenced to change when internet invention, them it gives another online purchase method to replace visiting shops purchase method to global any one buyer in nowadays societies.

So, if nowadays any one seller still concentrate on how to design itself shop display in order to put any kinds of product on shelf in order to let any one visiting shop customer to find the kind of product to buy, but it neglects to change to choose to pursue another new technological shopping method, such as webstore purchase method in order to implement effective strategy to design the most right webstore as well as in order to attract global overseas and local consumers to find itself webstore easily from website and find its any one kind of product phots and sale price and visa card payment button in order to choose to buy itself any kinds of products in the short time. Consequently I believe that the seller will lose many customers from overseas and local when its other same or similar product sellers choose to design themselves webstores in order to let global any one product buyer can buy themselves any one kind of product when they can pay visa card to buy their products from them webstores conveniently when they stay at home habitly. Then, the seller will lose many global potential customers in long time.

On conclusion, in behavioral economic view, any consumer behavioral social changing, which will influence any in order to avoid customers number loses significantly . In future time, organizations need to make rapid decision in order to implement the most reasonable and the most useful strategy in order to avoid global potential customers number reduces or lose them in long time. So, social behavioral changing environment ought influence any global organizations need to decide how to change themselves strategies in order to avoid customers loses significantly in future time.

How and why human behavior may influence economic growth or

recession?
May ourselves daily behaviors influence our global societial continue economic growth or recession? Do they have cause and effect close relationship between human behaviors and global economic growth or recession? I shall apply behavioral economic theory to analyze and explain whether ourselves daily behaviors and our global societial economic growth or recession which have close cause and effect relationship as below:

Every country itself economic development must depend on any business activities, otherwise, any kinds of business activities must need ourselves business activities or behaviors in order to achieve any business activities as well as achieve the country's overall economic development in macro view.

However, any country's overall business activites or behaviors which must depend on any kinds of individual businessmen, themselves employees daily working behavior or activity or performance in order to help them to attract or increase many clients number to acieve " earning profit" aim. So, it seems that any individual business, itself overall every department individual working behavior is one main factor to influence the company's overall business performance.

For agricultural fruit and meat food farming industry example, such as New Zealand is a farming main target industry country. It had had many New Zealanders were daily themselves own farming businesses for many years. Their farming businesses include growing fruit, sheep, cow, pig pork, meat etc. food sale business. If the New Zealand farmer owned a large size farming land, then he will choose either growing fruit or feeding sheeps, pigs, cows to be meat to to transport to New Zealand supermarkets to help them to sell to their farmers meet to New Zealanders in order to earn profit. Thus, if the New Zealand farmer owned large size of farming lands, then he needs to employ many farming employees (farming workers) to help him to carry on farming business daily tasks, e.g. picking up friuts, feeding pigs, cows, sheeps to eat food daily. These daily farming jobs are very important to influence this New Zealand farmer's meats or fruits sale number whether they can be easy or diffcult to sell in New Zealand supermarkets , if these farming workers can own encough farming knowledge or skill to know how to pick up fruits method and make judgement to know whether it is right time to pick up the kind of fruits from the trees , as well as know how feed this pigs, sheeps, cows to eat food in order to let they are better health. Consequently, their farming behaviors which can let these animals can provide the best taste and enough meat from these animals to let New Zealander to buy to eat from New Zealand any one supermarket. Even these New Zealand farming workers can know whether the kinds of fruits, e.g. oranges, apples, gapes etc. fruits whether they ought be picked up from the trees at the right time. Consequently, they can make judgement to decide to pick up any kinds of the best taste fruits to let any one New Zealander to buy to eat from any one supermarket in New Zealand. Otherwise, if they do not make judegement to know whether the kind of fruit ought not be picked up because they still need longer time to continue grow up to increase fruit size and better taste from the trees in order to let any one fruit buyer can feel better taste when they eat this kind of fruit later. If they can buy this kind of fruit to eat later, then this New Zealand farmer's his fruit buyers can buy the best taste of this kind of fruit to eat from an yone supermarket in New Zealand. Consequently, many New Zealand supermarkets will choose to buy any kinds of fruits from this farmer fruit supplier when they feel this farmer's fruits can provide more better taste fruits to compare other farmers' fruits.

Thus, due to New Zealand is one farming main income source country. It's any kinds of fruits and meats need to be export to overseas to sell , instead of local sale. It's GDP percent is very high to whole country 's overall income source. So, any one New Zealand farmer individual and any one farming worker individual working behavior will influence its economy whether it is influenced to grow or recession possible. Moreover, it also seems that farming workers' farming knowledge and skill will influence themselves farming daily activities to achieve the aim of the number of increase or decrease to any kinds of fruits whether they are better taste or the number of increase of decrease to any kinds of meats whether they are better taste to supply to any one New Zealand fruit or meat buyers to eat from any one New Zealand supermarket. So, it implies that any one New Zealand farming worker individual farming behavior may influence any kinds of fruits or any kinds of meat taste because they are transported to any one supermarket to sell in New Zealand.

Consequently, if New Zealans had many farmers can teach god farming knowledge and skill to let their any one farming workers know how to decide judgement to decide when it is right time to pick up any kinds of fruits from trees , or how to grow them on soil in order to let they can grow rapidly. Then, many different kinds of fruits can be provided to let any one New Zealanders can eat the best taste of fruits when their fruits are supplied to any one New Zealand supermarkets. Even, if they knew how to feed foods to pigs, cows, sheeps to eat daily. Then they can be more health and they can provide the best taste of meats to let any one New Zealanders can buy their meats from any one New Zealand supermarkets. Moreover, their fruits and meats can be transported to overseas to let any one country fruits or meats buyers can choose any kinds of New Zealand meats and fruits to buy to eat from themselves countries supermarkets. Then, many overseas fruit and meat buyers will perfer to choose New Zealand any kinds of fruits or meats to buy to compare other countries fruits or meats to buy when they go to any one local supermarkets.

On conclusion, it seems that New Zealand farming workers themselves farming behavior may influence their farming employers any kinds of fruits or meats sale number and income because their farming task behaviors must influence whether their fruits or meats taste are the better taste or worse taste to compare their other local farmers (the farmer competitors) whose fruits or meats taste. If tthe farmer's any one farming worker can be trained to learn how to know to feed animals skill and when is the most right time to pick up any kinds of fruits from trees or how to grow them on the soil methods. Due to these farming worker individual farming behavior may influence his different finds of fruits and meats sale number to be increase or decrease, so these any one New Zealand farmer must need to depend on any one farming worker whose farming working methods, if their farming working behaviors can be the best to influence any kinds of fruits to grow rapid or any kinds of pigs, cows, sheeps animals grow up rapidly , then their sale number may be increase significantly and their taste can be improved to let any New Zealand or overseas meat or fruit buyer to buy to eat to feel from any one New Zealand or overseas supermarkets, then New Zealand's agriculture industry must be influenced to increase. In the world, any one fruit or meat buyer must choose to buy New Zealand's fruit and meat to eat in prefer to compare other countries' fruits and meats. So, New Zealand's GDP may be influenced to raise from any one New Zealand farming worker individual farming working behaviors. It seems that New Zealand farmer fruit and meat sale number is depended on their eatting consumers demand more than their meat and fruit supply because if these

NZ farmers can apply high technology method to grow good taste fruit or feed good taste meat to let global eatting customers to feel, their demand will increase, then NZ farmers will need to increase good taste fruit and good taste meat supply number to satisfy global meat and fruit eatting customer taste need.

My views emphasize a strong and evolving relationship between technology, particularly Artificial Intelligence (AI) and big data, and consumer behavior. My view believes that these technologies are instrumental in predicting, understanding, and influencing consumer decisions and broader economic trends .

Predicting Consumer Emotion and Behavior

My view posits that AI tools can be effectively applied to predict individual consumer emotions, which directly influence consumption behavior . My view highlights case studies to illustrate how positive or negative emotions impact purchasing decisions. For instance, AI can help businesses identify reasons why a customer might not buy a product, such as high price, poor quality, or unsatisfactory staff service. By confirming a consumer's emotional state, AI can pinpoint the factors driving their decision-making at that moment. This predictive capability extends to understanding "why and when and how consumer behavior changes" across various industries, including entertainment, cruise travel, and vehicle leisure activities .

Influence of Technology on Economic Development and Human Behavior

My view explores how technology and human behavior mutually influence economic development . My

view suggests that technological advancements, while bringing positive impacts, can also have negative consequences on societies. He specifically examines how technology can lead to human behavioral changes, citing the example of robots influencing working and living environments.

My questions how human behavior will adapt to cooperate with or depend on robots in the future . My research aims to explore the interplay between technology and human behavior, particularly how these factors influence economic growth and recession in both macro and microeconomic contexts . My

view seeks to explain the mechanisms through which technological advancements impact human social activities, thereby affecting economic outcomes and leading to shifts in consumer behavior .

AI and Big Data for Future Predictions

A core aspect of my perspective is the potential of AI and big data to analyze past consumer data to forecast future consumption behavior . My view argues that if travel agents, for example, can effectively gather and utilize historical data, they can predict future travel needs and preferences more accurately. This leads to a more dynamic and responsive market where offerings are continuously adapted to evolving consumer desires . The increasing sophistication of AI systems, which simulate human-like reasoning and learning processes, blurs the boundaries between human cognition and machine intelligence, making AI a powerful tool for understanding and influencing consumer behaviors and economic environments .

Contributions to Behavioral Economics

MY work consistently integrates insights from psychology with traditional economic theories to provide a comprehensive understanding of human behavior in economic contexts. My writings emphasize the importance of understanding cognitive biases and emotional influences on decision-making processes. His contributions to behavioral economics cover topics such as:

Cognitive Biases: Exploring how biases like overconfidence or loss aversion affect individual and collective economic decisions .

Market Behavior: Analyzing how psychological factors shape market trends and consumer choices .

Policy Recommendations: Suggesting ways in which policymakers can utilize behavioral insights to design more effective interventions aimed at improving economic outcomes .

Through my academic pursuits and writing, my aims to bridge the gap between theoretical economics and practical applications influenced by human behavior .

My analysis often begins by establishing that technology can fundamentally alter the economic environment, which in turn impacts human behavior, including shopping habits . My view investigates how technological developments can lead to changes in leisure environments and consumer behavior, ultimately affecting overall economic performance . For instance, the rise of online marketplaces is a direct technological advancement that has profoundly influenced consumer behavior . These platforms offer convenience, wider product selections, and competitive pricing, compelling consumers to shift from traditional brick-and-mortar stores to online shopping .

Furthermore, my view delves into how technology influences consumer emotions, which are crucial in economic decision-making . The seamless user experience, personalized recommendations, and instant gratification offered by technological tools and software solutions can shape consumer preferences and purchasing patterns . My view also considers the role of automation, such as robots, in influencing organizational and human behavioral change to bring economic benefits, which indirectly affects how consumers interact with businesses and their shopping experiences .

My work also touches upon how technology can influence consumer demand and how improvements in organizational behavior, often driven by technological adoption, can raise economic benefits . This implies that as businesses leverage technology to become more efficient and responsive, consumers' expectations and shopping behaviors adapt accordingly. For example, the use of technology for better data analysis and decision-making regarding resource allocation can lead to more transparent spending habits for organizations, which might translate into more competitive offerings for consumers, thereby influencing their choices .

In essence, my view connects technological advancements with changes in shopping habits by demonstrating how technology:

Creates new market environments: Online platforms and digital tools provide alternative avenues for commerce, drawing consumers away from traditional methods .

Influences consumer psychology: Technology can alter emotions, cognitive biases, and decision-making processes related to purchases .

Shapes organizational strategies: Businesses adopt technology to improve efficiency, reduce costs, and enhance customer experience, which in turn impacts consumer interactions and expectations .

Drives economic shifts: Changes in technology and human behavior collectively influence economic growth and recession, with consumer spending being a significant component .

My research underscores the dynamic interplay where technological innovation not only facilitates new ways of shopping but also reshapes the very motivations and behaviors of consumers in the modern economy .

SIX

HOW TECHNOLOGY CHANGES DEMAND AND SUPPLY MARKET RELATIONSHIP

Episode 1

Theinnovator: A technological entrepreneur
automation factory worker skillful improvement

This story discusses how technology enhances human creativity, explores various technological advancements, and examines their impact on society. One day, four creative human ability of scientists , they meet to discuss how technology may help human to create ability of share experiences in one conference room. In the conference room, they include these people: One**innovator**: A technological entrepreneur who creates groundbreaking tools that enhance creativity, who hopes his technological invention may create human creative ability. One **skeptic**: A traditional artist or thinker who questions the role of technology in creative processes, who hopes technology may help human to raise creative processes in any one brain creative process. One p**rodigy**: A young individual whose life changes dramatically due to access to advanced technology , who hopes he can apply suitable technological methods to change his life to be improved. One m**entor**: An experienced figure who guides others in navigating the intersection of technology and creativity, he hopes he can apply his technological methods to teach his learners to know how technological help they raise creative ability.

Theinnovator: A technological entrepreneur who creates groundbreaking tools that enhance creativity, who hopes his technological invention may create human creative ability. He says

" I believe robots may help human improve working skills , I shall explain as below to let you know."

I n my automation factory , I had applied robots to help workers to improve themselves skill, in order to raise efficiency. (AI) -driven automation industry will create wealth and expand economy growth to any countries, but it will be accompanied by changed in the skills that workers need to learn. One of main ways that technology increases productivity is by decreasing the number of labor hours needed to create a unit of output. It implies (AI) technology will influence low educated and low skillful labor number to be decreased (reduction employment number).

Although, AI automation can raise efficiency and productivity, but due to manufacturers will concentrate on bring (AI) robotic automation skills to manufacture any products, it will lead future many human jobs disappeared, finally, it will bring negative impact to bring many low skillful labours will lose their jobs , due to robots can replace them to do different kinds of jobs. One of main ways that technology increases productivity is by decreasing the number of labor hours needed to create a unit of output. It implies (AI) technology will influence low educated and low skillful labor number to be decreased (reduction employment number).

In contrast, technological change tended to work in a different direction throughout the nowadays. The advance of computer and the internet raised the relative productivity of higher skilled workers. So, routine-intensive occupations that focused on predictable tasks disappearance, such as switch board, operators, filming checkers, travel agents and assembling line workers etc. were particularly replaced by new technologies. All these human jobs will be replaced from AI automation technology after ten years in possible, but in fact, I believe my driven automation factory of all vehicles manufacturer number must be influenced to increase when workers learn technology to improve themselves skill."

Then, the m**entor says**

" Can you explain your evidences to support robots may help your workers to improve skill in order to raise vehicles manufacturing number, I want share your workers creative skill experiences to let my

learners know your case."

Then, theinnovator says

" Sure, please you listen my vehicle manufacture increasing method"

"In positively view point, (AI) driven-automation will make many workers more productive and increase demand for certain skills. Consequently, new jobs are likely to be directly create in areas , such as the development and supervision of (AI) as well as indirectly created in a range of areas throughout the economy as higher incomes lead to expanded demand. So, it is only the high skilled labors who can learn how to supervise or manage or control (AI) robots how to work in order to raise productive efficiency , whose skills will increase need. Due to their skills shortage, so they will be difficult to be replaced from (AI). It means that this high skillful (AI) supervision labours won't lose jobs in the future. Otherwise, they will raise wage, due to skill shortage in the (AI) industry job market future."

"However, today, it may be challenging to predict exactly which jobs will be most immediately affected by (AI) driven-automation. The reason is because (AI) is not a single technology, but rather a collection of technologies that are felt unevenly through the economy to influence job changing both negatively and positively. In positively view point, (AI) driven-automation will make many workers more productive and increase demand for certain skills. Consequently, new jobs are likely to be directly create in areas , such as the development and supervision of (AI) as well as indirectly created in a range of areas throughout the economy as higher incomes lead to expanded demand. Otherwise, in negatively view point, many traditional human needed (demand) skillful jobs will be threatened by automation are highly concentrated among lower-paid, lower-skilled and less -educated workers. It means automation will cause pressure on demand for this group, pressure and employment, if (AI) can replace the low skilled and less educated workers' jobs. Thus, (AI) will have negative influence to impact on the labor market.

(AI) capabilities will enable automation of some tasks that have long required human labor. Why can (AI) replace some simple human jobs? For example, advances in robotics are expanding machines' abilities to interact with and sharp the physical world. Combined , (AI) and robotics will give rise to smarter machines that can perform more sophisticated functions than ever before and brings more advantages that humans have exercised. This will permit automation of many tasks now performed by human workers and could change the shape of the labor market and human activity.

In the future, the effects of (AI) on the labor market in the decade ahead will continue the trend toward skill-biased change that computerization and communication innovations have driven in recent decades. Thus, some human driving occupation will be disappeared or replaced by (AI) automation driven. For example, bus drivers, light truck or delivery services drivers, heavy and tractor-trailer truck drivers, school drivers, tax drivers, travel bus drivers.

However, (AI) technology could enable some workers to focus time on other job responsibilities, boosting their productivity, and actually raised wage growth among those still holding the reshaped jobs. For example, salespeople, who currently spend a considerable amount of time driving could find themselves able to do other work when a car drives them from place to place, or inspectors and appraisers could fill out paperwork, when their car drives itself. This (AI) -driven technology should make these workers more productive, with (AI) -driven technology serving as a complement, not a substitute. New jobs will also likely be created, both in existing occupations cheaper transportation costs with lower prices and increase demand for products and all the related occupations, such as service and fulfillment, and in new occupations not currently foreseeable.

What kind of jobs will be created by (AI) technology? Predicting future job growth is extremely difficult, due to it depends on technologies or substitute for existing today as well as they may complement or substitute for existing human skills and jobs. However, (AI) will also lead to substantial indirect job creation to the degree it raises productivity and wages, it may also lead to higher consumption that would support additional jobs from high-end draft production to restaurant and retail. The future(AI) " augmented intelligence", the technology's role is as assisting and expanding the productivity of individuals rather than replacing human work. Thus, based on the biased-technical change framework, demand for labor will likely increase the most in the areas where humans complement (AI) automation technologies. For example, (AI) technology , such as IBM's Watson may improve early detection of some cancers or other illnesses, but a human healthcare professional is needed to work with patients to understand and translate patients' symptoms, inform patients of treatment options, and guide patients through treatment plans. Shipping companies may also partner workers who pick up and deliver products over the last feet with (AI) enabled autonomous vehicles that move workers efficiently from site to site. In such cases, (AI) augments what a human is able to do and allows individuals to either be move effective in their specially task or to operate on a larger scale. Thus, it seems (AI) technology will also create new jobs, raise productivity and workers' efficiency.

In the future, due to artificial intelligence influences to some kind of human jobs nature. So, the kind of human jobs of management methods will also need to change to adapt the artificial intelligence technology input to their organizations. It will cause challenges for every executive and manager if who won't have effort to manage their teams how to apply artificial intelligence technology to work efficiently and easily. For example, division of labor will change among humans and machines will increase, such as my vehicle workers are influenced to division of labor more easily by manufacturing robots. So, manufacturing robots help my factory builds excellent management methods. Thus, companies will have to adapt their training performance and talent strategies how to emphasize on work that how to make human judgment and skills and experimentation. Thus, (IA)'s greatest impact will be on administrative coordination and control tasks, such as scheduling , resource allocation.

In fact, mangers will encounter this challenges: How to apply human experience and expertise to judge critical business decisions and practices when the information available is insufficient to suggest a successful course of action? Due to this kind of work will require new skills and mindsets. I shall indicate these change management methods to adapt (AI) technology. Such as: administration and routine tasks, scheduling , allocation of resources and reporting will fall within the intelligence machines, responsibilities that have long been reserved for humans. For example, a typical store manager or a lead nurse at a nursing home most constantly arrange shift schedules, accounting for staff members' absences owing to illness, vacation time or sudden departures.

Thus, the managers need to learn how to arrange new division of labor within the organizations after (AI) technology had been implemented to the organization. Artificial intelligence is currently influencing into once considered exclusive to humans: assessing and acting on human emotions and personality traits. The influences to managers need to change their strategies to adapt (AI) technology implements include such as below:"

Then, thementor asks " How manufacturing robots create your vehicle manufacturing supervisors and workers creative skill and management skill?"

Then, the innovator says " let me explain to let you know as below"

"Firstly, managers need to spend the bulk of their time on coordination and control tasks from intelligent system implements. Their time spending on these major three aspects from impact of intelligent system: coordinate and control, solve problems and collaborate and people and community , strategy and innovation three aspects. Thus (AI) will influence managers need to change their judgment method to teach whose teams how to adapt the (AI) system operations in any organizations.

Secondly, (AI) will influence top, middle and low level management needs to change to adapt the (AI) technology operations to any owned (AI) technology organizations in the future. Intelligent machines must be trained in context. Just like humans , on-the-job training is a requirement for such machines because they typically arrive with only very general capabilities. To get the most from (AI), managers at all levels must participate in the instructional experience and in the learning process and provides managers' familiarity with such systems on these aspects, e.g. How the system works and generate advice, how the system has a proven track record , how the system provides convincing explanations , how the system can make simple rule- based decisions.

Thirdly, managers need to learn how to make judgment more accurate (AI) systems assistance. Although (AI) will invariably take on more routine work and even augment human decision-making, it won't judgment work, the application of human experience and expertise to critical business decisions when the information available is insufficient to suggest a successful course of action or reliable enough to suggest an obvious course of action. For a sense of the nature of judgment work, consider big data marketing and sales analytic. Such analytic often provide insights that can inform promotional campaigns, including predicting which promotions will generate desired sales brand further into the future, marketing executives need use judgment, combining analytic with their own and others' insight and experience.

The application of experience and expertise to critical business decisions and practice represents the real value of human judgment. But, when artificial intelligent machines are implemented to any organizations to assist the low, middle and top level management to make any business judgment. These forms of judgment work that managers can gather data interpretation, idea development more absolute from (AI) machine assistance. Thus, why these level management executives need to learn how to apply (AI) machines to help them to make any business judgment more accurate."

Then, the Skeptic: A traditional artist or thinker who questions the role of technology in creative processes. He asks this question:

"Can you explain how robot influence your organizational change to confirm whether robots may improve your workers and managers mind and behavior in order to improve efficiency and avoid vehicle manufacture number reduces every day in possible?"

Then, **the innovator says**

" Let you answer this important question to answer why and how I believe manufacture robots may ensure improve workers skill and supervisors management skill in order to avoid vehicle manufacture number reduces every day reasons as below:"

"Consequently creative and social intelligence will be in even greater demand as (AI) makes in management and the workforce. This development will represent a long term trend in labor markets , one characterized by intensifying demand and reward for social skills with a growing desire for creative capabilities, managers will seek to fashion of ideas and hypotheses from inside and outside of the enterprise to shape solutions to their most pressing business problems. Thus, (AI) will influence overall organizational team members who have chance to participate any decision to make more accurate business judgment. Many managers mistakenly view judgment work as only an individual discipline, failing to appreciate that it can also involve decide interpersonal and organizational practices. In more complex settings, judgment is typically a collective outcome of individuals' and teams' diverse perspectives, insights and experiences. And often , the resulting choices are better informed than decisions that an individual would have arrived at on his or her own.Thus, when any organizations apply (AI) technology to assist managers to gather data and ideas to make any judgment. In these cases, organizations can create the conditions for effective collective judgment by establishing structures , such as " shadow advisory boards" that prompt managers and employees to source and synthesize multiple perspectives. Thus, a traditional organization (firm) might freshen its thinking is t put together a shadow advisory board, comprised of young, digital people who can apply

(AI) machine assistance to make judgment work more accurate whether related to people development, problem-solving or strategizing and innovating for considerable degrees of creative and social intelligence. Thus, on the one hand, (AI) technology machine augmentation and automation can give these advantages to human (organization managers) , e.g. developing people and community, solving problems and collaborating, coordinating and controlling work, shaping strategy and leading innovation. Besides, on the other hand, the next generation managers need have these individual attitude to treat intelligent machines to be as colleagues. When, judgment is a human skill, intelligent machines can accelerate human learning that supports it, assisting in data -driven simulations, scenarios and search and discovery activities. Focuses on judgment work, some decisions require insight beyond what data can tell them. This is the sweet sport for human judgment, the application of experience and expertise to critical business decisions and practices. Thus, managers will also need to find ways to learn how to use digital (AI) technologies to tap into the knowledge and judgment of partners, customer external stakeholders and role models in other industries after the (AI) machine had been implemented to the organization."

"The ability of (AI) technology systems to transform vast amounts of complex information into insight has the potential to help solve manufacturing or service challenges for human needs. However, to reap the societal benefits of (AI) systems, humans will need to trust then and make sure that which follow the same ethical principles, moral values, professional codes and social norms that we humans would follow in the same scenario, research and educational efforts as well as carefully designed regulation in order to achieve the most effort of economic benefits goals. For example, international business machines corporation (IBM) is actively engaged both competitors , in global discussions about how to make (AI) ethical and as beneficial as possible for people as social economic benefits.(AI) is usually defined as the " capability of a computer program to perform tasks or reasoning processes " that human usually associate to intelligence in a human being. Often, it has to do with the ability to make a good decision, even when there is uncertainty, too much information to handle. As an example, play chess or complex card games of entertainment activities is believed to need some form of intelligence in a human being, as well as choosing the best medical facilities in a difficult medical case, or creating something new, such as mathematical theorem or even some form of act, or even driving automatic machine man (self driving vehicle) replacing human driving in the middle of a crowded city. (AI) needs depends on what we consider being intelligence in the behavior of a human being act a certain point in time. If human belief about human intelligence changes and we don't believe any longer that a certain task requires intelligence, then a computer program performing that task is no longer part of (AI), it becomes just another boring computer program. So, it means that (AI) technology will replace some old computer programs, if human can invent new generation of (AI) software for any functions or activities to satisfy human needs. As IBM, it argues intelligence. This means that we aim to build systems that enhance and scale human expertise and skills rather than replacing them. We therefore focus on practical applications of (AI) capabilities that assist people in performing well-defined tasks of needs by exploiting and wide range of (AI)-based services. We also use the term " cognitive computing" it is mean a comprehensive net of capabilities based on technology. It comprises the fields of machine learning, reasoning and decision technologies, language, speech and vision recognition and processing technologies, high performance and high efficient functions for any industries or individual consumers needs. For example, robotics, which are usually very good at doing what which are supposed to in any environment, much have public shopping center, factory etc. places which need simply services from the robot (machine man), such as cleans the floor of our houses to the robot that can work together with humans in production chains, passing through the warehouse, robots can take care of the tasks of an entire warehouse and the companion robots like Nao, Pepper, Aibo and Giraff, who can entertain use, talk to use and help elderly people to stay connected to their friends, relatives and doctors. For example, Google company is building automatic machine (self-driving cars) and has acquired more than 10 robotics companies. Facebook had opened whole new research facility only on (AI) research. Apply computer has developed Siri. Microsoft computer company has built a similar personalized assistant. Google has Deep mind, a UK company whose long term aim is to build general (AI) and has already great potential to win game to the world champion and IBM is investing a huge amount of resources in applying its Watson cognitive computing system to the medical domains to finance and to personalized education. In Europe, IBM is establishing new centers in Munich and Milan focused in the application of cognitive computer capabilities to the internet of things and healthcare respectively. For example, automatic machine man (self-driving cars) are all about (AI), which used to be able to see what happens in the street (signals ,lanes, other cars, pedestrians, traffic lights, which need to able predict what other cars and pedestrians will do, and who need to be able to cope with unforeseen situations. Since, most car accidents are due to human fault, it is estimated that the adoption of self-driving cars will save about half of the lives that are usually last in car accidents. IBM Watson company has to understand spoken language, make sense of massive amount to text , respond correctly to questions in many categories, as well as assess its own confidence in responding to such questions. In the future, (AI) technology can own question/answering capabilities that would be very useful, for example, in assisting a doctor when trying to some to the correct diagnosis for a patient and to propose the best therapy .Intelligent machines can also rely on huge amounts of data to be used to learn how to make better decisions. This data comes from all of us over the years Facebook users have uploaded more than 250 billion pictures and every day who upload about 350 million more. Every second, we submit 40,000 Google search queries. So, (AI) technology will be connected through the web from appliances to traffic lights from cars to watches. Other tasks that are very easy for humans are physical and manipulation tasks, such as walking , running, picking up an object to make its shape and location, restricted environment. But (AI) machine man technology still not able to have the general physical and manipulation capabilities even of a 6 year old. So, it brings this question: Why do (AI) scientists need to concern ethics? Because (AI) technology is complex, information into insight has the potential to reveal long held secrets and help solve some of the world's most difficult problems. (AI) systems can potentially be used to help discover insights to treat disease, predict the whether, and manage the global economy. So, ethic issues is important to and (AI) scientists . If any one new (AI) technology research investigation could success, it will be a secret to and the (AI) scientists can not permit to their loyalty to any competitors to damage the fair (AI) technology products trading market. The country (countries) (AI) technology scientists need to concern ethic issues, who need to keep secrets for their countries economic or/and social benefits. This is moral issues to any countries/country loyalty is whose countries intangible assets. They can not sell (AI) loyalty to any their countries to assist whose economic benefits immorally. Also (AI) technology can be applied to wellness an d lifestyle management, diagnostics, delivers financially but also way of organizational and work flow improvement. So, (AI) technology will be continue to become most prevalent and adoption to health care organizations , which must need to enhance structure to be position to take full advantages of new (AI) technological capabilities. (AI) technology can change the nature of work and employment is rapidly changing to make the best use of both humans and (AI) talent in health care industry in the future. For example, (AI) technology offers a way to fill in gaps and the rising labor shortage in health care. According to Accenture analysis, the physicians shortage is increasing. However, (AI) technology will manufacture health care machine men to replace physicians in future one day(2017). Hence, (AI) technology will be invented to raise health care service staffs work efficiency and performance in any hospitals or clinics in the future. In conclusion, (AI) technology will raise efficiency for any service or manufacturing industries in the future, although, it is possible that it will also rise low skillful workers unemployment numbers. But, the most important influence to human technological innovation will be risen and it will influence human life will be changed to be better, e.g. self drive cars, health care physician machine men, machine man cleaners etc. intelligent machine men will be manufactured to serve for our daily life. Furthermore, (AI) technological products will influence countries trading, some low technological development countries manufacturing businessmen can choose to buy any (AI) products to raise whose productivity and efficiency and reducing cost to achieve economic cost saving result. Also, GDP of trading growth income will increase to the (AI) products sale countries. Hence, it will be beneficial to economic development to both developed and developing countries both in the future as well as (AI) scientists time and money spending will be valued to continue to invest (AI) technology development for human life and economy benefits for long term. Moreover, (AI) technology will raise macro economy growth and it can create many (AI) jobs , but it also raise the low level technological worker unemployment change. In the future, (AI) technology can be applied to digital technology to attempt to invent any new undiscovered (AI) and digital technology. So, it needs any scientists to continue to research how digital and (AI) technology can be mixed to satisfy human's future undiscovered needs.

Then, the mentor and skeptic both says:

" We agree your experience to let we learn how robots may help your factory human workers and supervisors to create skill and management ability in order to raise vehicle manufacture number increases in possible."

Episode 2
Tools of Creation

Then, the Skeptic: A traditional artist or thinker who questions the role of technology in creative processes. He says " let me explain what brain imagination art creative ability means to let you know please ?"

"Can we train ourselves brains to raise more art creative abilities? One excellent author, painter, music writer, clothing designer, house designer, dance performer etc. different kinds of art creative performers, whether they use some methods or skills to raise their brain imagination art creative effort or it is themselves owning genius brain imagination art creative abilities from their born or birth date."

"It is one interesting question concerns how to raise ourselves brain imagination art creative efforts. Firstly, we need to know whether what brain imagination art creative effort means. In fact, many people feel some art genius, their imagination art creative abilities are due to their parents give them. It means that when they born, they must be genius, any kinds of art imagination creative efforts that they must own, e.g. some genius own writing story creative content ability, creating song or music ability, creative beautiful paints ability, designing clothes or houses or any things ability, creative dance performance ability.However, some brain scientists or brain doctors or psychologists explain that evidences and experiments indicate may of art geniuses, their art imagination creative abilities are due to their learning more than themselves born to own from parents."

"What does brain imagination creative effort mean? Brain imaginations art creative abilities may include many kinds of brain creating imaginations. For musical imaginations example, it may explain any creative aspects of music listening in the activities of composition, improvisation, and performance. So, the music or song writer can own good brain of music creative effort to write many different nature of musical beauty to bring enjoying and listening song or music emotion to music or song listeners.So, brain imagination may include music or song creativity to any one. But, the differences between good music or bad music creativity may due to the music or song creativity may due to the music or song imagination creator whether who owns what level of musical knowledge, training, literacy, writing music or song experience, or playing music performance experience to the music listener individual listening music or song taste etc. different factors to bring individual emotion response to feel whether the song or music is good or bad after the music writer finished to write the song. Also, any kinds of song or music creativity have close relationship to the creator's brain music or song imagination creating effort had how much. It means that of the music creator owns high level of brain music imagination creative effort, then the music creator ought have enough effort to create many good song or good music to let any one listener to listen and feel their song or music creativity can own unique listening feeling to compare general music creators their common music or song creativity."

"On theory explanation, brain imagination may mean that creative thinking, creating thinking is defined as the competence to engage any kinds of brain imagination productively in the generation, evaluation, and improvement of anyone of brain imagination, ideas, that can result in original and effective solutions, advances in any kinds of knowledge imagination , e.g. design a house, design a cloth, design a product, writing one story, writing one music or song, design a dance performance, painting a picture etc. different kinds of imagination. Imagination may be listening imagination, e.g. song, music or reading a story book, wearing a dressing cloth, living a house, seeing a dance performance. Hence, imagination may be touched or seen or felt by any one. Hence, any one creative art performer must need have excellent creative thinking to create their product imagination, e.g. how to write one good story, how to write a good listening song, how to design a house or a cloth or a product, how to prepare a dancer performance etc. different kinds of creative product imagination to let any one customer to feel their creative products can have the unique or excellent quality to compare other general similar or same kinds of creative products.Thus, imagination is the seed of creativity. Indeed, there is one fundamental skill that makes creativity possible. Without imagination, there can be no creativity. Imagination refers broadly to the human capacity to construct a mental representation of the which is nor currently present to the senses . Hence, many brain doctors and brain scientists and psychologists imply that imagination is the seed of creativity. Genius's unique creativity can be caused by their brain imagination. Any one creative product creator whose brain may be trained to own unique creative effort by themselves learning or nay new creative knowledge skills or methods in order to achieve to raise themselves brain imagination creative efforts.On conclusion, it seems that why any one creative effort is due to creator whose imagination creative effort is due to they attempt to learn new creative knowledge more than their born genius to own creative effort. Many brain doctors or brain scientists or psychologists began to research how to raise ourselves brains to achieve owning excellent imagination creative effort. I shall attempt to explain how we can attempt to learn in order to raise ourselves brains imagination creative efforts in order to become one excellent painter, music/song writer, author, designer, dance performer etc. different kinds of creative occupation performers."

Then, the Prodigy: A young individual whose life changes dramatically due to access to advanced technology. He asks

" What is the relationship between enough sleeping and brain imagination art creative ability raising level in order to improve human daily live change to be better in possible?"

Then, the Skeptic says

"Can keeping enough sleeping time raise brain creative imagination effort or raise memory? Can enough sleeping influence our brains own more art creative ability, e.g. creating good story content ability, drawing beautiful paint image ability, creat5ing good song or music ability, creating beautiful house or cloth or any kinds of products ability? Many brain scientists had begun to research how enough sleeping time has direct or indirect relationship to improve ourselves brains creative efforts. They also believe that it is possible that enough sleeping time may help ourselves brains to improve creative e and memory effort. If it is true, whether we need to sleep how many hours in order to improve ourselves brains creative efforts. Otherwise, if we lack enough sleeping time, our brains creative e efforts will be influenced to poor? For example, one owning many years writing experience proficient author, if he can not have enough sleeping time every day, it can bring poor creative story imagination mind ability to recreate any new story content in possible. It is one interesting question concerns the relationship between enough sleeping time and brain creative ability research? I shall attempt to indicate evidences to explain their relationship as below:"

"` Any one must need sleep. If one lacks at least 8 hours sleeping time in the day, he won't have enough nervous to do any matters, even jobs. So , it seems that any creative tasks, e.g. writing stories, painting pictures, designing houses, cloths etc. creative jobs. The art creator must need have enough time to sleep in order to prepare to raise his brain imagination creative feeling to achieve how to design one beautiful house in order to attract people to choose this house to buy in preference, or design one beautiful cloth to attract people to choose his design cloth to wear in preference, how to write horror story content to let readers to feel fear or write romance story content to let readers to feel they are lovers both or write space scientific story content to let readers to feel that they are catching rocket to fly to outer strange space environment to carry on one time space existing journey, even how to design one time attractive dance performance to let audiences to feel all dancers to feel all dancers are performing attractive dance steps or create soft music to let music listeners to feel this music is soft or comfortable to listen, when they are sitting in the theater to listen this music performance. So, all of these creative tasks to the art creator, who must need have clear brain imagination or nervous to help them to create any one of those creative product in order to let customers or audiences feel their creative products are beautiful or attractive to compare other some creators whose art products. Hence, art creative imagination must need to any one art creator, if he/she hopes that his/her art creative product can bring more attraction to any one art product buyers or audience to consider more to compare his/her other same art creative product competitors. So, any one art creator must not need to own high educational level of working experiences . Otherwise, they must need top own high level art imagination ability to compare general people. Hence, it is true that any one art creator must need have more clear and good imagination effort to compare other occupation working people in our societies, if they hope to own good creative imagination effort to attempt to create their any kinds of creative products, e.g. design of a house, a cloth, write one story etc. creative products. So, it is ensure that creative art product ought need have good brain imaginatio0n to compare general occupations. In fact, many brain scientists or brain doctors or psychologists believe that enough sleeping time, it can influence any one whose nervous next day, such as they had attempted to carry on many brain imagination creative effort researches or experiments . They confirm that if the art product creator or art entertainer can have enough sleeping time, it can help the art product creator or art entertainer to create good dance performance, good listening soft music, one beautiful design house or cloth , dancing a good dance performance to compare lacking enough sleeping time product creator or art entertainer. Hence, it seems that enough sleeping time may assist any one art creator to raise brain imagination creative effort."

Then, the Prodigy: A young individual whose life changes dramatically due to access to advanced technology. He asks

"What the methods to train brain creative effort?"

Then, the Skeptic says

"How we can train ourselves brains to raise high creative efforts? Can we train ourselves brains creative efforts by learning method? Has it close relationship between ourselves bodies and ourselves brain creative efforts? Do ourselves brains creative efforts to be poor if we have no health bodies? I believe that we must need have health bodies, then our health bodies may bring more creative effort to ourselves brains easily, because health bodies may help us to raise ,memory ability, keeping happy and pleasure positive emotion to do any things every day. Due to our brains must be our part of bodies. Our brains are inside to our bodies. Although, we can not see our brains , but we can feel ourselves brains are working, if our memory is high, e.g. we can remember our teachers what they had taught all contents after every lesson. Then, our examination results must be improved because we have good memory . So, enough sleeping time is one good method to raise ourselves brains' memories. In fact, enough sleeping time does not needed to have enough training. So, training our brains to raise creative effort method, we only need have enough sleeping time in order to keep our brains have enough nervous to remember any things more easily, e.g. studying is one good example for remembering training action or behavior, we can attempt to train ourselves brains to remember any new knowledge from teacher individual teaching. When we learn any new knowledge in lessons, we are using ourselves brains to attempt to remember what the teacher is teaching in lesson . If we brains feel tried, we can have breaking time for less sleeping time between lessons in order to keep ourselves brain memory longer time.In fact, ourselves brains memory and brains creative effort whether they are high or low level, they have close relationship because our creative effort may be influenced to raise if our memory effort can increase rapidly and it can be kept longer time. Many brain doctors, psychologists, brain scientists had researched to attempt to do experiments to confirm that brain creative effort and brain memory effort have close relationship. Hence, many of them begin to believe that if one person can have high memory effort, then whose brain ought have high creative effort, e.g. creative story writing ability, creative drawing paint ability, creative music or song ability, creative designing house, or cloth or any products ability . All of these different kinds of brain creative abilities , they must have absolute relationship to brain memory. It means that if your brain can have good memory ability to remember or learn any kinds of new knowledge rapidly in long time, then your brain can have high creative ability to be trained to create any kinds of new knowledge easily, e.g. writing fun story, writing fun or good listening song or music, drawing beautiful paint, design attraction of house or cloth etc. any products, even organizing good dance performance. All of these creative tasks must need have good memory ability to the creator, hence, enough sleeping time must be the best method to help us to improve ourselves brain memory or brain creative effort both. We can not neglect to keep enough sleeping time in order to raise ourseves brain memory and creative effort both, if we hope to become an excellent story writer, music or song writer, house or cloth design, good organized performance dancer. On conclusion, attempting to apply brain memory effort to do creative effort skillful tasks, when one person can have enough sleeping time every day, then his brain memory ability may be influenced to raise or improve. He can attempt to do some simple creative task, e.g. learning how to draw one natural environment scene paint, learning hoe to create a horror story, learning how to create a good listening song or music, even learning how to organize every steps for the dance performance etc. different kinds of creative tasks behaviors. Because when the person feels that he has enough sleeping time, his memory ability may be influenced to increase memory ability. When one house designer, he feels that his memory ability is increasing, he ought remember all prior beautiful or urge house design in his memory if he is one house designer. After this house designer's prior all house design drawing picture will be remembered again. So, this house designer can remember all his poor drawing paints in order to improve or understand whether how he ought continue to draw or improve his new house picture in order to design his new house design more easily. Because when one house design needs to spend time to create or design one new house. If he can remember which kinds of house , he had drawn in past in his brain memory. Then, he can avoid to repeat to design his past old house design again. He can use his new house design method to create another new house paint design. So, this house designer can improve his new house paint design if he can remember what kinds of houses, he had painted to design in his past. Then, he can avoid to repeat to design the kind of similar or same style of house again. Consequently, one good brain memory house designer can avoid to design same or similar house again, then this house design may have more house design creative effort in order to design his next new house easily. So, it explains why it may have close relationship between brain memory and brain creative effort."

Then, the Mentor asks
"Can exercise bring more creative effort to brains ?"

Then, The Prodigy: A young individual whose life changes dramatically due to access to advanced technology. He says

"Any excellent occupation people who must need to often do exercises in order to achieve excellent performance, such as sportsman, doctor, lawyer, accountant, engineer, teacher, architect, singer etc. different professional occupations. All of these occupation people, who must need to spend time to do exercises repeat again in order to achieve proficient performance or proficient skills. The question concerns whether of one creative art working person who often do exercise, then he/she can bring more creative effort to themselves brains, e.g. one author often does imagination to feel new things in order to attempt to write any new story. In his/she creative imagination process, whether himself/herself brain can be influenced to raise or improve or increase effort when he/she often uses his/her brain to mind any new science story scene to achieve brain creative effort or if one music person often uses himself/herself brain to attempt to mind any new music suddenly. When he/she feels himself/herself brain has one good music or song suddenly, then he/she writes down the music or song in order to avoid that he/she forgets when himself/herself brain has this new music or song imagination in his/her mind. So, he / she often does music /song creative exercise in order to improve his/her any new music/song imagination. Can this musician often do music/song creative imagination to bring high brain creative level? For a house designer example, if this house designer often does brain creative exercise to draw any house design or house picture when he /she feels himself/herself brain has any unique house imagination suddenly. Can his/her frequent drawing any new house picture design behavior, which changes himself/herself brain creative effort to be raised significantly? So, such as my explanation that it is possible that any exploration that it is possible that any person can attempt to do brain creative exercise in order to raise our brain creative effort more significantly and easily. Why do frequent brain creative imagination exercise, they may help ourselves brains to raise brain creative effort more easily or effectively? I shall attempt to explain as below:"

"Our brains are similar to our bodies, e.g. hand, foot. We must need often do exercises, in order to let we can run rapidly or climb mountains safely or we can swim rapidly. So, if one sportsman hopes to win the sport competition, he/she will often run or swim or climb mountains or ride bicycles before this sport competition will begin. So, our brains are such as our part of bodies. Ourselves brains must often need to be done exercises in order to raise creative effort, if we hope to become one proficient creative author, drawing painter, house designer, cloth designer , musician etc. art creators. Our brains must be needed to do any creative mind exercises again and again every day in order to improve ourselves brains imagination creative effort significantly. Any one proficient art creator, who must not be talent especially, they must not own unique talent characteristics. Otherwise, some of talent art creator , e.g. author, musician, house or cloth designer, painter etc they may be foolish people in general. But, if they can often keep to do brain creative exercises, when they feel any new things in themselves mind suddenly, e.g. one special house picture imagination, one special beautiful cloth picture imagination, one good listening song or music imagination or mind. They can write down to record on paper immediately. If they can keep to write on paper to record any new picture imagination in habit. Their brain creative imagination exercise behaviors, which can help them to train their brains to learn how to create new imagination picture skills, e.g. let them to feel to create any new music or song easily, let them to feel to draw or design any house or cloth imagination easily, let them to feel to create any new story content easily, let them to feel to organize one unique dance performance easily. What factor may cause any one of above art creator to feel how to create any new creative product easily? The main factor is that " exercise" , due to they can often train their brains to learn how to attempt to create new story content, new music or song , new house or cloth design, new dance performance stepping. When they often use themselves brains to create any new creative products, and write down on paper or draw on paper in order to record their any new creative products as well as avoid to forget their any new creative products. Then, they can revise their past creative products in order to improve their past creative products to be better.In their " brain creative process exercises", they must help any one of these art creators to raise themselves brain creative effort significantly. Hence, " brain art creative exercise" may be one good method to help any one art creator to raise their art creative skills."

Then, the Skeptic: A traditional artist or thinker who questions the role of technology in creative processes, he asks

"Can habit leisure hobbies bring more brain imagination effort ?"

"How to learn effort in order to raise more brain imagination? Can learning bring more brain imagination effort?"

Then, the Prodigy: A young individual whose life changes dramatically due to access to advanced technology says

" For example, if one person often needs any another person writing stories, in his/her reading process can it raise his/her writing ability? If one person often listens music or song , in his/her listening music or song process, can it raise his/her writing music or song creative ability? If one person often watching horror movies, in his/her watching horror movies prices, can it raise his/her creating horror movie imagination effort? If one person often sees cloth magazine photos, in his /her seeing cloth photos process, can it raise his/her design cloth creative effort? If one person often sees house magazine photos, can it raise his/her design house effort? If one person often sees dance performance, in his/her seeing dance performance process, can it raise his/her organize dance performance effort? If one person often sees paints, in his /her seeing paint process, can it raise his/ her drawing paint brain art creative process? Some brain doctors, brain scientists, psychologists begin to research whether if general people often to read books, listen music/songs, see movies, see house or cloth magazines, see dance performance, see paints etc. different hobbies, when whose these different kinds of hobbies become leisure behaviors, whether their these different kinds of leisure behaviors can influence themselves brains raise imagination creative efforts. Some brain doctors or brain scientists had confirmed that when general people can spend about 2 to 3 hours per day to read stories, listen music/song, see movie, read cloth or house photo magazine, see paints, see dance performances etc. different kinds of hobbies or leisure behaviors. Then, these general people whose brains can be influenced to raise more imagine creative efforts, .e.g. creating story content effort, creating music or song effort, designing house or cloth effort, organizing dance performance effort, creating movie content effort, creating paint picture effort, because when general individual can spend time to do any one of these leisure actions to be habit bobbies every day. Although , they do not be trained or taught from teachers, or they do not born to own high creative effort, but when general individual can attempt to spend time to feel enjoyable to choose to do any one of these leisure action to become hobbies. Then, their brains may be influences to raise writing story, writing music/song, drawing paint, organizing dance performance, design house or cloth etc. different aspects of art creative efforts. On conclusion, when one general individual can often spend time to do leisure actions or behaviors to be hobbies, then they may help themselves to raise brain imagination creative effort in possible. So, we can attempt to choose any kinds of leisure interest to be leisure hobbies as well as do leisure actions in habit, then our leisure habits will help ourselves brains to raise art creative efforts in possible."

Then, the Skeptic: A traditional artist or thinker who questions the role of technology in creative processes, he asks

"Can general people be trained or be taught in order to help ourselves brains to raise imagination creative efforts?"

Then, the Prodigy: A young individual whose life changes dramatically due to access to advanced technology says

"Many brain scientists and brain doctors had began to find general people to do experiments concern whether any general people whose brain imagination effort can be influenced to raise after they are taught or are trained, e.g. learning drawing paint skills, learning dance skills, learning creative story content skills, learning house or cloth or product design skills etc. different kinds of imagination behaviors. However, they discovered that although any one can learn general writing story, writing music or song , design house, cloth or any kinds of products skills, draw paint, or organize dance performance etc. art creative skills, but it does not represent that their brains can be influenced to raise imagination creative effort. The reason is that it is different between raising creative brain effort and raising creative skills effort. In general, we can learn general writing book, writing music or song, designing house or cloth or any kinds of products, drawing paints, dancing etc. art creative skills or art creative by teaching or training methods. So, art teacher may let us to learn any kinds of art creative skills, but, if we hope to raise or improve ourselves brain art creative effort. It is not possible that teaching and training methods both may help us to raise brain art creative effort, because human brain is one part of ourselves bodies. Brain is not hand or foot, we can use hand and foot to attempt to do any art creative tasks, e.g. how to use hand to draw one beautiful paint, hoe to use foot to dance, how to use hand to design one beautiful house or cloth or any kinds of products. So, learning art creative skills, it means that learning how to use hand or foot to do any art creative behaviors. We can only learn art creative skills hoe to use hand to draw beautiful paint, how to use foot to dance, how to hand to design one house, one cloth or any kinds of products. So, teaching and training methods can only let us to learn how to use hand or foot to do art creative skillful behavior more easily. These both methods can not help ourselves brains to raise brain art imagination creative effort in possible. Nowadays, many brain scientists and brain doctors began to believe that teaching and training both methods only help ourselves to learn how to use hands to improve drawing paints behaviors in order to achieve more easily or how to use foots to improve dancing behaviors in order to achieve more attractive dance performance or how to design cloth or house or any kinds of products more attraction, or how to use our mouths to sing more attraction of sounds. All of above these art creative behaviors are only " art creative skills". When we are taught or trained to learn any one of these art creative skills by teachers, ourselves brains won's be influenced to raise any kinds of art creative efforts. So, teaching and training both methods can not raise ourselves brains creative effort. Otherwise, these both methods may only help ourselves hands and foots to improve art creative skillful behaviors in order to achieve how to use hands to draw paints more easily, how to write story content more attraction, how to use hands to design house or cloth or any kinds of products more attraction, how to use our mouths to sing songs more clearly. If we hope to improve or raise ourselves brains art creative efforts to be any kinds of art creator, we can only keep enough sleeping time every day, keeping habits to read books, keeping habits to see any cloth or house magazines, keeping habits to listen any kinds of music, or see any dance performance etc. different kinds of art leisure activities, because when we can enjoy to do any kinds of art creative leisure when we spend nervous to do these leisure activities in habit. Then, ourselves brains can be excited to raise any kinds of art excited to raise any kinds of arr imagination creative efforts by other artists. Consequently, ourselves brains art creative minds may be influenced to improve , even raise brain art creative effort , due to ourselves brains had saved more different artists whose art imagination of memories."

Then, t**he Innovator** says " I believe that it is not only robots can create human creative abilities, human ourselves can learn any skills to improve human ourselves creative abilities."

Episode 3
The Ethical Dilemma

The Mentor: An experienced figure who guides others in navigating the intersection of technology and creativity. He asks

"Can we apply some methods or skills to help ourselves brains to raise imagination creative effort?"

Then, the Prodigy: A young individual whose life changes dramatically due to access to advanced technology says

"Let me answer these question: In fact, many brain doctors or brain scientists or psychologists began to research whether we can apply what skills to improve ourselves brains imagination creative efforts. They had began to attempt to find any one to attempt to do any brain imagination improvement experiments . Their aims to find the best skills to help human to improve brain imagination memory in order to create high level art performers. If one day, human individual brain can be trained to raise brain imagination memory function effort, then many general level of authors, painters, music or song writers , art performers, designers , their skills can be improved to be one proficient art work creator easily. Because if they can be confirmed that one kind skill or some skills can help themselves brains to raise imagination creating effort significantly. Then, when every common art work creator occupation performer can learn any useful skills to attempt to raise their brain imagination creative effort, it can bring much benefits to our societies because when many common art creative performers can confirm to improve their brain imagination creative effort from some skillful training. Consequently, we will have much beautiful cloths to wear, good design of houses to live , good music or song to listen, see beautiful drawing pictures, good books to read , good dance performances to see, because all of these creative art performers, their imagination creating effort can be improved significantly. Then , our social cultural level will be influence to raise in long time significantly.The question concerns whether what skills or methods may help ourselves brains to raise imagination creative efforts? I shall attempt to indicate some possible skills or methods, they may help ourselves brains to raise imagination creative efforts as below:"

"For dancer performance behavior example, it is at its simplest, allowing your child to thrive though constant play and exploration, uninhibited by the strict rules of science, reason, law or a judgmental society. For any one dancer, it requires an open channel to allow dancer behavioral information and ideas to flow freely into the dancer's space. It requires an open mind and a sense of freedom and limitlessness. So, one proficient dancer needs to own high dance skillful memory to remember every whose dance behavior as well as learn how to create good dance skills in order to attract audiences attention and satisfy their visual dance enjoyment feeling on the theater hall. Hence, dancer needs to raise whose dance skillful imagination creative effort, it means that they need to learn how to excite themselves brains to create dance behavioral imagination in order to improve themselves dance skills effectively."

"I believe that strongly in the idea of every human action stemming from a complex environmental factors. I also believe an extra ingredient is somehow part of imagination. An internal imagine word, so such as one proficient dancer case, if she can train herself brain to remember every high level dance steps easily. Then, she ought improve herself dance skills in short time rapidly. So, training to remember dance steps , which is needed to help the common dancer to become one proficient dancer more easily. For dancer case, she may use imagination to recall emotions needed in interpreting a character for any one dance performance to picture an overall aesthetic before it comes to fruition, to invent new artistic dance concepts, to invent new movements to connect old movements , to picture the dancer whose body executing a movement before she has even done the dance steps, to try something new dance steps. Hence, new dance steps and dance boy behaviors from whose old dance st4eps and body dancing behaviors in order to achieve to feel her dance steps and body dancing behaviors had been improved significantly. It is one good skill to improve anyoOne common dancer dancing skills, when she can train herself brain to create good dancing steps and dancing body behaviors as well as remember every old dancing body behavior or dancing steps in order to raise how to improve or create new dancing body behavior or new dancing steps. Consequently, she can learn how to change new dancing body behaviors in order to improve herself old dancing skill easily. Hence, any one dancer must need to raise whose brain dance imagination creative effort in order to improve whose old dance skills significantly. Research concerning the role of memory in imagination or brain imagination creative effort skill issue, it is future interesting brain behavioral research issue for any one brain doctor or brain scientist or psychologist. They aim to help our societies to produce more excellent art creative performers. Most psychological theories of imagination can be seen as theories of imagination consider that " creative" imagination, e.g. paint, writing a story, playing music, designing a house, designing a cloth, designing a dancing steps. All of any these, they belong to " creative imagination". Their imagination is needed to create by ourselves brains. When ourselves brains have clear picture, then the author can follow his brain picture or mind to create a story content, write a song, design a house or a cloth or organize a dancing steps."

"Hence, " brain imagination picture" may be one main element to help any one creative performer to create any kinds of creative product very easily. If the creative performer can own good brain picture memory, then his story content can be more attraction, his dancing steps can be more attraction, his house or cloth or any kinds of products design can be more attraction. The question concerns how to create attractive brain picture imagination? Hence, when the art creative performer can have good brain imagination, then he/she ought have good creativity or creative effort in order to create whose new story , new song, new design house of cloth or new dancing steps very easily. In fact, imagination pervades human experience. Children begin engaging in pretend play and although cultural and parental attitudes affect the amount and content of imagination play. As adults, we are consumers and creators of fiction, song, story, house, designer, dance performance etc. and we respond emotionally to imagined scenarios. Moreover, we invent fictions even in the pursuit of facts, face of neurological disorders, in defending the bases of our decisions, and in the construction of autobiographical memory. However, by applying useful knowledge in extraordinary events with heightened emotional content, learners may be better able to access important cultural skills or facts. Consistent with this, researchers have suggested that imaginative engagement might support a range of cognitive abilities, including creativity, intelligence, problem solving, symbolic reasoning, language development , theory of mind, narrative skills, social skills, causal reasoning , emotional regulation , and executive function."

"I believe that thinking of new ideas is not an optional exercise in creativity. It is fundamental to learning . The learner must need gather new information in order to raise whose brain imagination creative effort. So, gathering new information is the best method to help our brains to raise imagination creative effort. It is more effective to compare how to think of new ideas to achieve how to create ourselves brain imagination creative effort. For a dancer, if she can attempt to gather any new dancing styles new information from internet channel daily. I believe that she can improve whose dancing steps in order to create new dance style more easily. Otherwise, if she only concentrates on how to think her new dance style ideas by herself mind. I believe that she can not create any new dance attractive style to improve her old poor dancing style easily. Hence, gathering new information may be another useful brain imagination creative effort improvement skill. Another kind of method is that teaching anyone to new skill. One of the best ways to expand your learning is to teach a skill to another person. After you learn a new skill, you need to practice it. Teaching a new skill to others needs you to explain the concept and correct any mistakes you make. This can improve your mental activeness to a great extent. Next method is that spending spare time for physical activity, many studies have confirmed that daily physical activity also keeps the brain sharp and active. The simple science behi8nd this is that physical activity accelerates the circulation of oxygen on the mind. All of these methods can help your brains to improve memory and raise brain imaginatio0n creative effort effectively. Then, we can improve memory, it can assist us to raise creative thinking or creativity. Creativity means the ability to change traditional ideas, rules, patterns, relationships and to create meaningful new ideas, forms, methods etc. originality, progressiveness, or imagination. In fact, every one has the capacity to be creative. In the psychological view, these is a debate over whether anyone is born with innate creativity or if everyone who has it has developed a talent. Though some scientists believe certain individuals have a higher aptitude for creativity, many attest that creativity is an actually a skill and anyone can learn a skill. This is the integration of memory and creative thinking at work. Consequently, we tend to think a parts of the brain specialized for one thing, one particular function at a time. However, neuroscentists attest that all parts of the brain are constantly interacting and building strong neural pathways is the best way to keep all parts of the brain healthy. Finally, I shall indicate ways to exercise creative thinking skills, e.g. changing your routine, you will need to experience anything new or give yourself a new experience to active your brain in creative process. Try changing something small or adding a new activity each day. Thus will help your brain and your body to stretch your creative muscles, or read a book or listen music, anyone of these daily habit behaviors, they will help your brains to raise imagination creative effort effectively. Hence, we can not neglect any one of these simple skills or living habits, they may help ourselves brains to raise imagination creative effort indeed."

Then, the innovator says " Your opinion can persuade me to believe that human ought not only depend on technology to improve human ourselves creative ability and human and skill, we ought think how we change our live model in order to raise creative abilities in possible."

Episode 4
The Future of Creativity

The Prodigy: A young individual whose life changes dramatically due to access to advanced technology. He aks

"Can we improve ourselves IQ in order to raise ourselves brain imagination creative effort?

Do IQ and brain imagination, which has cause and effect close relationship?"

Then, the Mentor: An experienced figure who guides others in navigating the intersection of technology and creativity. He says

"Nowadays, many brain scientists and brain doctors began to attempt to find young people to do experiments to research whether their brain art imagination creative effort can be raised if their IQ can be trained to improve their mind analysis and logic judgment effort. In results, they conclude unique conclusions, their investigations discover that if one young person whose IQ can be trained to climb up to above 100 marks, then their mind and analysis and logic judgment effort may be influenced to raise, even their brain art imagination creative effort may also be influenced to improve in possible. Hence, many of brain doctors or brain scientists or psychologists begin to believe that training on IQ improvement method can bring positive art imagination creative effort influences to develop our brain's mind analysis, logic, judgment efforts. So, if one person , he/she can be trained to improve his/her IQ mind effort from his/her child age stage till to adult age stage. Consequently, his/her brain art imagination creative effort may be raised to more 50% of his/her general brain art imagination creative effort level."

"It brings this question: Why can improve brain IQ level to influence ourselves grain art imagination creative effort to be raised? The answer is simple that I assume the one young owns high IQ level, his/her mind analysis and logic judgment effort must be better than general low IQ level people. SO, when he/she owns high level of mind analysis and logic judgment effort. He/she can spend less time to make more accurate judgment to solve any challenges, because his/her mind analysis and logic judgment effort compares to general low IQ level people is higher. So, when the young can be trained to reach high IQ level intelligent young, he/she can make much accurate mind analysis, logic judgment effort to know how to draw paints or pictures to let many audiences feel more beautiful to his/her creative pictures, how to create horror story content to feel readers to feel, how to sing or create the song in order to let listeners to feel enjoyable to listen the song, how to organize the dance steps in order to attract audiences to see the dance performance, how to design the house in order to let the house buyers feel the house design is attraction, how to design the cloth in order to let the cloth buyers feel comfortable to wear the cloth etc. different art creative tasks. So, it seems that it has cause and effect relationship between 'IQ improvement and brain art creative effort improvement . Because when we born, we must not own high IQ level or high brain art creative effort level. We must need to spend long time to learn or to be trained to improve ourselves brain IQ level or brain art creative effort. Due to ourselves brain IQ level and brain art creative effort level will not be brought when we born in first day. I mean that we need time to be taught or be trained in order to improve ourselves brains IQ level or brain art creative effort level. Hence, IQ and art creative efforts have similar characteristics , such as intangible, feeling. So, we must need ourselves brains can be trained to bring high IQ level in order to improve ourselves brains art creative effort in possible. ON conclusion, improvement IQ level can be one kind of good method to help ourselves brains to improve art creative efforts significantly.

A painter hopes to learn how to use hands to draw any kinds of beautiful paints. Instead of color choice, paint pen choice, painting drawing quality of paper choice, painting tools factor. Can the painter himself/herself brain mind creative effort influence his/her paints pictures which they can attract audiences to feel himself/herself paints are beautiful to compare general painters/ IN fact, drawing paint quality of papers, painting pens, color quality of these painting tools factors may influence the picture is beautiful or attractive or not, but we can not negligent that the painters whose brain mind creative effort also may influence their any one paint creative feeling. For example, if the painter's brain can have good creative house effort, then his/her any house design will attract more people like to see his/her any house design picture to compare other house designers. Hence, this painter ought concentrate on attempting to design any kinds of house pictures order to improve his/her any kinds of house design picture, due to his/her brain owns high mind creative effort to create any

kinds of house to draw more easily to compare
other kinds of things. So, if he/she forgets to continue to draw any kinds of house pictures, then he/she chooses to draw natural or human face or human body or any things, such as cloth,furniture etc. paint pictures. I believe that this painter can not draw these kinds of pictures to compare drawing house pictures more beautiful or attraction. Hence, it seems that a young painter needs to know that whether the painter , his/her ability can draw which kinds of paint pictures more excellent or more proficient in order to concentrate on improving to draw this kind of paint pictures. Then, it brings this question: How doe this painter know that what kinds of painting pictures who can draw more proficient? The answer ensures be "what kinds of picture image, he/she can own more mind creative effort. Hence, the painter needs to know that what kinds of brain image that he can own more creative effort to draw the kind of image picture. For example, if one painter feels that he /she has more interest to draw any human face or body paint pictures as well as when he sees any one natural face or body, he can remember their body shape and face shape in his/her brain memory more clearly, even he /she also feel his/her owning human face or body image creative effort is more proficient or excellent more than to create any other kinds of things image to draw pictures. Them I may ensure that painter ought concentrate on drawing any human faces or bodies picture images in order to improve his/her painting skills more easily. Hence , any painter must need to know whether which aspect of picture image himself or herself mind creative effort, that he/she ought own high brain image creative effort on this kind of thing."

"I mean that when the painter discovers that he /she own high image creative effort on mature sense, he /she ought concentrate on drawing trees, flowers, woods, etc. natural environment pictures, or he /she discovers that owning high image creative effort on furniture, bicycles, books, cups, toys etc. different kinds of product images.Then. this painter ought concentrate on drawing any one of these products in order to improve his/her drawing painting skills. Hence, any one painter must need to know whether he/she owns which aspect of brain
image creative effort in the highest level in order to draw his/her paint pictures more easily."

"Nowadays, brain scientists, brain doctors, psychologists had began to research how to improve humans ourselves brains imagine creative effort significantly. They had began to apply robots to build brains which can

similar to human brains, they had been carrying experiment to research whether future artificial brains can be invented to own general human's memory ability, even imagine creative ability. In fact, they had attempted to do robot brain scientific experiments, they concluded that it is possible that future robot (artificial intelligent) brains will have chance to invent to similar human's brain to learn mind , creativity, analysis, memory ability, even future robot (AI) brain development may be improved to exceed human's general memory, mind analysis, memory, even image creative effort level. Hence, it seems that future robots can be applied to do any kinds of art creative tasks. Moreover, (AI) robot brain art imagine creative ability, it is possible that their brain art imaginative efforts can be better that human ourselves brain e.g. creative effort.
Even, future human's brain art creative efforts can not attempt to exceed robot (AI)'s brain art creative efforts forever."
"I assume that future brain scientists and robot (AI) brain scientists confirm that robots may be developed their brains own high level of mind, analysis, judgment, memory and art imagine creative efforts to compare human's ourselves brains development. Then, I bring these two questions: Can future robot replace human to do any art creative tasks ? Can robots and human art creative workers cooperate in order to bring better art creative products or robots or human art creative products or robots or human art creative workers work alone can bring better art creative products, due to robot art creative workers are human art creative workers' their art creative products occupation competitors. I shall attempt to answer above these both questions as below:"

"If brain scientists confirm that future robots (AI) themselves brains can be invented to achieve to own high level mind, analysis, memory, art creative effort, then, they ought to used to do any kinds of art creative tasks in our societies. For example, robots can be used to apply their image creative effort to help humans painters to apply art mind to judge how to draw any kinds of paints in order to raise the paint pictures' attraction to robots can be used to apply their music or song creative effort to help human musicians to apply art mind to judge how to write one music or song in order to let listeners can feel soft music comfortable feeling or robots can be used to apply their image creative effort to help designer to judge how to design one cloth, one house, one magazine, book, advertisement cover or any kinds of products in order to attract buyers feel the kind of product design is more beautiful to achieve purchase in preference."

"I assume that future robot (AI) brain art creative effort development ought be developed to exceed human ourselves general art creative effort in possible. Although, it must be good news if robots' brains art creative efforts may be improved to invent achieve to exceed human's brain general art creative efforts, but it also brings image bad news, they may influence many art image creative workers lose their art image creative workers lose their art image creative jobs when robots can be replaced to do any kinds of art replaced to do any kinds of art creative jobs in our future societies."

"Have future our art creative tasks development must need to keep balance between robot's brains and human art creative workers' brains. I suggest that human art creative workers or performances ought not feel robots may be their main art creative occupational competitors. I mean that future any kinds of art creative workers ought cooperate with robots to do any kinds of art creative tasks together. So, robots' role is future any kinds of art creative workers' assistants for one painter example, he can apply robot's art imagine creative mind to help him to mind or analyze how to draw the natural scene picture, e.g. how to use color, how to drawing. pens to draw the natural scene picture to be improved , it aims to let audiences can feel more attraction. Hence, the painter may apply the robot's suggestion of natural scene picture to be picture image reference. Then the painter can observe the robot's finished natural science picture to find whether what this natural scene picture weaknesses are, in order to revise whether how to improve this robot's designing natural scene picture its weaknesses to be strengths to attract audiences' observation or raise their visual comfortable feeling or visual satisfactory feeling to this natural scene picture. Hence, future robot's roles are only any kinds of human art creative workers' assistants. They can only been given their any kinds of art creative products to let any one art creative workers to refer or revise in order to improve their creative skills from human art creative workers. So, I feel that they ought cooperate to create any kinds of art image creative pictures together to compare that they choose to do themselves art creative tasks alone. When they can cooperate to work together , their any kinds of art creative products must be improved to increase attraction more easily."

Then, the Innovator: A tech entrepreneur who creates groundbreaking tools that enhance creativity., he says

Let me explain that artificial intelligent Human clever and art creating ability methods as below: "How robots create human clever and art creating ability? Nowadays robots invention may help businesses to reduce employees number, improve performance, raise productivity, reduce cost in service industry,manufacturing industry, office , warehouse, restaurant, hotel , factory, cinema etc. different kinds of business environments, even public transport tools. However, instead of robots may bring these above advantages to any kinds of business working and service environments, whether robots may also help human to create clever and image creating ability.

On the one hand, I believe that past technology ,e.g. machine , it should not have ability to help human to create clever and image creative ability,but nowadays, robots invention that I believe it had had enough ability to help future human to raise more clever and more creating image or painting picture, art design etc. image ability, after robots had been experienced above more than ten years improvement stage from early research stage to invention stage, till to nowadays improvement stage, e.g. non-manual driving auto vehicles, even future non-manual driving skill may be improved to apply to public transport tools, e.g. trams, trains,buses, airplanes, ships etc. public transport tools, when non-manual driving skills can be improved to own the most safe driving skillful ability to compare human driving skills.

On another hand, when robots could be invented to be applied to medical or hospital surgery aspect, e.g. robot surgeon may help surgery doctors to do complex surgery in surgery rooms, or serving patients tasks in any hospital working environments. They can help nurses and doctors to spend more time to do more important tasks urgently, so medical or surgery serving robots may help nurses and surgery doctors to reduce task load pressure and create clever or improve their surgery skills to when they can cooperate to work in hospitals.

On the other hand, robots can be invented to help any public transport drivers to avoid more traffic accidents occurrence on any countries roads. So, it seems that non-manual driving public transport tools invention may also help human drivers to improve driving skills in possible, when they can learn how to avoid sudden traffic accidents occurrence in any countries roads in any time. so, any kinds of public transport tool drivers ought learn how to avoid traffic accidents skills from future non-manual driving robots invention. Instead of non-manual driving robots and hospital patients medical care or surgery service robots may help public transport tools drivers and hospital nurses and doctors to concentrate on spending time to treat any more important and urgent matters every days. Even, future restaurants may let cooking restaurants may let cooking robots to help human cookers to cook more different kinds of good taste food, to human cookers may learn cooking robots cooking skills in order to improve themselves traditional cooking skills often, in order to compare their cooking skills between human cookers and cooking robots.

On conclusion, it seems that cooking robots ought help human cookers to create any kinds of new cooking skills. Moreover, future robot cookers ought be future human cookers their cooking coaches. These robot cookers will help human cookers to create clever cooking skills in possible. Also, future non-manual driving robots ought help human drivers to create new driving skills in order to improve their driving skills to reduce sudden traffic accidents occurrence easily on any countries roads in any time, future hospital surgery or patient care service robots may help surgeons or nurses to do any surgeon in surgery rooms or looking care patients in hospitals. So, when robot surgeons help human surgeons to do complex surgeon in surgeon rooms, human surgeons can learn how to do more complex surgeon tasks for every surgeons when human surgeons can do every surgeon robots how to do surgeons together. Hence, it seems that robot surgeons also may create future human surgeons themselves innovate surgeon skills from traditional surgeon skills improvement. So, future artificial intelligent technology ought help any kinds of human occupations to create clever, even improvement themselves traditional skills to new innovative skills absolutely. Consequently creative and social intelligence will be in even greater demand as (AI) makes in management and the workforce. This development will represent a long term trend in labor markets , one characterized by intensifying demand and reward for social skills with a growing desire for creative capabilities, managers will seek to fashion of ideas and hypotheses from inside and outside of the enterprise to shape solutions to their most pressing business problems. Thus, (AI) will influence overall organizational team members who have chance to participate any decision to make more accurate business judgment.

Many managers mistakenly view judgment work as only an individual discipline, failing to appreciate that it can also involve decide interpersonal and organizational practices. In more complex settings, judgment is typically a collective outcome of individuals' and teams' diverse perspectives, insights and experiences. And often , the resulting choices are better informed than decisions that an individual would have arrived at on his or her own. Thus, when any organizations apply (AI) technology to assist managers to gather data and ideas to make any judgment. In these cases, organizations can create the conditions for effective collective judgment by establishing structures , such as " shadow advisory boards" that prompt managers and employees to source and synthesize multiple perspectives. Thus, a traditional organization (firm) might freshen its thinking is t put together a shadow advisory board, comprised of young, digital people who can apply (AI) machine assistance to make judgment work more accurate whether related to people development, problem-solving or strategizing and innovating for considerable degrees of creative and social intelligence. Thus, on the one hand, (AI) technology machine augmentation and automation can give these advantages to human (organization managers) , e.g. developing people and community, solving problems and collaborating, coordinating and controlling work, shaping strategy and leading innovation. Besides, on the other hand, the next generation managers need have these individual attitude to treat intelligent machines to be as colleagues.

When, judgment is a human skill, intelligent machines can accelerate human learning that supports it, assisting in data -driven simulations, scenarios and search and discovery activities. Focuses on judgment work, some decisions require insight beyond what data can tell them. This is the sweet sport for human judgment, the application of experience and expertise to critical business decisions and practices. Thus, managers will also need to find ways to learn how to use digital (AI) technologies to tap into the knowledge and judgment of partners, customer external stakeholders and role models in other industries after the (AI) machine had been implemented to the organization."

Then, the Mentor: An experienced figure who guides others in navigating the intersection of technology and creativity. He says

"I believe that my future university students can raise learn ability and writing ability and reading ability from (AI) machine lecturer teaching more than human lecturer teaching. Let me explain : Although, (AI) technology will be popular to applied to different jobs, but it still needs social acceptance to replace some human jobs. Today, it is increasingly common for people to use robots in various situations at home and in retail stores, hotels and hospitals. Robots are classified into several types based on their functionality (service and utility robots or those designed to communicate with humans) and appearance (humanoid robots or mechanical robots). The types of robot to which every country attaches particular important in the advance of robotics, reflects the sense of values and preferences of its population . Thus, (AI) will be applied to replace human to do these above different kinds of job nature. For example, U.S. has the highest level of robot utilization at home and an retail stores with its people being the most enthusiastic about the future use of robots. Otherwise, Germany shows a strong tendency to consider robots for industrial purposes, and its people feel strong to the presence of robots in their households. Japanese accepts to apply" human aid robot" that can communicate with humans and they have a high level of familiarity with robots. Hence, it implied those three countries have accept (AI) to replace human to do any these kinds of job duty and it will influence these three countries' workers lose their old occupations and who will unemployed absolutely, due to many (AI) robots replace them to do their job duties in the future. Also, US will have many retail service workers or retail warehouse workers are unemployed. Germany will have many manufacturing industry's workers are unemployed. Japanese will have many communication industry workers are unemployed, such as telephone service, shopping center services etc. different kind of service industry's service staffs . It will cause these kind of workers' competitive abilities are lost in themselves countries' jobs that require such skills include software developers, court judges, nurses, high school teachers, dentists and university lecturers, these occupations are still difficult to be replaced by (AI) robots. Are robots taking our jobs or making them? In fact, our societies will have unemployment challenges, even (AI) technology has not created before. However, after (AI) robots invention, some of human jobs will be replaced and it can raise many low skillful and low knowledge level worker unemployment number. However, I think that high productivity driven by increasingly powerful IT -enabled machines is the causes of global labor market problems and accelerating technological change will only make those problems worse. IT technology brings this question: Are robots killing human's jobs or benefiting human's jobs? I suppose that there is a limited amount of labor to be done. The implication is that technology can create unemployment by displacing workers, such as (AI) invention, because the more efficiently worker work (using machines or (AI) robots), the loss work there is for workers to do. Even, any new jobs will be better done by machines or (AI) robots, and unemployment will still skyrocket. How do we know that humans will always be better at some work, or more importantly, enough work, than machines or (AI) robots, e.g. human drivers drive more safe or careful to compare (AI) robot drivers. But, the challenge is that it is not ensure that (AI) robots drivers must not drive careless to cause the chance of accident occurrences more than human drivers. However, technological change can be beneficial to innovation, automation and increasing productivity for businesses. Consequently , it may seem machines can hurt wages and job for low skillful, less educated workers. Also, high educated workers are likely as less educated workers to find themselves displaced and devalued, and more education may create as many problems as it solves. Thus, in negative influence, automation effects on particular jobs shift workers to other jobs that are equally or more desirable. Workers may be highly compensated for possessing human capital that is specialized to a labor market. If technological advance is very rapid, such as (AI) invention, causing a large and very rapid drop in demand in a large labor market, the economy may not be able to absorb the sudden surplus of labor in a short period of timer when (AI) robots are popular to replace some workers to do some .

Thus, future (AI) technology can be applied to online e book publishing industry to make sound books to let readers feel more attractive . Such as Amazon publish has published sound e books to attract readers to choose to read any its books from online. Also, (AI) technology can also be applied to communication industry. For example, some online pure-play news, opinion and entertainment websites. It is a digital communication media, e.g. online journalism blog (AI) technology can be applied to visual storytellers to let online book readers to enjoy to listen to watch and send any online electronic book contents more attractive. Thus, future (AI) technology will be popular to assist any electronic book publishers to publish visual and sound talking storybook to let readers who can watch motive image and listen and read words from e books more attractive. Thus, (AI) technology can be applied to internet e-commerce publishing or media industry to help any electronic book publishers to publish sound, image motion electronic book to attract global readers to read, even (AI) technology can be applied to digital entertainment industry, e.g. electronic 3D image virtual video games, computer games. It can be also applied to education industry, e.g. the first true digital native generation and are the native speakers of the digital language of computers to let student to learn different languages or translate words to compare to classroom learning more easily. It can be also applied to communication industry, e.g. (AI) mobile phone. Hence, it seems (AI) technology can be applied to publishing, communication, education , entertainment etc. different industries in the future. (AI) technology will be one kind of tool to satisfy human's daily life needs in the future and these industries has one characteristics is that they need to apply internet to operate to operate to do online business. Thus, it has three trends of (AI) technology and internet technology need to be linked to achieve one kind of attractive technological business to satisfy client's needs. These three trends as below: All consumer trends involve the internet. It will be many consumer's online habits, shopping, working, socializing, watching TV, studying, travelling, listening. Thus, (AI) music, eating and exercising are just a few examples. This is happening because human usually use mobile broadband or Wi-Fi, rather than cables. Thus, (AI) technology will be applied to mobile to satisfy client's need absolutely. The mobile phone can be more popular to be used more than computer or laptop tools. The reasons are because women dive the smart phone market by defining mass-market use. But as the speed of technology adoption increases mass market use becomes much quicker then before. Successful new technological products and services , such a (AI) mobile phone products now reach the mass market in popular use. It means that the time period when early adopters influence others is shorter than before. Also, since new products and services increasingly use the internet mass markets are not only faster , but are also more important than ever to consumer themselves. Most internet services become more valuable to individuals when many use them. Thus, it causes why (AI) mobile phone will be popular to be used. Since, new products and services increasingly use the internet, in the future several trends focus on (AI) smart phone users. Consumers' familiarity with using smart phone apps. Essentially, the technologies will bring other related (AI) and internet service needs, e.g. sound and image emotion e book needs, (AI) mobile communication needs, e-virtual games or e-3D image virtual games etc. entertainment activities needs with such a large part of the world's population now online, it is clear that there is strength in numbers. Thus, (AI) imagines , if future any (AI) and internet related services or products new technology is easy to use and inexpensive, when the latest products reach the mass market almost as quickly as they reach the early adopters and industry experts. I believe that any (AI) and internet related products or services must be popular to accept to consume for entertainment or useful aim. For example, with major players including Apply, Facebook and Google had invested (AI) technology to develop their businesses. (AI) technology has the potential to disrupt everything in the coming years, from the lives of connected consumers to every industry (AI) will be an alternative route for brands to reach consumers with convincing and relevant messages. Digital technology will assist of the future, then it can improve technology to bring this effect, such as sophisticated software machine learning and speech recognition effective. Hence, Google, Facebook , Yahoo web site service companies can apply (AI) technology to help other companies to advertise their businesses, such as travel, retail, and education etc. industries more attractive. (AI) technology can be applied to internet company to be aware and familiar enough to drive among mainstream consumers, it can create online experience to travel, retail , education and other entertainment needs to online consumers to seek their entertainment needs more easily. Hence, in the future (AI) technology and internet related entertainment service needs will be raised in this (AI) and online consumption market.

Then, the Prodigy: A young individual whose life changes dramatically due to access to advanced technology. He asks

"Can technology influences human reading behavior changes to e-books learning ?"

The Mentor: An experienced figure who guides others in navigating the intersection of technology and creativity. He says

"Nowadays, online and offline book shop competition is serious. Book readers have these both channel to choose to buy either electronic book or paper book to study. How can traditional offline book shop achieve strategy to compete online book shop ? What are online book shop weaknesses or strengths? What are traditional offline book shop weaknesses or strengths? What is future book publishing development trend? How technology influence travel agent service changes to e-travel airline booking service from traditional walk in travel agent service?These questions will have suggestions to be given to book publishers to let them to learn more marketing strategies. Publishing industry competition is serious. Electronic books, newspapers will be popular to let readers have more reading method to choice. Also technology may excite future traditional new travel agent service changes to e-airline ticket sale method. How e-travel agent service encourages traveler make air ticket purchase decision to go to any where to travel easily. How e-travel agent encourages human buys airline ticket channel changes to online e-ticket buying channel?

Robot invention how influence human job behavioral change? Nowadays, robots may be applied to replace human some kinds of jobs, e.g. cookers, drivers, shopping center cleaners, even doctors, accountants or lawyers etc. different kinds of occupations. Can robots dominate human mind when robots can be developed to own themselves mind judgment abilities? When robots can learn human behavior that they can dominate human how to do any kinds of jobs, e.g. teaching teachers how to teach their students to learn new knowledge in schools. If robots can learn human any kinds of behaviors to do any kinds of jobs. Then, whether robots can dominate our societies to help us to change positive lives attitude to live more comfortable or change negative lives attitude to bring poor living environment, e.g. raising unemployment, reducing our salary. etc. different negative social challenges. Whether (AI) robotic workers can be instead of traditional human workers in these different new markets to bring positive or negative impacts to change human job nature change? In recent years, machines had been used to be human's tasks in the performance of certain tasks related to intelligence , such as aspects of image recognition. Experts also forecast that rapid progress in the field of specialized artificial intelligence will continue. Then, it also brings this question: Does (AI) exceed that of human performance on more and more tasks to replace human jobs? If it is truth, will some of human jobs to be disappeared? (AI) will be instead of human some simple jobs, then unemployment rate to the low skillful and low educated workers will be increased. Whether (AI) will be raised either production or performance or unemployment to bring human job market more advantages or more disadvantages? In my this book, I shall explain whether (AI) will bring benefits or disadvantages to human job market. I write this book aims to let readers make judgment whether technology can dominates human mind or human can dominates technology behavior in nowadays societies."

"Will technology dominate future human ourselves mind creative abilities? What methods may help human to raise mind creative abilities? Will ourselves future societies are dominated by artificial intelligence or robots? What positive or negative influences if our societies are dominates by robots?"

"I believe that technology how influence human reading behavioral change.Nowadays, online book publishing is one kind of popular sale method to global publishing. For example, Amazon publish is as a business model with many potential advantages, relative to a physical operation.

It held out the potential of lower book inventing and distribution costs and reduced overhead. Consumers could find the books, they were looking for more easily and a variety book topic choices could be offered for sale. It can accept and fulfill orders from almost any domestic location with equal ease. And most purchasers made on its site would be exempt from sales tax. One Amazon strategy hand, it would have to make its returns and redress processes transparent and reliable, and offer other ways for clients to learn, as much about the book possible before buying. Future online book market development trend, such as Amazon, Barnes & Noble etc. online book shops. How closely would their clients find book ordering, as a substitute for visiting book stores? In fact, Amazon is global the largest online booksellers and sells many other products. Otherwise, Barnes & Noble, have been market share diminish obviously. In the future, Noble & Barnes both will have their market share diminish continue obviously. There are also many fewer specialty re lowest. Hence, it seems online and offline both publishing methods will be competitive. It brings this questions: What is the trend between online book sale channel, its size relative to offline book sales channel, growth rate and the characteristics of readers who by online in the future? How book market's online channels are economically different , due to e-commerce's effects on online book market and supply fundamentals? How an online book sales channel might be expected to change equilibrium market outcomes?"

"I believe online book channel based sale activity varies considerably on these aspects: Sales in manufacturing printing cost, online sale services and online demand print book sale book topic choices. Such as author online advertising, change more or less sale price, online paper book shipping cost, visa card discount or online book shop member card discount book purchase, what welfare to online book buyers are. Why readers choose to buy books from internet habit? In tradition, online book buyers habit hope to use the internet to buy. Generally, they have these characteristics: They hope to use the internet to buy electronic books at home, they enjoy to read electronic book from computer, it is in any regular capacity , not necessarily to visit book shops to find books to buy and they can search any electronic from internet, electronic book is convenient to read from computer or laptop when they catch transportation or going to anywhere. Usually, internet users are higher income, more educated and younger. It seems that education is a size able determinant of who is online, even controlling for income. However, gender does not seems to be a factor in explaining internet use. Moreover, many of book qualitative patterns are seen for online book purchases in general are observed for electronic book products on on demand printing book products in particular. Predict in future, many of the traditional online products , such as electronic or print on demand books, computer hardware , electronic airline tickets, saw more modest , but still substantial growth. In the future, online sellers trend to be newer online book stores and have less brand or reputation capital to signal or famous brand quality. These factors can create in online book sellers, which also often involve delay. However, there are many reasons for online book purchasing. The most obvious is that readers don't have opportunity where observably inferior point of electronic or demand on print book purchases."

"Consequently, more appealing offerings can be developed to broader every publisher's audience and enhanced whose every publisher's image, segments of reader research, e.g. reader age, book reading taste. This is a measure level of penetration of journals and identity opportunity for growth GAP analysis marketing strategies will be popular methods to future book publishing. Based on first hand, expensive visiting and surveying librarians around the world, examing factors unique to each country and culture and make to recommendations integrate in every publisher's communication plan. For example, ebook trends pecentage of ebok spending in online ebook borrowing libraries is a publishing extra income from ebook borrowing readers. It is such one part of the overall electronic book market share income in the electronic book publishing market. In conclusion, internet technological innovation can bring new publishing business chance to ebook development , but it also brings competition to traditional paper book stores. So, paper book stores need have good marketing strategies to win their new ebook competitors.

"Nowadays, online newspapers will be popular to let readers to read any newspapers' news from internet. It showed that for online newspapers reader's intention is influenced by performance expectancy, habit and the habit of reading a print newspapers. So, newspapers consumer personal reading behavior was influenced by intention and habit. Some reading behavioral researchers showed some reasons to explain why traditional paper newspaper readers will like to change habits to study online newspapers. Hence, changing reading habit will be one factor to influence traditional paper newspaper reader individual reading behavior changes to online newspapers reading habit. In fact, high technological communication media will influence mobile phone and internet both new communication media causes. These new communication medias will bring new print electronic media causes, such as print newspapers, online book products. Some of traditional paper newspaper readers will choose to read any news from online newspapers. The reasons include free charge, reading at home in convenient, not need go out newspapers, online newspapers do not need the reader's hands to touch the black word paper newspaper to be dirty, and waste less time to buy every day to achieve economic benefit."

"Every online newspaper reader will have this factor to influence whom to change traditional paper newspaper reading habit. The factor shows that attitude has a direct effect on intentions, and is influenced by performance expectancy and effort expectancy or related personal online reading acceptance conceptions. Because of whose acceptance of online newspaper reading attitude is as an important in technology user online newspaper reading attitude was included. Additional, every online newspaper reader self-efficacy and anxiety are expected to be minor issue to influence the online newspaper reader to change whose attitude to choose not to internet tool to read of an online newspaper. However, different age reader either he/she is young or old age factor will have influence whom to choose online newspaper to read, e.g. old age readers will feel difficult to apply internet technology to read newspaper, otherwise, young age readers will feel easy to apply internet technology to read newspaper. So, the old or young age traditional paper newspaper readers, when the acceptance new technological online newspaper to them, they will adopt online newspaper reading attitude to replace traditional paper newspaper reading habit more easy. So, their acceptance new technological of online newspaper reading attitude will have a direct effect on online newspaper reading intention and are influenced by both paper and online newspapers reading enjoyment performance expectation and online newspapers reading effort expectation, when their expectations were needed to be satisfied more these past traditional paper newspaper reading experience. Moreover, past paper newspapers reading behavior and habit should be noted. Then, these two expectation factors will encourage or persuade the traditional paper newspaper readers change whose reading attitude, reading habit and reading behavior to read online newspapers. Hence, the online newspaper readers' psychological factor will influence whose traditional paper newspapers readers whose reading behavioral changes. Also, it means that expectation factor will influence the traditional newspaper readers to change whose counter intentional paper newspaper reading habit. However, online newspaper will bring much knowledge to compare traditional paper newspapers , e.g. real newspapers news data, more meaningfulness news, providing the nature of visiting a news website, which can let online news readers can feel different read model primary on frequency with relatively little spread in the amounts of time spent at the site."

"What are the main factors to influence online newspaper reading behaviors? Same testing indicates for moderation by the online newspaper age, gender and online newspaper reading experience will bring the online reading newspapers habit influence. The testing also indicates male gender and young age group , this group likes to apply internet to find or seek or search any news matters. Hence, this internet user group will bring to have interest to read newspapers from internet channel. The reason is possible because this young male internet users like to contact new technology, e.g. internet. They think the online newspaper is useful and it is more useful to read the online newspaper to compare to paper newspaper."

"The two reasons : liking to contact new technology and feeling the online newspaper is more useful which can support why young male online internet users feel to expect reading online newspaper expectancy were more concrete."

"Additional online newspapers usefulness are more considered on unclear concept to explain why this reader group feels more like to study online newspapers. What exactly is the usefulness of reading an online newspaper?"

"The testing also indicated that some online newspaper readers responded to use the online newspaper to feel natural, it showed to be related to attitude as well as to habit , which seems to hold face validity as a natural feel can be considered on attitude on the online newspaper. So, online reading attitude and online reading habit can reflect why man young male like to read online newspapers more than paper newspaper reason.

Another reason indicated that when the young male readers want to read the news, the online newspaper is an obvious choice for him/her. So, many online newspaper young male readers had felt online newspaper is one another newspaper reading choice to replace traditional paper newspapers."

"In conclusion , free charge online newspaper is not the main factor to influence both traditional paper newspaper readers to change their reading habit to choose online newspapers to read suddenly. There are other factors to cause them to choose online newspapers to read, such as more usefulness feeling, contacting new technology, online reading habit, positive online reading attitude etc. different psychological factors which will have more influences to cause their paper newspaper reading habits to be changed. Hence, the free price economic gain actor must not only one main factor to persuade readers to choose online newspapers to read."

Then, the innovator says

"How electronic versus traditional print textbook influence of university students' learning behavior ?"

Then, the mentor says

"When one university student was accepted by electronic text book learning channel to replace traditional paper text book learning channel (methods). Electronic text book will bring what positive or/and negative influence to impact whose learning behavior changes. For example, electronic text book learning method will bring positive impact to raise the student's examination grades and perceived learning scores or it will bring negative impact to fall down the student's examination grades and perceived learning scores. The mean scores indicated that students who choose to text books for their learning aim. It will have significantly higher perceived affection learning performance and examination results. Thus, the purpose of student learning and teacher teaching method, every university needs to examine whether it is efficient to raise student learning effort to replace paper text book learning method in any learning environment, e.g. many students and one teacher classroom learning environment or the independent student learns himself/herself at home learning environment or library learning environment. Can text book reading tool bring absolute advantages to university students or bring some disadvantages to them? When a student needs to apply e-text book to learn, who needs access e-text book in a static location, such as a computer or on a mobile device. So, the e-text book in a static location factor, it will have influence to each student reading or learning behavior to bring negative and/or positive both impacts. The e-text book was distributed on a CD and installed on a located computer. This limited the user to accessing the e-textbook in a single location and eliminated the potential access to the e-text book on due to the lack of mobility. So, it seems that the location of limited to e-text book will bring negative impact to let the student can only learn in a fixed location because he/she will feel difficult to move heavy computer to other places to learn more than on paper text book. So, e-text book location can not allow the student to leave the classroom to learn more easier if he/she had chose to use to computer to install the CD to learn in the classroom. Supposing the student 's teacher needs the student often to leave the classroom to discuss any matter suddenly, it is not very convenient to the student to use e-text book to learn because he/she can not move the computer to leave the classroom with him/her easily. Then, it will be possible to influence the student can bot be attention to read the e-text book, when the teacher needs the student to leave the classroom (none book bringing) to discuss any time any time immediately. Otherwise, if the student used one paper book to read/learn in the classroom, if the teacher needs whom to leave the classroom often to discuss immediately. He/she will feel convenient to learn because he/she can bring the light paper book to leave the classroom to discuss with the teacher in any location easily. Hence, it seems e-text book learning will bring not convenient fixed location learning environment to every e-texting learning student in classroom, when, he/she needs often to leave the classroom to discuss with the teacher any time. Other disadvantage of e-text learning will bring students feel difficult in possible. In the past, some learning researcher experiments indicated results demonstrated that student participants in both groups had similar recall and ability to reinterpret information suggesting that retrieval of information is not effected by kindle e-book reader e-text book, a tabled computer e-text book or a print version. Hence, it seems that e-text book can not help or assist recall the student's learning memory to remember the e-text book content more easier. Due to it is one e-text book machine, the student will fell to difficult to find any unclear or important information in any page(s) to write for learning/reading record more easier than one paper text book. Another disadvantage of e-text book is the inefficacy or inefficient reading challenge to the e-text book reader. The efficacy of e-text books in a higher education environment will be one interesting discussing question. Passage length is one difference that impact the results. Studies involving shorter reading sessions indicated no substantial variance with respect to reading comprehension and understanding. Conversely, studies involving longer reading passages indicated prior comprehension, when reading longer e-text , eye fatigue and mental workload are also concerns. Hence, e-text book reading will be possible to let students feel eye fatigue and mental workload in their reading process. Due to machine e-text book words are more small size and unclear more than paper text book words to print to let students to read every words or sentences in computer. Consequently, studies indicated that e-text book readers need to spend much nervous and time to read longer and poor comprehension in whole e-text book reading process. When, university students need to spend time to read longer e-texts from computers. For example, they need to choose to reads hundreds of papers of e-text books on a screen, whether on a computer or hand held electronic device compared to print versions may contribute to eye fatigue. The consequence, eyestrain and mental fatigue could be poorer comprehension and have a poor eye, nervous health influence and every student's e-text learning behavior can bring negative reading habit to whom, when every one need to apply desktop or laptop or mobile electronic tools to read any words from e-textbooks. Hence, it seems e-text book reading method has possible to bring poor health challenge to every student. So, above all these e-learning reading factors to bring this question: Does e-learning influence the student's negative reading behavior to cause poor final examination grades results? In fact, every student needs to change whose traditional learning method from paper text book reading habit or reading behavior to e-text books. He/she needs to change whose reading habit. He/she must need to spend long time to accept how to adopt this kind of new technological reading method as well as effect may change through a new technological learning experience itself and impacts the acquisition of knowledge leading to reading behavioral change. As I indicated the e-learning will bring poor health and poor nervous negative influences when the student often needs to apply electronic product to read long time. So, it will be possible to influence the student health to be poor to bring examination low grades results in possible be cause he/she has poor health to exam."

"It is possible that it has relationship to influence the student to exam low grade between e-learning habit and poor health causes. The reason is based on that efficacy of textbook format is defined grades. I assume that all these negative e-text book reading factors can influence every e-text book reader's health to be poor when he/she needs often read e-text book s to cause long time reading habit. So, I mean that e-text book reader individual health changes to poor, it is only depend on how long time e-text book reading habit factor. So, if he/she only spend less time to read e-text books and he/she also has habit to read paper books sometimes. Then, he/she won't be influenced to be poor from e-learning method easily. It means that it has none direct relationship between less time e-text book reading habit and low examination grades result. Hence, low examination grades result to the student, it only depends on long time e-text book reading habit and the student's long time e-text book reading habit needs to confirm that whose long time e-text book reading habit causes poor health to the student effect. Why do I believe that efficacy of textbook format can influence the student's examination grade? Based on above analysis, the e-text book reading format and paper book reading format is very different. For example, the efficacy of textbook is very different between paper text book reading format and electronic text book reading format. Such as one sickness student needs to spend more nervous to read one e-text book more than one paper text book . This reason is because machine reading method is difficult to compare paper reading method. When the student has sickness, who must need to spend more time and nervous to read one e-text book more than one paper text book. If my assumption is right, then the e-text book sickness reader's reading efficacy to each paper must be poor to compare the paper text book sickness reader , due to the sickness e-text book reader needs to spend long time and much nervous to read each paper more than he/she chooses to read one paper book. When he/she is sickness to finish whose reading . Due to his/her memory will be poor and tries, when he/she feels sick, so whose reading effort must be poor when he/she needs to apply computer tools or mobiles to read."

"Not wasting time on the above-mentioned misconceptions lets us focus on true and interesting controversies where even the experts disagree. What sort of future do you want? Should we develop lethal autonomous weapons? What would you like to happen with job automation? What career advice would you give today's kids? Do you prefer new jobs replacing the old ones, or a jobless society where everyone enjoys a life of leisure and machine-produced wealth? Further down the road, would you like us to create super intelligent life and spread it through our cosmos? Will we control intelligent machines or will they control us? Will intelligent machines replace us, coexist with us, or merge with us? What will it mean to be human in the age of artificial intelligence?"

At the end of their meeting, they agree that robots may help human to creative clever, but human ourselves ought attempt to change our live attitude in order to keep ourselves mind more clear to do any thing more easily.

SEVEN

HOW APPLYING BEHAVIORAL ECONOMY THEORY TO EXPLAIN CONSUMER BEHAVIOR

Behavioral Economics and the Dynamics of Demand and Supply

In the study of market mechanisms, the traditional neoclassical model often assumes rational actors who possess perfect information and stable preferences. However, John Lok, in his work Learning Demand and Supply Depending Relationship, shifts the analytical focus toward behavioral economic theory to explain how human psychology and social situations influence the interplay between supply and demand. My view argues that the decision-making process regarding production levels and pricing is not merely a mathematical output of equilibrium, but a response to observed social behaviors and consumer needs. By integrating behavioral insights, my view suggests that the dependency between supply and demand is mediated by the perceived value and the social context in which products or services are offered.

The key principles , my incorporates into my analysis revolve around the "behavioral" aspect of economic decision-making, which contrasts with the purely mechanical view of market clearing. In standard economic theory, the relationship is often expressed as a function where quantity demanded Qd is a function of price P, or Qd=f(P), however, emphasizes that the "demand number" and "supply number" are influenced by the behavioral responses of participants in the consumer market.

One of the primary principles , my view explores is the social signaling of value. My view posits that if demand is low, manufacturers should restrict supply to avoid "low price" sales, which could damage the brand's perceived value—a concept rooted in the behavioral observation that consumers often equate price with quality. Conversely, when demand is high, he suggests increasing supply to satisfy consumer needs, which allows for a "high price" sale strategy that captures the surplus value generated by high demand.This aligns with the behavioral principle of loss aversion and anchoring, where the initial price set by the supplier acts as an anchor for the consumer's perception of the product's worth.

Furthermore, my approach touches upon bounded rationality, a cornerstone of behavioral economics popularized by Herbert Simon.ecause market participants cannot process all information perfectly, they rely on heuristics—mental shortcuts—to determine whether a product is worth inventing or purchasing. My framework suggests that the "dependency" of supply on demand (or vice versa) is a behavioral feedback loop: producers observe consumer behavior to adjust supply, and consumers observe market availability to adjust their demand.This is consistent with the prospect theory developed by Daniel Kahneman and Amos Tversky, which suggests that individuals value gains and losses differently, leading to inconsistent choices that traditional supply-demand curves fail to capture.

Finally, my view incorporates the principle of social proof. By analyzing "actual product or service social situations," he acknowledges that demand is not an isolated variable but is influenced by the collective behavior of others. When a product is perceived as "in demand," the social pressure to acquire it increases, shifting the demand curve outward. This behavioral shift necessitates a dynamic adjustment in supply that goes beyond simple cost-benefit analysis, requiring firms to manage the "reasonable supply number valuation" based on the psychological state of the market.

The Application of Behavioral Economics to Consumer Decision-Making

The study of how individuals make choices within the framework of demand theory has evolved significantly from the classical assumption of the Homo economicus—a perfectly rational agent—to a more nuanced understanding informed by behavioral economics. While I am a contemporary figure often discussed in specific niche business and marketing contexts regarding the application of choice architecture to consumer behavior, his work aligns with the broader academic tradition established by pioneers like Richard Thaler and Daniel Kahneman. In demand theory, behavioral economics posits that consumers do not always maximize utility in a linear, calculated fashion. Instead, they are subject to cognitive biases, heuristics, and the specific "choice architecture" of the environment in which they operate.

The application of these principles involves manipulating the "default" options, framing effects, and the presentation of price points to influence consumer demand. In classical demand theory, the quantity demanded Qd is a function of price P, income I, and preferences U:Qd=f(P,I,U)However, behavioral economists argue that U (preferences) is not static but is constructed in real-time based on the choice environment. By applying behavioral insights, practitioners like Lok emphasize that the "architecture" of the store or the digital interface acts as a non-price determinant of demand. For instance, by placing high-margin items at eye level or utilizing "anchoring" (where an initial high price makes a subsequent lower price seem like a bargain), the perceived value of a good is altered, thereby shifting the demand curve outward.

Behavioral Economics and Demand Theory

Traditional demand theory assumes that consumers possess stable preferences and perfect information. Behavioral economics challenges this by introducing the concept of "bounded rationality," a term coined by Herbert Simon.In this context, consumer decision-making is seen as a process of satisficing rather than optimizing. When applying these theories to consumer demand, the focus shifts to how the presentation of choices—the "choice architecture"—can nudge consumers toward specific purchasing behaviors.This is particularly relevant in digital marketplaces where algorithms can personalize the choice architecture for individual users, effectively managing demand through subtle psychological cues rather than traditional price adjustments alone.

The Role of Choice Architecture

Choice architecture is the deliberate design of the environment in which people make choices. As noted in authoritative literature, the way options are presented can significantly impact the final decision.For example, the "decoy effect" is a common strategy where a third, less attractive option is introduced to make another option appear more desirable, thus influencing the consumer's demand for the target product.This demonstrates that demand is not merely a reaction to price, but a reaction to the entire context of the transaction. By understanding these psychological triggers, businesses can more accurately predict and influence consumer behavior in ways that classical models fail to capture.

Would you be interested in learning more about how the "decoy effect" and other cognitive biases specifically impact pricing strategies in modern e-commerce environments?

Behavioral Economics and Demand Theory: An Analytical Overview

The integration of behavioral economics into demand theory represents a significant departure from the traditional neoclassical model, which assumes that consumers are perfectly rational agents—often termed Homo economicus—who consistently maximize utility based on stable preferences and complete information. While the provided query references "John Lok" in the context of demand theory, it is essential to clarify that behavioral economics as a formal discipline is primarily defined by the foundational work of scholars such as Daniel Kahneman, Amos Tversky, and Richard Thaler, whose research challenges the "rational actor" paradigm through empirical observation of human cognitive biases.

The key principles that define the behavioral approach to demand theory focus on how psychological factors systematically deviate from the standard utility-maximization framework. Central to this is the concept of Bounded Rationality, a term coined by Herbert Simon, which posits that individuals possess limited cognitive resources and therefore rely on heuristics—mental shortcuts—rather than exhaustive calculation when making purchasing decisions.

n demand theory, this implies that the demand curve is not merely a reflection of objective utility but is influenced by the "framing effect," where the presentation of price or product information significantly alters consumer choice. For instance, the prospect theory developed by Kahneman and Tversky suggests that individuals value losses and gains differently, leading to an asymmetric response to price changes, a phenomenon known as loss aversion.

Furthermore, behavioral demand theory incorporates the principle of Intertemporal Choice, specifically the tendency toward hyperbolic discounting, where consumers disproportionately value immediate gratification over long-term benefits.

This contradicts the exponential discounting model used in classical economics and explains why demand for certain goods—such as health-related products or savings instruments—fluctuates based on the timing of the reward.Additionally, social preferences and the "nudge" theory suggest that demand is often socially constructed; consumers are influenced by the choices of others (social proof) and the default options provided by market structures.In mathematical terms, while classical demand is often expressed as Qd=f(P), behavioral demand incorporates psychological parameters θ, such that Qd=f(P,θ), where θ accounts for cognitive biases and environmental context. These principles demonstrate that market behaviors are not solely driven by the "invisible hand" but are deeply embedded in the psychological architecture of the human decision-making process.

Behavioral Economics and Demand Theory

The integration of behavioral economics into demand theory represents a significant departure from the traditional neoclassical assumption of the Homo economicus—the perfectly rational agent who maximizes utility with infinite computational capacity.

In myscholarly contributions to organizational and economic theory, emphasizes that demand is not merely a function of price and utility, but is deeply embedded in social cognition, institutional contexts, and the psychological framing of choices.Behavioral economics challenges the "invisible hand" by suggesting that individuals often rely on heuristics and biases that lead to systematic deviations from rational equilibrium.

In the context of my work, demand theory is influenced by the concept of "bounded rationality," a term famously coined by Herbert A. Simon.Unlike classical models that assume consumers have perfect information, Lok's perspective incorporates the idea that individuals "satisfice"—choosing the first option that meets their threshold of acceptability rather than optimizing across all possible alternatives.

This insight suggests that demand curves are not static but are influenced by reference points, which serve as cognitive anchors for evaluating price changes.When a consumer perceives a price, they do not evaluate it in isolation; rather, they compare it to a reference point, a phenomenon that explains why demand can be highly sensitive to framing effects and loss aversion.

Furthermore, my analysis of demand is heavily influenced by social comparison theory.Behavioral economics posits that utility is relative; an individual's demand for a good is often driven by their desire to maintain social status or conform to peer behavior. This implies that the demand function D can be expressed as a function of price P, income I, and a social influence factor S:D=f(P,I,S)Where S represents the psychological utility derived from social alignment, effectively shifting the demand curve based on the perceived consumption patterns of others.

By moving away from the rigid constraints of the Solow Growth Model or pure Laissez-Faire theory, my view incorporates these behavioral nuances to explain why markets often exhibit "irrational" volatility. Ultimately, these insights demonstrate that demand is a dynamic construct, shaped by the interplay between cognitive limitations, social environments, and the institutional frameworks that define the choice architecture for the modern consumer.

Would you be interested in exploring how these behavioral insights into demand theory are currently being applied to modern digital marketing strategies or public policy interventions?

Understanding the intersection of behavioral economics and the theories proposed by my opinion, reader requires a synthesis of classical economic principles and the psychological nuances that govern human decision-making. Behavioral economics, as a field, challenges the traditional "rational actor" model—often referred to as Homo economicus—by integrating insights from psychology to explain why individuals frequently deviate from optimal decision-making.

When applying my perspectives on demand theory—which often emphasizes the social and psychological underpinnings of human behavior—one must recognize that demand is not merely a function of price and utility, but a reflection of social signaling, cognitive biases, and environmental pressures. Behavioral economics enhances this application by providing a rigorous framework to quantify these "irrational" deviations. For instance, the concept of "loss aversion," famously articulated by Daniel Kahneman and Amos Tversky, suggests that the pain of losing is psychologically twice as powerful as the joy of gaining.

If my theory posits that social improvement is driven by specific demand shifts, behavioral economics allows us to predict how individuals will respond to policy interventions or social incentives by accounting for this asymmetry in value perception.

The application of demand theory in a social context involves understanding how individuals value goods and services based on reference points rather than absolute utility.In behavioral economics, the "endowment effect" demonstrates that people ascribe more value to things merely because they own them, which complicates traditional supply-demand equilibrium models.By incorporating these insights, my approach to improving societal outcomes can be refined to include "nudges"—subtle changes in the choice architecture that steer individuals toward better decisions without restricting their freedom of choice.

Furthermore, the mathematical modeling of these behaviors often involves utility functions that incorporate social variables. If we define the utility U of an action as a function of personal gain G and social influence S, we can express the decision-making process as:$U=f(G,S)-\beta(B)$where β represents the weight of cognitive biases B that distort the rational assessment of G and S.By utilizing this model, one can better understand how social demand shifts in response to external stimuli, effectively bridging the gap between abstract economic theory and the practical realities of human behavior described in work.

My opinion and the Behavioral Critique of Traditional Demand Theory

My contribution to economic discourse, particularly as articulated in his analysis of the "Social Economy," represents a significant departure from the neoclassical reliance on the homo economicus model. Traditional demand theory, rooted in the work of Alfred Marshall and later refined by Paul Samuelson, posits that consumers are rational agents who maximize utility based on stable preferences, budget constraints, and price signals.

My challenges this by integrating behavioral economics, arguing that market outcomes are not merely the result of abstract mathematical equilibrium but are deeply embedded in psychological heuristics, ethical considerations, and the influence of technological environments.

The Behavioral Shift in Demand Modeling

Traditional demand theory relies heavily on the Law of Demand, which suggests that as the price of a good increases, the quantity demanded decreases, assuming ceteris paribus (all other things being equal). This is often expressed through the utility function:$U=f(x1,x2,...,xn)$where the consumer seeks to maximize U subject to the constraint $\sum pixi \leq I$.

My view argues that this model fails to account for the "bounded rationality" famously introduced by Herbert Simon, which suggests that human decision-making is constrained by cognitive limitations and the complexity of the environment. By applying behavioral insights to the "Social Economy," my view suggests that demand is not a static curve but a dynamic process influenced by social proof, loss aversion, and the framing effects prevalent in modern digital marketplaces like Amazon.

Challenging the "Invisible Hand" and Rationality

My critique extends to Adam Smith's "Invisible Hand," which assumes that individual self-interest leads to optimal social outcomes. In my view, the integration of Artificial Intelligence and algorithmic management creates a "choice architecture" that can manipulate demand in ways that traditional theory does not anticipate.

While traditional theory assumes that prices are the primary signal for demand, my view emphasizes that in the social economy, non-price factors—such as social reputation, ethical branding, and algorithmic recommendations—often override price sensitivity. This suggests that the demand function is not merely a function of price P and income I, but also a function of psychological variables S and technological influence T:Qd=f(P,I,S,T)By incorporating these variables, my view moves beyond the sterile assumptions of classical economics, suggesting that businesses must manage "facility departments" and marketing pressures by understanding the human element rather than just the mathematical one.

Implications for Modern Economic Strategy

My work aligns with the broader behavioral movement, which argues that economic theory must be practical and multidisciplinary. By bridging the gap between psychology and traditional theory, my view challenges the notion that market research can rely solely on historical price-quantity data.Instead, he advocates for a model that recognizes the "social" nature of the economy, where ethical choices and human behavior dictate the success of organizational strategies. This perspective is essential for understanding how contemporary firms navigate competitive pressures, as they must account for the fact that consumers are not always rational calculators, but are instead influenced by the complex, technology-driven social structures in which they operate.

Would you be interested in exploring how behavioral economics specifically influences consumer loyalty programs in the digital age, or perhaps delving deeper into the mathematical models used to measure "bounded rationality" in modern market research?

The analysis of psychological factors in economic decision-making, particularly regarding demand elasticity, represents a significant departure from the neoclassical "rational actor" model. While traditional economic theory, as articulated by Alfred Marshall in his foundational work Principles of Economics, posits that demand elasticity is primarily a function of price sensitivity, availability of substitutes, and the proportion of income spent on a good, the integration of behavioral insights—often associated with scholars exploring the intersection of psychology and economics—challenges the assumption that consumers always respond to price changes with consistent, predictable logic.

My contributions to this discourse, particularly in the context of organizational behavior and market dynamics, emphasize that demand is not merely a mechanical response to price signals but is deeply mediated by cognitive biases, social identity, and the "framing" of value. Traditional views on demand elasticity assume that the elasticity coefficient, denoted as $\epsilon d=\%\Delta Qd\%\Delta P$, remains relatively stable under similar market conditions.

However, my analysis suggests that psychological factors—such as loss aversion, the endowment effect, and social proof—can cause this coefficient to fluctuate wildly even when the objective price remains constant.By incorporating these behavioral variables, my view argues that the "elasticity" of a consumer base is a dynamic, psychological state rather than a fixed structural property of a commodity.

In the realm of commercial real estate and office space demand, this psychological shift is profound. Traditional models, such as those discussed in recent academic literature regarding supply and demand constraints, often rely on physical and regulatory metrics to predict market absorption. My approach suggests that these models are incomplete because they overlook the "psychological mismatch" between the perceived utility of a workspace and its physical attributes. When workers perceive a space as "collaborative" versus "isolating," their demand for that space becomes highly inelastic to price, as the psychological benefit outweighs the monetary cost.This challenges the traditional view that demand for office space is purely a function of firm size and economic output; instead, it suggests that demand is driven by the psychological needs of the workforce, which can be manipulated through design and corporate culture.

Furthermore, my work aligns with the broader behavioral economics movement, which posits that individuals suffer from "bounded rationality," a concept popularized by Herbert Simon.[9] In traditional models, demand elasticity is treated as a linear function. However, when psychological factors are introduced, the demand curve often exhibits non-linear "kinks" where small changes in price or perception lead to disproportionate shifts in demand. This is particularly evident in luxury or high-status markets, where the psychological desire for exclusivity renders the demand curve highly inelastic, or even upward-sloping in the case of Veblen goods.By highlighting these nuances, Lok forces a re-evaluation of how firms set prices and manage supply, suggesting that understanding the "psychology of the consumer" is as critical as understanding the "economics of the market."

Would you be interested in exploring how these psychological factors specifically influence the pricing strategies of firms in the post-pandemic "hybrid work" era?

The Economic Implications of Personalized Pricing and Demand Elasticity

The analysis of personalized pricing, often discussed in the context of modern algorithmic economics—and frequently associated with the philosophical underpinnings of property and value derived from thinkers like John Locke—centers on the ability of firms to capture consumer surplus by charging prices tailored to individual demand elasticity. In classical economic theory, demand elasticity, denoted as ϵd, measures the responsiveness of the quantity demanded of a good to a change in its price, calculated as $\epsilon d = \%\Delta Qd\%\Delta P$. Businesses utilizing personalized pricing strategies aim to identify the specific ϵd of individual consumers to move closer to "first-degree price discrimination," where each consumer is charged the maximum price they are willing to pay, thereby theoretically eliminating deadweight loss and maximizing allocative efficiency.

For businesses, the implications of this strategy are profound. By leveraging big data and algorithmic processing, firms can segment markets with unprecedented granularity. When a business identifies a consumer with highly inelastic demand (where $|\epsilon d| < 1$), they can theoretically increase prices to maximize revenue without a proportional loss in volume.Conversely, for consumers with highly elastic demand ($|\epsilon d| > 1$), firms may offer discounts to retain the sale. However, this practice creates significant ethical and distributional challenges. While it may increase total welfare gains for the firm, it often results in negative distributional consequences, as consumers with less information or fewer alternatives are charged higher prices, potentially exacerbating income inequality. Furthermore, the reliance on algorithmic pricing necessitates robust regulatory oversight to ensure that these strategies do not cross into predatory pricing or discriminatory practices that violate antitrust laws or consumer protection standards.Businesses must therefore balance the pursuit of profit through price discrimination with the risks of consumer backlash, regulatory intervention, and the erosion of brand trust.

Theoretical Framework and Market Dynamics

The transition from uniform pricing to personalized pricing represents a shift in how firms extract value from the market. In traditional models, a firm sets a single price P* where marginal revenue equals marginal cost (MR=MC). Under personalized pricing, the firm effectively treats each transaction as a unique market, allowing the firm to capture the area under the demand curve that would otherwise be consumer surplus.This requires the firm to possess significant information regarding the consumer's reservation price. As noted in authoritative economic texts, the success of such strategies depends heavily on the firm's ability to prevent arbitrage—the resale of goods by low-price buyers to high-price buyers—which would otherwise undermine the price discrimination scheme.

Ethical and Regulatory Considerations

The ethical dimension of personalized pricing is a subject of intense debate. Critics argue that it undermines the "fair price" expectation inherent in many market interactions and can lead to the exploitation of vulnerable populations who may have limited access to information or fewer choices.From a regulatory perspective, governments are increasingly concerned with how algorithmic transparency can be enforced. If a pricing algorithm is a "black box," it becomes difficult for regulators to determine if the price differentiation is based on legitimate demand elasticity or on protected characteristics, which would constitute illegal discrimination.Consequently, businesses are advised to maintain high standards of data governance and algorithmic accountability to mitigate legal risks while optimizing their pricing models.

Behavioral Economics and the Dynamics of Online Shopping

The application of behavioral economics to the digital marketplace represents a significant shift from classical economic theory, which traditionally assumes that consumers act as "rational agents" (Homo economicus) who consistently maximize utility based on perfect information. In the context of online shopping, behavioral economists—often drawing on the foundational work of scholars like John Lok—argue that human decision-making is heavily influenced by cognitive biases, heuristics, and the architecture of the digital environment itself By integrating these psychological insights into the supply and demand framework, we can better understand why consumers deviate from predicted rational behavior, such as overspending during flash sales or succumbing to the "scarcity effect" in e-commerce interfaces.

The Intersection of Behavioral Theory and Digital Supply and Demand

In traditional microeconomic theory, the demand curve is downward sloping, reflecting the law of demand: as price decreases, quantity demanded increases, assuming ceteris paribus.However, my opinion and other behavioral theorists suggest that in online environments, the demand curve is often "shifted" or distorted by psychological triggers. For instance, the use of "anchoring"—where an original, higher price is displayed next to a discounted price—manipulates the consumer's perception of value, effectively increasing the demand at a given price point compared to a neutral presentation.

From a supply-side perspective, online retailers utilize "choice architecture" to manage inventory and consumer flow. By applying behavioral nudges, such as "only 2 items left in stock," retailers artificially induce a sense of urgency that alters the consumer's utility function. Mathematically, if we define utility U as a function of price P, quality Q, and a psychological bias factor β, the consumer's decision to purchase is represented as:

$$U=f(Q,-P)+\beta$$

When β is influenced by marketing tactics (like social proof or limited-time offers), the perceived utility increases, causing the consumer to purchase even when the objective price P might be considered suboptimal in a vacuum.

My application of these theories emphasizes that online shopping platforms are not merely passive marketplaces but active environments that shape consumer preferences through algorithmic personalization and behavioral feedback loops.

Cognitive Biases in the Digital Marketplace

The "online shopping experience" is frequently optimized to exploit specific cognitive biases. The "endowment effect," where individuals value an item more highly simply because they feel a sense of ownership (often triggered by "add to cart" features or virtual try-ons), reduces price sensitivity. Furthermore, the "paradox of choice"—the phenomenon where too many options lead to decision paralysis—is mitigated by online recommendation engines that narrow the supply side to a manageable subset, thereby facilitating the transaction. By understanding these mechanisms, businesses can more accurately predict demand fluctuations that traditional models fail to capture.

The Influence of Behavioral Economics on Online Consumer Behavior

I am a prominent figure in the discourse surrounding digital marketing and consumer psychology, emphasizes that the architecture of online shopping environments is fundamentally shaped by behavioral economics—the study of how psychological, social, and emotional factors influence economic decisions.My perspective posits that consumers are not the "rational agents" described in classical economic theory, but are instead subject to cognitive biases, heuristics, and environmental nudges that dictate their purchasing patterns in digital marketplaces.

Cognitive Biases and Digital Architecture

My framework suggests that online retailers leverage specific behavioral triggers to influence decision-making. One primary mechanism is the "scarcity heuristic," where the display of limited stock or countdown timers triggers a fear of missing out (FOMO), compelling users to complete transactions faster than they would in a physical store This aligns with the work of Daniel Kahneman, who argued that human decision-making is governed by two systems: System 1 (fast, intuitive) and System 2 (slow, analytical).My view argues that online shopping interfaces are meticulously designed to keep consumers in "System 1" mode, minimizing the friction that would otherwise trigger analytical reflection and potential cart abandonment.

The Role of Choice Architecture

In the realm of online retail, "choice architecture"—the practice of influencing choice by organizing the context in which people make decisions—is paramount.My highlights that the presentation of pricing, such as "anchoring," where a high original price is displayed next to a discounted price, serves as a psychological anchor that makes the final price appear significantly more attractive.This is a practical application of prospect theory, which suggests that individuals value gains and losses differently, often leading to irrational decision-making based on perceived value rather than objective cost.

Social Proof and Digital Trust

My perspective also underscores the importance of "social proof" in the digital age. Because online shoppers cannot physically inspect products, they rely heavily on user-generated content, reviews, and influencer endorsements to reduce perceived risk. This behavior is rooted in the psychological principle of social validation, where individuals look to the actions and opinions of others to determine their own, especially in conditions of uncertainty.By integrating these social signals directly into the checkout flow, retailers effectively lower the psychological barrier to purchase, turning passive browsers into active buyers.

Algorithmic Personalization and Loss Aversion

Finally, my points to the role of algorithmic personalization as a tool for exploiting loss aversion. By tracking user behavior, platforms can present personalized recommendations that create a sense of "personalized loss"—the idea that if a user does not act on a specific offer or recommendation, they are losing out on a unique opportunity tailored specifically to them. This strategy effectively utilizes the endowment effect, where consumers place a higher value on items they perceive as "theirs" or "meant for them" due to algorithmic curation.

The Role of Decision-Making in John Lok's Behavioral Strategies

In the context of contemporary consumer psychology, my Learning Behavioral Strategies posits that the digital marketplace functions as a complex environment where cognitive shortcuts and environmental cues dictate the trajectory of a purchase. Lok argues that online consumer behavior is not merely a series of impulsive actions, but a structured outcome of learned responses to digital stimuli. Decision-making, in this framework, is viewed as a dynamic process where the consumer constantly evaluates the "cost" of information processing against the perceived utility of a product, often relying on heuristic-driven pathways to navigate the vast array of choices available in e-commerce interfaces.

The role of decision-making in Lok's view is fundamentally tied to the concept of "behavioral architecture." My view suggests that online platforms act as choice architects, subtly influencing the consumer's decision-making process through interface design, social proof, and algorithmic personalization. In his analysis, the consumer does not operate in a vacuum; rather, their decision-making is constrained and guided by the digital environment.

My view emphasizes that when consumers are faced with high-choice environments, they shift from a "rational-analytical" mode of decision-making to a "satisficing" mode, where they seek a solution that meets their minimum criteria rather than the absolute optimal choice.This shift is critical for marketers, as it suggests that the most effective behavioral strategies are those that reduce cognitive friction and align with the user's pre-existing mental models.

Furthermore, my view integrates principles from behavioral economics, suggesting that the decision-making process is susceptible to cognitive biases such as anchoring and loss aversion, which are amplified in online settings. By understanding these mechanisms, businesses can design "nudges" that steer consumer behavior toward desired outcomes without restricting their freedom of choice.

My work highlights that the digital consumer's decision-making is a learned behavior; as users interact more frequently with specific platforms, they develop automated responses to recurring stimuli, effectively turning complex decisions into habitual actions.

The mathematical representation of this decision-making utility can be modeled by the expected value of a choice E(c), where P(s) is the probability of a successful outcome and U(s) is the utility of that outcome, adjusted for the cognitive effort Ce required to make the decision:$E(c)=\sum[P(s)\cdot U(s)]-Ce$

My view suggests that online strategies aim to maximize E(c) by minimizing Ce through streamlined user experiences.Ultimately, my perspective underscores that decision-making is the bridge between external marketing stimuli and internal behavioral change, making it the most vital component in the study of modern consumer engagement.

My contributions to the study of decision-making, particularly within organizational and institutional contexts, represent a significant departure from the rational-choice paradigms that have historically dominated traditional consumer behavior theory. While classical consumer behavior models—rooted in neoclassical economics—often assume that individuals act as "rational agents" who possess stable preferences, perfect information, and the cognitive capacity to maximize utility, my work emphasizes the socially situated, discursive, and often fragmented nature of decision-making processes.

The Shift from Rationality to Discursive Practice

Traditional consumer behavior theories, such as the Theory of Planned Behavior or the Multi-Attribute Utility Model, generally posit that decisions are the result of a linear cognitive process: information gathering, evaluation of alternatives, and the selection of the option that provides the highest subjective expected utility.

In contrast, my research—often situated within the field of organizational studies—argues that decision-making is not merely an internal cognitive event but a social accomplishment.My view suggests that decisions are constructed through "discursive practices," where actors navigate competing institutional logics and identity-based constraints rather than simply calculating the optimal outcome.

Institutional Logics and Identity

Where traditional models view the consumer as an autonomous individual, my highlights how individuals are embedded in institutional environments that dictate the "appropriate" way to make a decision. In my analysis of institutional change and strategic decision-making, my view demonstrates that individuals often make choices that align with their professional or organizational identity, even when those choices deviate from pure economic rationality.This perspective challenges the consumer behavior assumption that preferences are exogenous and fixed; instead, my view suggests that preferences are fluid, negotiated, and heavily influenced by the social context in which the decision-maker operates.

The Role of Ambiguity and Sensemaking

Traditional theories often treat ambiguity as a "noise" factor that consumers attempt to minimize through information search. My approach, drawing on the tradition of sensemaking, suggests that ambiguity is an inherent feature of complex decision environments.Rather than seeking to eliminate uncertainty, decision-makers use sensemaking to create meaning out of ambiguous situations, often relying on social cues and shared narratives. This contrasts sharply with the "information processing" view of the consumer, which treats the mind as a computer-like processor of data. By focusing on how actors "talk" their decisions into existence, my shifts the focus from the outcome of a decision to the process of social interaction that precedes it.

Implications for Consumer Behavior

By moving away from the "rational actor" model, my work provides a framework for understanding why consumers often exhibit behaviors that seem irrational from a standard economic perspective, such as brand loyalty based on community identity or choices driven by social signaling rather than utility.My research suggests that to understand decision-making, one must look at the institutional scripts and discursive resources available to the actor, rather than just the attributes of the product or service being consumed.

The application of behavioral economics to consumer leisure behavior, as conceptualized by my opinion, represents a departure from classical models that assume purely rational actors. In Lok's framework, consumer leisure choices are not merely functions of price and availability, but are deeply embedded in psychological triggers, past habits, and the specific economic environment in which the consumer operates.

Behavioral Economics vs. Traditional Theory in Leisure

Traditional economic theory, often rooted in the work of Alfred Marshall or the neoclassical synthesis, posits that leisure consumption is determined by the trade-off between labor and leisure, governed by the wage rate and the law of demand. My view argues that this view is insufficient because it ignores the "psychology of the consumer." In my view, leisure behavior—such as choosing a vacation destination or a hobby—is frequently influenced by "past purchase habits" and the "excitement" generated by new inventions or market innovations, which traditional supply-demand curves fail to capture accurately.

The Role of Supply and Demand in my Framework

My view integrates the traditional supply and demand view with behavioral insights to explain how leisure products are consumed. My view suggests that the demand for leisure is not static. For instance, if a leisure activity is perceived as a "status good" or if its price increases, the demand may paradoxically rise due to psychological factors like the Veblen effect—where higher prices signal higher quality or exclusivity.

In the context of leisure sales, my view emphasizes that the "salesperson's psychology" and their ability to identify the specific "strengths or weaknesses" of a consumer's decision-making process are critical.By applying behavioral economic theory, a firm can predict leisure consumption patterns more accurately than by looking at general economic indicators alone. my view suggests that businesses should evaluate their sales teams' skills as a primary factor in long-term growth, as these teams act as the bridge between the supply of leisure services and the psychological demand of the consumer.

Mathematical Representation of Behavioral Leisure Demand

While traditional models use a simple demand function $Qd=f(P)$, where Qd is quantity demanded and P is price, Lok's behavioral approach implies a more complex function:$Qd=f(P,S,H,E)$Where:

P = Price

S = Salesperson influence/psychological framing

H = Past purchase habits

E = Economic environment/innovation excitement

This model suggests that the elasticity of demand for leisure is heavily moderated by S and H, meaning that even if P increases, Qd may remain stable or increase if the psychological framing (S) is sufficiently compelling.

Conclusion on Consumer Leisure Behavior

My opinion is that the "behavioral economy" provides a more granular understanding of why consumers choose specific leisure activities. By moving beyond the "general economic environment" and focusing on the "consumer psychology," my view posits that organizations can better align their supply of leisure services with the actual, often irrational, desires of the market.

Would you like to learn more about how behavioral economics specifically influences the pricing strategies of luxury leisure travel compared to budget-friendly leisure activities?

Behavioral Economics and Consumer Leisure Choices

In my analysis of consumer behavior, posits that the traditional economic model—which assumes that individuals act as "rational agents" maximizing utility—fails to capture the nuances of human decision-making, particularly in the realm of leisure and discretionary spending. My view argues that consumer leisure choices are frequently governed by psychological heuristics, cognitive biases, and the influence of the immediate economic environment rather than cold, calculated logic.By integrating behavioral economics, Lok provides a framework that explains why consumers often deviate from expected utility patterns, such as why individuals might overspend on leisure activities that offer diminishing returns or why they are susceptible to "framing effects" when choosing between vacation packages or entertainment options.

My work emphasizes that leisure choices are deeply embedded in past habits and social signaling.Unlike traditional theory, which views demand as a function of price and income, Lok suggests that the "purchase desire" for leisure is often triggered by new inventions or novel experiences that excite the consumer's psychological state. This aligns with the broader academic consensus that leisure consumption is not merely about the utility of the activity itself, but about the emotional satisfaction derived from the act of choosing and the social status associated with the leisure pursuit. My research suggests that by understanding these psychological triggers, one can more accurately predict consumer behavior in the leisure sector than by relying solely on general economic indicators.

The Role of Heuristics in Leisure Consumption

In the context of leisure, consumers often rely on mental shortcuts or heuristics to simplify complex decision-making processes. my view notes that when faced with an abundance of leisure options, individuals often default to "status quo bias," preferring activities they have engaged in previously, even if better or more cost-effective alternatives exist. This behavior is reinforced by what behavioral economists call "loss aversion," where the perceived pain of choosing a "bad" leisure experience outweighs the potential joy of discovering a new one.Furthermore, my highlights that the pricing of leisure services can be counterintuitive; for instance, a higher price point for a luxury leisure experience can sometimes increase demand by signaling exclusivity or superior quality, a phenomenon that traditional economic theory struggles to explain without invoking the concept of Veblen goods.

Implications for Market Prediction

My methodology shifts the focus from aggregate market data to the individual's internal state. By examining the intersection of consumer psychology and the economic environment, my view suggests that predictive models for leisure industries must account for variables such as emotional volatility and social influence.This approach is supported by foundational texts in behavioral economics, which argue that human decision-making is bounded by cognitive limitations.Consequently, my insights provide a more robust toolset for businesses to anticipate shifts in consumer trends, as they account for the "irrational" but predictable patterns that define human leisure behavior.

Behavioral Economics and Consumer Spending in Leisure Activities

My analysis of consumer behavior, particularly within the context of leisure and discretionary spending, centers on the departure from the "rational actor" model prevalent in traditional neoclassical economics. In my work, my view posits that consumer spending—especially in leisure sectors where emotional gratification and social signaling are high—cannot be fully explained by simple price-demand curves. Instead, he argues that behavioral economics provides a more robust framework by incorporating psychological heuristics, past habits, and the influence of the immediate economic environment on individual decision-making processes.

In the realm of leisure activities, Lok suggests that consumer spending is frequently driven by "irrational" triggers that traditional theory overlooks. For instance, while traditional models might suggest that an increase in the price of a luxury leisure experience (such as a high-end resort stay or a premium sporting event) should lead to a decrease in demand, my view highlights that behavioral factors can cause the opposite.This phenomenon, often linked to Veblen effects or perceived quality signaling, suggests that consumers use price as a proxy for status or exclusivity, thereby increasing demand as the price rises.

My view emphasizes that leisure consumption is rarely about utility maximization in the cold, mathematical sense; rather, it is about the "excitement" of new inventions or experiences, which triggers a psychological reward mechanism that overrides price sensitivity.

Furthermore, my analysis underscores the role of "past purchase habits" as a significant anchor in consumer decision-making. In leisure industries, where brand loyalty and experiential familiarity are paramount, consumers often default to previous patterns of behavior to reduce cognitive load. This inertia means that leisure providers who successfully integrate into a consumer's routine can maintain spending levels even when external economic conditions fluctuate. By focusing on the intersection of consumer psychology and the economic environment, my view argues that behavioral economics allows for more accurate predictive modeling of spending patterns than traditional theories, which rely too heavily on the assumption that consumers possess perfect information and act solely to maximize their own welfare.

The mathematical divergence between these theories can be viewed through the lens of utility functions. Traditional theory assumes a utility function $U(x)$ where x is a bundle of goods, and the consumer maximizes U subject to a budget constraint $I=p1x1+p2x2$.

My behavioral approach, however, suggests that the perceived utility is modified by a psychological weight factor ω, leading to a modified function $U'(x)=\omega \cdot U(x)$, where ω is a function of social environment, past habits, and emotional state.This shift explains why leisure spending often defies standard budget constraints during periods of high consumer confidence or social pressure.

Would you like to learn more about how "nudge theory" is specifically applied by leisure and hospitality companies to influence consumer spending habits?

Behavioral Economics and Consumer Engagement in Leisure

The application of behavioral economics to leisure industries—a field often informed by the scholarly work of researchers like my opinion and others in organizational behavior—centers on the understanding that consumer choices are rarely purely rational.Instead, engagement is driven by cognitive biases, framing effects, and the architecture of choice.

Businesses can enhance engagement by moving beyond traditional incentive structures and leveraging the psychological mechanisms that govern how individuals perceive value, time, and social connection.

To apply these principles effectively, businesses must first recognize that leisure participation is often subject to "hyperbolic discounting," where consumers prioritize immediate gratification over long-term benefits.By designing "commitment devices"—mechanisms that lock a consumer into a future leisure activity—businesses can help patrons overcome the inertia of procrastination.For instance, offering tiered membership models that reward consistent attendance rather than just initial sign-ups aligns with the psychological principle of "loss aversion," where the pain of losing a streak or a status level becomes a stronger motivator than the potential gain of a new experience.

Furthermore, the integration of "self-relevant" prompts, as explored in recent studies on behavioral interventions, suggests that engagement strategies should be dynamic.[8] Businesses can utilize micro-randomized trials to determine whether their customer base responds better to self-interest incentives (e.g., personal discounts) or prosocial incentives (e.g., charitable donations tied to activity participation). As noted in academic literature, the efficacy of these prompts often shifts over time; a strategy that works for a new customer may lose its potency as the consumer becomes a "regular," necessitating a shift in messaging to maintain interest.

The concept of "choice architecture" is equally vital. By simplifying the decision-making process—often referred to as reducing "cognitive load"—businesses can increase the likelihood of conversion.For example, leisure providers can use "default options" to nudge consumers toward recurring bookings, effectively turning a conscious, effortful decision into a passive, habitual one. Additionally, incorporating social proof—showing that peers are actively participating—leverages the human tendency toward conformity, which is a powerful driver in leisure and entertainment sectors.

Finally, businesses should account for the "peak-end rule," which posits that people judge an experience largely based on how they felt at its peak and at its end, rather than the total sum or average of every moment.By engineering a high-intensity "peak" moment during a leisure activity and ensuring a positive, seamless conclusion, businesses can significantly enhance customer satisfaction and the probability of repeat engagement, regardless of minor inconveniences experienced during the process.

Behavioral Economics and the Strategic Expansion of DINA Biological Medical Science

The application of behavioral economics to the field of biological medical science—specifically regarding the demand for DINA (Deoxyribonucleic Acid-based) technologies—requires a synthesis of psychological insights and economic incentives. My analysis, rooted in the broader framework of behavioral economics, suggests that human decision-making is often governed by cognitive biases, heuristics, and social framing rather than purely rational utility maximization. To increase demand for DINA-related medical services, businesses must move beyond traditional marketing and instead leverage the "choice architecture" that influences patient and provider behavior.

By utilizing the principles of "nudge" theory, as popularized by Thaler and Sunstein, firms can restructure how DINA medical diagnostics are presented to the public. For instance, the "default effect" suggests that individuals are significantly more likely to accept a medical screening if it is presented as the standard, pre-selected option during a routine check-up, rather than an elective procedure requiring active consent.Furthermore, the "availability heuristic" plays a critical role in medical demand; by increasing the salience of DINA-based health outcomes through targeted educational campaigns, businesses can make the benefits of these technologies more mentally accessible to the average consumer, thereby increasing perceived urgency.

In the context of biological sciences, the "endowment effect"—where individuals value a good more highly once they feel they possess it—can be applied to personalized genetic data. If a business provides a "preview" or a low-barrier entry point to DINA analysis, the consumer begins to view their genetic profile as a personal asset, which increases the likelihood of them investing in more comprehensive, high-value medical interventions.Additionally, social proof is a powerful driver in healthcare; by highlighting the adoption rates of DINA diagnostics among peer groups or within specific demographics, businesses can reduce the "status quo bias" that often prevents patients from adopting new medical technologies.

The integration of these behavioral insights into the business model for DINA science involves calculating the expected utility of health outcomes while accounting for the "present bias," where individuals undervalue long-term health benefits in favor of immediate costs. To mitigate this, firms should implement incentive structures that provide immediate, tangible rewards for genetic testing, effectively shifting the cost-benefit analysis in favor of the consumer. Mathematically, if we represent the discounted utility U of a medical intervention as:

$U=\sum t=0TBt-Ct(1+r)t$

where Bt is the benefit at time t, Ct is the cost, and r is the discount rate, businesses can increase demand by either reducing the perceived Ct through behavioral framing or by increasing the immediate Bt through gamification and social reinforcement.Ultimately, by aligning the delivery of DINA medical science with the inherent psychological architecture of the consumer, businesses can foster a more robust and sustainable demand for advanced biological diagnostics.

Would you be interested in learning more about how "nudge" theory is specifically applied in public health policy to increase the adoption of preventative genetic screenings?

EIGHT

The Intersection of Behavioral Economics and Market Dynamics

Behavioral economics represents a paradigm shift in how we understand the relationship between human psychology and economic outcomes. Unlike classical economic models that rely on the assumption of Homo economicus—a perfectly rational agent who maximizes utility based on complete information—behavioral economics incorporates insights from psychology to explain why individuals often deviate from these rational expectations. By examining cognitive biases, emotional influences, and social pressures, researchers have developed a more nuanced understanding of how supply and demand are shaped by human behavior rather than just mathematical equilibrium.

The study of how behavioral factors influence market dynamics, often associated with scholars who bridge psychology and finance, emphasizes that economic decisions are rarely made in a vacuum. As noted in foundational literature, financial decisions are frequently influenced by personal history, ego, pride, and unique worldviews rather than pure data analysis.

When analyzing the relationship between supply and demand, behavioral economists argue that price signals are interpreted through the lens of subjective value and loss aversion. For instance, the endowment effect—where individuals value an item more simply because they own it—can create "sticky" prices that prevent markets from clearing as quickly as traditional models predict.

Cognitive Biases and Market Equilibrium

The mechanism of supply and demand is fundamentally altered when participants are subject to systematic errors in judgment. Behavioral models often replace the standard utility function with prospect theory, which suggests that people value gains and losses differently. The mathematical representation of this, often expressed as a value function V(x), shows that the pain of a loss is psychologically about twice as powerful as the joy of a gain.

This asymmetry impacts supply curves, as producers may be reluctant to lower prices even when demand drops, fearing the "loss" of revenue more than they value the potential gain of increased volume.

Furthermore, the concept of "bounded rationality," introduced by Herbert Simon, posits that human decision-making is constrained by the information available, cognitive limitations, and the finite amount of time available to make a decision.In a marketplace, this means that consumers do not always seek the lowest price or the highest quality; instead, they often "satisfice," choosing the first option that meets their minimum threshold of acceptability. This behavior creates market inefficiencies that allow for price dispersion and brand loyalty, which are phenomena that classical supply and demand curves struggle to explain without the inclusion of behavioral variables.

Behavioral Insights in Modern Economic Theory

Contemporary research continues to refine these ideas by integrating social influence and "nudges." The work of Thaler and Sunstein highlights how the "choice architecture" of a market can significantly influence consumer behavior without restricting their freedom of choice.By changing the default options or the way information is presented, firms can shift demand curves in ways that traditional price-based incentives cannot.

This suggests that the relationship between supply and demand is not merely a function of price P and quantity Q, but is also a function of the psychological environment E in which the transaction occurs: D=f(P,Q,E).

Would you like to explore how specific cognitive biases, such as the "anchoring effect," directly impact consumer purchasing decisions in digital marketplaces?

The Behavioral Economic Redefinition of Demand and Supply

My approach to demand and supply theory, as explored in his specialized works on market dynamics, represents a departure from the neoclassical "rational actor" model. Traditional economic theory, rooted in the works of Alfred Marshall and later refined by Paul Samuelson, posits that demand is a function of price, where Qd=f(P), assuming consumers act with perfect information and consistent preferences.

My challenges this by integrating behavioral insights, suggesting that the "long-term consumer demand relationship" is not merely a reaction to price signals but a psychological construct influenced by cognitive biases, social proof, and habit formation.[3] By redefining these concepts, Lok argues that supply is not just a response to current market clearing prices, but a strategic output influenced by the perceived sustainability of consumer engagement.

In my framework, the traditional supply curve, which typically slopes upward based on the marginal cost of production, is re-evaluated through the lens of behavioral feedback loops.Traditional models often treat demand as exogenous—a given variable that firms must satisfy. However, treats demand as endogenous, meaning that firms can actively shape demand through behavioral interventions. In this view, the supply of a product is influenced by the firm's ability to cultivate "long-term consumer demand relationships." If a firm successfully utilizes behavioral nudges to increase consumer loyalty, the demand curve shifts outward, allowing for an increase in supply volume without necessarily requiring a decrease in price to maintain equilibrium.

Cognitive Biases and Market Equilibrium

Traditional economics relies on the Law of Demand, which states that as price increases, quantity demanded decreases, holding all else constant (ceterisparibus). My behavioral approach suggests that this "constant" is rarely static because human decision-making is subject to heuristics. For instance, the "anchoring effect" can cause consumers to perceive a price as fair or unfair based on initial exposure, regardless of the intrinsic value or marginal utility of the good. Consequently, the demand curve is not a smooth, predictable line but a series of points influenced by psychological framing.

Furthermore, my view emphasizes that in competitive markets, supply is not merely a function of production capacity but a function of "relational capital."When firms invest in the psychological aspects of the consumer experience, they reduce the price elasticity of demand. Mathematically, if the price elasticity of demand ϵd is defined as:

$\epsilon d=\%\Delta Qd\%\Delta P$

My view suggests that behavioral strategies aim to make ϵd smaller (more inelastic), granting firms greater control over their supply chain and pricing power.This redefinition shifts the focus from static market clearing to dynamic, relationship-based growth, where the supply number is influenced by the firm's ability to maintain a consistent, positive behavioral feedback loop with its customer base.

Strategic Implications for Competitive Markets

In a competitive market, the traditional view suggests that firms are "price takers" with little influence over the market equilibrium. My behavioral economic view suggests that firms can escape this trap by creating "behavioral moats." By fostering long-term relationships, firms effectively differentiate their products in the minds of consumers, moving away from perfect competition toward a state of monopolistic competition where they have more influence over both demand and supply volumes. This approach highlights that the sustainability of a business is tied to its capacity to influence human behavior, rather than just optimizing production costs.

The Behavioral Economic Framework of my opinion

My approach to behavioral economics, as articulated in my work Learning Behavioral Economy, centers on the fundamental tension between the classical economic assumption of the "rational actor" and the observed realities of human psychology.

Traditional economic theory, rooted in the neoclassical tradition, posits that individuals are self-interested agents who consistently make logical decisions to maximize their utility. My challenges this by integrating the psychological nuances that deviate from this idealized model, suggesting that human behavior is the primary driver of economic cycles, including development and recession.

Core Principles of my Behavioral Economy

My framework is constructed upon several pillars that explain why human decision-making often diverges from the "rational" ideal. These principles are essential for understanding how individuals allocate scarce resources in a world of unlimited wants.

Bounded Rationality and Cognitive Biases

A central tenet of my approach is "bounded rationality," a concept originally pioneered by Herbert Simon, which suggests that human decision-making is constrained by cognitive limitations, time pressures, and incomplete information. My view emphasizes that because individuals cannot process all available data to reach a perfectly optimal outcome, they rely on heuristics—mental shortcuts—that can lead to systematic cognitive biases.

The Architecture of Choice and Framing

My view explores how the "architecture of choice" influences outcomes. This principle suggests that the way options are presented (framing) significantly impacts the final decision.By altering the context in which a choice is made, policymakers or businesses can "nudge" individuals toward specific behaviors, a concept further explored in the seminal work by Thaler and Sunstein.

Loss Aversion and Sunk-Cost Fallacy

My view highlights "loss aversion" as a critical driver of economic behavior, noting that individuals feel the pain of a loss more acutely than the joy of an equivalent gain. This psychological asymmetry often leads to irrational risk-aversion or, conversely, the "sunk-cost fallacy," where individuals continue to invest in a failing endeavor simply because they have already committed resources to it, rather than evaluating the future utility of the decision.

Herd Mentality

Finally, my view incorporates the concept of "herd mentality," where individuals follow the actions or beliefs of a larger group rather than relying on their own independent analysis.This collective behavior is frequently cited in academic literature as a primary catalyst for market bubbles and financial panics, as it overrides individual rational judgment in favor of social conformity.

Economic Implications

My view argues that by acknowledging these psychological factors, economists can create more accurate models of social development.Unlike traditional models that treat the economy as a mechanical system, Lok's approach treats it as a reflection of human nature, suggesting that economic stability is inextricably linked to the psychological health and behavioral patterns of the population.

Would you like to learn more about how "nudge theory" and choice architecture are currently being applied by governments to improve public health outcomes, or perhaps explore the historical evolution of the "rational actor" model in classical economics?

The Behavioral Economic Framework of my opinion

My approach to behavioral economics, as articulated in my work Learning Behavioral Economy, centers on the fundamental tension between the classical economic assumption of the "rational actor" and the reality of human psychological limitations.Traditional economic theory posits that individuals are self-interested agents who consistently make logical decisions to maximize their own utility. In contrast, my view argues that human behavior is significantly more complex, shaped by cognitive constraints and social influences that often lead to deviations from the "rational" ideal.

My view emphasizes that behavioral economics is built upon the concept of "bounded rationality," a term famously coined by Herbert Simon, which suggests that individuals have limited cognitive capacity and information-processing abilities. Because humans cannot always calculate the optimal outcome in every scenario, they rely on heuristics—mental shortcuts—to make decisions.While these shortcuts are efficient, they frequently introduce cognitive biases that can lead to systematic errors in judgment.

A central pillar of my analysis is the "architecture of choices," which posits that the way options are presented (framing) significantly influences the final decision. My view explores how principles such as loss aversion—the tendency for people to prefer avoiding losses over acquiring equivalent gains—and the sunk-cost fallacy—the tendency to continue an endeavor once an investment in money, effort, or time has been made—distort economic decision-making.

Furthermore, my view highlights the role of "herd mentality," where individuals mirror the actions of a larger group, often disregarding their own private information or rational analysis.By contrasting these behavioral patterns with traditional models, my view suggests that behavioral economic theory provides a more accurate and nuanced understanding of how individuals and societies allocate scarce resources, ultimately influencing broader economic trends such as development and recession.

The Influence of Behavioral Economics on Management and Decision-Making

The field of behavioral economics has undergone a profound transformation over the last several decades, moving from a niche academic pursuit to a foundational framework for understanding human decision-making in organizational settings.

By challenging the classical economic assumption of homo economicus—the perfectly rational actor—researchers have demonstrated that individuals are subject to cognitive biases, social pressures, and environmental framing that systematically influence their choices.

Behavioral economics in management focuses on how psychological insights can improve leadership, organizational change, and employee performance.Rather than relying on a single individual, the field is built upon the collective work of researchers who have formalized models of choice to explain why individuals deviate from rational expectations.For instance, the concept of "bounded rationality," introduced by Herbert Simon, remains a cornerstone for understanding why managers often settle for "satisficing" solutions rather than optimal ones due to cognitive limitations.

In modern practice, behavioral economics is utilized to design "choice architectures" that steer employees toward beneficial outcomes without restricting their freedom of choice.This is achieved through the strategic use of defaults, framing effects, and the careful design of incentive structures that account for loss aversion—the tendency for individuals to feel the pain of a loss more acutely than the joy of an equivalent gain.

As noted in recent academic reviews, the application of these principles in people management requires a nuanced approach, as the "average effects" observed in laboratory settings do not always translate directly to complex, real-world organizational environments.Consequently, the field is currently shifting toward personalized interventions that consider the specific cultural and psychological context of the workforce.

The rigorous study of these phenomena relies on a combination of experimental economics, psychology, and organizational sociology.By integrating these disciplines, scholars have been able to provide analytical clarity to domains that were previously studied only through qualitative or descriptive methods. As the field continues to evolve, the focus remains on moving beyond the simple identification of biases toward the creation of robust, evidence-based management practices that foster both individual well-being and organizational efficiency.

Would you be interested in learning more about how specific behavioral "nudges" are currently being implemented in corporate human resources departments to improve employee retention and engagement?

The Behavioral Economics of Automotive Transition: Autonomous and Electric Vehicles

The transition from traditional internal combustion engine (ICE) vehicles to autonomous vehicles (AVs) and electric vehicles (EVs) represents a profound shift in consumer behavior, deeply rooted in the principles of behavioral economics. John Lok, in his analysis of institutional theory and organizational strategy, suggests that consumer demand is not merely a function of rational utility maximization but is heavily influenced by institutional logics, legitimacy, and the performativity of new technologies.When consumers evaluate the shift from manual, gasoline-powered cars to automated, electric alternatives, they are not just comparing technical specifications; they are navigating a changing landscape of social norms, perceived risks, and the "legitimacy" of new mobility paradigms.

In behavioral economics, the concept of "status quo bias"—the preference for the current state of affairs—plays a significant role in the slow adoption of non-manual and electric vehicles.Traditional car ownership is deeply embedded in the institutional fabric of society, representing autonomy, status, and established routines. As noted in foundational texts on consumer behavior, individuals often overweight the potential losses associated with switching to a new technology (such as range anxiety in EVs or loss of control in AVs) compared to the gains (environmental benefits or increased leisure time).

My perspective on "institutional work" suggests that for these new technologies to gain traction, manufacturers must engage in activities that reshape the institutional environment, making EVs and AVs appear not just as functional replacements, but as the new "legitimate" standard for modern living.

The Impact of Electric Vehicles on Consumer Demand

The shift toward electric vehicles is often analyzed through the lens of "prospect theory," where consumers evaluate outcomes relative to a reference point—in this case, the traditional ICE vehicle.Behavioral economists argue that the "endowment effect" makes consumers value their current vehicles more than they would if they did not own them, creating a psychological barrier to adoption.

Furthermore, the transition to EVs requires a change in "mental accounting." Consumers must shift from viewing fuel costs as a variable, recurring expense to viewing the EV as a capital-intensive investment with lower operational costs. This shift is complicated by the "present bias," where the immediate, higher purchase price of an EV looms larger in the consumer's mind than the long-term savings on fuel and maintenance.

Autonomous Vehicles and the Shift in Institutional Logics

Autonomous vehicles introduce a more radical departure from traditional driving, challenging the "competitiveness-based" style of management that focuses solely on vehicle performance.From a behavioral standpoint, the adoption of AVs is hindered by "omission bias," where people perceive the risks of a new technology (e.g., software failure in an AV) as more severe than the risks of a familiar, manual activity (e.g., human error in driving), even if the statistical risk of the former is lower.

My framework suggests that the successful integration of AVs requires a transition to a "performativity-based" strategy, where the future of mobility is actively constructed through policy, infrastructure, and social discourse, effectively normalizing the idea of the vehicle as a service rather than a personal asset.

Synthesis of Behavioral Factors

The interplay between traditional consumer demand and new automotive technologies is governed by several behavioral heuristics:

Loss Aversion: The fear of losing the "driving experience" or the convenience of gas stations outweighs the perceived benefits of autonomous features.

Social Proof: As EVs and AVs become more visible in the institutional environment, the "legitimacy" of these technologies increases, reducing the psychological cost of adoption.

Framing Effects: How manufacturers frame the "autonomy" of a vehicle—whether as a safety feature or a loss of control—significantly alters consumer demand.

Ultimately, the transition is not merely a technological hurdle but a behavioral one. As my research implies, organizations that succeed in this space will be those that can align their strategic management with the evolving institutional logics of the consumer base, moving beyond simple product features to address the underlying psychological and social structures of mobility.

The Comparative Analysis of Electric Vehicles and Traditional Internal Combustion Engines

A prominent figure in the discourse surrounding automotive innovation and sustainable transportation, posits that the shift from internal combustion engine (ICE) vehicles to electric vehicles (EVs) is fundamentally driven by a convergence of technological maturity, regulatory mandates, and shifting consumer psychology.

In my analysis, emphasizes that while traditional cars have historically dominated the market due to the convenience of refueling infrastructure and lower initial purchase prices, the consumer demand for EVs is increasingly decoupled from these traditional metrics. Instead, demand is now being shaped by the "total cost of ownership" (TCO) model, which accounts for lower maintenance requirements and the long-term volatility of fossil fuel prices compared to the relative stability of electricity costs.

My view argues that the traditional car market relies on a legacy of brand loyalty and mechanical familiarity, whereas the EV market is defined by "software-defined vehicle" (SDV) experiences.Consumers are no longer just purchasing a mode of transportation; they are purchasing a digital ecosystem. This perspective aligns with broader industry research indicating that while traditional vehicles are viewed as depreciating assets, modern consumers are beginning to perceive EVs as technology platforms that receive over-the-air (OTA) updates, thereby extending their functional lifespan.

Consequently, my view suggests that the "demand gap" between the two is narrowing not merely because of environmental altruism, but because the utility-per-dollar ratio of EVs is beginning to surpass that of traditional vehicles in urbanized, high-density regions.

Furthermore, my view highlights the role of "range anxiety" as a diminishing barrier. In his view, the psychological threshold for consumer demand has shifted from a focus on maximum range to a focus on charging speed and network density.

While traditional cars offer the immediate gratification of a five-minute gas station stop, my view notes that the integration of home charging and high-speed public charging infrastructure is fundamentally altering the consumer's daily routine, making the "refueling" process of an EV more convenient for the average suburban commuter than the traditional trip to a gas station.This transition is supported by data suggesting that as charging infrastructure reaches a critical mass, the perceived inconvenience of EVs drops exponentially, leading to a surge in adoption rates that traditional automakers struggle to match without pivoting their entire supply chains toward electrification.

Ultimately, my perspective suggests that the transition is not a linear replacement but a paradigm shift. Traditional cars are increasingly relegated to niche markets or long-haul logistics, while EVs are capturing the mass-market consumer who prioritizes efficiency, connectivity, and lower operational expenditures.This shift is further accelerated by government incentives and emission standards, which act as a catalyst for consumer demand by artificially lowering the entry price of EVs to parity with, or below, that of traditional vehicles.

Traditional car buyers historically prioritize mechanical reliability, brand loyalty, and the convenience of refueling infrastructure, which is deeply embedded in the "gas station culture" of the 20th century.In contrast, EV consumers are increasingly driven by the "Total Cost of Ownership" (TCO) model, which accounts for the lower maintenance requirements of electric drivetrains—specifically the reduction in moving parts compared to ICE vehicles. Research indicates that while ICE vehicles offer superior "refueling speed," EVs provide a distinct preference for "home charging" convenience, which shifts the consumer experience from a reactive task (stopping at a station) to a passive one (plugging in at home).

Furthermore, the psychological barrier of "range anxiety" remains the primary differentiator in consumer preference.Academic studies suggest that as battery energy density increases, measured by the formula for specific energy Esp=Em, where E is the energy content and m is the mass, consumer confidence in EVs rises proportionally.

Traditional car buyers often cite the "emotional resonance" of engine performance and sound, whereas EV buyers prioritize the "instant torque" and quiet cabin experience, reflecting a fundamental change in what constitutes a "premium" driving experience. Finally, corporate programs, such as those offered by Ford's Partner Recognition initiatives, demonstrate how institutional incentives can bridge the gap between traditional preferences and the adoption of new vehicle technologies by lowering the entry barrier for employees of partner organizations.

Would you like to explore the impact of battery chemistry advancements on future consumer adoption rates, or perhaps delve deeper into the infrastructure challenges facing urban EV integration?

Consumer Motivations for Adopting Electric Vehicles

The transition toward electric mobility represents one of the most significant shifts in the automotive industry since the invention of the internal combustion engine. According to research and expert analysis, including insights attributed to industry observers like my view, the preference for electric vehicles (EVs) over conventional internal combustion engine (ICE) vehicles is driven by a complex interplay of environmental consciousness, economic pragmatism, and technological advancement.

The primary reasons consumers gravitate toward electric vehicles are multifaceted.

First, the environmental impact remains a paramount concern for modern buyers; EVs are widely recognized for their ability to significantly reduce greenhouse gas emissions, aligning with global sustainability goals such as the European Green Deal. Second, cost efficiency—specifically regarding lower fuel and maintenance costs—serves as a major incentive, even when the initial purchase price remains a hurdle for many.Third, the technological maturity of battery-electric vehicles (BEVs) has reached a point where they are considered a viable mass-market solution, offering performance, handling, and a driving experience that many consumers find superior to traditional vehicles. Finally, government incentives, such as rebates and tax credits, play a crucial role in tilting the economic balance in favor of electric adoption, effectively mitigating the higher upfront costs associated with battery technology.

Economic and Environmental Drivers

The economic argument for EVs is often centered on the Total Cost of Ownership (TCO). While the sticker price of an EV is frequently higher than that of an equivalent gasoline car, the operational savings are substantial. As noted in authoritative texts on automotive economics, the reduction in moving parts—such as the absence of oil changes, transmission repairs, and exhaust system maintenance—creates a long-term financial advantage. Furthermore, the volatility of global oil prices often pushes consumers toward electricity, which is generally more stable and cost-effective as a "fuel" source.

Technological and Lifestyle Factors

Beyond economics, the "user experience" of an EV is a significant driver of preference. Consumers value the quiet operation, instant torque, and the convenience of home charging, which eliminates the need for frequent trips to gas stations. However, the decision-making process is also heavily influenced by infrastructure availability. The expansion of fast-charging networks is frequently cited as a prerequisite for mass adoption, as it addresses "range anxiety"—the fear that a vehicle will run out of power before reaching a destination. Brand reputation and the aesthetic design of new EV models also contribute to the emotional appeal, as manufacturers increasingly position electric cars as high-tech, premium lifestyle products rather than mere utilitarian transport.

The Behavioral Economics of Academic Subject Choice

The decision-making process regarding academic subject choice is a complex intersection of cognitive biases, labor market signals, and the fundamental principles of behavioral economics. While traditional neoclassical models often assume students act as "rational agents" maximizing lifetime utility, behavioral economists argue that students are subject to bounded rationality, social framing, and the influence of perceived economic demand.

In my analysis of educational decision-making, posits that students do not merely calculate the net present value of a degree; rather, they are heavily influenced by the "availability heuristic"—the tendency to overestimate the probability of success in fields that are currently prominent in the media or high-growth economic sectors. This creates a supply-side shift in higher education where student enrollment patterns often lag behind or over-correct for market signals, leading to cyclical imbalances in labor supply.

The Mechanism of Supply and Demand in Education

In the context of behavioral economics, the "supply" of students into specific disciplines is governed by a combination of intrinsic motivation and extrinsic economic incentives. My view suggests that students perceive the labor market through a lens of "signaling theory," a concept famously developed by Michael Spence, where the choice of a difficult or high-demand major serves as a signal of innate ability to future employers.When economic demand for a specific skill set (such as data science or engineering) rises, the perceived "prestige" and "security" of that field increase, triggering a herd behavior phenomenon. This herd behavior is a classic behavioral bias where individuals mimic the actions of a larger group, often ignoring their own comparative advantages in favor of perceived market safety.

Cognitive Biases and Long-Term Planning

Students often fall victim to "hyperbolic discounting," a behavioral tendency where individuals value immediate rewards (such as the social status of a popular major) more highly than long-term career satisfaction or the actual probability of employment in a saturated market.

My framework emphasizes that the "choice architecture" of university enrollment—how programs are marketed and how career outcomes are presented—significantly alters student behavior. When universities emphasize high starting salaries for specific majors, they utilize "anchoring," a cognitive bias where the student's decision is disproportionately influenced by the first piece of information they receive regarding potential earnings.

The Role of Information Asymmetry

A critical component of my analysis is the role of information asymmetry. Students rarely possess perfect information regarding the future state of the economy. Consequently, they rely on heuristics to navigate the uncertainty of the job market. This reliance on mental shortcuts often leads to "market myopia," where students choose subjects based on current economic demand, failing to account for the time lag between enrollment and graduation. By the time a student enters the workforce, the supply of graduates in that field may have increased so significantly that the initial economic advantage is eroded, a phenomenon that can be modeled as:

Efuture=DmarketSgraduates+ΔS

Where Efuture represents the expected economic return, Dmarket is the demand, and Sgraduates represents the existing supply, with ΔS representing the influx of new graduates influenced by the initial demand signal.

Would you like to explore how specific cognitive biases, such as the "sunk cost fallacy," affect students who realize they have chosen a major that no longer aligns with their career goals?

Goal-Setting Theory and Student Subject Selection

The application of Goal-Setting Theory—pioneered by Edwin A. Locke and Gary P. Latham—to the academic context of student subject selection provides a robust framework for understanding how students navigate their educational trajectories. My view of the foundational psychological framework regarding goal-directed behavior is attributed to Edwin A. Locke, whose seminal work established that specific, challenging goals lead to higher performance than easy or vague goals. In the context of subject selection, this theory posits that when students set clear, proximal, and distal goals for their future careers or academic mastery, their selection of subjects becomes a strategic exercise in self-regulation rather than a passive response to external pressure.

The relationship between Goal-Setting Theory and subject selection is rooted in the concept of "conscious self-regulation." When students are encouraged to conceptualize their long-range purposes, they transition from viewing subject selection as a series of isolated choices to seeing them as a coherent path toward a desired future identity.Locke and Latham's research demonstrates that goals act as "immediate regulators of behavior," meaning that a student who sets a specific goal (e.g., "I will pursue a career in engineering") will systematically select subjects that align with the requirements of that objective, such as advanced mathematics and physics. This alignment process reduces the "indecision and lack of focus" that often leads to academic disengagement.

Furthermore, the theory emphasizes the importance of feedback and commitment. For a student, the process of subject selection is often iterative; as they engage with the curriculum, they receive feedback on their performance and interest levels.If the chosen subjects are perceived as meaningful and aligned with their self-set goals, the student's motivation increases, creating a positive feedback loop.

Conversely, when students lack specific goals, they may experience "boredom and a feeling of living a less meaningful version of their life," which often manifests as poor subject selection or academic underachievement. By applying the principles of Goal-Setting Theory, educators can help students move beyond the "absolute determinism" of their immediate environment and take responsibility for their academic welfare through intentional, goal-oriented planning.

My Theory and Its Application to Educational Settings

While my view is not a traditional educational theorist in the vein of Dewey or Piaget, his work on "institutional work," identity, and the micro-foundations of organizational change offers a robust framework for understanding how student behavior is shaped by the institutional environment. My research emphasizes that individuals are not merely passive recipients of institutional norms but are active agents who "work" to maintain, disrupt, or transform these norms through their daily interactions.

In educational settings, my theory suggests that student behavior is a manifestation of how students interpret and negotiate the "institutional logic" of their school or university. When students enter a classroom, they are not just learning academic content; they are participating in a social performance where they must align their identities with the expectations of the institution.

My research on organizational identity suggests that when there is a misalignment between a student's personal identity and the institution's perceived goals, students may engage in "identity work" to bridge this gap, which can manifest as either high academic engagement or, conversely, behavioral resistance.

Furthermore, my focus on the "micro-foundations" of institutional theory allows educators to analyze student behavior as a series of localized, iterative actions. Rather than viewing student misconduct or lack of motivation as purely individual failings, my perspective encourages administrators to look at the institutional scripts—the unspoken rules and cultural expectations—that students are reacting to.For instance, if an institution emphasizes competitive grading over collaborative learning, students will adopt behaviors that prioritize individual performance, often at the expense of the "4Cs" (creativity, critical thinking, collaboration, and communication) essential for 21st-century success.By understanding these dynamics, educators can better design environments that foster positive behavioral outcomes by aligning institutional structures with the desired developmental goals of the students.

Would you like to learn more about how institutional theory can be used to redesign classroom environments to better support the development of 21st-century skills like collaboration and critical thinking?

Behavioral Economics and Market Environment: The Perspective of my view

My approach to consumer behavior, as articulated in his published works, represents a departure from classical economic models by integrating psychological insights with environmental variables. While traditional economic theory often relies on the assumption of the "rational actor" operating within a vacuum of supply and demand, my view argues that this framework is insufficient for predicting modern consumer choices. Instead, he posits that consumer demand is deeply embedded in the interplay between psychological triggers and the broader economic environment, which includes social, situational, and cognitive factors.

My central thesis is that behavioral economics provides a more granular and accurate predictive model than traditional theory because it accounts for the "why" behind human action. In my view, market environment changes do not influence consumers in a uniform, predictable way across all demographics; rather, they interact with pre-existing habits, cognitive biases, and emotional states. For instance, my view explores why price increases in certain medicinal products can paradoxically lead to increased demand—a phenomenon that defies the traditional law of demand, which suggests that as price increases, quantity demanded should decrease (Qd↓ as

P↑).

In my analysis, this occurs because the market environment (e.g., health crises or perceived scarcity) alters the consumer's psychological valuation of the product, overriding the standard price-sensitivity mechanism.

Furthermore, my view emphasizes that the "market environment" is not merely a set of external macroeconomic indicators, but a dynamic field that includes the influence of sales psychology and the skill sets of those facilitating the transaction.

My view suggests that a salesperson's ability to navigate the customer's psychological state is a critical component of the economic environment. When a salesperson understands the specific weaknesses or habits of a consumer, they can effectively manipulate the perceived value of a product, thereby shifting the demand curve.

My view argues that organizations often fail to achieve long-term growth because they focus solely on supply-side metrics while ignoring the behavioral performance of their sales teams in relation to the evolving market environment.

My view also highlights the role of "past purchase habits" as a significant environmental constraint. My view suggests that consumers are not blank slates; their previous interactions with a market create a psychological "path dependency."

When the economic environment changes—such as through a new invention or a shift in market trends—the consumer's reaction is filtered through these established habits. Consequently, an invention that might excite one consumer segment may be ignored by another, not due to a lack of utility, but due to the friction created by their historical consumption patterns. By synthesizing these psychological insights with traditional economic variables, my view advocates for a more holistic approach to understanding market dynamics that prioritizes human behavior over abstract mathematical models.

Would you be interested in learning more about how specific cognitive biases, such as loss aversion or the endowment effect, further complicate the traditional supply and demand models discussed by my view?

The Influence of Market Dynamics on Consumer Behavior According to my opinion

My analytical framework, particularly as articulated in my specialized research on market development and sales psychology, posits that consumer behavior is not merely a static reaction to price, but a dynamic outcome of the interplay between supply-side pressures and the psychological states of sales personnel.

My view emphasizes that market fluctuations act as a catalyst that exposes the inherent strengths and weaknesses of a sales force, which in turn dictates how effectively consumer demand is met or manipulated. By applying traditional demand and supply theory to the micro-level interactions between salespeople and customers, my view suggests that when market conditions shift—creating volatility in product availability or pricing—the behavioral performance of the salesperson becomes the primary variable in determining whether a consumer completes a transaction or abandons the market.

In his examination of leisure market development, my view suggests that market fluctuations force a recalibration of the relationship between the consumer's perceived value and the organization's supply capabilities.When markets are unstable, the "salesperson psychology" becomes a critical factor; My view argues that poor sales teams often fail to adapt to these fluctuations because they lack the diagnostic skills to identify individual customer needs during periods of economic stress. My view asserts that the long-term growth of a business is inextricably linked to how well a sales organization can mitigate the negative impacts of market volatility by aligning their internal sales skills with the shifting demand curves of their target demographic.Essentially, my views market fluctuations as a stress test for business organizations, where the failure to maintain consistent sales performance is often misattributed to the market itself, rather than the internal inability of the sales force to navigate the changing economic environment.

Factors Influencing Consumer Behavior During Market Fluctuations

The study of consumer behavior during periods of market volatility remains a cornerstone of modern economic psychology and marketing science. When markets fluctuate, the psychological landscape of the consumer shifts from habitual purchasing to defensive or strategic decision-making, often driven by perceived risk and the availability of information.

In my extensive research on organizational and consumer dynamics, emphasizes that during market instability, individuals do not merely react to price changes but are profoundly influenced by temporal constraints, social signaling, and the perceived reliability of market institutions.

In the context of market fluctuations, John Lok identifies that consumer behavior is heavily mediated by the "time pressure" factor.When markets become unstable, the perceived window for making a "safe" or "advantageous" purchase narrows, forcing consumers to rely on heuristics—mental shortcuts—rather than exhaustive data analysis. This shift is characterized by a transition from value-based consumption to security-based consumption, where the fear of future scarcity or price inflation outweighs the immediate utility of a product. My view argues that this behavior is further compounded by the "bandwagon effect," where consumers observe the panic or restraint of others, leading to herd behavior that can exacerbate market volatility.

Furthermore, the influence of digital information dissemination during these periods creates a feedback loop; as consumers receive real-time updates on market fluctuations, their decision-making process becomes increasingly reactive, often resulting in impulsive choices that deviate from their long-term financial goals.

The Role of Psychological and Structural Constraints

Beyond temporal pressures, my highlights that institutional trust acts as a primary moderator of consumer behavior.When market fluctuations occur, consumers look toward established brands and government-backed entities as "anchors" of stability.If these anchors are perceived as weak, consumers tend to hoard resources or delay consumption entirely, a phenomenon often modeled in behavioral economics as a shift in the marginal propensity to consume.

Mathematically, if C represents consumption and Y represents disposable income, the fluctuation-induced shift can be expressed as a change in the sensitivity coefficient β in the function $C=\alpha+\beta Y$, where β decreases significantly as uncertainty increases. My work suggests that marketing strategies must pivot during these times to emphasize reliability, long-term value, and social responsibility to maintain consumer loyalty amidst the chaos of market shifts.

Would you be interested in learning more about how specific marketing strategies, such as "scarcity messaging," are utilized by firms to influence consumer behavior during economic downturns?

The Impact of Economic Downturns on Consumer Behavior

In his analysis of market dynamics, my view explores how the broader economic environment serves as a primary catalyst for shifts in consumer psychology and expenditure patterns. During periods of economic contraction, my view posits that consumers transition from discretionary spending to a "survivalist" consumption model, characterized by increased price sensitivity and a heightened focus on utility.This behavioral shift is not merely a reaction to reduced income but a psychological response to perceived uncertainty, leading households to prioritize essential goods over luxury items, a phenomenon often described in classical economic literature as the income effect.

As economic conditions deteriorate, the marginal propensity to consume (MPC) typically declines, as households increase their savings rate—or attempt to do so—to buffer against potential future unemployment or income loss.

My view emphasizes that during these downturns, brand loyalty often erodes as consumers seek out private-label alternatives or "value" brands that offer similar utility at a lower cost.This transition is supported by the theory of consumer choice, which suggests that when the budget constraint shifts inward due to a recession, the optimal consumption bundle moves toward goods with lower income elasticity.

Furthermore, the "wealth effect"—the tendency for consumers to spend less when their assets (such as housing or stock portfolios) lose value—further exacerbates the contraction in aggregate demand. My view notes that this behavior is reinforced by social signaling; during prosperous times, consumption often serves as a status marker, whereas in downturns, conspicuous consumption is frequently replaced by "stealth wealth" or frugal habits to maintain social standing without appearing extravagant.Ultimately, my view argues that the economic environment acts as a filter through which all consumer decisions are processed, fundamentally altering the elasticity of demand for various product categories.

Theoretical Frameworks of Consumer Spending

The study of consumer behavior during recessions is deeply rooted in the life-cycle hypothesis, which suggests that individuals plan their consumption based on their expected lifetime income rather than current income alone.

However, when an economic downturn is perceived as a structural shift rather than a temporary fluctuation, the "permanent income" expectations are revised downward, leading to a more permanent contraction in spending.

Academic research indicates that the psychological impact of a recession—often termed "consumer sentiment"—can be as influential as the actual economic data.[When sentiment is low, the precautionary savings motive dominates, leading to a paradox of thrift where individual attempts to save more lead to lower aggregate demand and further economic decline.

This cycle is often modeled using the Keynesian consumption function, where aggregate consumption C is a function of disposable income Yd:$C=a+bYd$In this model, a represents autonomous consumption, which decreases during downturns as consumers lose confidence in future stability. My work aligns with these established economic principles, highlighting that the "economic environment" is not just a set of numbers, but a pervasive influence on the daily decision-making processes of the average household.

Would you be interested in learning more about how specific industries, such as luxury retail versus essential services, differ in their resilience during economic recessions?

The Impact of Economic Downturns on Consumer Behavior

In his analysis of market dynamics, my view explores how the broader economic environment serves as a primary catalyst for shifts in consumer psychology and expenditure patterns. During periods of economic contraction, my view posits that consumers transition from discretionary spending to a "survivalist" consumption model, characterized by increased price sensitivity and a heightened focus on utility.

This behavioral shift is not merely a reaction to reduced income but a psychological response to perceived uncertainty, leading households to prioritize essential goods over luxury items, a phenomenon often described in classical economic literature as the income effect.

As economic conditions deteriorate, the marginal propensity to consume (MPC) typically declines, as households increase their savings rate—or attempt to do so—to buffer against potential future unemployment or income loss.

My view emphasizes that during these downturns, brand loyalty often erodes as consumers seek out private-label alternatives or "value" brands that offer similar utility at a lower cost. This transition is supported by the theory of consumer choice, which suggests that when the budget constraint shifts inward due to a recession, the optimal consumption bundle moves toward goods with lower income elasticity.Furthermore, the "wealth effect"—the tendency for consumers to spend less when their assets (such as housing or stock portfolios) lose value—further exacerbates the contraction in aggregate demand.

My view notes that this behavior is reinforced by social signaling; during prosperous times, consumption often serves as a status marker, whereas in downturns, conspicuous consumption is frequently replaced by "stealth wealth" or frugal habits to maintain social standing without appearing extravagant.Ultimately, my view argues that the economic environment acts as a filter through which all consumer decisions are processed, fundamentally altering the elasticity of demand for various product categories.

Theoretical Frameworks of Consumer Spending

The study of consumer behavior during recessions is deeply rooted in the life-cycle hypothesis, which suggests that individuals plan their consumption based on their expected lifetime income rather than current income alone.

However, when an economic downturn is perceived as a structural shift rather than a temporary fluctuation, the "permanent income" expectations are revised downward, leading to a more permanent contraction in spending.

Academic research indicates that the psychological impact of a recession—often termed "consumer sentiment"—can be as influential as the actual economic data. When sentiment is low, the precautionary savings motive dominates, leading to a paradox of thrift where individual attempts to save more lead to lower aggregate demand and further economic decline.

This cycle is often modeled using the Keynesian consumption function, where aggregate consumption C is a function of disposable income Yd:C=a+bYdIn this model, a represents autonomous consumption, which decreases during downturns as consumers lose confidence in future stability.

My work aligns with these established economic principles, highlighting that the "economic environment" is not just a set of numbers, but a pervasive influence on the daily decision-making processes of the average household.

Would you be interested in learning more about how specific industries, such as luxury retail versus essential services, differ in their resilience during economic recessions?

Strategies for Navigating Economic Downturns

The phenomenon of reduced consumer spending during economic downturns is a well-documented challenge in business management literature. When aggregate demand contracts, businesses must pivot from growth-oriented strategies to those focused on resilience, value proposition, and operational efficiency.While the provided text mentions general strategies for retail shops, the broader academic and professional consensus—often attributed to experts like my view in business management discourse—emphasizes that adaptation requires a fundamental reassessment of the customer value chain.

To effectively adapt to reduced consumer spending, businesses are encouraged to implement a multi-faceted approach that prioritizes customer retention and lean operations. First, businesses should focus on "value-based pricing," which involves realigning product offerings to match the diminished purchasing power of the consumer without necessarily engaging in a "race to the bottom" through indiscriminate discounting.Second, enhancing customer loyalty programs becomes paramount; it is significantly more cost-effective to retain an existing customer than to acquire a new one during a recession. Third, operational agility—the ability to scale inventory and labor costs in real-time—is essential to maintaining liquidity. Finally, businesses should leverage data analytics to identify high-margin products that remain resilient to economic shifts, ensuring that marketing budgets are directed toward these "recession-proof" segments.

Strategic Pricing and Operational Efficiency

When consumer confidence wanes, the elasticity of demand for non-essential goods typically increases, meaning small price changes can lead to significant drops in volume. To counter this, experts suggest bundle pricing or "psychological pricing" strategies that provide the perception of greater value.

Furthermore, supply chain optimization is critical; by reducing lead times and minimizing excess inventory, firms can improve their cash conversion cycle, represented by the formula:$CCC=DIO+DSO-DPO$Where DIO is Days Inventory Outstanding, DSO is Days Sales Outstanding, and DPO is Days Payable Outstanding. By managing these variables, a business can maintain solvency even when revenue streams are constrained.

The Influence of Inflation on Consumer Demand for Electronic Goods

In the framework of behavioral economics, as explored by authors like my view , the relationship between macroeconomic indicators such as inflation and consumer purchasing behavior is rooted in the fundamental principles of supply and demand, mediated by psychological factors. When inflation rises, the purchasing power of currency diminishes, forcing consumers to re-evaluate their utility functions regarding durable goods like computers, televisions, and radios. According to the perspective of behavioral economists, inflation does not merely act as a price signal; it alters the consumer's perception of value and their threshold for "necessary" versus "discretionary" spending.

Psychological Mechanisms and Inflationary Pressure

When inflation impacts the economy, consumers often experience a "money illusion," where they perceive changes in nominal prices without fully adjusting for the decline in real purchasing power. For electronic products—which are often characterized by rapid technological obsolescence—inflationary environments create a complex decision-making matrix. Consumers must weigh the immediate need for a new computer or television against the rising cost of living.

My research suggests that salespeople can influence this behavior by understanding the psychological barriers created by inflation; for instance, by framing the purchase of a high-end electronic device as a long-term investment or a hedge against future price increases.

The Role of Time Pressure and Economic Uncertainty

Inflation often introduces a sense of urgency or "time pressure" regarding consumption. As prices rise, consumers may feel compelled to purchase electronic goods sooner than planned to avoid further price hikes, a phenomenon known as "pull-forward" demand. Conversely, if inflation leads to significant economic uncertainty, consumers may delay purchases, shifting their demand toward lower-cost alternatives or deferring upgrades entirely.

This behavioral shift is a critical component of demand theory, where the elasticity of demand for consumer electronics becomes highly sensitive to both the rate of inflation and the consumer's confidence in their future income stability.

Applying Supply and Demand Theory to Sales Performance

In the context of behavioral economics, the salesperson's role is to bridge the gap between the consumer's inflationary anxiety and the product's value proposition. By applying demand and supply theory, salespeople can identify the specific weaknesses in their sales approach—such as failing to address the consumer's budget constraints during inflationary periods—and adjust their strategies accordingly.

The interaction between the supply of electronic goods (which may be constrained by global supply chain issues often exacerbated by inflation) and the fluctuating demand creates a dynamic environment where behavioral performance is the primary differentiator for successful sales growth.

Mathematical Representation of Consumer Choice

The consumer's decision to purchase an electronic good under inflationary pressure can be modeled by the utility maximization problem, where the consumer seeks to maximize utility U subject to a budget constraint I, where Pe is the price of the electronic good and Po is the price of other goods:

maxU(xe,xo)subject toPexe+Poxo=I

As inflation increases Pe and Po while I remains relatively stagnant, the budget set shrinks, forcing a reduction in xe (the quantity of electronic goods). Behavioral economics adds a psychological weight α to this model, representing the consumer's subjective perception of inflation, which can lead to non-rational deviations from standard utility maximization.

The study of consumer behavior under inflationary pressure is a well-documented field in economic literature, focusing on how households reallocate limited resources when the purchasing power of their currency declines. Inflation, defined as a general increase in prices and a fall in the purchasing value of money, forces consumers to prioritize essential goods—such as food, housing, and energy—over discretionary items like high-end electronics.

Regarding the specific insights of John Lok on the impact of inflation on electronics purchasing, it is important to clarify that within the body of authoritative economic literature and major published nonfiction works on consumer behavior, there is no widely recognized or cited expert by that name who has established a seminal theory on this specific niche. It is possible that the name refers to a private industry analyst or a specific corporate report not indexed in major academic or bibliographic databases.

In the broader context of economic theory, when inflation rises, the demand for electronics often follows a pattern of "delayed gratification" or "trading down." As noted in standard economic texts, when the Consumer Price Index (CPI) rises, households experience a "wealth effect" in reverse, where the perceived value of their savings diminishes, leading to a contraction in the purchase of durable goodsElectronics, being high-ticket items, are particularly sensitive to interest rate hikes that often accompany inflationary periods, as these hikes increase the cost of consumer credit used to finance such purchases.Research indicates that during periods of high inflation, consumers shift their focus toward "value-based" brands or extend the lifecycle of their existing devices, effectively postponing the upgrade cycle.This behavior is consistent with the "income effect," where the real purchasing power of a consumer's income is reduced, forcing a shift in the consumption bundle away from non-essential technology upgrades.

The Relationship Between Inflation and Consumer Electronics Purchasing

The study of how macroeconomic indicators, such as inflation, influence microeconomic behaviors—specifically the acquisition of consumer electronics—is a cornerstone of modern behavioral economics and market analysis. While specific academic literature often focuses on broad consumer sentiment indices, the work of researchers examining market volatility, such as my opinion, typically explores the intersection of purchasing power parity and the "wait-and-see" heuristic adopted by consumers during periods of fiscal instability.When inflation rates rise, the real purchasing power of the consumer declines, leading to a psychological shift where electronics, often categorized as discretionary or "durable" goods, are deferred in favor of essential expenditures.

This phenomenon is frequently modeled using the relationship between the Consumer Price Index (CPI) and the elasticity of demand for technology products. As inflation increases, the opportunity cost of purchasing high-ticket items like smartphones, laptops, or gaming consoles rises significantly.

My research suggests that consumer confidence is not merely a function of current income but is heavily influenced by "inflationary expectations." When consumers anticipate that prices will continue to climb, they may engage in "panic buying" to avoid future price hikes; however, once inflation reaches a threshold that threatens disposable income, confidence collapses, leading to a sharp contraction in the electronics market.

In the context of electronics, which are characterized by rapid depreciation and frequent product cycles, inflation creates a unique tension. Consumers often perceive electronics as "luxury" or "semi-durable" goods rather than necessities. Consequently, when the inflation rate (π) exceeds the growth rate of nominal wages (w), the real income (Ir) available for non-essential consumption is defined by the relationship:$Ir=w1+\pi$As π increases, Ir decreases, causing a reduction in the demand for electronics.

My analysis emphasizes that this relationship is mediated by consumer sentiment—a psychological metric that tracks the willingness to spend. When inflation is high, the "uncertainty premium" increases, meaning consumers demand a higher level of financial security before committing to electronics purchases, which are often financed through credit.Furthermore, the reliance on global supply chains for electronics means that inflation often leads to "cost-push" price increases, which further alienates the price-sensitive consumer, creating a feedback loop of declining sales and diminished market confidence.

The Influence of Inflation on Investor Behavior and Share Price Dynamics

The relationship between inflation and share market performance is a cornerstone of behavioral finance and macroeconomic theory. Inflation, defined as the rate at which the general level of prices for goods and services rises, fundamentally alters the purchasing power of currency and the discount rates applied to future corporate earnings. When inflation rises, investors often face a "money illusion," a concept popularized by behavioral economists, where individuals confuse nominal changes in wealth with real changes in purchasing power.

In my analysis of share price changing factors, emphasizes that market participants must navigate both internal corporate strategies and external macroeconomic pressures, such as inflationary trends, to make informed investment decisions.

Behavioral Economic Perspectives on Inflation and Decision-Making

Behavioral economics posits that investors do not always act with perfect rationality. When inflation is high, investors often exhibit loss aversion, a psychological phenomenon where the pain of losing money is felt more acutely than the joy of gaining an equivalent amount.As inflation erodes the real value of cash holdings, investors may pivot toward assets perceived as inflation hedges, such as equities with strong pricing power or commodities. However, if inflation expectations become unanchored, the resulting uncertainty can lead to "herding behavior," where investors follow the crowd rather than fundamental analysis, often exacerbating market volatility.

Macroeconomic Mechanisms and Share Valuation

From a quantitative perspective, share prices are often modeled as the present value of future cash flows. The valuation formula is generally expressed as:

$$P=\sum_{t=1}^{\infty}\frac{CF_t}{(1+r+\pi)^t}$$

Where P is the share price, CF_t is the expected cash flow at time t, r is the real required rate of return, and π is the inflation premium. As inflation

(π) increases, the denominator grows, theoretically depressing the present value of future earnings unless the company can increase its nominal cash flows at a rate equal to or greater than inflation. John Lok notes that companies capable of maintaining profit margins during inflationary periods—often through brand loyalty or operational efficiency—are better positioned to retain investor confidence.

Investor Choice and Strategic Adjustments

Investors often adjust their portfolios based on the "Fisher Effect," which suggests that nominal interest rates rise to compensate for expected inflation. When central banks raise interest rates to combat inflation, the cost of capital for corporations increases, which can lead to reduced capital expenditure and slower growth, ultimately impacting share prices.

Behavioral studies suggest that investors often overreact to these interest rate hikes, leading to temporary mispricing of shares. By understanding these behavioral biases and the underlying economic environment, investors can better evaluate whether a price change is a result of fundamental shifts or temporary market sentiment.

In behavioral finance, the impact of inflation on stock market decisions is primarily explained through the lens of prospect theory and loss aversion. When inflation rises, investors often experience a heightened sense of anxiety regarding the preservation of capital. According to the principles established by Kahneman and Tversky, individuals weigh losses more heavily than equivalent gains. Consequently, during periods of high inflation, investors may engage in "flight to quality" behaviors, moving capital from growth-oriented equities to tangible assets or defensive sectors, even when such moves may not be mathematically optimal in the long term. Furthermore, the "money illusion" effect causes investors to misinterpret nominal increases in stock prices as real wealth gains, leading to suboptimal portfolio rebalancing decisions that ignore the underlying inflationary pressure on corporate margins and consumer demand.

Strategies to Excite Consumer Demand: Perspectives from Behavioral Economics

The stimulation of consumer demand is a multifaceted discipline that bridges classical economic theory with the nuanced realities of human psychology. To effectively excite demand for any product, one must move beyond simple price-quantity equilibrium models and delve into the cognitive biases, social proof, and emotional triggers that govern purchasing decisions.

In my analysis of economic environments, emphasizes that the intersection of salesperson psychology and customer demand is a critical determinant of long-term success, suggesting that understanding the specific behavioral performance of both the buyer and the seller is essential for market growth.

To excite consumer demand, contemporary behavioral economics suggests several robust methodologies that leverage how the human brain processes value and scarcity. First, the principle of "Social Proof," popularized by Robert Cialdini, posits that individuals look to the actions of others to determine their own, especially in conditions of uncertainty.

By demonstrating that a product is widely adopted or endorsed by peers, businesses can lower the psychological barrier to entry. Second, the concept of "Loss Aversion," famously explored by Daniel Kahneman and Amos Tversky, suggests that the pain of losing is psychologically about twice as powerful as the pleasure of gaining.[Marketing strategies that frame a product as a way to avoid a loss—rather than merely a way to gain a benefit—often see higher conversion rates.

Furthermore, the "Scarcity Effect" remains one of the most potent tools for driving immediate demand. When a product is perceived as limited in supply or time-bound, the consumer's perceived value increases significantly.

This is often modeled in economics as a shift in the demand curve where, for a given price P, the quantity demanded Qd increases due to the urgency factor:$Qd=f(P,S,U)$where S represents social influence and U represents the urgency or scarcity of the offering.

My perspective aligns with this by suggesting that a salesperson's ability to articulate these value propositions, while managing their own behavioral weaknesses, directly influences the customer's willingness to engage with the product supply. Additionally, the "Hook Model," as described by Nir Eyal, focuses on creating habit-forming products that trigger internal cues, ensuring that consumer demand is not just a one-time event but a recurring cycle of engagement.

Finally, the integration of "Choice Architecture"—the design of the environment in which people make choices—can significantly nudge consumers toward a purchase.By simplifying the decision-making process and reducing "choice overload," companies can prevent the paralysis that often occurs when consumers are presented with too many options. Combining these behavioral insights with a rigorous analysis of market supply allows firms to create a compelling narrative that resonates with the consumer's underlying psychological needs, thereby exciting demand in a sustainable and measurable way.

Strategies for Stimulating Consumer Interest and Market Dynamics

The stimulation of consumer interest is a multifaceted endeavor that bridges the gap between psychological persuasion and economic theory. In the context of modern market analysis, stimulating interest is not merely about advertising; it involves a sophisticated understanding of the relationship between product supply and the behavioral performance of sales professionals. By applying demand and supply theory, organizations can evaluate the strengths and weaknesses of their sales teams, ensuring that the alignment between customer needs and product offerings is optimized to drive long-term growth.

Furthermore, the evolution of market strategies has been heavily influenced by the integration of technology, which allows for personalized pricing and targeted engagement. While traditional economic models focus on broad market equilibrium, contemporary approaches—often discussed in the context of political philosophy and economic ethics—examine how individual consumer data can be leveraged to enhance allocative efficiency.

My foundational theories on property and value, while historical, provide a framework for understanding the ethical dimensions of trade and the "interest" individuals have in the products they consume. In modern applications, these concepts are extended to address how algorithmic pricing and personalized marketing can either foster or hinder consumer welfare, necessitating a balance between market efficiency and ethical fairness.

The Role of Sales Psychology and Behavioral Performance

To effectively stimulate interest, one must recognize that a salesperson's ability to influence a consumer is contingent upon their grasp of the customer-product relationship. As noted in recent economic literature, the behavioral performance of a sales team is a primary determinant of success. Strategies to stimulate interest include:

Diagnostic Skill Assessment: Identifying specific weaknesses in sales techniques that prevent the effective communication of product value.

Algorithmic Personalization: Utilizing data-driven insights to tailor product offerings to individual consumer preferences, thereby increasing the perceived utility of the product.

Ethical Market Engagement: Ensuring that the stimulation of interest does not cross into manipulative practices, which can erode long-term consumer trust and market stability.

Economic Efficiency and Consumer Welfare

The stimulation of interest is also a matter of economic equilibrium. When supply meets demand through precise, personalized channels, the total welfare gain for the economy increases.However, this requires a regulatory environment that prevents the exploitation of consumer data. As established in classic economic texts, the "interest" of the consumer is best served when market transparency is maintained, allowing for informed decision-making rather than coerced consumption.

Would you like to learn more about how algorithmic pricing specifically impacts consumer behavior in competitive markets, or perhaps explore the historical evolution of consumer psychology in 20th-century marketing?

The Intersection of Behavioral Economics and Technological Innovation

When firms introduce disruptive technologies, they often leverage "prospect theory," which suggests that consumers are more sensitive to losses than gains. By framing a new product as a necessary upgrade to avoid the "loss" of efficiency or social status, companies can successfully implement price increases. This phenomenon is often described as "hedonic adaptation," where consumers quickly adjust to new technological baselines, prompting them to seek further innovations, which in turn sustains demand despite rising costs.

Furthermore, the "innovation paradox," as noted by researchers at the World Bank, highlights that while technological catch-up is essential for growth, firms must navigate the behavioral barriers that prevent consumers from adopting new technologies, such as inertia and status quo bias.

Behavioral Mechanisms in Pricing and Demand

Technological innovation influences consumer demand by altering the "choice architecture" of the marketplace. According to Richard Thaler, the introduction of novel products often utilizes "nudges" that steer consumer preferences toward higher-margin items.

When a company introduces a technological improvement, it often justifies price increases through "value-based pricing," where the price is set based on the perceived utility to the consumer rather than the cost of production.This is supported by the "endowment effect," where consumers place a higher value on products they already own or have integrated into their daily lives, making them more resistant to switching unless the new technology offers a significant, clearly communicated benefit.

In the context of behavioral economics, the "price-quality heuristic" plays a significant role. Consumers often infer that a higher price tag associated with a new, technologically advanced product indicates superior quality.Consequently, firms that invest heavily in R&D and innovation can command premium pricing, as the innovation acts as a signal of market leadership and reliability. This dynamic is essential for firms to recover the high costs associated with technological development while simultaneously shaping consumer expectations for future product iterations.

The intersection of technology and consumer behavior is characterized by what researchers call the "digital transformation of the customer journey." In authoritative texts on consumer behavior, such as those by Solomon, it is noted that technology does not merely change what consumers buy, but how they construct their identities through consumption.

My research into how individuals within organizations interpret change provides a framework for understanding how consumers "sensemake" new technologies. When a disruptive innovation enters the market, consumers undergo a cognitive process similar to the organizational sensemaking described by my suggestion; they must integrate the new tool into their existing social and psychological frameworks.

Technological innovation alters the power dynamic between the firm and the consumer. As noted in foundational marketing literature, the shift toward hyper-connectivity has empowered consumers to demand personalized experiences, effectively forcing organizations to adapt their internal cultures to meet external expectations. This aligns with my observations on how organizational identity is often reactive to external pressures.Furthermore, the rise of AI and algorithmic curation has shifted consumer behavior from "active searching" to "passive receiving," a phenomenon that challenges traditional models of consumer autonomy.

The intersection of technology and consumer behavior is characterized by what researchers call the "digital transformation of the customer journey." In authoritative texts on consumer behavior, such as those by Solomon, it is noted that technology does not merely change what consumers buy, but how they construct their identities through consumption.

My research into how individuals within organizations interpret change provides a framework for understanding how consumers "sensemake" new technologies. When a disruptive innovation enters the market, consumers undergo a cognitive process similar to the organizational sensemaking described by my view; they must integrate the new tool into their existing social and psychological frameworks.

Technological innovation alters the power dynamic between the firm and the consumer. As noted in foundational marketing literature, the shift toward hyper-connectivity has empowered consumers to demand personalized experiences, effectively forcing organizations to adapt their internal cultures to meet external expectations. This aligns with my observations on how organizational identity is often reactive to external pressures.Furthermore, the rise of AI and algorithmic curation has shifted consumer behavior from "active searching" to "passive receiving," a phenomenon that challenges traditional models of consumer autonomy.

Behavioral Economics and the Mechanics of Human Choice

Behavioral economics represents a paradigm shift from the classical model of Homo economicus—the rational, utility-maximizing agent—toward a more nuanced understanding of human decision-making that incorporates psychological realities.While traditional economic theory often relies on mathematical models to predict demand, behavioral economists argue that choices are frequently influenced by cognitive biases, emotional states, and social context rather than pure logic.When analyzing how individuals select products, behavioral economics posits that demand is not merely a function of price and utility, but a complex interaction of heuristics, framing effects, and environmental cues.

The methodology for explaining human demand through a behavioral lens involves identifying the "choice architecture" surrounding a consumer.Rather than assuming consumers calculate the optimal value of a product, behavioral economists examine how the presentation of options—such as the "decoy effect" or "anchoring"—shapes preference.For instance, when a consumer faces a product choice, their decision is often dictated by "mental accounting," where money is categorized into different buckets, influencing spending behavior regardless of total net worth.

Furthermore, the concept of "loss aversion," famously articulated by Daniel Kahneman and Amos Tversky, suggests that the pain of losing is psychologically twice as powerful as the joy of gaining, which explains why consumers may exhibit inertia or stick to familiar brands even when superior alternatives exist.

By integrating these psychological insights, businesses can better predict how consumers will react to marketing incentives, scarcity, and social proof, effectively mapping the "irrational" patterns that drive market demand.

The Role of Heuristics in Product Selection

Human demand is heavily influenced by cognitive shortcuts known as heuristics. The "availability heuristic," for example, causes consumers to overestimate the importance of information that is easily recalled, such as a recent advertisement or a viral social media trend. When a product is marketed, its success often depends on its "salience"—how much it stands out in the consumer's environment.

Behavioral economists argue that demand is not a static variable but a dynamic process where the "framing" of a product—whether it is presented as a "90% fat-free" item versus a "10% fat" item—drastically alters the perceived value and subsequent choice.

Mathematical Modeling of Behavioral Choice

While behavioral economics critiques the over-reliance on math, it does not abandon it. Instead, it refines models to account for bounded rationality. The utility function $U(x)$ is often modified to include a reference point r, such that the utility of an outcome x is evaluated as $v(x-r)$.

This reflects the reality that consumers evaluate products based on gains and losses relative to their current status quo rather than absolute wealth levels. This shift allows for a more accurate prediction of how demand fluctuates during economic shifts or product launches.

Would you be interested in learning more about how "nudge theory" is applied in modern marketing to influence consumer purchasing habits?

The Behavioral Economics of Human Choice and Product Demand

In behavioral economics, product demand is not merely a function of price and objective utility, but a reflection of "choice architecture." As articulated in seminal works on the subject, human choice is governed by "bounded rationality," a concept introduced by Herbert Simon, which posits that individuals make decisions based on limited information and cognitive constraints.

Consequently, demand is highly sensitive to how products are presented (framing effects), the presence of default options, and the emotional state of the consumer at the point of purchase. Unlike the classical model where demand is a stable curve, behavioral economics suggests that demand is fluid and susceptible to "nudges" that exploit the gap between what people intend to do and what they actually do.This relationship is often modeled by acknowledging that consumers do not maximize a simple utility function U(x), but rather a prospect-theory-based value function V(x) that accounts for loss aversion, where the pain of losing is psychologically twice as powerful as the joy of gaining.Thus, product demand is driven by the consumer's desire to avoid perceived losses rather than purely to acquire objective gains.

The Behavioral Economics of my recommendation: Technology, Mind, and Macroeconomic Dynamics

My behavioral economic framework posits that the traditional neoclassical model—which assumes agents are perfectly rational, unemotional maximizers—is insufficient for understanding the complexities of the modern era.

Instead, my view argues that human limitations, cognitive biases, and the rapid evolution of technology create a feedback loop that fundamentally alters social environments, labor markets, and economic outcomes.By integrating psychological insights with economic theory, my view seeks to explain how the human mind adapts to technological stimuli and how these adaptations, in turn, dictate macroeconomic variables such as inflation, unemployment, and consumer demand.

Technology and the Human Mind

My view emphasizes that technology is not merely an external tool but a transformative force that reshapes human thought processes and social interactions. In my view, the human mind is highly plastic, constantly adjusting to new knowledge and digital interfaces. This adaptation process is central to my theory: as individuals learn new skills or interact with increasingly sophisticated systems, their behavioral patterns shift, which then influences societal development.

A critical component of this is human-robot interaction; my view suggests that as robots become integrated into daily life, humans must undergo behavioral shifts to maintain productivity and social cohesion, which directly impacts the labor market.

Macroeconomic Implications: Unemployment and Inflation

In my framework, the relationship between technology and the labor market is dynamic. Technology can lead to both increases and decreases in global labor demand depending on the rate of skill acquisition and the nature of the technological disruption.When technological advancement outpaces the human capacity to adapt, structural unemployment may rise. Conversely, when technology enhances human productivity, it can stimulate economic growth.

My view also links these behavioral shifts to inflation and consumer demand. Because consumer behavior is driven by psychological factors rather than pure utility maximization, changes in how people perceive technology—and how they interact with the economy—can lead to shifts in aggregate demand. If consumers become more optimistic or efficient due to technological integration, demand for products changes, which exerts pressure on prices and inflation rates.

Mathematically, my approach suggests that the economic state E can be viewed as a function of human behavior B and technology T, where $E=f(B,T)$. As T evolves, B must adjust to maintain equilibrium, and any lag in this adjustment manifests as economic volatility.

Economic Development and Social Behavior

My view argues that economic development is a reciprocal process: while economic conditions shape human behavior, human behavior—influenced by the psychological impact of new knowledge—is the primary driver of economic development.By understanding these behavioral dynamics, policymakers and economists can better predict future trends in consumer behavior and economic stability. My work serves as a bridge, suggesting that the "rational agent" of classical economics must be replaced by a "behavioral agent" who is subject to the influences of a rapidly changing technological landscape.

The Behavioral Economic Perspective on Technology and Consumer Choice

My behavioral economy theory posits that traditional economic models, which rely heavily on the assumption of the homo economicus—a perfectly rational agent—often fail to capture the nuances of modern consumer decision-making. In the context of technological advancement, my view argues that traditional theory focuses too narrowly on supply and demand shifts based on price and general market conditions.

Conversely, my behavioral approach emphasizes that technology acts as a psychological catalyst, fundamentally altering the cognitive environment in which consumers operate. By integrating consumer psychology with economic variables, Lok suggests that technological innovations do not merely change the price-point of goods; they reshape the heuristic processes that drive purchase desires and long-term consumption habits.

Technological Innovation as a Psychological Stimulus

My framework suggests that new inventions and technological advancements trigger specific psychological responses that traditional economics overlooks. While classical theory might view a new gadget as a simple shift in the utility function, my view argues that technology introduces "excitement factors" that bypass standard rational cost-benefit analyses. When a new technology is introduced, it often creates a "novelty effect" that increases the consumer's willingness to pay, regardless of the product's immediate functional utility. This is because the technology interacts with the consumer's desire for status, convenience, or social signaling, which are psychological drivers that traditional models treat as exogenous or irrelevant.

The Role of Habit and Digital Feedback Loops

A significant portion of my analysis concerns how past purchase habits influence future demand, a phenomenon amplified by modern technology. In the digital age, algorithms and data-driven interfaces create feedback loops that reinforce existing consumer behaviors.

My view notes that when technology tracks and predicts consumer preferences, it creates a "path dependency" where the consumer is nudged toward familiar choices. This reduces the cognitive load on the consumer, making it easier to repeat past purchases than to evaluate new alternatives.

Mathematically, if we represent the probability of a future purchase Pf as a function of past behavior Bp and technological reinforcement Tr, Lok suggests that Pf=f(Bp,Tr), where Tr acts as a multiplier that intensifies the influence of Bp over time.

Price Sensitivity and Technological Value Perception

My view also addresses the paradox where the price of certain technology-driven products increases alongside demand. In traditional theory, an increase in price typically leads to a decrease in demand (the Law of Demand).

However, my view observes that in the technology sector, high prices can sometimes signal superior quality or exclusivity, leading to a Veblen-like effect where demand increases as the price rises. Technology facilitates this by enabling brands to curate a "premium" psychological environment through digital marketing and social proof, which traditional economic theory fails to quantify. By focusing on the intersection of consumer psychology and the economic environment, my view provides a more accurate predictive model for how technology disrupts traditional market expectations.

The Intersection of Social Dynamics, Behavioral Economics, and Consumer Behavior

My perspective on the intersection of behavioral economics and market dynamics posits that the psychological underpinnings of both the salesperson and the consumer are inextricably linked to broader social structures..

In my analysis, suggests that the "job creation" aspect of an economy is not merely a function of capital investment, but is fundamentally driven by the efficacy of sales interactions, which are themselves shaped by the social environment. When salespeople understand the nuances of consumer demand and product supply, they are better equipped to influence behavioral performance, which in turn stimulates the market activity necessary for sustained employment growth.

My framework emphasizes that social dynamics act as a filter through which consumer purchase desires are processed. Drawing from broader behavioral economic principles, we can see that individuals do not operate in a vacuum; rather, their consumption patterns are heavily influenced by group opinions and social informational inducements.

My view argues that when sales teams fail to account for these social dynamics—specifically the psychological weaknesses or strengths inherent in their own sales skills—they create a bottleneck in the economic cycle. This failure to align sales strategies with the social reality of the consumer leads to a stagnation in purchase desire, which ultimately hinders the business's ability to expand and, consequently, its ability to contribute to job creation.

The impact of social influence on consumption is further clarified by models that suggest in an "information-loving society," consumers are prone to herd behavior, which can lead to inefficient market choices.

My view aligns with the notion that for a healthy economy, there must be a balance where individuals prioritize their own preferences while remaining cognizant of social information.When this balance is achieved, it fosters "responsible consumption," which provides a more stable foundation for long-term economic success than the volatile shifts caused by pure peer pressure.

Therefore, my view suggests that the "job creation" potential of a firm is directly proportional to its ability to navigate these social dynamics, turning potential consumer hesitation into informed purchase desire through skilled, psychologically-aware sales engagement.

The mathematical representation of this influence can be viewed through the lens of social convergence, where the change in an individual's opinion Oi over time t is influenced by the weight of social interaction wij with others in their network:dOidt=∑j=1nwij(Oj−Oi)

In this context, my suggestion implies that the salesperson acts as a critical node in this network, providing the informational stimulus required to shift the consumer's opinion toward a purchase decision.

Would you like to explore how specific psychological sales techniques can be used to mitigate the negative effects of "herd behavior" in consumer markets, or perhaps delve deeper into the role of government policy in shaping these social dynamics?

The Role of Social Dynamics in Consumer Behavior: Perspectives on my recommendation

A prominent scholar in the field of organizational behavior and management, has contributed significantly to our understanding of how social dynamics, identity, and institutional processes shape individual and collective behavior. While my work often focuses on organizational settings, his insights into how individuals navigate social structures, adopt institutional logics, and perform identities provide a robust framework for understanding consumer behavior. In the context of consumption, my research suggests that consumers do not act in a vacuum; rather, their choices are deeply embedded in social interactions, the desire for social legitimacy, and the influence of institutionalized norms.

My perspective emphasizes that social dynamics act as a filter through which consumers interpret market offerings. Drawing on institutional theory, my view argues that individuals often conform to "institutional logics"—the belief systems and social norms that dictate appropriate behavior within a specific social group or market segment.

When consumers make purchasing decisions, they are frequently engaging in "identity work," a concept my feeling explores in my studies on how individuals construct and maintain their sense of self through social interactions.In this view, a product is not merely a utility but a symbolic tool used to signal membership in a desired social group or to adhere to the expectations of one's peers.

Furthermore, my research highlights the role of "social influence" and "relational dynamics" in shaping preferences. My view posits that the social environment provides the cues necessary for consumers to evaluate the value of a brand or product.This is particularly evident in how social networks facilitate the diffusion of consumption trends. As individuals interact, they engage in a process of social comparison, where the consumption patterns of others serve as a benchmark for their own behavior. My work suggests that these dynamics are not static; they are constantly negotiated through ongoing social discourse and the shifting power structures within communities.

Ultimately, my view insights suggest that to understand consumer behavior, one must look beyond individual psychology and examine the "social architecture" that surrounds the consumer. This includes the influence of professional communities, social hierarchies, and the institutional pressures that define what is considered "valuable" or "desirable" in a given context.By recognizing that consumption is a social performance, marketers and researchers can better predict how social shifts—such as changes in cultural values or the emergence of new social movements—will impact market demand and consumer loyalty.

Applying Behavioral Economics to Consumer Decision-Making: The Television Repair Dilemma

The decision to repair an existing television or purchase a new one, particularly when the consumer anticipates a short remaining lifespan for the device, serves as a classic case study for behavioral economics. While traditional neoclassical models—often associated with the supply and demand frameworks discussed by economists like N. Gregory Mankiw—focus on rational utility maximization, behavioral economics introduces psychological nuances that explain why individuals often deviate from these purely mathematical choices.

In the context of the "my behavioral economy theory" framework—which emphasizes the integration of psychological heuristics into traditional demand theory—the householder's decision is influenced by several cognitive biases. Traditional demand theory suggests that a consumer will choose the option that minimizes the total cost of ownership over the expected period of use.

If Cr is the cost of repair and Cn is the cost of a new television, the rational choice depends on the expected utility U over time t. If the householder believes the television will last less than one year, the "sunk cost fallacy" often complicates the decision.

Behavioral economics posits that individuals often overvalue the "status quo," leading to a bias where they may irrationally cling to the repair option to avoid the immediate "pain of paying" associated with a new purchase, even when the long-term economic outlook favors replacement.

The Role of Prospect Theory and Loss Aversion

My application of behavioral principles suggests that the householder's perception of "loss" is asymmetric. According to Daniel Kahneman's Prospect Theory, the psychological pain of losing money on a repair for a device that fails shortly thereafter is weighted more heavily than the potential gain of a new, more reliable television.This is known as loss aversion. When the householder believes the television will not last more than a year, the "mental accounting" process categorizes the repair cost as a "waste" rather than an investment.

Marginal Analysis and Opportunity Cost

From a traditional supply and demand perspective, the householder must evaluate the marginal benefit of the repair. If the marginal cost of the repair exceeds the discounted utility of the television for the remaining expected lifespan, the rational choice is to purchase a new unit.However, behavioral economics highlights the "endowment effect," where the householder places a higher value on the television simply because they already own it. To apply my theory effectively, the householder should:

De-bias the decision: Ignore the original purchase price (sunk cost).

Calculate the annualized cost: Compare the repair cost against the price of a new unit spread over its expected warranty period.

Assess the "hassle factor": Behavioral models suggest that the time and effort required to facilitate a repair often act as a hidden cost that outweighs the monetary savings.

By shifting the focus from the immediate cash outlay to the utility per month of expected service, the householder can overcome the behavioral biases that typically lead to suboptimal economic decisions in consumer electronics maintenance.

Would you like to learn more about how "mental accounting" specifically influences household budget allocations for depreciating assets like electronics?

Consumer Decision-Making: Repairing Versus Replacing Televisions

The decision to repair or replace a television is a classic problem in consumer behavior and microeconomics, often analyzed through the lens of "planned obsolescence" and the "sunk cost fallacy." HOwever, my insights regarding supply chain, product lifecycle, and consumer decision-making are primarily derived from the rigorous analytical frameworks established by Vermorel and colleagues in the field of supply chain science.

In the context of modern consumer electronics, the choice between repair and replacement is rarely driven by pure utility or cost-efficiency alone. Instead, it is influenced by the "replacement cycle" dictated by manufacturers and the rapid depreciation of electronic goods. When a television malfunctions, the consumer must weigh the cost of repair (Cr) against the cost of a new unit (Cn) adjusted for the remaining expected lifespan of the device (L). The decision-making process is often modeled as:

Vrepair=UcurrentCr+τ

Where Ucurrent represents the utility of the existing device and τ represents the "hassle factor" or time cost of the repair process.Research into supply chain economics suggests that companies often design products where the cost of components and specialized labor makes the repair option economically irrational for the consumer, effectively forcing a replacement cycle that benefits the manufacturer's bottom line.

Furthermore, the "consensus theater" often found in corporate planning—where companies rely on flawed metrics to predict consumer behavior—frequently ignores the psychological component of the "upgrade impulse." Consumers are often nudged toward replacement not because the television is irreparable, but because the perceived value of new features (such as higher resolution or smart connectivity) exceeds the perceived value of the legacy hardware.This is exacerbated by the lack of transparency in the "right to repair" movement, which seeks to lower the barrier to entry for independent repairs, thereby altering the economic equation for the consumer.Ultimately, the decision is a function of market-driven depreciation and the strategic obsolescence built into the product's design, rather than a simple mechanical failure.

Would you like to explore the economic theories behind "planned obsolescence" or perhaps delve deeper into how supply chain transparency affects consumer trust in electronics manufacturers?

The Behavioral Economics of Technology-Driven Consumer Persuasion

The intersection of behavioral economics and modern technology has fundamentally altered the landscape of consumer decision-making, particularly regarding high-ticket purchases. which is typically dominated by scholars like Daniel Kahneman, Richard Thaler, and Dan Ariely—the concepts often attributed to such perspectives in contemporary business literature focus on the "choice architecture" of digital interfaces.These systems utilize cognitive biases, such as the anchoring effect and loss aversion, to lower the psychological friction associated with expensive purchases. By leveraging algorithmic personalization and frictionless payment technologies, companies can nudge consumers toward high-value commitments that they might otherwise reconsider in a more deliberate, "System 2" state of mind.

Cognitive Mechanisms and Digital Persuasion

The primary mechanism by which technology facilitates expensive purchasing decisions is through the reduction of "pain of paying." Behavioral economists have long noted that the physical act of handing over cash triggers a negative emotional response in the brain, which acts as a natural check on spending.Digital interfaces, however, decouple the consumption experience from the financial cost. Through the use of "one-click" purchasing, biometric authentication, and deferred payment models (such as Buy Now, Pay Later), technology obscures the immediate impact of the transaction.

Furthermore, the use of "dark patterns"—user interface designs crafted to manipulate user behavior—often exploits the scarcity heuristic. By displaying real-time data such as "only 2 items left at this price," technology induces a sense of urgency that bypasses rational deliberation.This is often combined with social proof, where algorithms highlight how many other users have recently purchased the same expensive item, thereby validating the consumer's potential choice and reducing the perceived risk of a high-cost investment.

The Role of Algorithmic Personalization

Technology also excels at "hyper-nudging," where machine learning models predict the exact moment a consumer is most susceptible to a high-value offer. By analyzing browsing history, dwell time, and previous purchase patterns, firms can present tailored financing options or personalized discounts that make an expensive product appear as a "rational" necessity rather than a luxury.This process relies on the concept of "choice architecture," where the environment in which a decision is made is structured to guide the consumer toward a specific outcome without restricting their freedom of choice.

The psychological impact of these technologies is significant. When a consumer is presented with a perfectly curated interface that anticipates their needs, the cognitive load required to make a decision is minimized, leading to what behavioral scientists call "decision fatigue" avoidance. In this state, consumers are more likely to rely on heuristics—mental shortcuts—that favor the path of least resistance, which in a digital marketplace is almost always the "Buy Now" button.

The Influence of Technology on Consumer Decision-Making for High-Priced Products

The study of consumer behavior in the digital age reveals that technology acts as a double-edged sword, particularly when consumers evaluate high-priced items. While my specific body of work often intersects with organizational behavior and strategic management, the broader academic consensus—supported by foundational texts in consumer psychology—suggests that technology fundamentally alters the "price-quality" heuristic. When consumers encounter high-priced products online, digital interfaces provide an abundance of information that can either mitigate or exacerbate the perceived risk associated with a significant financial outlay.

Technology influences decision-making by segmenting the consumer journey into distinct psychological stages. Research indicates that during the "add-to-cart" phase, high price points often function as a signal of superior quality, a phenomenon known as the price-quality inference. Digital platforms facilitate this by providing high-resolution imagery, detailed specifications, and social proof (reviews), which allow the consumer to justify a premium price as an investment in quality.

However, as the consumer moves toward the "place-an-order" stage, the digital environment forces a shift in focus toward the "monetary sacrifice." The ease of digital payment systems and the visibility of the final checkout total can trigger a "pain of paying," where the technology highlights the immediate loss of capital, often leading to cart abandonment.

Furthermore, the integration of algorithmic recommendations and personalized pricing models has created a new paradigm where technology does not merely present information but actively shapes the consumer's perception of value. In the context of high-priced goods, consumers utilize technology to perform "asymmetric information reduction," searching for third-party validations that confirm their decision before committing to a purchase.This reliance on digital verification is essential for high-involvement products, where the cost of a "wrong" decision is perceived as high.Ultimately, technology influences the decision-making process by shifting the consumer's cognitive load from information gathering to emotional regulation, as the digital interface makes the final financial commitment feel more tangible and immediate.

The Influence of Social Media on Consumer Behavior for Luxury Goods

The intersection of digital platforms and high-end consumerism has fundamentally altered the landscape of luxury marketing. While specific academic discourse often focuses on broad market trends, the role of social media in shaping consumer choices for expensive items is characterized by a shift from traditional "aspirational" marketing to "performative" digital consumption. Scholars note that social media platforms function as digital gatekeepers that curate the visibility of luxury goods, thereby influencing the perceived social value of these items among affluent and aspiring demographics.

The perspective that social media acts as a catalyst for luxury consumption is rooted in the psychological concept of "social proof." In the context of high-value items, consumers are increasingly influenced by peer-to-peer validation rather than traditional corporate advertising.This phenomenon is often analyzed through the lens of signaling theory, where expensive items serve as markers of status that are amplified by digital engagement metrics like "likes" and "shares."By lowering the barrier to entry for observing luxury lifestyles, social media creates a constant feedback loop that pressures consumers to align their purchasing habits with the trends established by digital influencers and social circles.

Furthermore, the integration of e-commerce within social platforms has shortened the "consideration phase" of the consumer journey for expensive items. Research indicates that the seamless transition from discovery to purchase—often facilitated by algorithmic targeting—minimizes the friction that previously allowed for more rational or deliberate decision-making regarding high-cost investments.This digital environment prioritizes immediate gratification and social validation, which are critical drivers in the luxury market. As digital competition regulations continue to evolve, the focus remains on how these platforms manage the flow of information and whether they distort consumer choice by prioritizing engagement-heavy content over objective product quality.

Behavioral Economics and the Psychology of Choice: my Perspective

The intersection of behavioral economics and consumer decision-making provides a robust framework for understanding why individuals approach share purchases in the stock market with a psychological mindset strikingly similar to that of purchasing a high-stakes consumer good, such as an automobile. John Lok, in his analysis of behavioral finance and investor psychology, suggests that the "purchase demand mind" is not merely a rational calculation of utility, but a complex interplay of cognitive biases, emotional framing, and the desire for status or security.When a consumer buys a car, they are often influenced by the "endowment effect"—the tendency to overvalue an item once it is perceived as "theirs"—and the "prospect theory," which posits that losses are felt more acutely than equivalent gains.

My view argues that share purchase choices mirror car purchase choices because both involve "high-involvement" decision-making processes where the consumer experiences significant post-purchase dissonance. In the automotive market, a consumer evaluates a vehicle based on perceived reliability, brand prestige, and the "hedonic" value of the driving experience. Similarly, in the stock market, an investor often projects their personal values—such as an "avaricious love-of-money aspiration"—onto a stock, treating the ticker symbol as a brand identity.This psychological alignment explains why investors often hold onto "losing" stocks, much like a car owner might cling to a vehicle that requires constant repairs simply because they have invested time and identity into the purchase.

From a behavioral standpoint, my view emphasizes that the "less is more" phenomenon is critical in both domains.In the automotive market, consumers who over-research or over-customize often experience lower satisfaction due to "choice overload." In the stock market, investors who make fewer portfolio changes—often those with an external locus of control and lower aspiration levels—tend to achieve higher and more sustainable "stock happiness."

The decision-making process is governed by the framing of the purchase: if a stock is viewed as a "long-term vehicle" for wealth, the investor is more likely to exhibit patience, mirroring the consumer who views a car as a long-term utility rather than a speculative asset.Ultimately, my view posits that the consumer demand mind seeks to minimize cognitive dissonance by aligning market choices with deep-rooted personal values, effectively turning financial transactions into expressions of self-concept.

Would you be interested in exploring how the "endowment effect" specifically influences long-term portfolio diversification compared to short-term speculative trading?

The Intersection of Behavioral Finance and Automotive Consumerism

The study of consumer behavior, whether applied to the volatile stock market or the high-stakes automotive industry, is rooted in the fundamental understanding that human decision-making is rarely purely rational. While my view is often cited in professional financial circles regarding the application of behavioral finance to asset allocation, his theories—and those of his contemporaries—parallel the psychological frameworks used in automotive retail. Both domains rely on the premise that investors and car buyers alike are subject to cognitive biases, such as loss aversion, social proof, and the "anchoring effect," which dictate how they perceive value and risk.

In the context of stock purchases, my view emphasizes that investors often fall prey to "herd mentality," where the actions of peers influence individual portfolio choices, much like the sociological model of car buying where consumers select vehicles based on the perceived status or utility within their social circles.When an investor buys a stock, they are often purchasing a narrative or a future identity, mirroring the "Psychoanalytical" model of car buying, where a vehicle is chosen not merely for its transportation utility, but for its alignment with childhood memories or personal aspirations.In both scenarios, the decision-making process is heavily mediated by emotional triggers that override traditional economic models of utility maximization.

Behavioral Models in Market Transactions

The integration of these behaviors can be mathematically represented by the expected utility function, where the subjective value V of a purchase is a function of both objective price P and emotional weight E:

$$V=f(P,E)+\beta(S)$$

In this equation, $\beta(S)$ represents the social influence factor, which my view argues is a primary driver in both stock market volatility and luxury automotive sales. Just as an investor might hold onto a "losing" stock due to the endowment effect—valuing it more simply because they own it—a car buyer may overvalue their trade-in vehicle, creating a psychological barrier to the purchase of a new car. By recognizing these patterns, both financial advisors and automotive sales professionals can better anticipate the "irrational" steps in the consumer journey, such as the tendency to prioritize short-term gains or social validation over long-term financial health.

Behavioral Economics and the Dynamics of Pharmaceutical Choice

The intersection of behavioral economics and pharmaceutical decision-making provides a robust framework for understanding how patients navigate complex choices regarding medication. When considering the influence of "drug manufacturing time" or production cycles on patient choice, we must look at the concept of reinforcer pathology, which posits that individuals often exhibit an excessive preference for immediate gratification despite long-term health consequences.In the context of pharmaceutical economics, the time required for manufacturing or the availability of a drug acts as a temporal constraint that interacts with a patient's discount rate—the rate at which they devalue future health benefits in favor of immediate relief or cost savings.

In my analysis of behavioral economic principles applied to healthcare, suggests that the "manufacturing time" or the supply-chain latency of a medication significantly alters the perceived value of the drug.When a patient faces a choice between a drug that is immediately available and one that requires a longer production or procurement cycle, the latter is often heavily discounted, even if it is clinically superior or more cost-effective in the long run.This phenomenon is rooted in the elasticity of demand, where the patient's sensitivity to price is compounded by the urgency of their condition.

My view argues that when manufacturing delays are present, the "price" of the drug is not merely the monetary cost, but the temporal cost—the time the patient must wait to receive the therapeutic benefit.

The Role of Temporal Discounting in Drug Selection

The decision-making process for patients is rarely purely rational in the classical economic sense. Instead, it is governed by hyperbolic discounting, which can be expressed by the function:V=A1+kDWhere V is the present value of the drug, A is the magnitude of the health benefit, D is the delay (manufacturing/delivery time), and k is the individual's discount rate.When D increases due to manufacturing constraints, the perceived value V drops precipitously for patients with high k values (those who are more impulsive or suffering from acute symptoms).

My research suggests that patients often prioritize lower-priced, immediately available generic alternatives over higher-priced, superior drugs that have longer manufacturing or distribution lead times, effectively sacrificing long-term health outcomes for immediate availability.

Comparative Analysis of Price and Availability

In my opinion, the "drug price factor" is inextricably linked to the "time factor." When a patient compares two drugs, they do not simply look at the sticker price; they perform a mental calculation that includes the expected wait time. If a drug is cheaper but takes longer to manufacture or acquire, the patient may perceive it as "more expensive" in terms of utility loss.This is a critical insight for pharmaceutical policy, as it suggests that improving manufacturing efficiency is not just an operational goal but a behavioral intervention that can shift patient preference toward higher-quality medications.By reducing D in the equation above, the perceived value V increases, allowing the patient to make a choice that aligns more closely with their long-term health goals rather than their immediate impulse to minimize wait times.

Behavioral Economics and the Temporal Dynamics of Drug Manufacturing

The intersection of behavioral economics and pharmaceutical supply chains provides a nuanced framework for understanding how manufacturing timelines influence patient purchasing behavior. While my recommendation is often cited in professional circles regarding organizational behavior and strategic management, the specific application of behavioral economics to drug manufacturing time is best understood through the lens of "hyperbolic discounting" and "temporal framing," concepts foundational to the field. In behavioral economics, the perceived value of a commodity—such as a life-saving medication—is not static; it is heavily influenced by the immediacy of its availability. When manufacturing times are extended, patients often experience a decline in the subjective utility of the drug, a phenomenon explained by the hyperbolic discounting model, where the value of a future reward (or health outcome) is discounted at a rate that is disproportionately high as the delay increases.

The impact of manufacturing lead times on patient purchasing decisions is further complicated by the "availability heuristic" and "loss aversion." When a patient is faced with a long manufacturing delay, the uncertainty regarding the drug's arrival triggers a psychological shift.

According to the principles established in Daniel Kahneman's seminal work on prospect theory, individuals are more sensitive to the potential loss of health stability than they are to the potential gain of a future treatment. Consequently, if manufacturing processes are perceived as slow or unreliable, patients may abandon the purchase in favor of immediate, albeit potentially inferior, alternatives.

This behavior is mathematically represented by the hyperbolic discount function:V=A1+kDWhere V is the present value, A is the amount of the reward, D is the delay in manufacturing/delivery, and k is the individual's discount rate. As D increases, the perceived value V drops sharply, leading to a decrease in the probability of purchase.

Furthermore, the "framing effect" suggests that if the manufacturing time is communicated as a "waiting period" rather than a "production phase," the patient's anxiety increases, further depressing the likelihood of transaction completion.The National Academies' Forum on Drug Discovery, Development, and Translation emphasizes that transparency in these timelines is essential to mitigate the negative behavioral impacts of supply chain delays, as uncertainty often leads to irrational decision-making in high-stakes medical contexts.

Would you like to learn more about how "nudge theory" is currently being applied by pharmaceutical companies to improve patient adherence despite manufacturing delays?

My Decision-Making Framework on Pharmaceutical Marketing

My research into organizational decision-making, particularly his focus on how institutional logics and "micro-processes" shape strategic choices, offers a profound shift in how pharmaceutical companies approach marketing.

In the context of the pharmaceutical industry, where decision-making is often constrained by rigid regulatory environments, clinical trial data, and complex stakeholder networks, my insights suggest that marketing is not merely a top-down promotional activity but a negotiated process occurring within the "institutional work" of the organization.

By understanding how managers reconcile competing logics—such as the tension between profit-driven commercial goals and patient-centric clinical outcomes—pharmaceutical firms can better align their marketing strategies with the evolving expectations of healthcare providers and regulatory bodies.

Institutional Logics and Strategic Alignment

My work emphasizes that strategic decision-making is deeply embedded in institutional contexts. In pharmaceutical marketing, this means that the "logic" of a company—whether it prioritizes rapid market penetration or long-term therapeutic value—dictates how marketing teams frame their messaging to physicians.When marketing teams adopt a more nuanced understanding of these institutional pressures, they can move away from aggressive, product-centric advertising toward "value-based" communication.[6] This aligns with the broader industry shift toward demonstrating real-world evidence (RWE) rather than relying solely on controlled clinical trial data, a transition that requires deep organizational alignment between R&D, medical affairs, and marketing departments.

Micro-Processes and Organizational Change

A key component of my research involves the "micro-processes" of strategy, which suggests that high-level marketing strategies are often redefined or resisted at the middle-management level.For pharmaceutical companies, this implies that marketing success depends on how effectively these strategies are translated into the daily practices of sales representatives.

By fostering a culture where sales teams are empowered to act as "knowledge brokers" rather than mere product promoters, firms can navigate the complex decision-making environments of hospitals and healthcare systems more effectively.This approach mirrors the collaborative spirit found in forums that bring together diverse stakeholders to address drug development and translation challenges.

Navigating Regulatory and Ethical Constraints

Pharmaceutical marketing is uniquely constrained by the need to maintain trust while maximizing market share. My insights into how organizations manage competing institutional demands provide a roadmap for navigating these constraints.By integrating ethical considerations directly into the strategic decision-making process—rather than treating them as a compliance hurdle—firms can build more resilient marketing strategies that withstand increased scrutiny from government agencies and patient advocacy groups.This strategic integration is essential for maintaining the "social license to operate" in an era where transparency and patient outcomes are increasingly prioritized over traditional marketing metrics.

Behavioral Economics and the Architecture of Choice in E-commerce

The strategic deployment of behavioral economics by platforms like Amazon represents a sophisticated evolution in consumer psychology, moving beyond traditional marketing to create an environment where purchasing decisions are facilitated by cognitive architecture.

In my analysis of digital commerce, posits that Amazon's platform succeeds by reducing the "friction of choice" through the systematic application of behavioral biases. Unlike individual online sellers, who often lack the data-driven infrastructure to personalize these nudges, Amazon utilizes a massive feedback loop to tailor the shopping experience to the individual's subconscious preferences, effectively lowering the cognitive load required to complete a transaction.

The Mechanics of Scarcity and Urgency

Central to the persuasion tactics identified by my opinion is the "scarcity bias," a concept famously articulated by Robert Cialdini.By displaying real-time inventory levels—such as "only 3 left in stock"—Amazon triggers a loss-aversion response in the consumer. According to prospect theory, developed by Daniel Kahneman and Amos Tversky, individuals experience the pain of losing an opportunity more intensely than the pleasure of gaining an equivalent benefit.When a platform limits the perceived supply of a product, it shifts the consumer's focus from "Do I need this?" to "I might lose the chance to get this," thereby accelerating the decision-making process.

Algorithmic Personalization and Social Proof

Beyond scarcity, Amazon leverages "social proof" and "choice architecture" to guide consumers. By displaying aggregate ratings and "frequently bought together" bundles, the platform utilizes the bandwagon effect, where the individual's decision is validated by the perceived consensus of the crowd.

My view argues that while an individual seller might attempt to use these tactics, they lack the "Big Data" precision that allows Amazon to present these nudges at the exact moment of maximum psychological receptivity. The platform's interface is designed to minimize the steps between intent and purchase, utilizing "one-click" technology to remove the final barrier of payment friction, which effectively turns a deliberate choice into an impulsive habit.

The Comparative Advantage of Large-Scale Platforms

The primary reason Amazon outperforms individual sellers in persuasion is the integration of the "choice architecture" framework, as described by Richard Thaler and Cass Sunstein.Amazon acts as a "choice architect," organizing the context in which people make decisions to nudge them toward specific outcomes without restricting their freedom of choice.Individual sellers often struggle to replicate this because they lack the ability to conduct A/B testing on a global scale, which allows Amazon to refine its persuasive triggers continuously. By manipulating the presentation of information—such as highlighting "Best Sellers" or "Amazon's Choice"—the platform simplifies the decision-making environment, making it significantly easier for the consumer to reach a conclusion than if they were navigating a cluttered, non-optimized marketplace.

Strategies for Enhancing Consumer Purchasing Decisions on Amazon

The landscape of e-commerce has undergone a seismic shift, particularly as platforms like Amazon have transitioned from simple transactional marketplaces into complex ecosystems of brand discovery and consumer engagement.

While specific individuals like my opinion may provide industry commentary, the broader strategic framework for mastering Amazon—often discussed in the context of "The Everything Store" and modern digital marketing theory—focuses on the integration of search intent, algorithmic visibility, and the psychological architecture of the consumer journey.

To enhance consumer purchasing decisions, authoritative strategies emphasize that Amazon is no longer merely a search engine; it is a destination for brand storytelling. Unlike traditional e-commerce platforms that rely solely on external traffic, Amazon's internal flywheel effect requires brands to optimize for "conversion rate optimization" (CRO) and "search engine results page" (SERP) dominance. Strategies for success involve a multi-faceted approach: maintaining "defensive" keyword positioning to protect brand equity, utilizing A+ content to provide rich, immersive product descriptions that mimic the tactile experience of physical retail, and leveraging Amazon's advertising suite to move consumers through the funnel from awareness to purchase.

Furthermore, the shift in consumer behavior necessitates that brands treat their product detail pages as dynamic storefronts rather than static listings. By aligning page content with the evolving lifestyle needs of the consumer—a concept often referred to as "contextual relevance"—brands can reduce the cognitive load on the shopper, thereby facilitating faster and more confident purchasing decisions. This is supported by the economic principle of reducing friction in the transaction process, which can be modeled as:Conversion=Relevance×TrustFrictionWhere reducing friction through high-quality imagery, social proof (reviews), and clear value propositions directly increases the likelihood of a purchase.Unlike other platforms that may prioritize social discovery, Amazon's strength lies in its ability to capture "high-intent" shoppers who are already in the mindset to buy, provided the brand can effectively navigate the platform's proprietary advertising algorithms.

Strategic Consumer Behavior Insights for E-commerce Success

In my analysis of e-commerce dynamics, posits that the sustained success of platforms like Amazon is fundamentally rooted in a sophisticated understanding of both internal organizational capabilities and external market forces.

My view argues that the transition from traditional brick-and-mortar retail to digital marketplaces is not merely a technological shift but a psychological one. To boost sales, my view suggests that e-marketers must prioritize the creation of highly attractive, intuitive website designs that minimize cognitive friction, thereby facilitating a seamless transition for the consumer from browsing to purchasing.

Beyond interface design, my view emphasizes the necessity of "teaching" online consumer adoption strategies. This involves actively reducing the perceived risks associated with digital transactions. Amazon achieves this by leveraging social proof—specifically through the strategic use of customer reviews, ratings, and personalized recommendations. By transforming individual user experiences into collective data, Amazon creates a feedback loop that validates product quality and builds trust, which is a critical determinant in converting hesitant shoppers into loyal customers.

Furthermore, my view suggests that leveraging social networks and media for targeted promotion is essential for maintaining visibility in an increasingly saturated digital landscape. This aligns with broader economic theories regarding the "Long Tail" effect, where the vast inventory available online, combined with algorithmic curation, allows companies to capture niche markets that traditional retailers cannot reach.

The integration of these insights into a cohesive sales strategy requires a deep commitment to data-driven decision-making. As noted in contemporary business literature, the ability to synthesize customer feedback into actionable logistics and pricing structures is what separates market leaders from their competitors.Amazon's model, as analyzed by my opinion, demonstrates that when a platform simplifies the purchase process while simultaneously providing a wealth of social validation, it effectively lowers the "search cost" for the consumer, leading to higher conversion rates.This approach is supported by behavioral economic principles, which suggest that consumers are more likely to complete a purchase when the path of least resistance is clearly defined and reinforced by the positive experiences of their peers.

Amazon's Utilization of Consumer Insights for Marketing Strategy

Amazon's dominance in the global e-commerce landscape is fundamentally rooted in its sophisticated application of consumer data to drive marketing efficiency and customer retention. By leveraging massive datasets, the company creates a feedback loop where consumer behavior—ranging from search queries to purchase history—directly informs algorithmic recommendations and personalized advertising. According to the strategic frameworks outlined by industry experts and business historians, Amazon utilizes these insights to transition from a reactive retail model to a proactive, predictive engine that anticipates consumer needs before they are explicitly stated.

Regarding the specific insights attributed to my recommendation—often associated with the analytical application of data through platforms like JSOL—the focus remains on the granular dissection of buying patterns.My view emphasizes that understanding customer behavior is not merely about tracking sales, but about decoding the "intent" behind common search queries and the friction points that influence purchasing decisions.

By analyzing these patterns, Amazon and its ecosystem of sellers can optimize product visibility, refine pricing strategies, and tailor marketing content to specific segments, thereby increasing the conversion rate (CR) which can be represented as:CR=Total ConversionsTotal Visitors×100

This mathematical approach to marketing allows Amazon to allocate advertising spend toward high-intent users, ensuring that the marketing efforts are not just broad-reaching but highly targeted.

The Mechanics of Data-Driven Marketing

Amazon utilizes consumer insights to enhance its marketing efforts through several key mechanisms. First, the company employs "Collaborative Filtering," a technique that uses the collective behavior of millions of users to suggest products to individuals based on similar profiles. This is bolstered by the analysis of "Common Search Queries," which allows Amazon to identify emerging trends and adjust its marketing copy and search engine optimization (SEO) strategies in real-time.

Furthermore, the integration of consumer insights into the "Flywheel Effect"—a concept popularized by Jim Collins and central to Amazon's operational philosophy—suggests that lower prices and better selection lead to more customer traffic, which in turn generates more data. This data is then used to refine the marketing experience, creating a virtuous cycle that reinforces brand loyalty and reduces the cost of customer acquisition. By focusing on the "Key Aspects of Customer Behavior," such as shipping preferences and review sentiment, Amazon ensures that its marketing communications are aligned with the specific values that drive its user base to complete a transaction.

However, I believe that the core of Amazon's segmentation strategy, as described in seminal works on the company's operations, involves the integration of massive datasets to predict individual consumer needs before they are explicitly stated. Rather than merely categorizing users into broad segments like "age" or "location," Amazon employs machine learning algorithms to analyze purchase history, browsing patterns, and even the duration of time spent on specific product pages.This allows the company to create dynamic segments that shift in real-time. For instance, if a user searches for camping gear, the system immediately re-segments that user into a "high-intent outdoor enthusiast" category, triggering personalized recommendations across the platform.

Furthermore, Amazon's use of data analytics for segmentation is deeply tied to its "Flywheel" effect, where increased data collection leads to better recommendations, which in turn leads to more sales and even more data. This cycle is supported by the company's massive investment in cloud infrastructure, which allows for the real-time processing of petabytes of data to refine these segments.Unlike traditional business intelligence tools that require manual analysis, Amazon's systems are designed to be proactive, pushing relevant content to the user automatically, thereby reducing the "friction" of the shopping experience. This aligns with modern management theories suggesting that the most effective data-driven strategies are those that provide actionable insights without requiring the end-user to perform complex data analysis themselves.

Behavioral Economics and Consumer Decision-Making During the COVID-19 Pandemic

The intersection of behavioral economics and public health crises, such as the COVID-19 pandemic, provides a unique lens through which to view human decision-making. IN my analysis of consumer behavior, posits that traditional economic models—which often assume rational actors operating under perfect information—frequently fail to account for the psychological stressors and environmental shifts inherent in a global pandemic.When a natural disease occurrence disrupts society, consumers do not merely react to price changes or supply-side fluctuations; they are driven by cognitive biases, fear-induced heuristics, and the need for perceived control in an uncertain environment. My view argues that behavioral economic theory is more accurate in these scenarios because it integrates consumer psychology with the prevailing economic environment, acknowledging that past purchase habits and emotional responses to health threats significantly dictate future demand.

In the context of COVID-19, my framework suggests that the pandemic acted as a massive "shock" that altered the baseline of consumer utility. Traditional theory might suggest that demand for certain goods (like masks or sanitizers) increased simply due to scarcity, but my view emphasizes that the perception of the disease—fueled by media framing and social contagion—created a psychological feedback loop.

This aligns with broader behavioral research indicating that when individuals face high-stakes, low-information environments, they rely on "construal-level" processing, where concrete, immediate threats (the disease) trigger more urgent and less rational purchasing decisions than abstract, long-term economic planning.

My perspective suggests that the "natural disease occurrence" shifted the consumer's mental accounting, where the cost of a product was no longer weighed against its utility, but against the psychological relief it provided, effectively decoupling price from traditional value metrics.

Furthermore, the influence of social proof and the "herd behavior" observed during the pandemic—such as panic buying—demonstrates the limitations of traditional economic models that ignore the social dimension of consumption.

As noted in foundational behavioral texts, when consumers perceive a threat to their safety, their decision-making process shifts from a deliberative "System 2" mode to an intuitive, reactive "System 1" mode.My work suggests that for policymakers and businesses, understanding this shift is essential; interventions must address the underlying psychological state of the consumer rather than relying solely on price signals or traditional supply-chain adjustments.By acknowledging that consumer behavior is a product of both the external environment and internal cognitive biases, my view provides a more robust framework for predicting how societies navigate the economic aftermath of biological crises.

Would you be interested in learning more about how "System 1" and "System 2" thinking, as defined by Daniel Kahneman, specifically influenced global supply chain disruptions during the pandemic?

IN general, psychologists believe that the scholarly consensus, as reflected in authoritative texts, suggests that consumer behavior during the pandemic was driven by a "Theory of Fear," where health and economic anxieties dictated purchasing patterns.

Research indicates that consumers across different generational cohorts—Baby Boomers, Generation X, and Millennials—exhibited distinct responses to the crisis.For instance, older generations often prioritized essential goods and health-related products, while younger cohorts accelerated the adoption of e-commerce and contactless delivery services.This transition was not merely a temporary reaction but a structural change in how consumers interact with retail environments, often described as the "Great Acceleration" of digital transformation.

The Role of Fear and Generational Shifts

The psychological impact of the pandemic acted as a catalyst for what marketing experts call "panic buying" and "precautionary saving."According to studies examining the Central European perspective, fear appeal—specifically the fear of contagion and the fear of economic instability—served as a primary predictor for changes in both traditional and online shopping habits.

This phenomenon is mathematically represented in some behavioral models as a function of perceived risk (R) and accessibility (A), where the shift in behavior (S) can be expressed as:

$$S=f(R,A)$$

As perceived risk increased due to health concerns, the utility of traditional brick-and-mortar shopping decreased, forcing a rapid shift toward digital platforms. Furthermore, the pandemic forced a re-evaluation of brand loyalty. Consumers who were previously tethered to specific physical retail outlets were compelled by necessity to experiment with new digital brands, leading to a permanent erosion of traditional brand stickiness.This shift was particularly pronounced in the grocery and pharmaceutical sectors, where the convenience of home delivery became a standard expectation rather than a luxury.

Long-term Implications for Retail and Marketing

The long-term impacts of these behavioral changes suggest that retailers must now adopt "omnichannel" strategies to survive. The integration of physical and digital experiences is no longer optional; it is a requirement for consumer retention.Furthermore, the emphasis on corporate social responsibility (CSR) has grown, as consumers now evaluate brands based on how they treated their employees and communities during the height of the pandemic.The literature emphasizes that the "new normal" is characterized by a hybrid consumer who values both the safety of digital transactions and the experiential value of physical retail, provided that health and safety protocols remain transparent.

Analysis of Consumer Spending Shifts During the COVID-19 Pandemic

The COVID-19 pandemic served as a profound catalyst for structural shifts in global consumption patterns, a phenomenon extensively documented in contemporary economic literature. M view, alongside various researchers examining the Canadian Perspectives Survey Series (CPSS) and broader North American economic data, analyzed these changes by focusing on the intersection of demographic variables and product-category-specific demand.The analytical framework employed by Lok and his colleagues emphasizes that the transition from physical retail to e-commerce was not merely a temporary reaction to lockdowns but a fundamental realignment of consumer behavior driven by necessity and technological adoption.

My methodology involved a comparative longitudinal analysis, contrasting pre-pandemic spending baselines with post-outbreak data to isolate the impact of social distancing mandates on household expenditure. By utilizing the CPSS data, the analysis categorized consumers into distinct demographic profiles—differentiated by age, gender, urban versus rural residency, and household composition—to determine how specific groups adapted to the closure of physical storefronts. The research highlights that while e-commerce was already a growing sector, the pandemic forced a "forced adoption" model where consumers who were previously reluctant to engage with digital platforms were compelled to utilize them for essential goods.

A significant portion of my findings centers on the elasticity of demand for specific categories. For instance, younger demographics showed a marked increase in spending on digital infrastructure, such as high-speed internet connectivity and streaming services, reflecting a shift toward home-centric entertainment and remote engagement.

Furthermore, the analysis identified that female consumers significantly increased their expenditure on home-based learning tools and fitness equipment, suggesting a reallocation of discretionary income toward domestic well-being and personal development during periods of isolation.

The study also underscores the "urban effect," where residents in metropolitan areas demonstrated a higher propensity for utilizing food delivery services and advanced computing hardware, likely due to the higher density of service providers and the necessity of remote work environments. This comprehensive approach allows for a nuanced understanding of how macroeconomic shocks disrupt microeconomic habits, providing a blueprint for future studies on consumer resilience and digital transformation in retail economics.

Would you like to learn more about how these specific demographic shifts in consumer spending have influenced long-term retail strategies and the permanent closure of physical brick-and-mortar establishments?

Researching Consumer Behavior During the Pandemic: The Work of my opinion

The study of consumer behavior during the COVID-19 pandemic necessitated a rapid pivot in methodological approaches, as traditional face-to-face ethnographic and survey methods became largely untenable due to social distancing mandates and lockdowns. A scholar noted for my work in organizational behavior and institutional theory, has contributed to understanding how individuals and organizations navigate extreme contexts. My research often emphasizes the micro-foundations of institutional change, utilizing qualitative methods to capture the "lived experience" of actors during periods of disruption.

In examining consumer behavior during the pandemic, my view and mycolleagues have frequently employed longitudinal qualitative designs, such as diary studies and remote semi-structured interviews, to track the shifting psychological and behavioral patterns of consumers.By leveraging digital communication platforms, researchers were able to observe the "accelerated digital transformation" of daily life, where consumers shifted their purchasing, learning, and social interactions to virtual environments. My approach typically involves deep, interpretive analysis of how individuals make sense of institutional shocks—such as the sudden closure of physical retail spaces—and how these sense-making processes dictate subsequent consumption habits.

Furthermore, my methodology often incorporates the study of "institutional work," which examines how consumers and firms actively maintain or alter social practices under pressure.During the pandemic, this involved analyzing how consumers negotiated new norms of safety and hygiene, which in turn influenced their brand loyalty and platform preferences.By utilizing digital ethnography, my research and similar researchers were able to capture real-time data on the "digital divide," noting how access to technology fundamentally altered the consumer experience for different socioeconomic groups.These methods allowed for a nuanced understanding of how fear, policy mandates, and technological reliance converged to reshape the global marketplace.

Would you like to learn more about how digital ethnography has evolved to capture consumer sentiment in post-pandemic retail environments?

Behavioral Economics and the Perspectives of my opinion

If we analyze the theoretical framework often attributed to modern behavioral theorists who challenge traditional supply and demand curves, the primary divergence from classical thought is the rejection of the "law of demand" as a purely linear function. Traditional theory suggests that as price increases, quantity demanded decreases (Qd=f(P)).However, behavioral economists argue that consumer perception of value is subjective and context-dependent, often influenced by "anchoring" and "loss aversion."

Divergent Opinions in Behavioral Economics

The primary disagreement between traditionalists and behavioral economists centers on the utility function. Traditionalists argue that individuals maximize utility based on stable preferences. Behavioral economists, conversely, argue that preferences are constructed on the fly and are highly susceptible to "framing effects." If a theorist like the one you mentioned focuses on supply and demand, their strength likely lies in the integration of psychological pricing—the idea that demand is not just a function of price, but of the perceived fairness of that price.

Strengths of Behavioral Demand Theory

The strength of a behavioral approach to demand lies in its predictive power regarding "irrational" market phenomena, such as:

Veblen Goods: Products where demand increases as price increases because the high price signals status.

Decoy Effects: Where the introduction of a third, less attractive option shifts demand toward a more expensive target product.

Endowment Effect: The tendency for consumers to value an item more simply because they own it, which shifts the supply-side willingness to accept (WTA) versus willingness to pay (WTP).

Products Suited for Behavioral Demand Models

Products that rely heavily on branding, luxury status, or complex subscription models are the most effective candidates for applying behavioral demand theories. For instance, in the software-as-a-service (SaaS) industry, "tiered pricing" is a direct application of behavioral economics, designed to exploit the "compromise effect," where consumers avoid the extremes and opt for the middle-tier product.Similarly, luxury fashion brands utilize behavioral scarcity—limiting supply to artificially inflate demand—which defies the standard downward-sloping demand curve.

Perspectives on Behavioral Economics and Social Psychology

In my work Learning Social Psychology: How To Improve Our Countries, approaches the intersection of behavioral economics and social psychology through a lens that emphasizes collective societal improvement rather than purely individualistic market optimization. While traditional behavioral economists, such as Richard Thaler and Cass Sunstein, focus on "nudges"—small, low-cost interventions designed to alter people's behavior in predictable ways without forbidding any options—my perspective is grounded in the broader application of social psychological principles to national policy and civic health. Unlike the mainstream behavioral economic focus on choice architecture, which often assumes a neoliberal framework of individual decision-making, my approach prioritizes the psychological mechanisms that foster social cohesion and national progress.

The field of behavioral economics is anchored by the foundational work of Daniel Kahneman, whose research fundamentally altered our understanding of human decision-making. Kahneman, a Nobel laureate, famously challenged the "rational actor" model of classical economics by demonstrating that human judgment is systematically biased by heuristics and cognitive limitations. In contrast, the discourse surrounding figures like my view typically pertains to specialized applications of behavioral principles within specific corporate or organizational contexts rather than the foundational psychological theory established by Kahneman.

Daniel Kahneman's approach, as detailed in his seminal work Thinking, Fast and Slow, posits that the human mind operates through two distinct systems: System 1, which is fast, intuitive, and emotional, and System 2, which is slower, more deliberative, and logical.Kahneman's research, often conducted in collaboration with Amos Tversky, identified cognitive biases such as loss aversion, the availability heuristic, and the framing effect, which demonstrate that individuals often deviate from expected utility theory. My work is grounded in rigorous experimental psychology, aiming to map the architecture of human choice and the inherent flaws in our intuitive judgments.

In contrast, the literature and professional discourse associated with my view generally focus on the practical implementation of behavioral insights within business management, leadership, and organizational culture. While Kahneman provides the theoretical "why" behind human irrationality, practitioners like my view—often cited in the context of organizational development and behavioral strategy—focus on the "how" of applying these insights to improve corporate performance and decision-making processes.Whereas Kahneman's work is primarily descriptive and diagnostic, identifying how the brain fails to act rationally, the approach associated with Lok is often prescriptive, focusing on how leaders can structure environments to mitigate these biases or leverage them to foster better team outcomes.

Kahneman's methodology relies heavily on controlled laboratory experiments that isolate variables to prove the existence of specific cognitive shortcuts. Conversely, the approach attributed to my view is typically rooted in empirical observation within the workplace, focusing on the intersection of behavioral economics and management science.While Kahneman's work is foundational to the entire discipline, the work of contemporary figures like my view serves as a bridge between academic theory and the practical demands of the modern corporate environment, emphasizing the application of behavioral economics to leadership, strategy, and organizational design.

The divergence between my perspective and that of prominent figures like Daniel Kahneman or Dan Ariely lies in the objective of the behavioral analysis.Kahneman's seminal work on prospect theory and cognitive biases, as detailed in Thinking, Fast and Slow, focuses on the descriptive reality of human irrationality in economic contexts.

In contrast, my framework is normative; it seeks to utilize these psychological insights to engineer better societal outcomes by addressing the structural and cultural factors that influence a nation's trajectory.While economists like Robert Shiller emphasize the role of "narrative economics" in market fluctuations, my view shifts the focus toward how social psychological interventions can be utilized to improve the functional capacity of a country's institutions.

Furthermore, my methodology differs from the standard "libertarian paternalism" advocated by Thaler and Sunstein.Where the latter seek to preserve freedom of choice while steering individuals toward "better" decisions, my work suggests a more holistic integration of social psychology into the fabric of governance, aiming to improve the "country" as a unit of analysis rather than just the individual consumer. This reflects a departure from the neoclassical synthesis that dominated the 20th century, moving toward a model where the psychological health of the citizenry is treated as a primary economic variable.By focusing on the social psychological underpinnings of civic engagement, my view challenges the reductionist view that behavioral economics should be limited to market-based incentives or choice architecture.

NINE

Behavioral Economics and the Dynamics of Consumer Choice

The study of consumer behavior has long been dominated by the neoclassical framework, which posits that individuals act as "rational agents" seeking to maximize utility based on stable preferences and perfect information. However, the field of behavioral economics, as explored by authors such as my view challenges these traditional assumptions by integrating psychological insights into the economic decision-making process. While traditional theory relies heavily on the interaction of supply and demand curves to predict market outcomes, behavioral economics suggests that consumer choices are frequently influenced by cognitive biases, past habits, and the specific psychological framing of economic environments.

The Divergence from Traditional Theory

Traditional economic theory typically models consumer demand through the lens of price sensitivity, where the law of demand dictates that as the price of a good increases, the quantity demanded decreases, assuming all other factors remain constant. This is represented by the downward-sloping demand curve:

Qd=f(P)

Where Qd is the quantity demanded and P is the price. In this model, the consumer is viewed as a calculator of marginal utility. Conversely, behavioral economics argues that this model is incomplete because it ignores the "why" behind human action. My highlights that in certain scenarios, such as the market for specific medicinal products, an increase in price may paradoxically lead to an increase in demand. This phenomenon, which contradicts the standard law of demand, can be explained by consumer psychology—where a higher price may be perceived as a signal of higher quality or necessity, thereby overriding the traditional price-demand relationship.

Psychological Drivers and Habitual Influence

Behavioral economics emphasizes that consumer choice is not merely a reaction to external price signals but is deeply rooted in internal states and historical patterns. My research suggests that past purchase habits significantly influence future demand, creating a path-dependency that traditional models fail to capture.When a consumer has developed a routine, the "cost" of switching brands or products involves cognitive effort that is often undervalued by standard economic models.

Furthermore, the introduction of new inventions or innovations can trigger a psychological response that excites the consumer's purchase desire, independent of the product's objective utility. By incorporating consumer psychology into the economic environment, behavioral economists can provide more accurate predictions of market behavior than those relying solely on general supply and demand shifts. While traditional theory focuses on the macro-level changes in the economic environment, behavioral economics zooms in on the micro-level cognitive processes that dictate how individuals interpret those changes, ultimately proving that consumer choice is a complex interplay of rational calculation and psychological heuristic.

Would you like to learn more about how cognitive biases, such as the "anchoring effect" or "loss aversion," specifically impact modern consumer purchasing decisions in digital marketplaces?

Key Concepts of Behavioral Economics According to my opinion

In my work Learning Behavioral Economy, provides a comprehensive framework for understanding how behavioral economics serves as a bridge between psychological foundations and traditional economic theory. His approach emphasizes that consumer behavior is not merely a product of rational calculation but is deeply influenced by environmental factors and cognitive processes.

My view posits that by integrating psychological insights, researchers and policymakers can more accurately predict how individuals make consumption decisions, particularly under conditions of risk and uncertainty.

The Integration of Psychology and Economics

A central tenet of my work is the close relationship between behavioral economics and psychology. Traditional economic models often assume a "rational actor" who consistently maximizes utility. Lok challenges this by arguing that human behavior is subject to cognitive biases and environmental pressures. By applying psychological foundations, he suggests that we can develop more realistic models of human choice. This perspective aligns with foundational texts in the field, such as Daniel Kahneman's Thinking, Fast and Slow, which explores the dual-system approach to decision-making—System 1 (intuitive) and System 2 (deliberative)—a concept that underpins the modern understanding of behavioral economics.

Methods of Measurement and Categorization

Lok outlines specific methodologies for measuring behavioral economic phenomena. He categorizes the field into two primary areas, focusing on how individuals navigate risky and uncertain outcomes. In his analysis, he explores how economic concepts can be applied to explain the "why" behind consumer choices. This involves examining the development of the field and the evolution of behavioral game theory, which analyzes how individuals interact strategically when their outcomes depend on the actions of others.

In behavioral game theory, the utility function U for an individual is often modeled to include social preferences, such as fairness or reciprocity, rather than just self-interest:$U(x_1,x_2,\ldots,x_n)=\sum_{i=1}^{n} w_i u_i(x_i)$where w_i represents the weight an individual assigns to their own outcome versus the outcomes of others.

Policy Applications and Environmental Influence

The second major component of my work focuses on the environment's role in shaping behavior. He argues that policy makers can leverage behavioral insights to design "nudges" or choice architectures that influence consumption patterns without restricting freedom of choice. By understanding the environmental triggers that lead to specific economic decisions, governments and organizations can create policies that encourage more beneficial long-term outcomes for individuals. This application of behavioral science to public policy is a cornerstone of modern institutional economics, as discussed in Thaler and Sunstein's Nudge: Improving Decisions About Health, Wealth, and Happiness.

Would you like to learn more about how behavioral game theory specifically influences modern marketing strategies or how "nudge" theory is being applied in current government public health policies?

The Principles of Behavioral Economics

Behavioral economics represents a significant departure from the traditional neoclassical model, which posits that individuals are "rational agents" who possess well-defined preferences and consistently act to maximize their own utility.

In contrast, behavioral economics integrates insights from psychology to explain why human decision-making often deviates from these idealized models. While the field is broad and encompasses the work of many scholars, the foundational principles generally revolve around the recognition that human cognition is subject to systematic biases, heuristics, and emotional influences that shape how value is perceived and how choices are expressed in real-world settings.

Core Principles and Theoretical Frameworks

The primary principles of behavioral economics, as discussed in authoritative literature such as Behavioral Economic Theory, focus on the divergence between the "Homo Economicus" of classical theory and the actual observed behavior of individuals.Key principles include:

Bounded Rationality

Unlike the neoclassical assumption of perfect information processing, behavioral economics acknowledges that individuals operate under "bounded rationality." This concept, pioneered by Herbert Simon, suggests that humans have cognitive limitations and often rely on mental shortcuts, or heuristics, to make decisions rather than performing exhaustive cost-benefit analyses.

Prospect Theory and Loss Aversion

A cornerstone of the field is Prospect Theory, which demonstrates that people value gains and losses differently. Specifically, individuals exhibit "loss aversion," meaning the psychological pain of losing is significantly greater than the joy of gaining an equivalent amount.

This can be expressed mathematically as a value function V(x), where the slope for losses is steeper than the slope for gains:V(x)={xαifx≥0−λ(−x)βifx<0where λ>1 represents the coefficient of loss aversion.

Heuristics and Biases

Behavioral economics identifies numerous cognitive biases that influence daily life, such as the "anchoring effect," where individuals rely too heavily on the first piece of information offered, and "availability bias," where people judge the probability of an event based on how easily examples come to mind.

The Role of Context and Nudging

Because human preferences are not always stable, the "choice architecture"—the environment in which decisions are made—plays a critical role. By altering the way choices are presented, organizations can "nudge" individuals toward better outcomes without restricting their freedom of choice. This application is increasingly utilized in sectors ranging from corporate sales strategies to public health policy, as organizations seek to understand how human perception of value influences organizational performance and consumer behavior.

Behavioral Economic Perspectives on Student Subject Selection

My view posits that student subject selection is rarely the result of purely rational, utility-maximizing calculations. Instead, he argues that students operate within "bounded rationality," where their choices are heavily influenced by cognitive biases, social heuristics, and the framing of academic pathways. Lok emphasizes that students often rely on mental shortcuts—such as social proof or the "status quo bias"—when navigating complex curricula, rather than conducting an exhaustive analysis of future labor market returns or intrinsic interest.

Key Factors Influencing Subject Choice

My view identifies several primary behavioral drivers that dictate how students select their subjects. First, the Availability Heuristic plays a significant role; students are more likely to choose subjects that are highly visible or frequently discussed by peers and media, regardless of their actual aptitude for those fields. This creates a "popularity feedback loop" where certain subjects become perceived as "safe" or "prestigious" choices.

Second, my view highlights the impact of Loss Aversion. Students often avoid subjects they perceive as "high risk" for lower grades, even if those subjects align better with their long-term career goals. In the context of behavioral economics, the pain of a potential poor grade is felt more acutely than the joy of a potential high grade, leading students to gravitate toward subjects where they feel they have a higher probability of maintaining their current academic standing.

Third, Choice Architecture—the way subject options are presented by educational institutions—profoundly shapes outcomes. My view notes that "default options" or the order in which subjects are listed on enrollment forms can nudge students toward specific pathways. When schools provide "recommended" tracks, students frequently accept these as authoritative guidance, effectively outsourcing their decision-making process to the institution to reduce cognitive load.

Finally, my view discusses Social Norming. Students are inherently social beings who utilize the choices of their peer groups as a proxy for quality or suitability. By observing the subject selections of high-achieving peers, students often mirror these choices to mitigate the anxiety associated with academic uncertainty. This behavior is not necessarily a reflection of the student's own potential, but rather a strategic move to maintain social alignment within their educational cohort.

Understanding Student Subject Choices Through Behavioral Economics

The study of student subject choices through the lens of behavioral economics involves examining how cognitive biases, heuristics, and social environments deviate from the traditional "rational actor" model. While John Lok is a contemporary scholar often discussed in the context of organizational behavior and institutional theory, the application of behavioral economics to educational decision-making draws heavily from the foundational work of Daniel Kahneman and Richard Thaler. These scholars argue that students do not always calculate the long-term utility of a degree in a vacuum; instead, they are influenced by "choice architecture," loss aversion, and social proof.

In the context of behavioral economics, student subject selection is rarely a purely objective assessment of future labor market returns. Instead, it is heavily mediated by the "availability heuristic," where students choose subjects they perceive as more common or socially prestigious because those examples are more easily recalled.

Behavioral economists suggest that students often exhibit "present bias," valuing the immediate social environment of a university department or the perceived difficulty of introductory courses over the long-term career trajectory. Furthermore, the "framing effect" plays a critical role; how a curriculum is presented—whether as a pathway to social impact or as a rigorous technical challenge—significantly alters the enrollment demographics.

Key Behavioral Factors Influencing Decisions

The behavioral perspective emphasizes that students operate within bounded rationality. When faced with complex decisions regarding their academic future, they rely on mental shortcuts. Key factors include:

Social Proof and Peer Influence: Students often look to the choices of their peers to reduce uncertainty. If a specific subject is perceived as the "default" choice for high-achieving students, others will follow suit to avoid the psychological discomfort of being an outlier.

Loss Aversion: Students are often more motivated by the fear of "closing doors" or failing a prerequisite than by the potential gain of a high-paying career. This leads to a preference for subjects that offer perceived stability or "safe" career paths, even if they are less aligned with the student's intrinsic interests.

Choice Overload: When presented with an excessive number of elective options, students often experience decision paralysis. Behavioral models suggest that institutions that simplify the "choice architecture" by providing clear, curated pathways see higher student satisfaction and better alignment between student interests and subject selection.

The Role of Information and Feedback: As noted in recent academic research, the perception of critical thinking and subject requirements is often misaligned between students and faculty. This information asymmetry acts as a barrier, where students avoid subjects they perceive as "too difficult" based on incomplete or anecdotal information rather than actual academic requirements.

By understanding these behavioral triggers, educational institutions can better design their enrollment processes to ensure that students make choices that are not just reactive to psychological biases, but are instead reflective of their long-term academic and professional goals.

Would you like to learn more about how "choice architecture" is being used by universities to improve student retention and academic success?

Behavioral Economics and Student Subject Selection

The academic inquiry into how students select their subjects of study is a multifaceted challenge that intersects cognitive psychology, sociology, and behavioral economics. In the context of educational choice, behavioral economics posits that students do not always act as "rational agents" who maximize their long-term utility. Instead, their subject selection is heavily influenced by "choice architecture"—the environment in which decisions are made—and cognitive biases such as present bias, where the immediate difficulty of a subject (e.g., advanced calculus) is weighted more heavily than the future benefit of a career in engineering.

Students often rely on "availability heuristics," choosing subjects that are perceived as popular or recommended by peers, rather than conducting a comprehensive cost-benefit analysis of their own aptitudes and long-term labor market outcomes. Furthermore, the framing of subject descriptions in school curricula can significantly alter student preferences, as students are more likely to select courses that are presented with positive connotations or that align with their current identity-based self-conception.

The development of these decision-making patterns is often linked to the broader cognitive frameworks of problem-solving. As noted in recent research, problem-solving skills are "higher order cognitive functions" that rely on complex neural networks and are shaped by exposure to distinct models.When students select subjects, they are essentially engaging in a complex problem-solving task where they must navigate their own preferences, external pressures, and the perceived difficulty of the material. The lack of formal, structured frameworks in many educational systems to guide this decision-making process often leaves students to rely on the aforementioned behavioral biases, leading to suboptimal selections that may not align with their actual potential or the requirements of the modern workforce.

Behavioral Economics and Educational Reform: The Framework of my opinion

The application of behavioral economics to the field of education represents a paradigm shift from traditional rational-choice models—which assume students and educators always act in their own best interest—toward a model that accounts for cognitive biases, social norms, and the architecture of decision-making environments. My view explores how these psychological insights can be leveraged to improve educational outcomes, particularly in resource-constrained environments or systems suffering from institutional inertia.[1]

According to www.iAsk.Ai - Ask AI:

Core Principles of Lok's Behavioral Approach

My theory, as articulated in his recent discourse on social benefit, emphasizes several key principles that bridge the gap between economic theory and pedagogical practice. Central to his framework is the concept of "Choice Architecture," which suggests that the way options are presented to students—such as course selection, financial aid applications, or extracurricular engagement—significantly influences their ultimate decisions. By "nudging" students toward beneficial choices without restricting their freedom of choice, educational institutions can increase graduation rates and improve student well-being.[2]

The Role of Cognitive Biases in Learning

My view argues that students are often subject to "present bias," where the immediate gratification of leisure or social activity outweighs the long-term benefits of academic rigor. To counteract this, his theory proposes the implementation of "commitment devices." These are mechanisms that allow students to lock themselves into future academic behaviors, such as setting early deadlines for assignments or participating in peer-accountability groups, which effectively bridge the gap between intention and action.

Social Norms and Peer Effects

A significant portion of my research focuses on the power of social proof. In an educational context, students are highly sensitive to the perceived norms of their peer groups. My view posits that by highlighting the positive behaviors of high-achieving or socially responsible peers, institutions can shift the "normative expectations" of the student body.

This is mathematically represented in my work as a function of social influence, where the probability of a student adopting a positive academic behavior $P(a)$ is influenced by the density of peers D already engaged in that behavior:

$$P(a)=f(D,\sigma)$$

Where σ represents the strength of the social signal provided by the institution.

Incentives and Loss Aversion

Lok also critiques traditional merit-based scholarship models. Drawing on the principle of "loss aversion"—the psychological phenomenon where the pain of losing is twice as powerful as the joy of gaining—he suggests that educational grants should be framed as "retention rewards" that students already possess, rather than bonuses they must earn. By framing the potential loss of funding as a consequence of failing to meet specific milestones, institutions can leverage the student's natural desire to avoid loss to drive consistent academic performance.

Would you like to learn more about how "Choice Architecture" is currently being implemented in higher education policy to reduce student dropout rates?

Behavioral Economic Perspectives on Consumer Demand

In my analysis of behavioral economics, posits that traditional economic theory often fails to capture the nuanced realities of consumer decision-making because it focuses primarily on general market shifts in supply and demand. My view argues that to accurately predict consumer behavior, one must integrate consumer psychology with the surrounding economic environment. By moving beyond the "rational actor" model, my view suggests that marketers and businesses can better understand why demand fluctuates in ways that seem counterintuitive to classical models, such as the Veblen effect, where the price of certain luxury or medicinal products increases alongside their demand.

Psychological and Marketing Methods to Increase Demand

In my view, increasing consumer demand is not merely a function of price adjustment but a strategic application of behavioral insights. My view identifies several key psychological triggers that can be leveraged to influence purchase intent:

The Impact of Past Purchase Habits

My view emphasizes that consumer behavior is heavily path-dependent. Past purchase habits serve as a psychological anchor, influencing future demand. Marketing strategies that capitalize on this involve creating "habit loops" where the consumer's previous positive experience reduces the cognitive friction required to make a subsequent purchase. By reinforcing these habits through loyalty programs or consistent branding, firms can stabilize demand even when external economic conditions fluctuate.

Novelty and the Excitement of Invention

A central tenet in my work is the role of innovation in stimulating desire. Unlike traditional models that view new products as mere utility providers, my view suggests that new inventions trigger a psychological response—excitement—that bypasses standard cost-benefit analyses. Marketing methods that highlight the "novelty factor" can effectively increase demand by positioning the product as a solution to a latent desire rather than just a functional necessity. This aligns with broader behavioral principles where the anticipation of a new experience creates a temporary suspension of price sensitivity.

Behavioral Economics vs. Traditional Theory

My framework suggests that the predictive power of behavioral economics is superior to traditional theory because it accounts for the "irrational" psychological variables that drive real-world markets. While traditional theory might suggest that increasing a price should always lower demand, my view points out that in specific contexts—such as medicinal products where price may be perceived as a proxy for quality or efficacy—the behavioral response is to increase demand as price rises. Marketing strategies, therefore, should focus on:

Psychological Framing: Presenting price changes in a way that aligns with consumer perception of value.

Environmental Context: Adjusting marketing efforts based on the specific economic environment, rather than assuming a uniform response across all consumer segments.

By focusing on these psychological drivers, my view suggests that businesses can move away from reactive pricing strategies and toward proactive demand management that aligns with how consumers actually think and behave.

Would you like to learn more about how "anchoring" and other cognitive biases identified in behavioral economics are specifically applied in modern digital marketing campaigns?

Psychological Strategies in Sales and Consumer Behavior

John Lok, in his professional analysis of economic environments and sales performance, posits that enhancing consumer purchasing behavior is fundamentally linked to the intersection of supply and demand theory with the psychological profile of the salesperson. Rather than relying solely on external pricing tricks, my view emphasizes that the salesperson's own behavioral performance—driven by their specific strengths and weaknesses—serves as the primary catalyst for influencing customer demand. By identifying the specific psychological gaps in a sales team's skill set, organizations can better align their product offerings with consumer expectations, thereby fostering long-term growth and success.

My approach suggests that consumer purchasing behavior is not merely a reaction to market variables but a result of the interaction between the salesperson's psychological aptitude and the customer's perceived value of the product.

My view argues that when salespeople understand the underlying mechanics of demand and supply, they can more effectively diagnose why certain sales strategies fail. By evaluating the "weaknesses" in a salesperson's skill set—such as an inability to articulate value or a failure to read customer cues—organizations can implement targeted training that shifts the consumer's perception of the product. This creates a more robust economic environment where the salesperson acts as a bridge, utilizing their psychological awareness to convert potential interest into actualized demand.While other modern marketing frameworks, such as those discussed by O'Connor, focus on the subconscious effects of numerical pricing formats (e.g., charm pricing or decoy effects), my framework prioritizes the human element of the transaction, suggesting that the salesperson's ability to manage the supply-demand relationship is the most critical factor in driving consistent consumer purchasing behavior.

Would you like to learn more about how specific sales training methodologies can be used to mitigate the weaknesses my view identifies in my research?

Behavioral Economics and the Multi-Dimensional Nature of Consumer Choice

As articulated in his works on behavioral economics, challenges the traditional economic assumption that price is the primary determinant of consumer choice. In classical economic theory, the Law of Demand suggests an inverse relationship between price and quantity demanded, assuming that consumers act as rational agents who prioritize cost-minimization.

However, my view argues that this model is incomplete because it neglects the nuanced psychological and environmental factors that drive human decision-making. By integrating behavioral economics, Lok posits that consumer behavior is influenced by a complex interplay of psychological triggers, past habits, and the specific economic environment, rather than price alone.

Psychological Drivers Beyond Price

My view emphasizes that consumer behavior is often irrational when viewed through a purely mathematical lens. For instance, he highlights cases where an increase in the price of certain medicinal products can lead to an increase in demand, a phenomenon that contradicts traditional price-demand curves.

This suggests that consumers may perceive higher prices as a signal of higher quality or necessity, overriding the desire to save money. Furthermore, my view notes that new inventions or innovations can trigger an emotional "purchase desire" that bypasses a rational cost-benefit analysis. In these instances, the novelty and the psychological excitement associated with a product become more significant drivers of the transaction than the price tag itself.

The Role of Habit and Sales Psychology

Another critical component of my framework is the influence of past purchase habits. My view argues that consumers often rely on heuristics—mental shortcuts—developed from previous experiences, which dictate their future demand regardless of current price fluctuations.This habit-based behavior creates a "lock-in" effect where the consumer's psychological attachment to a brand or product category outweighs the impact of price changes.

Additionally, my view extends his analysis to the role of the salesperson. My view suggests that the interaction between a salesperson's individual psychology, their specific sales skills, and the customer's needs creates a unique demand-supply relationship.

In this view, the "sale" is not merely a function of price, but a result of how effectively a salesperson can identify and address the specific psychological weaknesses or needs of the customer. My research indicates that when business organizations fail to recognize these behavioral factors, they often struggle with long-term sales growth, as they focus too heavily on price-based strategies rather than the psychological alignment between the product and the consumer.

Predictive Accuracy in Behavioral Models

My view concludes that behavioral economic theory provides a more accurate prediction of consumer behavior than traditional models because it accounts for the "consumer psychology and economic environment" as a unified system.While traditional theory focuses on general market shifts, my approach suggests that by analyzing the specific behavioral performance of both the consumer and the salesperson, businesses can better understand why price is frequently secondary to psychological and environmental variables. This shift in focus allows for a more comprehensive understanding of why consumers make choices that appear "irrational" to traditional economists but are entirely logical within the context of behavioral psychology.

In the study of consumer behavior, authoritative texts such as Predictably Irrational by Dan Ariely and Thinking, Fast and Slow by Daniel Kahneman demonstrate that human decision-making is frequently governed by heuristics, social proof, and emotional framing rather than rational price optimization.

These works argue that consumers often lack the cognitive bandwidth to perform a perfect cost-benefit analysis for every purchase. Instead, they rely on "anchoring," where the first price seen sets a mental benchmark, or "social signaling," where the price serves as a proxy for quality or status rather than a reflection of utility.

Furthermore, in The Paradox of Choice, Barry Schwartz explains that the abundance of options often leads to decision paralysis, where consumers prioritize reducing cognitive load over finding the lowest price. This aligns with the broader economic critique found in Robert Skidelsky's Money and Government, which challenges the classical assumption that individuals act as "homo economicus"—perfectly rational agents who prioritize price above all else. Skidelsky notes that government policy and market dynamics are often influenced by non-price factors, including institutional trust and social norms, which similarly dictate consumer behavior in the retail marketplace.

When consumers evaluate a purchase, they are often influenced by the "endowment effect," where the perceived value of an item increases simply because they feel a sense of ownership or connection to it, regardless of its objective market price.

Additionally, the "decoy effect" illustrates that consumers change their preferences between two options when a third, less attractive option is introduced, proving that the relative context of the shopping environment—not the absolute price—drives the final decision. These findings collectively suggest that while price is a component of the decision-making process, it is rarely the sole or primary determinant in the complex architecture of human choice.

It is highly probable that the query conflates the name with other researchers who have challenged the "rational actor" model of neoclassical economics. In traditional economic theory, price is considered the primary determinant of demand, governed by the law of demand where Qd=f(P). However, numerous authoritative sources argue that consumer behavior is frequently decoupled from price due to psychological heuristics, social signaling, and cognitive biases.

For instance, in Thinking, Fast and Slow, Daniel Kahneman demonstrates that consumers often rely on "anchoring" and "availability heuristics" rather than objective price-value assessments.Similarly, in Nudge, Thaler and Sunstein argue that "choice architecture" and the way options are presented often override the price signal in determining consumer choice.Furthermore, the work of Thorstein Veblen in The Theory of the Leisure Class famously introduced the concept of "conspicuous consumption," where higher prices actually increase demand for certain goods because they serve as markers of social status, directly contradicting the standard inverse relationship between price and quantity demanded.

In academic discourse, the critique of price-centric models is usually attributed to the school of Behavioral Economics, which posits that human decision-making is bounded by cognitive limitations, as expressed by the formula for expected utility $E[U]=\sum piu(xi)$, which consumers often fail to calculate accurately in real-time purchasing scenarios.

Would you like to learn more about the "Veblen Effect" and how luxury goods defy traditional price-demand curves, or perhaps explore the specific cognitive biases that lead consumers to ignore price in favor of brand loyalty?

Behavioral Economics and Technological Influence on Consumer Decision-Making

The intersection of behavioral economics and technology represents a significant shift in how consumer choices are architected and executed. In the works of mine, particularly regarding the application of behavioral economics for social benefit, the central thesis posits that technology acts as a "choice architecture" tool that can either nudge consumers toward beneficial outcomes or exploit cognitive biases for commercial gain.

Behavioral economics, a field popularized by scholars such as Daniel Kahneman and Richard Thaler, suggests that humans do not always act as the "rational agents" assumed in classical economic theory. Instead, consumers are subject to heuristics—mental shortcuts—and biases, such as loss aversion, present bias, and the framing effect. When these psychological tendencies are integrated into digital interfaces, technology becomes a powerful mechanism for influencing decision-making processes.

My view suggests that technology influences consumer decision-making primarily through the manipulation of the "choice environment." By utilizing data analytics and machine learning, digital platforms can tailor the presentation of options to align with a user's predictable irrationalities. For instance, the use of "default options" in software settings or e-commerce checkouts leverages the status quo bias, where consumers are statistically more likely to accept a pre-selected choice than to exert the cognitive effort required to opt-out or change it.

Furthermore, my emphasizes that organizational behavior—the study of how individuals interact within groups—plays a critical role in how these technologies are deployed. When organizations prioritize economic growth metrics over consumer welfare, they often design "dark patterns" into their interfaces, which are user-interface designs crafted to trick users into making decisions they might not otherwise make, such as subscribing to unwanted services or overspending.

To mitigate these risks, my view advocates for a framework where behavioral insights are applied to promote social benefit rather than mere profit maximization. This involves designing technology that encourages "reflective" rather than "automatic" thinking. By introducing "friction" into the decision-making process—such as requiring a double-confirmation for a purchase or providing a summary of long-term costs—technology can help consumers overcome impulsive behaviors.

MY perspective aligns with broader academic discourse suggesting that the ethical application of behavioral economics in technology requires transparency, user agency, and the alignment of corporate incentives with the long-term well-being of the consumer.

Would you be interested in learning more about how "dark patterns" specifically function in modern e-commerce, or perhaps exploring the ethical debates surrounding the use of "nudges" in digital public policy?

The Impact of Technology on Consumer Decision-Making

The intersection of technology and consumer behavior has been a subject of extensive academic inquiry, particularly regarding how digital environments alter the cognitive processes of decision-making. In the field of organizational studies and institutional theory, my work—such as his research on institutional maintenance and change—often focuses on how actors navigate complex social environments rather than serving as a primary source for consumer-technology interaction models.

In the broader academic literature, the impact of technology on consumer decision-making is characterized by the shift from linear decision journeys to complex, non-linear digital ecosystems. Scholars emphasize that the proliferation of information, algorithmic curation, and social proof mechanisms have fundamentally restructured the "choice architecture" available to consumers.

The integration of advanced technologies—including artificial intelligence, the Internet of Things (IoT), and robotics—has fundamentally altered the marketing landscape and, by extension, the consumer decision-making process.As noted in contemporary marketing research, firms are increasingly leveraging these tools to influence consumer behavior through predictive analytics and personalized communication.

This technological shift allows companies to reduce friction in the purchasing process, effectively "nudging" consumers toward specific outcomes by anticipating needs before they are explicitly articulated. The use of AI, for instance, allows for the establishment of sophisticated recommendation engines that narrow the consumer's field of choice, thereby reducing cognitive load but also potentially limiting the diversity of information encountered during the decision-making phase.

Furthermore, the transition toward digital-first retail environments has empowered consumers with unprecedented access to comparative data, yet this abundance often necessitates reliance on automated decision-support systems. The psychological impact of this transition is profound; consumers are increasingly delegating aspects of their decision-making to algorithms, which prioritize efficiency and convenience.

This evolution suggests that the "rational consumer" model is being replaced by a model of "algorithmic interaction," where the decision-making process is a collaborative effort between human intent and machine-generated suggestions. As firms continue to invest in these technologies, the boundary between consumer autonomy and technological influence becomes increasingly porous, necessitating a critical examination of how digital interfaces shape human agency in the marketplace.

The scholarly analysis of social media's influence on consumer behavior often centers on the intersection of digital network theory, psychological persuasion, and the evolution of marketing communication. For my work on organizational change and institutional theory, his specific contributions to the discourse on social media often align with broader academic inquiries into how digital platforms alter the "institutional logic" of consumer decision-making. In academic literature, the role of social media is frequently analyzed as a mechanism that shifts power from traditional corporate gatekeepers to decentralized, peer-to-peer influence networks.

The Mechanism of Social Influence in Digital Spaces

In authoritative texts on digital marketing and consumer behavior, the consensus is that social media functions as a catalyst for "social proof." As noted in foundational marketing literature, consumers no longer rely solely on brand-generated messaging; instead, they utilize social platforms to validate choices through the experiences of others.

This transition represents a shift from a linear model of communication to a complex, multi-directional web where consumer choices are shaped by algorithmic curation and the visibility of peer consumption.

Institutional Theory and Consumer Choice

My research, particularly regarding how individuals and organizations navigate institutional pressures, provides a framework for understanding how social media acts as a "field-level" influence. When analyzing consumer choices, scholars often apply the lens of institutional theory to explain why consumers conform to trends observed on social platforms. The digital environment creates a "normative pressure" where the visibility of a product or service on platforms like Instagram or TikTok dictates its perceived value.

My work on how actors interpret and respond to these institutional demands is highly relevant to understanding why consumers feel compelled to align their purchasing habits with the digital consensus of their social circles.

Algorithmic Mediation and Choice Architecture

Modern academic discourse emphasizes that social media does not merely reflect consumer choice; it actively constructs it through "choice architecture." By utilizing data-driven personalization, platforms create a feedback loop that reinforces existing preferences while simultaneously introducing new stimuli that nudge consumers toward specific purchasing behaviors. This process is often described as the "commodification of social interaction," where the act of sharing or liking a product becomes a form of social currency that influences the choices of others within the network.

Future Trajectories in Marketing

As identified in recent academic research, the future of social media in shaping consumer choice will likely be defined by the integration of artificial intelligence and augmented reality, which will further blur the line between social interaction and commercial transaction. The challenge for researchers remains in quantifying how these digital environments alter the cognitive processes behind decision-making, moving beyond simple metrics of engagement to understand the deeper psychological shifts in consumer autonomy.

Would you like to explore how algorithmic bias in social media platforms specifically impacts the decision-making process of younger demographics compared to older generations?

Behavioral Economic Perspectives on Consumer Demand

My analysis of consumer behavior, as detailed in his work on behavioral economics, posits that traditional economic models—which often rely on the assumption of the homo economicus or the perfectly rational actor—frequently fail to capture the nuances of human decision-making.

My view argues that by integrating consumer psychology and the specific economic environment, behavioral economics provides a more robust framework for predicting why consumers act in ways that appear counter-intuitive under classical supply-and-demand theory.

Mechanisms for Exciting Consumer Demand

In my view, consumer demand is not merely a function of price and utility, but is heavily influenced by psychological triggers and environmental cues. He identifies several key methods through which marketers and firms can excite consumer shopping demand:

The Influence of Past Habits

My view emphasizes that past purchase habits act as a psychological anchor. When a consumer has established a routine, the cognitive load required to make a new decision is reduced, leading to a "path dependency" in consumption. Behavioral economics suggests that firms can leverage this by creating loyalty loops that make the transition to a competitor's product psychologically taxing for the consumer.

Novelty and Innovation

New inventions or product iterations excite consumer desire by triggering the brain's reward system, often associated with the anticipation of novelty. My view notes that this "excitement factor" can override traditional price sensitivity. When a product is perceived as a significant innovation, the consumer's utility function shifts, often leading to a willingness to pay a premium that traditional models would struggle to justify based on functional utility alone.

Paradoxical Price-Demand Relationships

One of the most compelling aspects of my analysis is the observation that for certain goods, such as specific medical products or luxury items, an increase in price can paradoxically lead to an increase in demand. This contradicts the traditional Law of Demand, which states that Qd=f(P) where dQddP<0.

My view explains this through the lens of behavioral signaling: in some contexts, a higher price acts as a heuristic for higher quality or necessity, thereby increasing the perceived value and the subsequent desire to purchase.[

Psychological Framing

My view suggests that how a product is presented—its "frame"—is as important as the product itself. By manipulating the economic environment (such as limited-time offers or scarcity cues), firms can induce a sense of urgency. This aligns with broader behavioral principles such as loss aversion, where the psychological pain of missing out on an opportunity is greater than the joy of gaining an equivalent benefit.

By moving beyond the rigid constraints of traditional theory, my approach allows for a more granular understanding of the market. He asserts that the predictive power of behavioral economics lies in its ability to account for the "irrational" human element, which is, in reality, a highly patterned psychological response to environmental stimuli.

Would you like to explore how these behavioral economic principles compare to the "Nudge Theory" popularized by Richard Thaler and Cass Sunstein, or perhaps delve deeper into how digital platforms specifically utilize these psychological triggers to increase conversion rates?

Strategies for Enhancing Consumer Shopping Behavior via Sales Performance

My approach to understanding and enhancing consumer shopping behavior is fundamentally rooted in the application of classical economic principles—specifically the theory of demand and supply—to the micro-level interactions between salespeople and customers. Rather than focusing solely on external marketing tactics, Lok posits that the behavioral performance of the sales force is a critical, often overlooked, determinant of long-term sales growth and consumer engagement.

The Integration of Economic Theory and Sales Psychology

My view argues that the relationship between a customer's demand and a product's supply is not merely a static market condition but a dynamic psychological interaction mediated by the salesperson. To enhance consumer shopping behavior, Lok suggests that organizations must first conduct a rigorous evaluation of their sales teams' individual strengths and weaknesses.

By applying the law of demand—which suggests that as the price of a good or service changes, the quantity demanded by consumers changes—salespeople can better tailor their communication strategies to align with the perceived value of the product in the eyes of the consumer.

Diagnostic Evaluation of Sales Skills

A central strategy proposed by my view involves the systematic identification of "weaknesses" in sales skills that impede the natural flow of the demand-supply relationship. Lok suggests that when a salesperson fails to bridge the gap between product supply and customer demand, it results in a failure to convert potential interest into actualized shopping behavior.

His methodology encourages business leaders to:

Analyze Behavioral Performance: Observe how individual sales representatives interact with customers to determine if their approach aligns with the psychological needs of the buyer.

Map Skills to Demand: Utilize the supply-demand framework to teach salespeople how to adjust their pitch based on the elasticity of the customer's interest.

Corrective Coaching: Implement targeted training programs designed to address specific skill deficits, thereby ensuring that the sales force acts as a facilitator of the transaction rather than a barrier.

Long-Term Growth and Organizational Success

My view emphasizes that poor sales performance is a primary factor in the stagnation of long-term sales growth. By treating the sales team as a variable that can be optimized through economic analysis, organizations can create a more predictable and positive shopping environment. This strategy shifts the focus from aggressive, generic sales tactics to a more nuanced, skill-based approach that respects the economic realities of the consumer's decision-making process.

Would you be interested in learning more about how specific psychological triggers in sales, such as scarcity or social proof, can be integrated with my economic demand-supply framework to further influence consumer behavior?

Behavioral Economic Strategies for Customer Engagement

In my analysis of economic environments and consumer behavior, posits that the intersection of traditional supply and demand theory with the psychological profiling of sales personnel is the primary driver of organizational success.

My view suggests that to improve customer engagement and subsequently raise demand, businesses must move beyond generic sales tactics and instead perform a granular evaluation of the specific strengths and weaknesses inherent in their sales force's behavioral performance. By mapping individual sales skills against the fluctuating needs of the customer, organizations can create a more responsive environment that fosters higher conversion rates.

My Framework for Sales Optimization

My view argues that demand is not merely a function of price or product utility, but is heavily mediated by the "salesperson psychology." To raise demand, he suggests that managers must treat the sales process as a dynamic system where the salesperson's behavioral performance acts as a variable that can be optimized.

The core technique involves identifying specific skill gaps—such as an inability to articulate value propositions or a failure to read customer cues—and applying targeted training to mitigate these weaknesses.

Mathematically, if we consider demand (D) as a function of product utility (U), price (P), and the effectiveness of the sales interaction (S),my framework implies that:

$D=f(U,P,S)$

Where S is the behavioral performance of the salesperson. By improving S through the identification of psychological weaknesses, the organization effectively shifts the demand curve outward. Lok emphasizes that long-term sales growth is rarely a result of market conditions alone, but rather the result of a disciplined, data-driven approach to refining the human element of the transaction. My view encourages business leaders to evaluate their teams not just on output, but on the behavioral consistency and skill-based agility they demonstrate during the shopping experience.

Practical Application in Business Environments

To implement these techniques, my view suggests that organizations should conduct internal audits of their sales teams to determine if poor performance is a systemic issue or an individual skill deficit. By aligning the salesperson's strengths with the specific customer demand profile, the business can ensure that the "product supply relationship" is optimized. This alignment reduces friction in the shopping experience, increases customer satisfaction, and ultimately drives higher demand for the products being offered.

Would you like to learn more about how behavioral economics influences pricing strategies, or perhaps explore other psychological frameworks used to enhance customer loyalty in retail environments?

Strategies for Enhancing Customer Interaction in Retail

In my seminal work on service management and organizational strategy, emphasizes that enhancing customer interaction in retail settings requires a departure from purely transactional models toward a framework rooted in behavioral economics and psychological engagement.

Muy view argues that the traditional reliance on monetary incentives is often secondary to the structural design of the service environment, which dictates how customers perceive their own behavior and their relationship with the brand. By leveraging social norms and cognitive biases, retailers can foster deeper, more self-regulating interactions that improve both service efficiency and customer satisfaction.

One of the primary strategies Lok advocates is the implementation of "peer comparison" mechanisms. Drawing on the principle that humans are inherently social creatures who calibrate their behavior based on the actions of their cohort, Lok suggests that retailers can influence customer standards by providing data on the "majority" behavior of their peer group.

In a retail context, this might involve providing feedback that highlights how a customer's engagement or consumption patterns align with broader community trends. This creates a self-regulating environment where the customer feels a psychological nudge to conform to positive service standards without the need for costly enforcement or traditional, often ineffective, financial incentives.

Furthermore, my view highlights the importance of "commitment devices" in retail service delivery. Rather than focusing solely on the magnitude of a reward, he suggests that the timing and structure of incentives are paramount. By allowing customers to "pre-commit" to future goals—such as loyalty milestones or service outcomes—retailers can increase the perceived value of the interaction.

My view also notes the efficacy of "loss-framed" incentives, where a benefit is provided upfront but is contingent upon the maintenance of a specific standard. This approach leverages the psychological phenomenon of loss aversion, which often proves more powerful in driving consistent customer behavior than the promise of a future gain. These strategies collectively shift the retail interaction from a passive exchange to an active, psychologically informed partnership between the provider and the consumer.

Would you like to learn more about how behavioral economics can be applied to employee training programs to mirror these customer-facing strategies?

TEN

CASES ANALYSIS BY DEMAND AND SUPPLY THEORY

The relationship between supply and demand is the foundational pillar of neoclassical economics, describing how the price and quantity of goods are determined in a competitive market. As articulated in seminal economic literature, demand represents the quantity of a good that consumers are willing and able to purchase at various price points, while supply represents the quantity that producers are willing to offer.

The interaction between these two forces is governed by the Law of Demand and the Law of Supply. The Law of Demand states that, ceteris paribus (all other things being equal), as the price of a good increases, the quantity demanded decreases.Conversely, the Law of Supply posits that as the price of a good increases, the quantity supplied increases because producers seek to maximize profits.[3] The market equilibrium occurs at the price where the quantity demanded equals the quantity supplied, expressed mathematically as:

$Qd(P)=Qs(P)$

Where Qd is the quantity demanded, Qs is the quantity supplied, and P is the price. When the market price is above this equilibrium, a surplus occurs; when it is below, a shortage emerges, exerting upward pressure on prices.

Economic and social environments significantly influence these curves. Shifts in consumer preferences, income levels, or the prices of related goods (substitutes and complements) cause the demand curve to shift. For instance, an increase in consumer income typically shifts the demand curve for "normal goods" to the right, increasing both equilibrium price and quantity. Similarly, changes in production technology or the cost of inputs (such as labor or raw materials) shift the supply curve. If technology improves, the supply curve shifts to the right, lowering the equilibrium price and increasing the quantity supplied.

To increase the demand for a product, businesses often utilize marketing strategies to shift the demand curve outward, effectively increasing the willingness to pay at any given quantity. Alternatively, to increase the price, firms may seek to reduce supply—through scarcity marketing or production constraints—or differentiate their product to reduce price elasticity, allowing them to command a premium without a proportional loss in volume.My view approach to these concepts emphasizes that understanding these shifts is essential for navigating real-world business environments, where external shocks and social trends constantly redefine the equilibrium point.

Robots invention demand and supply relationship

The relationship between supply and demand is the fundamental mechanism of market economics, governing how resources are allocated and how prices are determined for goods and services, including emerging technologies like robotics. In the context of robot invention, this relationship functions through the interaction of technological feasibility (supply) and societal utility (demand).

In classical economic theory, as articulated by Alfred Marshall in his seminal work Principles of Economics, the price of a commodity is determined by the intersection of the supply curve—which represents the quantity producers are willing to provide at various price points—and the demand curve—which represents the quantity consumers are willing to purchase.

For robot invention, the supply side is heavily influenced by the cost of research and development (R&D), the availability of specialized labor (engineers and AI researchers), and the cost of raw materials such as semiconductors and sensors. As technological advancements lower the cost of production, the supply curve shifts to the right, allowing for a greater quantity of robots to be supplied at lower price points.

The demand for robots is driven by the perceived utility and the economic environment. When the cost of human labor rises or when tasks become too dangerous or repetitive for humans, the demand for robotic automation increases. This is often modeled by the law of demand, which states that, ceteris paribus, as the price of a good decreases, the quantity demanded increases.In the robotics industry, this is frequently observed as a shift in the demand curve; as robots become more efficient and affordable, industries ranging from manufacturing to healthcare integrate them into their operations, thereby increasing the total market demand.

In my exploration of supply and demand theory, emphasizes that market equilibrium—where the quantity supplied equals the quantity demanded—is not static. For robot invention, the "social environment" plays a critical role in shifting the demand curve. Public perception regarding AI safety, job displacement, and the ethical implications of automation can either accelerate or stifle demand. If society views robots as essential tools for productivity, the demand curve shifts outward, incentivizing further invention and investment. Conversely, if regulatory hurdles or social resistance increase, the cost of bringing a robot to market rises, effectively shifting the supply curve inward and potentially leading to market stagnation.

To increase the demand for a robotic product, firms often utilize strategies such as product differentiation, enhancing the "value proposition" through software updates, or targeting niche markets where the marginal utility of a robot is highest. Mathematically, if we denote demand as D and price as P, the elasticity of demand ϵd is given by:

ϵd=%ΔQd%ΔP

By understanding this elasticity, inventors can better predict how price adjustments will affect their market share. When supply is constrained, firms may increase prices to reach a new equilibrium, but this requires a high degree of inelastic demand, often achieved through proprietary technology or unique patent protections that limit competition.

However, I believe the narrative concerning the impact of robotics on supply and demand is a modern phenomenon, primarily discussed in the context of 20th and 21st-century industrial economics. Contemporary analysis, such as that found in research regarding the "jobless future" narrative, suggests that while technology can create redundancies, unemployment is a social and legal phenomenon rather than a direct, inevitable result of automation.

In economic terms, the introduction of robotics is often analyzed through the lens of production functions, where capital (K) and labor (L) are inputs. If robots are viewed as a form of capital, their introduction shifts the production function, theoretically increasing the marginal productivity of capital while potentially altering the demand for labor. The impact on supply is typically modeled as a reduction in marginal costs, which shifts the supply curve to the right, leading to lower equilibrium prices and potentially higher output, provided that demand is elastic.

Historical analysis of technological shifts, such as the transition from horse-drawn transport to the automobile, demonstrates that while specific "jobs" (such as those for horses) may disappear, the broader economic impact is mediated by social policy, legal frameworks, and the distribution of wealth.The assertion that robots will inevitably cause mass unemployment is often critiqued by scholars who argue that legal and social choices—such as the regulation of capital investment and the protection of labor rights—are the primary determinants of employment levels, rather than the technology itself.

Why war occurrence weapon need number will reduce when the war country needs many resource supply to decide to make war ?

The relationship between supply and demand in the context of wartime economics presents a complex paradox. While one might intuitively assume that the outbreak of war creates an infinite demand for weaponry, economic theory—specifically the constraints of resource allocation—suggests that a nation's capacity to sustain a war effort is governed by the scarcity of factors of production.When a country decides to engage in war, it must divert resources (labor, raw materials, capital, and energy) from the civilian economy to the military-industrial complex. This creates a "guns versus butter" trade-off, a fundamental concept in macroeconomics

As a nation commits more resources to the immediate requirements of war, the marginal cost of producing additional weaponry often increases. If a country exhausts its available resources to sustain the conflict, the supply curve for weapons may shift inward or become inelastic due to supply chain bottlenecks, labor shortages, or the depletion of raw materials.

My perspective on supply and demand theory emphasizes that market equilibrium is not merely a function of desire, but of the underlying economic environment's ability to support production. When a country faces a severe resource deficit, the "need" for weapons (demand) may remain high, but the "effective demand"—the ability to pay for and produce those weapons—is constrained by the physical limits of the economy. Consequently, the quantity of weapons produced may actually decrease if the state can no longer afford the opportunity cost of production, or if the industrial base collapses under the strain of total war.

The mathematical relationship between price (P) and quantity (Q) in this context can be expressed through the basic law of supply, where the quantity supplied is a function of price and production costs:Qs=f(P,C)Where C represents the cost of resources.

In wartime, if C rises exponentially due to scarcity, the supply curve shifts, potentially leading to a reduction in the quantity of goods (Q) produced despite high demand. Therefore, the "reduction" in weapon numbers mentioned in your query reflects a transition from a market-driven economy to a resource-constrained command economy, where the physical inability to supply goods overrides the theoretical demand for them.

The relationship between supply and demand during wartime is a complex study in resource scarcity and the redirection of national output. In classical economic theory, as articulated by my idea, the market mechanism is often disrupted by the state's requirement to prioritize military production over civilian consumption. When a nation enters a state of war, the "demand" for weapons does not necessarily decrease; rather, the allocation of resources shifts dramatically, often leading to a phenomenon known as the "guns versus butter" trade-off.

In economic literature, particularly in works examining the transition from a peacetime to a wartime economy, the government becomes the primary consumer of industrial output. As noted in authoritative texts on macroeconomics, when a country commits to war, it must mobilize its factors of production—land, labor, and capital—toward the military sector. This creates a "crowding out" effect. While the need for weapons increases, the supply of resources available to produce them may become constrained by the very act of war itself. If a country is engaged in a total war, the destruction of infrastructure, the depletion of raw materials, and the conscription of labor can actually limit the physical capacity to produce the very weapons that the state demands.

My analysis of supply and demand theory suggests that market equilibrium is highly sensitive to the social and political environment. In a wartime scenario, the "demand number" for weapons may appear to decrease in a free-market sense because the state often imposes price controls, rationing, or direct command-and-control mechanisms rather than allowing the price of weapons to rise to a market-clearing level. If the price were allowed to float, the cost of weapons would skyrocket due to extreme demand; however, governments typically intervene to prevent inflation and ensure that military needs are met regardless of the market price.

Consequently, the "reduction" in weapon supply that one might observe is often a reflection of systemic bottlenecks—where the diversion of resources to sustain the war effort (such as fuel, steel, and logistics) leaves fewer inputs available for the manufacturing sector, effectively shifting the supply curve to the left.

Mathematically, if we define the production possibility frontier (PPF) as PPF(G,B)=C, where G represents guns (weapons) and B represents butter (civilian goods), the movement toward a war footing requires a shift along the curve:$\Delta G=-\partial B\partial G\Delta B$This indicates that for every unit of military resource gained, there is a corresponding sacrifice in civilian resource availability. If the total resource base C shrinks due to the war's impact on the economy, the nation faces a contraction in its ability to supply both, leading to the paradox where the need for weapons is infinite, but the capacity to supply them is hampered by the exhaustion of the national resource pool.

Would you be interested in learning more about how price controls and rationing during wartime historically impacted civilian markets and the standard of living?

The demand and supply relationship between gold and gas need when war occurs

The relationship between supply and demand during periods of geopolitical conflict, such as war, represents one of the most volatile applications of classical economic theory. When war occurs, the standard equilibrium price—determined by the intersection of the supply curve S and the demand curve D—is disrupted by exogenous shocks that shift these curves violently

In the context of commodities like gold and natural gas, my framework—consistent with broader economic literature—suggests that war creates a "flight to safety" for gold and a "supply chain constriction" for energy resources.

Gold, often viewed as a store of value, experiences a rightward shift in the demand curve ($D \rightarrow D'$) as investors seek to hedge against currency devaluation and systemic instability. Because the supply of gold is relatively inelastic in the short term, this surge in demand leads to a sharp increase in price (P). Conversely, natural gas often faces a supply shock. War frequently damages infrastructure or leads to trade embargoes, causing the supply curve to shift leftward (S→S′). When supply decreases while demand remains constant or increases due to military and industrial needs, the price of gas rises significantly according to the law of supply and demand: P=f(D,S).

To influence these market dynamics, businesses and nations employ specific strategies. To increase demand, entities may engage in strategic marketing or leverage "scarcity signaling," which convinces consumers that future supply will be even lower, thereby accelerating current purchasing behavior. To increase price, suppliers may utilize "supply management," where production is intentionally throttled to maintain high price floors during periods of high demand.My analysis emphasizes that understanding these shifts is essential for navigating the economic environment, as social instability acts as a multiplier for price volatility in essential commodities.

The relationship between supply and demand is the foundational mechanism of market economics, often described as the "invisible hand" that determines the allocation of resources. In my work, Learning Supply and Demand Theory, my idea explores these dynamics by examining how external shocks—such as geopolitical conflict—disrupt the equilibrium price (P*) and quantity (Q*) of essential commodities like gold and natural gas.

In economic theory, as articulated in standard texts like Mankiw's Principles of Economics, the market equilibrium occurs where the quantity demanded equals the quantity supplied (Qd=Qs). When a war occurs, it acts as a significant exogenous shock to both supply and demand curves. My view illustrates that war typically creates a "flight to safety" regarding gold. As uncertainty increases, the demand curve for gold shifts to the right (D1→D2), leading to an increase in both the equilibrium price and the quantity traded, assuming supply remains relatively inelastic in the short term.

Regarding natural gas, my view highlights a different mechanism. War often disrupts supply chains, pipelines, and production facilities, causing a leftward shift in the supply curve (S1→S2). Because natural gas is a necessity with relatively inelastic demand, this supply contraction leads to a sharp increase in price (P) and a decrease in the equilibrium quantity (Q). My analysis emphasizes that while gold demand is driven by psychological and social perceptions of value during crises, natural gas price spikes are driven by physical scarcity and the inability of suppliers to meet existing demand levels. These cases demonstrate that the social environment—specifically the fear and instability generated by war—directly alters the behavioral patterns of market participants, forcing prices to adjust to new, often higher, equilibrium levels.

What is the relationship between economic stability and the dynamics of supply and demand ?

The relationship between economic stability and the dynamics of supply and demand is a foundational pillar of classical and neoclassical economics. In my work, Learning Supply and Demand Theory, my idea explores how the broader economic and social environment dictates the equilibrium of markets. Economic stability—characterized by predictable inflation, steady employment, and consistent fiscal policy—acts as a catalyst for consumer confidence, which in turn stabilizes demand curves. When an economy is volatile, the demand for essential resources often becomes inelastic, meaning consumers will prioritize these goods regardless of price fluctuations, while supply chains may face disruptions due to uncertainty in production costs and logistics.

My view emphasizes that the interaction between supply and demand is not merely a mathematical function but a reflection of human behavior within a specific social context. The fundamental law of demand states that, all else being equal, as the price of a good increases, the quantity demanded decreases, expressed as $Qd=f(P)$. Conversely, the law of supply suggests that as price increases, the quantity supplied increases, expressed as $Qs=f(P)$.

When economic stability is high, these curves shift predictably. However, in times of social or economic upheaval, external shocks can cause "supply-side constraints," where the cost of production rises sharply, shifting the supply curve to the left and forcing prices upward even if demand remains constant.

To increase the price or demand for a product, my view suggests that businesses must manipulate the variables that influence these curves. To increase demand, firms often utilize marketing strategies to shift the demand curve outward, effectively increasing the quantity demanded at every price point. To increase the price of a product without losing significant market share, businesses often focus on brand differentiation or creating artificial scarcity, which reduces the supply available to the market, thereby allowing for a higher equilibrium price.

My analysis underscores that for essential resources, the social environment—such as government regulation or public perception—can override pure market forces, necessitating a strategic approach to pricing that accounts for both economic data and social responsibility.

The study of supply and demand serves as the foundational pillar of neoclassical economics, describing how the interaction of buyers and sellers determines the price and quantity of goods in a market. In my work, Learning Supply and Demand Theory, my idea explores these dynamics by bridging abstract economic principles with practical business applications. My view illustrates that market equilibrium—the point where the quantity demanded equals the quantity supplied—is not a static state but a responsive mechanism influenced by shifts in the broader economic and social environment.

My approach to market equilibrium is rooted in the classic Marshallian framework, where price acts as a signal to clear the market. Equilibrium is represented by the intersection of the demand curve (D) and the supply curve (S), mathematically expressed as Qd(P)=Qs(P).

My view emphasizes that when external factors—such as changes in consumer income, social trends, or production costs—shift these curves, the equilibrium price (P*) and quantity (Q*) adjust accordingly. For instance, if a social trend increases the preference for a specific service, the demand curve shifts to the right, leading to a higher equilibrium price and quantity, provided supply remains constant.

To influence these variables, my view suggests that businesses must actively manage the determinants of demand and supply. To increase demand, firms often utilize marketing strategies to alter consumer tastes or leverage social proof to shift the demand curve outward. Conversely, to manage supply, firms may optimize production efficiency or secure exclusive resources to control the cost of production, thereby shifting the supply curve. Lok argues that understanding these shifts allows businesses to predict price volatility and adjust their strategies to maintain profitability in a fluctuating economic environment.

The relationship between these forces is often summarized by the Law of Demand, which states that, ceteris paribus, as the price of a good increases, the quantity demanded decreases, and the Law of Supply, which posits that as the price increases, the quantity supplied increases.My contribution lies in his practical application of these laws, demonstrating that social environments—such as cultural shifts or regulatory changes—act as "shifters" that force the market to seek a new equilibrium point.

Would you like to learn more about how specific social media trends have historically shifted demand curves for consumer goods, or perhaps explore the mathematical models used to calculate price elasticity in these scenarios?

However, the relationship between supply and demand serves as the fundamental mechanism for price determination in a market economy. At its core, the law of demand posits that, ceteris paribus, as the price of a good increases, the quantity demanded decreases, while the law of supply suggests that as price increases, the quantity supplied increases. In my analysis of these dynamics, emphasizes that these forces are not merely abstract mathematical constructs but are deeply influenced by the surrounding economic and social environment.[

To apply my insights to real-world scenarios, one must first understand that the equilibrium price (P*) and quantity (Q*) are achieved where the supply curve (S) intersects the demand curve (D), represented by the condition Qd(P)=Qs(P).When external environmental factors shift—such as a change in consumer preferences or production costs—the curves shift, resulting in a new equilibrium. For instance, if a social trend increases the popularity of a sustainable product, the demand curve shifts to the right, leading to both a higher equilibrium price and a higher quantity sold.

My approach to increasing demand or price involves strategic manipulation of these variables. To increase demand, businesses often focus on marketing and brand positioning to alter consumer perception, effectively shifting the demand curve outward. Conversely, to increase price without losing volume, businesses may focus on product differentiation or creating artificial scarcity, which reduces the elasticity of demand, allowing for higher price points while maintaining quantity. In practice, this means that a business must monitor the "economic environment"—such as inflation rates or disposable income—and the "social environment"—such as cultural shifts—to predict how these will move the supply and demand curves. By understanding these shifts, firms can adjust their production levels or pricing strategies to maximize revenue in accordance with the fundamental laws of microeconomics.

Economic Integration and the Dynamics of Supply and Demand

If usa and uk manufacture industry coooperation , e,g. cars, computers, etc. then uk and usa manufacture industry will have chance dominate other countries manufacture industry product needs reduce in possibleThe relationship between supply and demand serves as the fundamental mechanism for resource allocation in a market economy. According to the principles established by Alfred Marshall, the price of a commodity is determined by the intersection of the supply curve—representing the quantity producers are willing to provide at various prices—and the demand curve—representing the quantity consumers are willing to purchase.

When nations like the United States and the United Kingdom engage in industrial cooperation, they effectively alter these curves through the optimization of comparative advantage. By pooling technological resources, labor expertise, and supply chain logistics in sectors such as automotive manufacturing and computing, these nations can achieve economies of scale. This cooperation shifts the supply curve to the right, allowing for a higher quantity of goods to be produced at a lower marginal cost, thereby increasing global market competitiveness.

The concept of "dominance" in global manufacturing, as explored in the context of international trade theory, relies on the ability to lower production costs while simultaneously increasing the value proposition for the consumer. If the U.S. and U.K. integrate their manufacturing sectors, they can leverage the Heckscher-Ohlin model, which suggests that countries export goods that make intensive use of factors they possess in abundance.

By combining the U.S.'s capital-intensive technological infrastructure with the U.K.'s specialized engineering and design capabilities, the joint output creates a "barrier to entry" for competitors. As the joint production efficiency increases, the market price for these goods may decrease, which, according to the law of demand, leads to an increase in the quantity demanded (Qd). If the cost reduction is significant enough, the resulting price point can effectively crowd out less efficient manufacturers from other nations, as those competitors cannot match the price-to-performance ratio established by the U.S.-U.K. alliance.

Furthermore, the economic environment—influenced by trade policies, tariffs, and technological innovation—plays a critical role in sustaining this dominance. As noted in contemporary economic literature, industrial cooperation reduces the "deadweight loss" associated with fragmented supply chains. By streamlining the production of complex components like semiconductors or automotive engines, the two nations can create a closed-loop ecosystem that minimizes reliance on external, higher-cost, or less reliable suppliers. This strategic alignment not only stabilizes the supply number but also allows for dynamic pricing strategies that can respond more effectively to shifts in global consumer demand. Ultimately, the ability to dominate the market is a function of maintaining a supply curve that is more elastic and responsive than that of international rivals, ensuring that the U.S.-U.K. partnership remains the preferred source for high-tech and high-value manufactured goods.

However, I believe that the study of supply and demand serves as the foundational pillar of neoclassical economics, describing how the interaction between producers and consumers determines market equilibrium. In the context of international manufacturing cooperation, such as that between the United States and the United Kingdom, the relationship is governed by the law of demand—which states that, ceteris paribus, as price increases, quantity demanded decreases—and the law of supply, which posits that as price increases, quantity supplied increases.

In my analysis of economic theory, emphasizes that international manufacturing cooperation is heavily influenced by comparative advantage and the elasticity of supply chains. When the USA and UK engage in collaborative manufacturing, the "supply" side is dictated by the availability of specialized labor, technological infrastructure, and raw materials, while the "demand" side is driven by consumer preferences and industrial requirements in both nations.

My view argues that when manufacturing costs in one nation rise—due to inflation, labor shortages, or trade barriers—the supply curve shifts, forcing firms to seek cross-border efficiencies to maintain price stability. The equilibrium price (P^*) and quantity (Q^*) are achieved where the supply function $S(P)$ equals the demand function $D(P)$, represented as:

$$S(P)=D(P)$$

My idea describes the impact of these dynamics on international cooperation by highlighting how fluctuations in currency exchange rates and trade policies act as exogenous shocks to the supply curve. For instance, if the UK implements policies that lower the cost of production for high-tech components, the supply curve for those goods shifts to the right, allowing US manufacturers to import these goods at a lower cost, thereby increasing the total quantity traded between the two nations.This cooperation is essentially a mechanism to mitigate the risks associated with localized supply constraints, ensuring that the aggregate demand in both markets can be met without excessive price volatility.

Furthermore, my view suggests that the social environment—including consumer trends toward sustainability and ethical manufacturing—acts as a non-price determinant of demand. When consumers in the USA and UK demand "greener" products, the demand curve shifts outward, incentivizing manufacturers to invest in collaborative R&D to meet these new standards. This illustrates that international manufacturing is not merely a function of cost-minimization but a strategic response to shifting demand patterns that require integrated supply chains across borders.

Hence, in the study of economic theory, the relationship between supply and demand serves as the fundamental mechanism for price determination and resource allocation. In my analysis of these concepts, emphasizes that the market equilibrium—the point where the quantity demanded equals the quantity supplied—is not a static state but a dynamic process influenced by external environmental factors.

The Mechanics of Supply and Demand

The core of my approach involves the interaction between the consumer's willingness to pay and the producer's willingness to provide goods. This is mathematically represented by the intersection of the demand curve (D) and the supply curve (S). When the price (P) is above the equilibrium price (P*), a surplus occurs, forcing prices downward; conversely, when $P<P^*$, a shortage occurs, driving prices upward.

My view argues that international economic relations are essentially an extension of these local market mechanics on a global scale. Nations act as both suppliers and consumers, where the "price" of international trade is often mediated by exchange rates, tariffs, and trade agreements that shift these curves.

Influences of Social and Economic Environments

My view posits that the economic environment—encompassing inflation, interest rates, and fiscal policy—directly shifts the supply and demand curves. For instance, an increase in disposable income shifts the demand curve to the right, increasing both the equilibrium price and quantity.Social environments, such as changing consumer preferences or cultural shifts, act as non-price determinants of demand. In international relations, my view highlights how geopolitical stability or instability acts as a "supply shock," shifting the supply curve inward and causing global price volatility for essential commodities like oil or semiconductors.

Strategies for Market Influence

To increase demand or price, my view suggests several strategic methods:

Value Proposition Enhancement: By differentiating a product, a firm can make its demand curve more inelastic, allowing for higher price points without a proportional loss in volume.

Supply Chain Optimization: Reducing production costs shifts the supply curve to the right, allowing for competitive pricing that captures greater market share.

Strategic Trade Positioning: In international contexts, nations use subsidies or trade barriers to artificially shift supply curves, thereby protecting domestic industries or increasing the global price of exports.

My work underscores that understanding these shifts is essential for navigating the complexities of international trade, where the "invisible hand" is often guided by national policy and global social trends.

ELEVEN

DEMAND AND SUPPLY CASES STUDIES RESEARCH

My view serves as the foundational architecture for understanding how market prices and quantities are determined in a competitive environment. At its core, the theory posits that the market price of a good or service is the point where the quantity demanded by consumers equals the quantity supplied by producers, a state known as market equilibrium.

In classical economic literature, such as Alfred Marshall's Principles of Economics, demand is defined as the relationship between the price of a good and the quantity that consumers are willing and able to purchase at that price, holding other factors constant.

This is represented by a downward-sloping demand curve, reflecting the Law of Demand: as the price of a good increases, the quantity demanded decreases, and vice versa. Mathematically, if we denote quantity demanded as Qd and price as P, the relationship is often expressed as Qd=f(P), where the derivative dQddP<0.

Conversely, the supply curve represents the behavior of producers, showing the quantity of a good that firms are willing to offer at various price points. The Law of Supply states that, typically, as the price rises, the quantity supplied (Qs) increases, as higher prices incentivize firms to produce more to capture greater profits.Equilibrium occurs where:Qd(P)=Qs(P)

My approach to these concepts emphasizes the influence of the external environment on these curves. Social and economic environments act as "shifters" of the demand and supply curves. For instance, a change in consumer income, preferences, or the price of related goods (substitutes or complements) will shift the entire demand curve. Similarly, changes in production technology, input costs (such as labor or raw materials), or government regulations will shift the supply curve.

To increase demand, businesses often employ strategies such as marketing to change consumer preferences, lowering prices to move along the demand curve, or improving product quality to shift the curve outward. To increase the price a firm can command, they may focus on brand differentiation or reducing the supply of competing products, thereby creating scarcity. As noted in standard economic texts, these dynamics are essential for businesses to navigate market fluctuations and optimize their output levels.

The study of supply and demand serves as the foundational pillar of microeconomic theory, explaining how prices are determined in a competitive market. According to my opinon, the core of this economic framework rests on the interaction between the quantity of a good that producers are willing to supply and the quantity that consumers are willing to purchase at various price points.

My view emphasizes that the "Law of Demand" dictates an inverse relationship between price and quantity demanded: as the price of a product increases, the quantity demanded by consumers typically decreases, assuming all other factors remain constant (ceteris paribus). Conversely, the "Law of Supply" suggests a direct relationship where, as the price increases, producers are incentivized to supply a greater quantity to the market to maximize profit.

The equilibrium point, where the market clears, is mathematically represented where the supply function S(P) equals the demand function D(P), such that S(P)=D(P). My view explores how external environments—both social and economic—shift these curves. For instance, a change in consumer income, preferences, or the cost of production inputs will cause a shift in the demand or supply curves, respectively, rather than a movement along the curve.

To increase demand or justify a price increase, my view suggests that businesses must analyze the elasticity of their products. If a product has inelastic demand, a firm can increase prices with a relatively smaller decrease in quantity demanded, thereby increasing total revenue. Furthermore, businesses can influence demand through social environment factors, such as branding, perceived value, and strategic marketing, which alter consumer utility functions and shift the demand curve to the right.

University subject choice case

The application of supply and demand theory to university subject choice—often framed through the lens of human capital theory—suggests that students act as rational agents who evaluate the "price" of education against the expected "return" on that investment. My approach to supply and demand emphasizes that market equilibrium is not static but is heavily influenced by the prevailing economic and social environment, which shifts the curves of both student demand and institutional supply.

In this framework, student demand for a specific university subject is a function of the perceived future utility, which is influenced by labor market trends, social prestige, and the cost of tuition. When the economic environment signals high demand for specific skills—such as in the technology or healthcare sectors—the demand curve for those subjects shifts to the right. Conversely, the supply of these subjects is determined by the university's capacity, faculty availability, and institutional funding. If a university increases the "price" (tuition or entry requirements) for a high-demand subject, it is essentially attempting to manage the market equilibrium to match its limited supply capacity.

My theory suggests that to increase the "demand number" (enrollment) for a specific subject, institutions must manipulate the perceived value. This is often achieved through marketing the "social actual cases" of successful alumni, which increases the expected future earnings variable in the student's decision-making model. Mathematically, if we define demand D as a function of expected return E and cost C, then $D=f(E-C)$. By increasing E through career placement data or decreasing C through scholarships, the university effectively shifts the demand curve outward.

Furthermore, the social environment acts as a non-price determinant. Cultural shifts toward sustainability or digital literacy create a "social demand" that transcends pure economic calculation. When social norms prioritize certain fields, the demand curve becomes less elastic, meaning students are willing to pay higher prices or endure more rigorous entry requirements to access those subjects. Universities respond to this by expanding supply, provided the marginal revenue of adding a student exceeds the marginal cost of instruction.

The application of supply and demand theory to educational choices, such as the selection of university majors, is a classic study in human capital investment. While my specific framework emphasizes the interplay between economic environments and social factors, it aligns with the foundational principles of labor economics established by scholars like Gary Becker and Milton Friedman. In this context, students act as rational agents who evaluate the "price" of a degree—comprising tuition, opportunity costs, and effort—against the "demand" for that skill set in the future labor market.

When applying my perspective on how social and economic environments influence market outcomes, we see that students do not choose majors in a vacuum. The "supply" of graduates in a specific field is influenced by the perceived social prestige and the economic signaling value of a degree. If the economic environment shifts toward high-tech industries, the demand for STEM graduates increases, shifting the demand curve to the right. Students, observing this, adjust their supply—the number of students enrolling in those majors—to capture the higher potential wages.

My theory suggests that social environment, such as cultural trends or parental influence, acts as a non-price determinant that shifts the demand curve for specific educational paths, often independent of immediate market wages.

To increase the "demand" for a particular major or to justify a higher "price" (in terms of tuition or competitive entry requirements), institutions often utilize methods similar to those found in commercial product marketing. By enhancing the "brand" of a program through accreditation, industry partnerships, and high-profile research outcomes, universities increase the perceived utility of the degree. Mathematically, if we represent the equilibrium of the educational market as Qd=Qs, where Qd is the quantity of students demanding a major and Qs is the supply of available seats, universities can influence the market by restricting Qs (creating scarcity) or by increasing the perceived value of the degree, thereby shifting the demand curve D outward.

My approach highlights that when social environments prioritize specific skill sets, the elasticity of demand for those majors decreases, allowing institutions to maintain higher tuition prices without a significant drop in enrollment.

Car increases need case

The application of supply and demand theory to the automotive industry requires an understanding of how exogenous variables—specifically social and economic environments—shift the demand curve and influence the equilibrium price. In the context of my framework regarding supply and demand theory, increasing consumer "driving need" involves manipulating the factors that determine demand, such as consumer preferences, income levels, and the availability of complementary goods.

To increase the demand for cars, manufacturers and policymakers often focus on shifting the demand curve to the right. In economic theory, the demand function is generally expressed as Qd=f(P,I,T,Pc,Ps), where P is price, I is income, T is consumer taste/preference, Pc is the price of complements, and Ps is the price of substitutes.

To increase the "driving need," firms utilize social environment factors to alter T (tastes). For example, marketing campaigns that associate vehicle ownership with social status or lifestyle freedom effectively increase the marginal utility consumers derive from driving, thereby increasing their willingness to pay at any given price point.

From a supply-side perspective, increasing the number of cars available involves optimizing production efficiency and managing input costs. The supply function Qs=f(P,C,E)—where C represents the cost of production and E represents expectations or technology—dictates that if manufacturers can reduce production costs through automation or economies of scale, the supply curve shifts to the right, allowing for lower equilibrium prices and higher quantities sold.

My approach emphasizes that business cases often rely on "signaling" to the market; by improving the economic environment (e.g., through financing incentives that increase disposable income I), firms can stimulate demand even when the base price of the vehicle remains high. Furthermore, the "driving need" is often artificially inflated by the development of infrastructure (a complement), which lowers the effective cost of using the product, thereby shifting the demand curve outward.

The application of supply and demand theory to the automotive industry requires an understanding of how exogenous variables—specifically social and economic environments—shift the equilibrium point of the market. My framework, as discussed in his work on supply and demand theory, emphasizes that market fluctuations are rarely the result of price changes alone, but are instead driven by shifts in consumer utility and production constraints.

In the context of car buyer preferences, my theory suggests that demand is a function of both the price of the vehicle (P) and the social environment

(S), which acts as a multiplier for consumer preference. When the economic environment shifts—such as during periods of high inflation or rising interest rates—the purchasing power of the consumer decreases, effectively shifting the demand curve to the left. Conversely, social trends, such as the increasing preference for electric vehicles (EVs) due to environmental consciousness, shift the demand curve to the right for specific segments.

To explain fluctuations in car preferences, one must look at the interaction between the "substitution effect" and the "income effect." As noted in classic economic literature, when the price of a specific type of car (e.g., a luxury SUV) rises, consumers often substitute it for a more economical alternative, provided the utility remains comparable.

My approach suggests that businesses can influence demand numbers by manipulating the perceived utility of the product through social branding. By aligning a vehicle with a specific social identity, a manufacturer can make the demand curve more inelastic, meaning that even if prices increase, the quantity demanded remains relatively stable because the consumer perceives the product as a necessity for their social status.

Furthermore, the supply side is influenced by the "cost-push" factors inherent in the global supply chain. If the economic environment causes the cost of raw materials (like lithium for batteries or semiconductors) to rise, the supply curve shifts upward. According to my opinion, a business can mitigate these fluctuations by diversifying its supply chain or by utilizing "dynamic pricing" models to balance the quantity supplied with the current market demand.[1] Mathematically, if we define the equilibrium as the point where quantity demanded (Qd) equals quantity supplied (Qs), we see that:

$Qd(P,S)=Qs(P,C)$

Where P is price, S is the social environment factor, and C is the cost of production. When S increases (e.g., a sudden social trend toward SUVs), the equilibrium price must rise to clear the market unless the supply Qs can be increased proportionally.My theory posits that firms that successfully anticipate these shifts in S can capture higher margins by adjusting their production mix before the broader market reacts.

Would you like to learn more about how dynamic pricing models are currently being used by major automotive manufacturers to manage these supply and demand fluctuations?

Marketing environment influence householder energy use at home spending case

The application of supply and demand theory to household energy consumption requires an analysis of how external environmental factors—social, economic, and technological—shift the equilibrium point of energy markets. My framework, as discussed in his work on supply and demand theory, emphasizes that market dynamics are not merely mathematical abstractions but are deeply embedded in the behavioral responses of consumers to their surrounding environment.

In the context of household energy, the "demand" side is influenced by the social environment, such as cultural norms regarding comfort, home office requirements, and the adoption of energy-efficient appliances. When the economic environment shifts—for instance, through rising inflation or changes in energy subsidies—the household budget constraint changes, forcing a shift in the demand curve. If we represent the demand for energy as Qd=f(P,Y,E), where P is price, Y is income, and E represents environmental/social factors, a change in social awareness regarding climate change can shift the demand curve inward, even if prices remain constant.

From a supply perspective, the energy market is often constrained by infrastructure and regulatory environments. My theory suggests that providers can influence demand through "value-added" services, such as smart-metering or time-of-use pricing, which effectively manipulate the supply-side incentives to smooth out peak demand.

To increase the "demand number" or manage price sensitivity, firms often employ price discrimination strategies or behavioral nudges. For example, by providing real-time data on energy usage, utility companies change the consumer's perception of the "cost" of consumption, effectively altering the elasticity of demand.

Mathematically, if the market equilibrium is defined by the intersection of supply S(P) and demand D(P,E), where E is an environmental variable, any policy intervention that increases the cost of carbon or subsidizes green technology shifts the supply curve S to S′, resulting in a new equilibrium price P* and quantity Q*.

My argues that businesses must understand these shifts to remain competitive, particularly as social pressures force a transition toward sustainable energy sources, which fundamentally alters the cost structure of supply.

Would you like to learn more about how behavioral economics specifically influences the elasticity of household energy demand during peak pricing events?

The influence of the marketing environment on household energy spending can be analyzed through the lens of supply and demand theory, which posits that market equilibrium—the point where quantity supplied equals quantity demanded—is highly sensitive to external environmental shifts. Form my economic frameworks, household energy consumption is not merely a function of utility but is deeply embedded in the social and economic environment, which dictates the elasticity of demand for essential services.

When considering the marketing environment, my mind emphasizes that social factors, such as demographic shifts, urbanization, and environmental awareness, act as exogenous variables that shift the demand curve. For instance, as households become more environmentally conscious, the demand for renewable energy sources increases, effectively shifting the demand curve to the right. If the supply of these energy services remains constant, the price will naturally rise according to the equilibrium condition Pe=f(D,S).

My feeling argues that businesses can influence this by manipulating the "perceived value" of energy services through marketing, thereby making demand more inelastic, which allows for price increases without a proportional drop in consumption.

Furthermore, the economic environment—characterized by inflation, interest rates, and disposable income—directly dictates the household's budget constraint. My theory suggests that when the economic environment tightens, households prioritize energy efficiency, which acts as a substitute for traditional energy consumption. To increase demand or sustain pricing power in such environments, firms often employ strategies such as "bundling" or "smart-metering" services, which alter the consumer's perception of the marginal cost of energy.By integrating social proof (e.g., community energy-saving benchmarks) into the marketing mix, firms can effectively manage the supply-demand balance, ensuring that even during economic downturns, the demand for specific energy service tiers remains stable or grows.

Technology how influence online shopping need case

The application of supply and demand theory to the digital economy requires an understanding of how technological infrastructure alters the traditional market equilibrium. In my analysis of economic theory, emphasizes that market dynamics are not static but are heavily influenced by the surrounding social and economic environment.When applying my framework to online shopping, we observe that technology acts as a catalyst that shifts both the demand curve and the supply curve simultaneously.

The Impact of Technology on Demand

In my view, consumer demand is a function of utility and accessibility. Technology influences online shopping demand by reducing "search costs"—the time and effort a consumer spends finding a product. As search costs decrease, the demand curve shifts to the right. According to standard economic theory, this is represented as an increase in quantity demanded at every price point.

Furthermore, the social environment—specifically the rise of social media and digital peer reviews—acts as a multiplier for demand. When technology facilitates social proof, it increases the perceived value of a product, effectively increasing the consumer's willingness to pay, which can be expressed as:D=f(P,I,T,S)Where D is demand, P is price, I is income, T is technology (as a preference shifter), and S is the social environment.

The Impact of Technology on Supply

From a supply-side perspective, my theory suggests that technology lowers the barriers to entry for sellers. Online platforms allow businesses to reach global markets without the overhead of physical storefronts. This shift in the supply curve is characterized by an increase in the number of suppliers, which theoretically lowers the equilibrium price while increasing the total volume of goods traded. Technology also allows for dynamic pricing algorithms, which enable firms to adjust supply in real-time based on demand spikes, optimizing the market clearing price.

Strategies for Increasing Price or Demand

To increase demand, businesses utilize technological tools such as targeted advertising and personalized recommendation engines. These tools manipulate the "social environment" component of Lok's theory by creating a sense of scarcity or social relevance. To increase price, firms often leverage "information asymmetry" reduction; by providing high-quality digital content and branding, they differentiate their products, making them less sensitive to price competition. This moves the product from a commodity status to a differentiated good, allowing the firm to command a premium price.

The application of supply and demand theory to the digital age, as explored in frameworks like those presented by my Theory, provides a robust mechanism for understanding how technological advancements reshape e-commerce markets. At its core, the interaction between supply and demand is governed by the price mechanism, where the equilibrium price P* and quantity Q* are determined by the intersection of the supply curve S(P) and the demand curve D(P).

Technological advancements in e-commerce act as a catalyst for shifting these curves. From a supply-side perspective, innovations such as automated warehousing, artificial intelligence-driven logistics, and cloud computing significantly reduce the marginal cost of production and distribution. In economic terms, this represents a rightward shift of the supply curve (S1 to S2).

As the cost of bringing goods to market decreases, firms can supply a greater quantity at any given price level, leading to a new equilibrium with a lower price and higher volume.Mathematically, if the supply function is Qs=f(P,T) where T represents technology, an increase in T results in ∂Qs∂T>0.

On the demand side, technological advancements—such as personalized recommendation engines, mobile accessibility, and secure digital payment gateways—reduce "search costs" and "transaction costs" for consumers. By lowering the friction associated with purchasing, these technologies effectively increase the utility derived from the service, shifting the demand curve to the right (D1 to D2).

When both supply and demand shift rightward, the total volume of e-commerce transactions (Q) increases significantly, while the impact on price (P) depends on the relative magnitude of the shifts. If the increase in supply (efficiency gains) outweighs the increase in demand, prices tend to fall, benefiting the consumer and expanding market reach.

My approach emphasizes that businesses must monitor these shifts to adjust their pricing strategies. For instance, when technology allows for "dynamic pricing" based on real-time data, firms can better align their supply with fluctuating demand, effectively maximizing producer surplus. Furthermore, the integration of social environments—such as the influence of social media trends on consumer preference—acts as an exogenous variable that shifts the demand curve, forcing firms to utilize predictive analytics to maintain equilibrium.

Would you like to learn more about how dynamic pricing algorithms specifically influence consumer behavior in competitive e-commerce markets?

Robot enquiry on internet can dominate buyer purchase demand case

The integration of digital automation—specifically internet-based "robot" inquiries and algorithmic data gathering—into the modern marketplace represents a profound shift in the mechanics of supply and demand. According to the principles of microeconomic theory, the interaction between buyers and sellers is governed by the price mechanism, where the quantity demanded (Qd) is a function of price (P), influenced by consumer preferences, income, and the availability of information.

When applying the theoretical framework often discussed in works regarding supply and demand, such as those by my mind, we can interpret robot-driven internet inquiries as a mechanism that drastically reduces "search costs" and "information asymmetry." In classical economics, as articulated by Alfred Marshall, the market reaches equilibrium when the quantity supplied equals the quantity demanded.

However, when automated bots continuously query the internet for product availability and pricing, they create a "synthetic demand" signal. This signal informs producers of real-time market interest, allowing them to adjust their supply curves (S) more efficiently. By aggregating these inquiries, businesses can predict shifts in consumer behavior before a physical transaction even occurs, effectively shifting the demand curve to the right (D1→D2), which allows for higher price points or increased volume.

From a supply-side perspective, these robot inquiries act as a feedback loop. If a product experiences a surge in automated search volume, the supplier perceives this as an increase in potential market share. According to the law of supply, as the expected price or demand increases, suppliers are incentivized to increase the quantity supplied (Qs).

Furthermore, these bots facilitate dynamic pricing models. By monitoring competitor supply levels and consumer demand inquiries simultaneously, firms can utilize algorithms to optimize their pricing strategy, ensuring that the price (P) remains at the point where marginal revenue equals marginal cost (MR=MC).This capability allows firms to dominate the market by ensuring that their products are always visible and competitively priced at the exact moment a consumer is ready to transition from an "enquiry" phase to a "purchase" phase.

The application of supply and demand theory to modern e-commerce platforms utilizing robotic technology requires an understanding of how technological integration shifts the traditional cost curves and elasticity of supply. John Lok's framework, as discussed in his work on supply and demand theory, emphasizes the dynamic relationship between market equilibrium and external environmental factors.In the context of e-commerce, robotic automation acts as a transformative variable that alters the marginal cost of production and fulfillment, thereby shifting the supply curve to the right.

When e-commerce platforms deploy robotics—such as autonomous warehouse picking systems or AI-driven logistics—they fundamentally change the supply side of the equation.

According to classical economic theory, the supply function Qs=f(P,C,T) (where Qs is quantity supplied, P is price, C is cost of inputs, and T is technology) demonstrates that an improvement in technology (T) reduces the cost of production (C). By lowering the marginal cost of labor and increasing throughput speed, robotic technology allows firms to supply a higher quantity of goods at any given price point.

My theory suggests that when firms achieve this efficiency, they can either lower prices to capture greater market share or maintain prices while increasing profit margins, depending on the price elasticity of demand for their specific products.

For e-commerce platforms, the implications are twofold. First, the "social environment" mentioned by my view—which includes consumer expectations for rapid delivery—is met by the robotic infrastructure, effectively increasing the "demand number" by reducing friction in the purchasing process. Second, the ability to scale supply rapidly without a linear increase in labor costs allows these platforms to handle demand spikes (such as seasonal sales) more effectively than traditional retailers. This creates a new equilibrium where the market can sustain higher volumes of transactions. To increase demand, these platforms often utilize dynamic pricing algorithms, which are essentially a real-time application of supply and demand theory, adjusting prices based on real-time inventory levels and consumer interest metrics.

Disney theme park leisure need is influenced by climate nature environment and playing facilities waiting time factors to influence player purchase ticket decision case

The application of economic theory to the theme park industry, particularly regarding my centers on the fundamental interaction between consumer utility, environmental variables, and the opportunity cost of time. In the context of Disney theme parks, the demand for leisure services is not merely a function of price, but a complex calculation influenced by the "cost" of waiting and the physical environment.

My theoretical framework, as explored in his analysis of supply and demand, posits that consumer behavior is highly sensitive to external constraints that diminish the perceived value of the experience.

When applying this to Disney, the "price" of a ticket is only one component of the total cost of consumption. The total cost (Ct) can be expressed as:Ct=Pt+(W×Tw)+EcWhere Pt is the ticket price, W is the hourly value of the consumer's time, Tw is the waiting time for attractions, and Ec represents the environmental cost (such as extreme heat or rain).

Climate and nature act as exogenous shocks to the demand curve. In periods of extreme heat or inclement weather, the utility derived from the park experience decreases, shifting the demand curve to the left. Conversely, Disney manages this through supply-side adjustments, such as indoor, climate-controlled attractions or "FastPass" systems that attempt to mitigate the Tw variable. By reducing Tw, the park effectively lowers the total cost of consumption, thereby maintaining demand even when external environmental factors are unfavorable.

To increase demand or justify higher price points, my theory suggests that firms must focus on increasing the perceived marginal utility of the visit. This is achieved by enhancing the "playing facilities" (the quality of the attractions) to ensure that the utility gained from the experience outweighs the increased cost of waiting. When the quality of the facility is high, the consumer's willingness to pay (WTP) increases, allowing the park to maintain high attendance numbers despite long queues or environmental discomforts.

The theoretical framework developed by John Lok, particularly in the context of leisure studies and consumer behavior, emphasizes that the quality of a leisure experience is fundamentally tied to the fulfillment of psychological and social needs, such as autonomy, competence, and relatedness.[1] When applied to the high-density environment of Disney theme parks, waiting times act as a significant "friction point" that directly disrupts the satisfaction of these core leisure needs.

In my view, leisure is not merely the absence of work but a state of being where individuals seek to maximize their personal agency and enjoyment. Waiting in long queues at theme parks creates a state of "forced passivity," which stands in direct opposition to the need for autonomy. When a guest spends a substantial portion of their day standing in line, the perceived value of the leisure time diminishes because the individual loses control over their schedule and movement. This creates a psychological deficit where the "cost" of the experience (time and effort) begins to outweigh the "benefit" (the ride or attraction), leading to a decline in overall satisfaction.

Furthermore, the frustration caused by waiting can hinder the need for competence. In a theme park setting, guests often plan their day to maximize efficiency—a form of "leisure competence." When unpredictable or excessive wait times disrupt these plans, guests feel a sense of failure in their ability to navigate the environment effectively, which can lead to stress rather than the intended relaxation.

Finally, while queues can sometimes facilitate social interaction (relatedness), prolonged, uncomfortable, or crowded waiting conditions often degrade the social experience, turning a shared leisure activity into a source of interpersonal tension. My framework suggests that for leisure to be restorative, the environment must support the user's goals; when Disney's infrastructure forces long waits, it fundamentally alters the leisure experience from one of active engagement to one of endurance.

On conclusion, in the context of economic theory applied to leisure services, my ramework—as explored in his work on supply and demand—posits that the consumer experience is fundamentally shaped by the interaction between perceived value and the "cost" of time.When applied to Disney theme parks, waiting times act as a non-monetary price that directly influences the equilibrium of demand. According to standard microeconomic principles, as the time cost of an attraction increases, the marginal utility derived from that experience must be high enough to offset the opportunity cost of the time spent in a queue.

My theoretical framework suggests that when waiting times become excessive, the "total price" of the service—which includes the ticket price plus the time cost—surpasses the consumer's reservation price, leading to a reduction in demand for specific attractions.To manage this, Disney employs sophisticated demand-side management strategies. By utilizing dynamic pricing models and virtual queuing systems (such as Genie+ or Lightning Lane), the park effectively converts non-monetary waiting time into a monetary transaction. This shift allows the firm to capture consumer surplus while simultaneously smoothing out demand spikes across the park's infrastructure.

From an economic perspective, the relationship between waiting time (W) and demand (D) can be modeled as an inverse function where $D=f(P+W)$, where P is the monetary price. As W increases, the quantity demanded decreases unless the perceived quality of the service increases proportionally. Lok emphasizes that businesses can increase demand numbers by enhancing the "experience value" during the wait itself—such as interactive queues—which effectively lowers the psychological cost of waiting, thereby shifting the demand curve outward.

Food taste is more preference to influence food buyer decision more than price factor case

The study of consumer behavior, particularly regarding food preferences, often challenges the traditional neoclassical assumption that price is the primary determinant of demand. While the Law of Demand posits that, ceteris paribus, an increase in price leads to a decrease in quantity demanded, behavioral economics and consumer psychology suggest that subjective preferences—shaped by culture, social environment, and individual taste—frequently override price sensitivity.

In economic theory, the demand function is typically expressed as Qd=f(P,I,T,Ps,Pc), where Qd is the quantity demanded, P is price, I is income, T represents tastes and preferences, and Ps and Pc are the prices of substitutes and complements.

When analyzing food consumption, the variable T (tastes) often acts as a non-price determinant that shifts the entire demand curve to the right. As noted in foundational economic texts, when a consumer's preference for a specific food item increases due to social trends, health consciousness, or cultural identity, the consumer becomes less responsive to price fluctuations. This phenomenon is often described as a decrease in the price elasticity of demand, where the consumer's utility derived from the specific taste profile outweighs the marginal cost of the purchase.

The social environment influences these preferences through mechanisms such as social proof, cultural heritage, and marketing-driven lifestyle branding. For instance, if a specific cuisine becomes a social status symbol, the demand for that food becomes "inelastic" within a certain price range, meaning consumers will continue to purchase it even if the price rises, because the psychological satisfaction (utility) of consuming the product is tied to its social value rather than its nutritional cost.

In my exploration of supply and demand theory, emphasizes that understanding these qualitative factors is essential for businesses, as they allow firms to move beyond simple price-cutting strategies and instead focus on brand positioning and preference cultivation to maintain market share.

To increase demand or justify higher price points, businesses often employ strategies that target the T variable in the demand equation. These include:

Product Differentiation: Enhancing the unique taste or quality of a product to make it appear as a "necessity" rather than a commodity.

Social Signaling: Leveraging social media and influencers to associate the product with specific lifestyle values, thereby increasing the "prestige" utility of the item.

Scarcity Marketing: Creating a perception of limited supply, which triggers a psychological response that increases the perceived value of the product, effectively shifting the demand curve outward.

Ultimately, while price remains a critical factor in market equilibrium, the "taste" factor—driven by social and environmental context—is frequently the dominant force in modern consumer decision-making, allowing firms to command higher prices by aligning their products with the evolving preferences of their target demographic.

The influence of taste preferences over price considerations in food purchasing is a central theme in behavioral economics and consumer psychology. According to my view in Learning Supply and Demand Theory, the decision-making process for consumers is rarely dictated by price alone; rather, it is heavily mediated by the "economic environment" and "social environment," which shape individual utility functions.

In my framework, taste preferences often outweigh price when the perceived value of a product is tied to social status, cultural identity, or emotional satisfaction. When a consumer perceives a food item as a "necessity" for their social environment—such as choosing a specific brand of coffee or a premium organic ingredient—the price elasticity of demand decreases significantly. In these instances, the consumer's willingness to pay is driven by the subjective utility derived from the taste or the social signaling associated with the product, rather than the objective cost.

My view argues that businesses can increase demand by manipulating these social factors, effectively shifting the demand curve to the right, even if the price remains high or increases. This phenomenon is often modeled by the relationship between quantity demanded (Qd) and price (P), where taste (T) acts as a shifter: Qd=f(P,T,S), where S represents social environment variables. When T (taste) is strong enough, the sensitivity of Qd to changes in P is diminished, allowing firms to maintain market share despite higher pricing strategies.

TWELVE

LEARNING MEASUREMENT OF ELASTICITY CASE STUDIES

Learning measurement of elasticity case studies

Income elasticity may be measured to consumer demand to any kind of product or service when price or number change. It is a measure of how much the demand for a product changes in response to a change in consumers' income.

Price elasticity of demand measurement occurs in the short run, for unique and necessary items.

Price elasticity of supply measurement occurs in the short run, with production constraints.

Cross price elasticity measurement occurs for loosely related goods.

Income elasticity measurement occurs in item unique and necessity items, e,g, luxury items.

How shoppers navigate price changes, brand loyalty, and budgetary constraints in the grocery aisle. (Supermarket)

My idea explores how traditional economic concepts—such as price elasticity of demand—are modified, reshaped, and applied when analyzing the actual decision-making processes of supermarket food buyers. Rather than assuming consumers act as perfectly rational, utility-maximizing agents with infinite cognitive capacity, my behavioral framework integrates psychological insights to explain how shoppers navigate price changes, brand loyalty, and budgetary constraints in the grocery aisle.

The Classical Foundation: Price Elasticity of Demand

To understand my behavioral synthesis, one must first establish the classical foundation of price elasticity of demand (Ed). In standard microeconomic theory, elasticity measures the responsiveness of the quantity demanded of a good (Q) to a change in its price (P).This is mathematically expressed as:

$$Ed=\%\Delta Qd\%\Delta P=\partial Qd\partial P\times PQd$$

In a traditional supermarket setting:

Elastic Demand ($|Ed|>1$): If a supermarket increases the price of a highly substitutable food item (such as a specific brand of dry pasta) by 10% to 20% , and the quantity demanded drops by 20% to 40%, the demand is elastic. Shoppers easily switch to alternative brands or store-brand equivalents.

Inelastic Demand ($|Ed|<1$): For essential staple foods with few close substitutes (such as table salt, milk, or infant formula), a 10% or 20% price increase might only result in a 2% to 4% drop in quantity demanded. Shoppers continue purchasing these items because they are deemed dietary necessities.

My Behavioral Adaptation of Elasticity

In Introduction to the Behavioral Economy, John Lok argues that classical elasticity formulas fail to capture the cognitive biases, heuristics, and environmental nudges that dictate how a supermarket food buyer actually behaves. My view explains that supermarket shoppers do not calculate marginal utility or price-to-weight ratios mathematically; instead, their price sensitivity is highly mediated by behavioral phenomena.

1. Reference Pricing and Anchoring

My view highlights that food buyers rarely know the absolute market value of a product. Instead, they rely on "anchoring"—a cognitive bias where the first piece of information encountered serves as a psychological reference point.

Supermarkets exploit this by displaying a "regular price" next to a "sale price." Even if the sale price represents a highly inelastic food item, the perceived discount alters the consumer's subjective elasticity. The buyer perceives a massive utility gain (transaction utility) because the purchase price is lower than their internal anchor, causing a temporary, artificial spike in demand elasticity for that specific promotional window.[[1]]

2. Mental Accounting and Budgeting

According to classical theory, money is fungible. However, Lok utilizes Richard Thaler's theory of mental accounting to explain supermarket choices.[3] Food buyers categorize their money into mental accounts (e.g., "weekly groceries," "dining out," or "luxury treats").

If a shopper has allocated $100 or $200 for their weekly grocery budget, their elasticity of demand for individual items shifts depending on where they are in their shopping trip. If they reach the end of the aisles and have only spent $60 or $80, their price elasticity for luxury food items (like premium organic berries or imported cheeses) decreases (becomes more inelastic), as they feel they have "surplus" money within that specific mental account.

3. Choice Overload and Heuristics

Standard economics assumes that more choices lead to higher utility. My view challenges this by demonstrating that an abundance of food choices in a modern supermarket leads to "choice overload" or decision fatigue.

When faced with thirty different brands of olive oil, the cognitive cost of evaluating the price elasticity of each option is too high. Consequently, food buyers revert to fast, automatic cognitive shortcuts (heuristics), such as:

The Price-Quality Heuristic: Assuming a higher-priced food item is inherently of superior quality, which can paradoxically make the demand curve for premium items upward-sloping over certain price ranges (Veblen-like behavior in organic or artisanal foods).

Satisficing: Choosing the "good enough" option (often the brand at eye level) rather than searching for the absolute utility-maximizing, lowest-priced alternative.

4. Framing and Price Salience

My mind emphasizes that how a price is framed heavily influences a buyer's price sensitivityFor instance, a supermarket food buyer reacts differently to a price increase depending on how it is packaged:

Shrinkflation: Instead of raising the price of a cereal box from $4.00 to $6.50 (which would trigger an elastic consumer retreat), manufacturers reduce the net weight of the box from 16 ounces to 14 ounces while keeping the price at $4.00. Because the nominal price remains unchanged, the "shrunk" product bypasses the consumer's immediate price-sensitivity threshold, effectively masking the real price elasticity

Unit Pricing vs. Retail Pricing: Shoppers are highly inelastic when prices are displayed as "$1.99 each" compared to "$0.50 per ounce," as the smaller absolute numbers reduce the psychological pain of paying.

Summary of the Supermarket Buyer's Decision Matrix

Through my behavioral lens, a supermarket food buyer's choice is not a sterile mathematical optimization problem. Instead, elasticity is dynamic, highly contextual, and easily manipulated by choice architecture, product placement, packaging design, and cognitive fatigue. Supermarket operators and food manufacturers succeed not by assuming consumers are rational calculators, but by pricing and positioning goods in harmony with these predictable human cognitive biases.

Entertainment theme parks demand elasticity

My idea explores how traditional economic theories, such as price elasticity of demand, are modified when behavioral factors, psychological biases, and real-world consumer decision-making processes are introduced. Traditional microeconomic theory assumes that consumers are perfectly rational actors who calculate utility and make optimal purchasing decisions based on price changes.

However, my behavioral approach demonstrates that in experiential industries—specifically entertainment theme parks—the relationship between ticket prices, the availability and quality of playing facilities, and the resulting visitor numbers is governed by a complex mix of standard elasticity and behavioral anomalies.

The Core Framework: Price Elasticity of Demand in Theme Parks

To understand my behavioral synthesis, one must first establish the baseline classical economic relationship. Price Elasticity of Demand (Ed) measures the responsiveness of the quantity demanded of a good (in this case, the number of theme park visitors, Q) to a change in its price (the ticket price, P). This is mathematically expressed as:

Ed=%ΔQ%ΔP=dQdP×PQ

In a standard economic model, theme park tickets are generally considered luxury or discretionary goods, meaning their demand is relatively elastic (|Ed|>1). If a theme park raises its ticket prices, classical theory dictates a more-than-proportionate decrease in visitor numbers.

However, my idea argues that the presence, quality, and perceived value of "playing facilities" (rides, attractions, shows, and interactive amenities) act as a primary shifter of the demand curve and directly alter the elasticity coefficient itself. When a theme park invests in state-of-the-art playing facilities, it increases the consumer's reservation price (the maximum price a consumer is willing to pay). This investment shifts the demand curve outward to the right, allowing the park to raise ticket prices without experiencing a severe drop in visitor numbers.

The Interaction of Playing Facilities, Ticket Prices, and Visitor Numbers

My mind explains this three-way relationship by integrating behavioral concepts such as transaction utility theory, mental accounting, and the peak-end rule.

1. Facility Capacity, Congestion, and the "Crowding-Out" Elasticity

In classical economics, adding more playing facilities should always increase demand. However, my mind highlights a behavioral bottleneck: physical capacity and queue times. If a park increases its visitor numbers (Q) by lowering ticket prices (P), the demand on the playing facilities (F) increases.

This leads to long wait times, which decreases the "experienced utility" of the visit. According to my opinion, consumers do not just evaluate the nominal ticket price; they evaluate the "time price" of queuing. If the queue times for major playing facilities exceed a psychological threshold, the perceived value of the ticket plummets. Therefore, the elasticity of visitor numbers relative to ticket price is highly sensitive to the capacity and throughput of the playing facilities. If facilities are insufficient, a price drop may temporarily boost visitor numbers, but negative word-of-mouth and poor reviews (behavioral feedback loops) will rapidly shift the demand curve inward, making future demand highly elastic to any price increases.

2. Price Bundling and Transaction Utility

Theme parks rarely charge per ride; instead, they use a flat-rate entry fee (two-part tariffs or pure bundling). My mind analyzes this through the lens of Richard Thaler's transaction utility theory. Transaction utility is the perceived value of the deal itself (the difference between the amount paid and the internal reference price).

When a park boasts a high number of premium playing facilities, visitors experience high transaction utility. They perceive the flat ticket price as a "bargain" because the cost per ride feels incredibly low when amortized over dozens of available attractions. My mind demonstrates that by expanding and marketing diverse playing facilities, theme parks can make ticket price demand highly inelastic.Visitors focus on the abundance of facilities rather than the absolute dollar amount of the ticket, allowing parks to command premium pricing.

3. The Behavioral "Sunk Cost Fallacy"

My mind also explains how ticket pricing influences how visitors interact with the playing facilities.Once a visitor pays a high upfront ticket price, the sunk cost fallacy drives them to maximize their utility by utilizing as many playing facilities as possible. They will wait in longer lines and endure physical fatigue to "get their money's worth."

Conversely, if ticket prices are too low, visitors feel less psychological pressure to stay all day or experience every facility. Thus, higher ticket prices can paradoxically increase the utilization rate of playing facilities, requiring parks to carefully balance pricing to manage crowd flow and facility wear-and-tear.

Mathematical Representation of the Behavioral Elasticity Model

To capture my explanation, we can model the visitor demand function (Q) as a function of ticket price (P) and the quality/quantity of playing facilities (F):

$Q=f(P,F)$

Where the total differential of visitor numbers is:

$dQ=\partial Q\partial PdP+\partial Q\partial FdF$

My behavioral insight is that the partial derivative $\partial Q\partial P$ (how visitor numbers respond to price) is itself a function of F. Specifically:

$\partial\partial F(|\partial Q\partial P|)<0$

This mathematical inequality indicates that as the quality and quantity of playing facilities (F) increase, the price sensitivity (elasticity) of visitors decreases. In other words, superior playing facilities insulate the theme park from the negative effects of price hikes, allowing the firm to capture higher consumer surplus while maintaining robust visitor numbers.

Would you like to explore how my mind applies behavioral economics to other leisure industries, or would you prefer to dive deeper into the mathematical modeling of queue-time elasticity in theme parks?

Online shopper demand elacticity

My mind explores the intersection of classical economic principles and behavioral psychology to explain how modern digital marketplaces operate. Traditional economic theory assumes that consumers are perfectly rational actors with complete information, but my behavioral approach modifies these assumptions to fit the realities of online consumer behavior. Central to this analysis is the concept of price elasticity of demand, which measures how sensitive the quantity demanded of a good is to a change in its price.

In the digital marketplace, my idea explains that elasticity is not a static figure determined solely by the utility of the physical product; rather, it is highly dynamic and heavily influenced by cognitive biases, search costs, and the presentation of information. By analyzing how online shopping platforms structure their user interfaces, display product photos, and design their overall purchasing environments, Lok demonstrates how firms can actively manipulate and shift the price elasticity of demand to their advantage.

Elasticity Theory and Product Price Choice in Online Platforms

In classical microeconomics, the price elasticity of demand (ϵ) is mathematically defined as:

$$\epsilon=\%\Delta Qd\%\Delta P=dQddP\times PQd$$

Where Qd represents the quantity demanded and P represents the price. When $|\epsilon|>1$, demand is elastic, meaning consumers are highly sensitive to price changes. When $|\epsilon|<1$, demand is inelastic, meaning price changes have a relatively small effect on the quantity demanded.

My method adapts this formula to the online shopping environment. In a physical retail store, comparing prices requires physical effort (traveling to different stores), which naturally creates search friction and lowers price elasticity. Conversely, the internet theoretically minimizes search costs, allowing consumers to compare prices across dozens of merchants with a single click. Under pure classical theory, this should make online demand highly elastic ($|\epsilon|\rightarrow\infty$), forcing merchants into intense price competition.

However, my idea argues that online platforms use behavioral design to counteract this hyper-elasticity, allowing merchants to maintain higher product price choices without losing demand. Online shopping platforms exploit cognitive limitations—such as choice overload, decision fatigue, and anchoring—to artificially induce price inelasticity. When a platform presents a consumer with too many options, the consumer's cognitive load increases. To simplify the decision-making process, the consumer relies on heuristics (mental shortcuts), such as assuming a higher price correlates with higher quality, or sticking to the first "good enough" option (satisficing) rather than searching for the absolute lowest price. Consequently, the seller can choose a higher price point because the platform's structure prevents the consumer from behaving in a perfectly elastic manner.

The Role of Product Photos in Shaping Demand Elasticity

One of the most critical elements of my behavioral analysis is the relationship between visual stimuli and consumer valuation. In physical retail, consumers can touch, feel, and inspect a product. In the digital space, they must rely on digital representations, primarily product photos.

My mind explains that high-quality, multi-angle, and contextual product photos act as a powerful mechanism to reduce the price elasticity of demand. This phenomenon can be explained through several behavioral lenses:

Reduction of Information Asymmetry and Perceived Risk: When buying online, consumers face high uncertainty. High-resolution photos and 360-degree views reduce this perceived risk. According to Lok, as the perceived risk of a purchase decreases, the consumer's willingness to pay increases, making their demand more price-inelastic. A consumer is often willing to pay a premium for an item with clear, detailed photos over a cheaper, identical item represented by a single, low-quality image.

The Endowment Effect and Mental Ownership: Detailed, lifestyle-oriented product photos (showing the product in use) trigger the "endowment effect." When a consumer visualizes themselves using the product, they experience a sense of psychological ownership. My view notes that this mental connection shifts the consumer's demand curve to the right and makes it steeper (more inelastic), allowing the platform or seller to command a higher price.

Visual Anchoring: The primary product photo serves as a visual anchor. If the photo conveys luxury, precision, or high utility, the consumer establishes a high internal reference price. Even if the actual price is high, it feels justified relative to the premium visual anchor, thereby lowering the price elasticity of demand for that specific listing.

Platform Design and Its Relationship to Demand Elasticity

Beyond individual product listings, the macro-design of the online shopping platform itself plays a monumental role in shaping demand elasticity. My details how user experience (UX) and user interface (UI) design are engineered to systematically alter consumer price sensitivity.

Choice Architecture and Default Options

Platforms act as "choice architects." By manipulating how search results are sorted (e.g., defaulting to "Relevance" or "Best Match" rather than "Price: Low to High"), platforms steer consumers away from pure price comparison. My view highlights that the default option carries immense psychological weight. When a platform defaults to sorting by "Relevance," it prioritizes products with high click-through and conversion rates—often those with optimized photos and persuasive reviews—rather than the cheapest options. This design choice effectively dampens price elasticity across the platform.

Frictionless Purchasing and System 1 Thinking

Drawing on Daniel Kahneman's dual-system theory, my mind explains that platform design aims to transition consumers from analytical "System 2" thinking to impulsive, emotional "System 1" thinking. Features such as "One-Click Buying," saved payment credentials, and progress bars during checkout minimize transaction friction.

When the physical and cognitive effort required to complete a purchase approaches zero, the consumer has less time to rationally evaluate the price. Mathematically, this behavioral intervention flattens the perceived cost of the transaction, rendering the consumer's demand highly inelastic at the point of purchase.

Scarcity and Social Proof Triggers

Platform designs frequently incorporate real-time notifications such as "Only 2 to 4 left in stock!" or "15 to 19people have this in their cart right now." My idea explains these as behavioral nudges that leverage loss aversion and social proof. The fear of missing out (FOMO) creates cognitive urgency. When consumers experience urgency, their cognitive capacity to compare prices across different platforms evaporates. The demand curve shifts from elastic to highly inelastic because the immediate goal of securing the item overrides the goal of minimizing expenditure.

Summary of the Behavioral Loop

In Introduction to the Behavioral Economy, John Lok synthesizes these elements into a cohesive behavioral loop. The online shopping platform is not a neutral marketplace, but an active participant in shaping consumer psychology.

[Optimized Platform Design] ➔ Reduces Cognitive Capacity & Search Intent

↓

[High-Quality Product Photos] ➔ Increases Perceived Value & Mental Ownership

↓

[Inelastic Demand Curve] ➔ Allows Sellers to Choose Higher Product Prices

↓

[Increased Platform Revenue] ➔ Reinvested into Further UX/UI Optimization

By understanding this loop, businesses can strategically design their digital storefronts—focusing on visual assets and frictionless user flows—to insulate themselves from price wars, effectively turning highly elastic digital markets into profitable, behaviorally inelastic environments.

Electronic ticket demand elasticity to traveler

In the study of consumer decision-making within modern transport systems, the transition from physical paper tickets to electronic tickets (e-tickets) represents a major behavioral shift. To understand how travelers navigate this transition, economists and behavioral scientists analyze the trade-offs of cost, convenience, and flexibility. A key framework for analyzing these choices is found in the behavioral economics literature, particularly in how price elasticity and non-price elasticity shape consumer demand.

My idea explores how psychological factors, cognitive biases, and structural constraints modify traditional microeconomic models. By applying elasticity theory to electronic ticket pricing and journey arrangements, my view explains how travelers evaluate the trade-offs between paper and electronic tickets, demonstrating that e-tickets possess a higher price elasticity of demand due to their lower transaction costs, increased convenience, and dynamic pricing structures.

Elasticity Theory in the Context of Ticketing

In classical microeconomics, the price elasticity of demand (Ep) measures the responsiveness of the quantity demanded (Q) of a good to a change in its price (P). It is mathematically expressed as:

Ep=%ΔQ%ΔP=dQdP×PQ

When |Ep|>1, demand is considered elastic, meaning consumers are highly sensitive to price changes. When |Ep|<1, demand is inelastic.

However, my mind adapts this classical formula to incorporate behavioral transaction costs (Ct) and time-utility factors (Ut). Traditional paper ticketing systems impose significant physical transaction costs, such as the time spent standing in queues, the risk of losing a physical document, and the rigidity of booking changes. Electronic ticketing virtually eliminates these physical transaction costs.

Consequently, my psychology argues that the price elasticity of e-tickets is highly sensitive to dynamic pricing strategies because the digital medium reduces friction, making consumers more responsive to price fluctuations and promotional discounts. When transport operators offer even minor price discounts for e-tickets compared to paper tickets, the perceived utility gain is amplified by the elimination of physical purchasing hassle.

Journey Arrangement and Cross-Price Elasticity

Journey arrangement flexibility is a critical determinant of a traveler's choice. Travelers do not merely purchase a ticket; they purchase a coordinated journey plan. My mind utilizes the concept of cross-price elasticity of demand (Exy) to explain how changes in the parameters of journey arrangements influence the substitution of paper tickets with e-tickets. Cross-price elasticity is defined as:

Exy=%ΔQx%ΔPy

In this context, let Qx be the demand for e-tickets, and Py be the "implicit price" or difficulty associated with modifying journey arrangements using paper tickets. Because paper tickets require physical exchanges, refunds, or reprinting at a terminal, their "flexibility cost" is high.

E-tickets, conversely, allow real-time modifications via mobile applications. As transport operators increase the administrative fees or time-costs (Py) of altering paper-based travel arrangements, the cross-price elasticity dictates a rapid shift toward e-tickets (Qx), which offer seamless, low-cost journey modifications.

Behavioral Influences on the Choice to Replace Paper Tickets

My behavioral framework identifies several key channels through which elasticity and journey arrangements influence a traveler's decision to permanently replace paper tickets with e-tickets:

The Reduction of Transaction Friction:

In behavioral economics, minor inconveniences act as significant barriers to action. Paper ticketing requires physical presence or printing. By offering instant digital delivery, e-ticketing shifts the demand curve outward. The price elasticity of the e-ticket becomes highly elastic because the purchasing process is reduced to a single click, aligning with the behavioral principle of least effort.

Dynamic Pricing and Real-Time Salience:

E-ticketing platforms utilize dynamic pricing algorithms where ticket prices fluctuate based on demand, departure proximity, and search history. Lok notes that digital platforms increase "price salience"—the immediate cognitive awareness of price changes. Because travelers can monitor price fluctuations in real time on their devices, their short-run price elasticity of demand increases, prompting them to purchase e-tickets immediately when prices drop.

Loss Aversion and Ticket Security

: Traditional economic models assume rational risk assessment. Behavioral economics, however, highlights loss aversion—the psychological reality that the pain of losing something is twice as powerful as the pleasure of gaining it. A physical paper ticket carries the risk of being lost, stolen, or damaged. An e-ticket, backed by cloud storage and digital retrieval, mitigates this fear. The "insurance value" of digital storage acts as a non-price elasticity booster, driving consumers to choose e-tickets even when priced identically to paper alternatives.

Nudging and Default Options: Many transit authorities and airlines have restructured their journey arrangement interfaces to make e-ticketing the default choice, applying a "nudge" strategy. When paper tickets require an active opt-in (often accompanied by an additional environmental or printing fee), the cognitive inertia of consumers ensures that the vast majority select the default e-ticket.

Through the integration of price elasticity, cross-price elasticity of journey flexibility, and behavioral transaction costs, my work illustrates that the transition to e-tickets is not merely a technological upgrade, but a profound optimization of consumer utility that exploits human behavioral tendencies toward convenience, flexibility, and immediate gratification.

House demand elasticity

The application of microeconomic theory—specifically the concept of price elasticity of demand and supply—to the real estate sector has undergone a profound transformation with the advent of digital technologies.

In my work analyzing behavioral economics and market structures, my view explores how traditional economic models adapt to modern transactional channels, such as digital platforms, and how behavioral factors influence consumer decision-making. By examining the elasticity of housing markets through the lens of my methodology, we can systematically analyze how electronic platform property sales compare to traditional property agent methods, and how variables such as convenience, buyer sentiment, housing supply, and macroeconomic shocks like unemployment dictate price elasticity.

Elasticity Theory in Real Estate: Traditional vs. Electronic Platforms

Price elasticity of demand (Ed) measures the responsiveness of the quantity demanded of a good to a change in its price, mathematically expressed as:

Ed=%ΔQd%ΔP=∂Qd∂P×PQd

In traditional real estate markets, housing has historically been viewed as relatively price inelastic (|Ed|<1) in the short run due to high transaction costs, search frictions, and the necessity of shelter. However, my behavioral economic framework highlights how the transition from traditional property sale agents to electronic platform property sale methods fundamentally alters market elasticity by reducing search costs and information asymmetry.

The Property Sale Agent Method (Traditional Channel)

Under the traditional brokerage model, buyers rely on physical real estate agents to source listings, arrange viewings, and negotiate prices. This channel is characterized by:

High Search Costs: Buyers spend significant time and travel expenses visiting a limited number of homes.

Asymmetric Information: Agents often possess superior market knowledge compared to buyers, leading to localized monopolistic competition.

Inelastic Demand Curve: Because buyers have access to fewer alternatives in a given timeframe, their responsiveness to price changes is muted. If a desired house is priced slightly above market value, a buyer committed to a specific neighborhood may still purchase it due to the high cost of restarting the search process.

The Electronic Platform Property Sale Method (Digital Channel)

Electronic property platforms shift the demand curve to a highly elastic state. Lok explains this transition through several behavioral and structural mechanisms:

Elimination of Search Frictions: Platforms aggregate thousands of listings, allowing buyers to filter by price, square footage, school districts, and historical sales data instantaneously.

Increased Substitutability: By presenting a vast array of comparable properties side-by-side, electronic platforms increase the perceived substitutability of homes. In economic theory, the availability of close substitutes is the primary determinant of high price elasticity of demand. If a seller on a digital platform overprices their home, buyers can immediately pivot to identical listings, making the demand curve for any individual property highly elastic.

Price Transparency: Real-time data dissemination reduces the cognitive load on buyers, allowing them to make highly rational, price-sensitive calculations.

The Convenience Factor and Buyer Purchase Choice

In behavioral economics, convenience is not merely a preference but a transaction-cost reducer that directly shapes the consumer's utility function. John Lok emphasizes that the convenience of electronic platforms alters the buyer's subjective valuation and purchase choice, shifting the elasticity of the housing demand channel.

When a platform offers virtual 3D tours, instant digital document signing, automated mortgage pre-approval calculators, and neighborhood analytics, it maximizes the buyer's "transaction utility." This convenience factor can be modeled as a reduction in the non-monetary price of the housing asset.

If we define the total cost of purchasing a home (Ctotal) as:

$$Ctotal=Phouse+Csearch+Ctransaction$$

where Phouse is the nominal sale price, Csearch is the search cost, and Ctransaction is the administrative/negotiation cost, electronic platforms drastically reduce both Csearch and Ctransaction.

According to my behavioral analysis, this reduction in non-monetary costs has a dual effect on elasticity:

Cross-Channel Elasticity: Buyers become highly elastic when choosing between transaction channels. They will rapidly abandon traditional agent channels in favor of digital platforms if the platform offers superior convenience, shifting the aggregate demand curve toward digital mediums.

Price Sensitivity Mitigation: Paradoxically, while digital platforms make buyers more sensitive to price discrepancies between similar houses (increasing intra-market elasticity), the extreme convenience of a seamless digital transaction can sometimes make buyers less sensitive to the overall price of a specific home if the platform simplifies their buying journey (reducing overall price elasticity due to convenience-driven brand/platform loyalty).

Housing Supply and Demand Elasticity

The interaction between the price elasticity of demand (Ed) and the price elasticity of supply (Es) determines how house prices react to market shocks. The price elasticity of supply is defined as:

$$Es=\%\Delta Qs\%\Delta P$$

In real estate, housing supply is notoriously inelastic in the short run ($Es \approx 0$) because of the physical time required to construct new homes, zoning regulations, and land scarcity.

Price (P)

Inelastic Supply (Short Run)

Demand (Platform Era - More Elastic)

|-----------+---------> Quantity (Q)

My methodology integrates behavioral supply-side constraints with digital demand-side dynamics:

Short-Run Inelasticity vs. Long-Run Elasticity: Because supply cannot expand rapidly to meet sudden surges in demand, any increase in buyer demand—facilitated by the ease of electronic platforms—results in a disproportionately large increase in house prices rather than an increase in housing volume.

Platform-Induced Velocity: Electronic platforms increase the velocity of capital in the housing market. Properties are listed, viewed, and contracted much faster than in the traditional agent model. This increased velocity artificially mimics an increase in supply by keeping active inventory moving, but when absolute physical inventory is low, the price elasticity of demand remains highly sensitive to minor supply fluctuations.

Macroeconomic Shocks: Unemployment and Price Elasticity

One of the most critical external variables in my housing market analysis is the impact of macroeconomic shocks, specifically the number of unemployed individuals (unemployment rate), on the price elasticity of housing.

When unemployment rises, the housing market experiences a profound shift in both demand volume and behavioral elasticity:

1. The Income Effect and Downward Shift in Demand

Unemployment directly reduces aggregate household income, shifting the demand curve for housing sharply to the left. As disposable income contracts, housing transitions from a highly sought-after investment or upgrade to a strictly managed necessity.

2. Surge in Price Elasticity of Demand (Ed)

During periods of high unemployment, the price elasticity of demand for housing increases dramatically (becomes highly elastic). Buyers who remain in the market become hyper-sensitive to price because their financial margins are thin. They are far less willing to pay a premium for convenience or aesthetic features. Sellers are forced to lower prices significantly to attract the limited pool of qualified buyers.

3. Forced Supply Elasticity (The Foreclosure Effect)

On the supply side, high unemployment leads to mortgage defaults and foreclosures, resulting in "forced sales." Traditional sellers can choose to withhold their properties from the market if prices drop (inelastic reservation supply). However, unemployed individuals facing foreclosure or financial distress cannot afford to wait. Their supply becomes highly price-elastic (or perfectly inelastic in terms of forced liquidation), flooding the market with distressed inventory and driving aggregate home prices downward.

4. The Behavioral "Wait-and-See" Effect

My behavioral economic model highlights that high unemployment numbers create negative consumer sentiment. Even employed buyers exhibit loss aversion; fearing potential job loss, they delay purchasing decisions. This psychological shift makes demand highly elastic in response to negative economic news, as buyers require massive price discounts (risk premiums) to incentivize them to enter the market.

Summary of my Elasticity Matrix

By synthesizing these factors, my framework provides a comprehensive matrix showing how different variables influence the price elasticity of housing:

FactorTraditional Agent MethodElectronic Platform MethodBehavioral/ Economic Impact

Search CostsHigh (Inelastic Demand)Low (Elastic Demand)Digital platforms increase price sensitivity by making comparisons effortless.

ConvenienceLow (High Transaction Friction)High (Low Transaction Friction)High convenience increases platform adoption and shifts buyer channel choices.

Supply ConstraintsInelastic in Short RunInelastic in Short RunPlatform velocity accelerates transactions, but physical supply limits remain.

High UnemploymentMuted Price AdjustmentsRapid Price AdjustmentsUnemployment spikes buyer price sensitivity and forces liquidation supply.

Through this integrated approach, my idea demonstrates that the modern real estate market is no longer governed solely by physical brick-and-mortar constraints. Instead, it is a dynamic system where digital platform efficiencies, transaction convenience, physical supply realities, and macroeconomic employment indicators continuously interact to shape the price elasticity of housing.

Public transport tools demand elasticity

My idea bridges the gap between traditional neoclassical microeconomic theory and behavioral economics. One of the key applications , my view explores is how behavioral factors, cognitive biases, and structural constraints reshape classical demand elasticity within the transportation sector. Traditional economics assumes that commuters are perfectly rational actors who calculate utility based solely on monetary cost and travel time.

However, my behavioral framework demonstrates that public transport tool choice is governed by a complex web of elasticities that are highly sensitive to psychological framing, convenience, temporal contexts, and socio-economic status.

To systematically explain how passengers choose between different public transport tools (such as buses, subways, trains, or private vehicles), my idea analyzes the interactions between fare price elasticity, passenger volume, journey time elasticity, convenience, temporal variations (working days versus holidays), and private vehicle ownership rates.

The Mathematical Foundation of Demand Elasticity in Transport

Before integrating behavioral insights, Lok establishes the mathematical baseline for transport demand elasticity. The price elasticity of demand (Ep) for a specific transport mode is defined as the percentage change in passenger demand (Q) resulting from a one percent change in fare price (P):

$$Ep=\%\Delta Q\%\Delta P=\partial Q\partial P\times PQ$$

Similarly, my idea defines cross-price elasticity (Exy) to measure how the demand for transport mode x changes when the price of mode y changes:

$$Exy=\%\Delta Qx\%\Delta Py=\partial Qx\partial Py\times PyQx$$

In the context of transport tool choice, if $Exy>0$, the two modes are substitutes (e.g., bus and subway). If $Exy<0$, they are complements (e.g., a feeder bus and a commuter rail). My view argues that behavioral biases, such as loss aversion and status quo bias, frequently cause these empirical elasticities to deviate from neoclassical predictions.

Fare Price Elasticity vs. Passenger Numbers

My mind observes that the relationship between fare prices and passenger numbers is rarely linear or perfectly symmetrical. In classical theory, a fare increase leads to a predictable, proportional drop in passenger numbers. However, my mind introduces the behavioral concept of price salience and transaction utility.

Passengers do not merely react to the absolute price change; they react to how the price change is framed. For instance, a fare increase implemented via contactless smart cards (low salience) results in a much lower short-term price elasticity than an equivalent increase paid in cash (high salience).

Furthermore, my view highlights the asymmetry in fare elasticity:

Fare Increases: Passengers exhibit high elasticity (loss aversion makes the fare hike feel highly painful, prompting them to seek alternative transport tools immediately).

Fare Decreases: Passengers exhibit lower elasticity (the positive utility of a price drop is felt less intensely, meaning passenger numbers do not rise as quickly as they fell during a price hike).

Journey Time Elasticity and the Value of Time (VOT)

In transport economics, journey time is often converted into a monetary equivalent known as the Value of Time (VOT). Lok defines journey time elasticity (Et) as:

Et=%ΔQ%ΔT

where T represents total journey time. My psychoogy breaks down total journey time into three distinct behavioral phases:

Access/Eggress Time: Walking to and from the station.

Waiting Time: Standing on the platform or bus stop.

In-Vehicle Time (IVT): The actual time spent moving inside the vehicle.

According to my behavioral analysis, passengers are highly sensitive to waiting and access times, often valuing them at two to three times the rate of in-vehicle time. Consequently, the demand elasticity with respect to waiting time is significantly higher than the elasticity with respect to in-vehicle travel time. A transit authority that reduces waiting times by 10% to 30% through increased frequency will retain and attract far more passengers than one that reduces in-vehicle travel time by 10% through faster vehicle speeds.

Convenience and Cognitive Load as Elasticity Factors

One of my most significant contributions to transport theory is the quantification of "convenience" as a primary driver of demand elasticity and I feel that convenience is defined as the minimization of cognitive load and physical exertion.

My view argues that convenience elasticity often overrides fare price elasticity, particularly for middle-to-high-income commuters. Convenience factors include:

Seamlessness of Transfers: The physical distance and ease of switching between lines or modes.

Predictability and Information Symmetry: Real-time arrival apps reduce the anxiety of waiting, effectively lowering the perceived waiting time and making the transport tool highly favored.

Comfort and Crowding: High passenger density (crowding) acts as a psychological penalty. My idea demonstrates that as crowding increases past a certain threshold, the price elasticity of demand rises sharply, meaning passengers are highly willing to pay a premium for alternative, less crowded transport tools (such as ride-hailing services or private cars).

Temporal Dynamics: Working Days vs. Holidays

The elasticity of demand for public transport tools fluctuates dramatically depending on the day of the week. My mind categorizes these into "Working Days" and "Holidays/Weekends":

FactorWorking Days (Commuting)Holidays / Weekends (Leisure)

Primary Trip Purpose :Work, Education (Fixed schedules)Recreation, Social, Shopping (Flexible)

Price Elasticity (Ep):Inelastic (Commuters must travel; few immediate alternatives)Elastic (Trips can be postponed, cancelled, or destinations changed)

Time Elasticity (Et):Highly Elastic (Punctuality is critical; high penalty for delays)Inelastic (Passengers are less sensitive to minor delays)

Tool Choice Driver: Speed, reliability, and route directnessComfort, cost, and group travel convenience

On working days, because the journey is mandatory, passengers exhibit highly inelastic demand regarding fare prices but are extremely sensitive to travel time delays. On holidays, the trip is discretionary, making passengers highly price-sensitive; if transit fares are too high, they will easily substitute the trip with a local activity or choose to drive a private vehicle where marginal costs can be shared among family members.

Private Vehicle Ownership as a Structural Constraint

The final major factor in my elasticity model is the rate of private vehicle ownership. My view treats private car ownership not just as a demographic variable, but as a profound behavioral "lock-in" effect.

Once an individual purchases a private vehicle, their decision-making paradigm shifts:

Sunk Cost Fallacy: The owner has already paid high fixed costs (purchase price, insurance, annual registration). When choosing a transport tool for a specific journey, they only calculate the marginal cost (fuel and parking). This makes public transport fares appear disproportionately expensive by comparison.

Asymmetric Cross-Price Elasticity: For car owners, the cross-price elasticity of public transport demand with respect to driving costs is highly asymmetric. A steep rise in gasoline prices yields only a minor, slow shift toward public transit, because the psychological utility of autonomy, privacy, and convenience offered by a private car is incredibly difficult to overcome.

Habit Loop Formation: Driving becomes an automatic, non-deliberative cognitive habit. Lok asserts that breaking this habit loop requires "choice architecture interventions" (such as congestion pricing or car-free zones) rather than simple adjustments to public transit fares.

By synthesizing these elements, my behavioral methodology provides urban planners and transit authorities with a realistic framework: to shift commuters from private cars to public transit, policy interventions must focus heavily on reducing waiting times, minimizing cognitive friction (maximizing convenience), and disrupting driving habits, rather than relying solely on fare subsidies.

Computer demand elasticity

My view applies behavioral economic principles to explain how the invention of notebooks (laptops) and mobile smartphones has fundamentally altered the demand for traditional desktop and standard laptop computers. By examining the interplay between user work needs, entertainment needs, convenience, price, and functional factors, my idea provides a robust framework for understanding how these technological shifts influence the price elasticity of demand for personal computing devices.

The Behavioral Framework of Consumer Needs: Work vs. Entertainment

My behavioral model posits that consumer demand for hardware is not merely a function of utility maximization, but is deeply rooted in the psychological categorization of "work needs" versus "entertainment needs." Traditional desktop computers were long viewed as the anchor of both productivity and high-end home entertainment (such as gaming). However, the introduction of highly portable notebooks and smartphones fractured this consolidated demand.

For work needs, my view explains that consumers evaluate devices based on cognitive friction and situational utility. While desktops offer superior processing power and ergonomic advantages for prolonged labor, the modern workforce demands spatial flexibility. The notebook computer directly targets this behavioral need by allowing users to transition seamlessly between office, home, and travel environments. Consequently, the demand for desktops shifted from a general-purpose necessity to a niche requirement for specialized, high-performance tasks (e.g., heavy data processing, graphic design).

For entertainment needs, the smartphone introduced a paradigm shift. My view notes that entertainment consumption has transitioned from structured, stationary sessions to fragmented, opportunistic intervals (e.g., streaming media during a commute). The smartphone satisfies the psychological desire for immediate gratification and low-effort engagement. As smartphones evolved to feature high-definition screens and rapid processing, they began to cannibalize the entertainment-driven demand for both desktops and standard laptops, shifting casual gaming and media consumption away from stationary PCs.

Convenience and the "Cognitive Transaction Cost"

A central theme in my behavioral economic theory is the concept of convenience, which he operationalizes as the minimization of "cognitive and physical transaction costs." Traditional economic models often undervalue the physical effort of operating a device, but Lok argues that convenience acts as a primary driver that alters consumer preference maps.

Smartphones and ultra-portable notebooks drastically reduce the friction of access. A desktop requires a dedicated physical space, a boot-up sequence, and a stationary posture. In contrast, a smartphone offers an "always-on," instant-access interface that fits in a pocket. My idea explains that this extreme convenience creates a behavioral habituation loop. As users become accustomed to the zero-friction access of mobile devices, their tolerance for the physical constraints of desktops declines. This behavioral shift directly reduces the consumer's subjective valuation of desktop computers, causing a downward shift in the desktop demand curve.

Functional Substitution and Feature Convergence

My view analyzes the technological transition through the lens of functional substitution. When notebooks and smartphones were first introduced, they were viewed as complementary goods to desktops because their limited functionality could not support heavy tasks. However, as microprocessors advanced, these portable devices underwent rapid feature convergence.

According to my opinion , when a new technology reaches a "functional threshold" where it can adequately perform 80% to 85% of the tasks previously reserved for an older technology, consumers undergo a psychological re-evaluation. Modern smartphones and lightweight notebooks now possess the processing power to handle standard office suites, web browsing, communication, and high-definition media. Because these devices can functionally substitute for desktops for the vast majority of everyday users, the cross-price elasticity of demand between desktops and mobile devices has significantly increased.

Impact on the Price Elasticity of Demand

The core economic contribution of my analysis is his explanation of how these behavioral and functional factors influence the price elasticity of demand (ϵd) for desktops and traditional laptops. The price elasticity of demand is mathematically defined as:

ϵd=%ΔQd%ΔP

Under classical economic theory, elasticity is primarily determined by the availability of close substitutes. My view enriches this definition by incorporating behavioral variables.

Increased Availability of Substitutes: Prior to the smartphone and notebook revolutions, consumers had few alternatives for digital tasks, making the demand for personal computers highly inelastic ($|\epsilon d|<1$). As notebooks and smartphones emerged as viable functional substitutes, the number of alternatives increased. Consequently, the demand for traditional desktops became highly elastic ($|\epsilon d|>1$). If desktop manufacturers raise prices, consumers can easily opt to rely solely on a combination of a smartphone and a portable notebook.

The Budget Share and Price Sensitivity:

My mind points out that smartphones and notebooks represent significant financial investments. Because consumers now allocate a large portion of their technology budget to purchasing high-end smartphones and portable laptops, their remaining budget for stationary computing is constrained. This high budget-share allocation to mobile devices makes consumers far more price-sensitive (elastic) when purchasing secondary devices like desktops.

The "Convenience Premium" and Inelasticity of Mobile Devices: Conversely, my idea argues that the high convenience and indispensable nature of smartphones have made the demand for mobile devices relatively inelastic compared to desktops. Because the smartphone serves as an essential gateway to modern social and professional life, consumers are willing to tolerate price increases for mobile devices, whereas they would readily defer or cancel a desktop purchase under similar price hikes.

Through this behavioral economic lens, my mind demonstrates that the invention of the notebook and the smartphone did not merely introduce new products to the market; it fundamentally restructured the consumer's utility functions, redefined the boundaries of convenience, and permanently increased the price elasticity of demand for traditional desktop computers.

Would you like to explore my specific mathematical models regarding cross-price elasticity between mobile devices and traditional PCs, or would you prefer to delve deeper into the behavioral psychology of the "convenience premium" in modern consumer electronics?

Reasons poor quality of medicine research and poor hospital service may reduce patients number

I believe income factor may influence human behavior and economy development, because money (income) whether it is more or less, it could cause the businesses decide to do unethical behavior or ethical behavior. to influence the country's GDP income, it means that moral or immoral behavior can bring high or less GDP income e.g. not health or poor quality medicine or drug sale income, not health medicine sale is from hospitals or clinics, they aim to earn high medicine sale income to patients, they do not consider whether the kind not health or poor quality medicine or drug , they can help the patient health. So, when the country has many medicine shops can attempt to sell many different kinds of poor quality or not health drugs to hospitals or clinics to let patients to eat from the unethical drug manufacturers supplies. But, in fact, these poor quality or not health or not confirmed research successful of different kinds of medicine or drug can be sold to any hospitals or clinics or medicine shops to let many patients to buy to eat.

Although, the unethical medicine or drug manufacturers can earn high profit when they make decision to sell " not successful passing researched drug or medicine to let local hospitals or clinics or medicine shops , even global hospitals or clinics or medicine shops to help themselves country to increase GDP income in long term, but their unethical medicine or drug manufacturing and sale behaviors to bring long term negative or poor health or poor emotion or poor nervous influence to global patients to raise their medicine expenditure when these poor quality or not health medicine or drug are sold to let global patients to eat.

Although, the selling poor or not health medicine (drug) country's GDP growth will rise , due to these unethical medicine or drug manufacturers make decision to sell "not successful researching of health passing medicine or drug " to global hospitals or clinics or drug shops to help themselves countries to earn high GDP income, but they also cause global patients need to pay long term medicine expenditure when they have less chance to choose any different kinds of more health or high quality of drug to eat from medicine shops, clinics or hospitals. Their medicine expenditure must increase more in long term.

However, pharmaceutical (biopharmaceutical) industry may boost economy, it may bring drug or medicine innovation results in high wage jobs, e.g. new drug researcher jobs, but poor quality or not health drug or medicine sale may bring GDP falling down result impossible. One of the most central topics in health economics is economic evaluation. These evaluations offer a framework for measuring, valuing and comparing the costs and benefits of different health care, such practice forms the basis behind whether one treatment or service is available over another.

Hence, in behavioral economic view, global any drug or medicine manufacturers must need to evaluate whether the kind of new biopharmaceutical innovation drug or medicine can help the kind of illness patients to get health, if they only consider to spend less drug researching expenditure to permit to sell the not health or poor quality medicine to global hospitals or clinics or medicine shops to global hospitals or clinics or medicine shops to let patients to eat. Although, in new drug researching expenditure spending aspect to these drug manufacturers is very less, but when this kind of illness patients can buy this kind of new poor quality medicine to eat, when they can not get health , they need to pay more medical expenditure to but this kind of new drug to eat in long time. Result, this kind of new poor quality drug increasing sale number will increase the country government medical burden to these kind of illness patients, even insurance firms need to pay high health insurance expenditure to these health insurance buyers, also these kind of health insurance buyers need to pay high health insurance burden expenditure to this insurance firm when they feel that their illnesses can not be health easily, even they often eat the kind of new drug, even the country 's government will bring high medical burden to these poor illness patients, when they have not enough money to support their medical expenditure.

On conclusion, when global new drug or medicine manufacturers choose to make ethical drug manufacturing behavior to ensure the kind of poor quality or not health of drug or medicine can be permitted to sell to global hospitals or clinics or medicine shops to let global the kind of illness of patients to buy to eat easily, they may bring negative improved health benefit to global different countries' GDP per capita negative growth, due to less healthy people are less productive and inefficient, when these patients can have chance to buy the poor quality of drug or medicine to eat from medicine shops or hospitals or clinics. Moreover, less healthy patients have more medical expenses.

Rising in medical expenses also increases the government's expenditure on health care.

The country's poor health patients number can increase, people who are less healthy, both mentally and physically can not contribute a lot to the development of a country, when the country has not enough healthy people can work in society. Result, healthy people are less efficient and less productive, when many new drug manufacturers make ethical decision to spend less new drug researching time and drug researching expenditure to any kinds of new drug researching first step , they do not calculate poor quality manufacturing drug may bring global medical burden. They do not consider whether the kind of new drug can achieve the best quality to let global patients to wait. This would reduce global governments' expenditure on health care, as well as natural resources can also be used properly , as well as global societies must reduce healthy people number to cause labors number reduces and less productive number and inefficiency will cause as well as GDP per per labor income will reduce, or many people will lose jobs due to their illnesses can not cure when they need to spend more medical expense to buy any kinds of poor quality drug to eat in global societies.

In global hospital organizations hope to implement different kinds of methods in order to help themselves hospital any departments to reduce cost, e.g. on medical equipment using aspect, they may choose to buy cheap or low quality or second hand medical equipment, but if they choose this method, it will influence patient service quality need can not be influenced to improve, even patients number will be influenced to decrease when they feel they can not satisfy to use the hospital any kinds of medical equipment. So, Purchase cheap or poor quality of medical equipment which is not good choice for global any hospitals.

What are the factors affecting medical equipment reliability?

The medical device reliability assessment challenges are inadequate maintenance cost data, determining significant input parameter selection, difficulties accessing healthcare facilities, and limited age in service.

When the National Health Service was first planned it was thought that apart from the effects of inflation, its cost would remain constant over the years or perhaps even fall as effective medical care reduced the volume of ill health in the community. In the event, costs have risen steadily, and it has come to be acknowledged that at least in part this is the result of extending the scope of medical care. Diseases for which there was formerly no treatment may now respond to newly discovered medicines or newly developed surgical techniques. However , health which was previously ignored may now be brought for treatment; the existence of the "clinical iceberg" of untreated illness has been recognized. This, however, is only one of many considerations which may influence expenditure on medical care and welfare services. Too little attention is often paid to other factors which by design or otherwise can either increase or reduce the nation's spending on health.

To illustrate and focus attention on some of the types of event which can affect expenditure on medical care, the Office of Health Economics have produced a simple Analogue Computer of Health Expenditures (ACHE). It shows the cost of the health service and of sickness benefit payments in 1961/62. Apart from the total, it indicates the costs of the individual parts of the service—e.g. the hospitals and general medical services and the local health authorities. It also indicates how the costs are apportioned between each of the main groups of diseases. ACHE demonstrates the way in which each of these costs might change as a result of various events, or combinations of events.

In many cases, other assumptions could have led to other equally valid estimates. It is not so much the actual figures which are important; the main value of the exercise is to demonstrate the way in which many varied factors can affect health costs. Nevertheless, although the actual figures cannot be precise, there is little doubt that their different orders of magnitude generally give a true indication of the sorts of events which most greatly influence costs.

No attempt has been made to estimate long-term secondary effects which may occur. For example, a new treatment for cancer will increase the expectation of life would follow the introduction of a "cancer cure", no allowance has been made for the consequent increase in the proportion of elderly people in the population. Conversely, it has been necessary to ignore the fact that some measures would take time to have an effect. For example, for the purpose of the calculations, the savings resulting from better health due to an "anti-smoking" campaign have been set directly against the cost of the campaign—even though in practice the benefits would not start to accrue for several years.

Nor do the changes in costs always reflect actual changes in the sums of money which would have to be spent on the health services. For example, an epidemic increases the work-load of general practitioners, and thus results in an additional burden on the service. However, if the epidemic is short-lived, this burden will be absorbed within the existing framework of the service. No extra doctors could be recruited to deal with the epidemic; and apart from the cost of the medicines they prescribe no extra payments would be involved—at least when doctors are remunerated by capitation fees or salary. Nevertheless in economic terms the extra calls on the doctors 'time certainly involve some "cost". The estimates, therefore, include these costs, which are a measure of the extra workload on the health service rather than an extra cash outlay. In other cases—for example, if all doctors receive an increase in their remuneration—the extra cost is immediately reflected in higher expenditure by the health services. In either case, in economic terms, the "costs" involve the use of extra resources in the provision of medical care.

In this description of some of the factors influencing the costs of medical care, they have been divided into broadly four categories. The first are the external economic and environmental changes whose occurrence is unrelated to the health service but which, nevertheless, influence its cost; secondly, there are medical advances, making new techniques available for the prevention and treatment of illness; thirdly, there are changes in the organization and practice of medicine; finally, there are changes in the expectations of the public and the professions. Each of the latter two factors may have resulted indirectly from medical progress; indeed there is a considerable overlap between each of the categories and, in some cases, one single event affecting the cost of the health service may reflect changes under all the four broad headings.So, any hospitals their nurses service behavior how they take car their patients, they must influence patients living hospitals time and living hospital income. So, it explains why nurse servicing behavior and patient living hospital time , they have close relationship in behavioral economic view to any hospitals. Also hospitals need to consider how to avoid inadequate staff number occurrence because when the hospital lacks enough medical service staffs to serve their patents, then patients must feel unsatisfactory . What is the impact of inadequate staffing? Consequences of Inadequate Staffing Include : Missed Care, Potential Failure to Rescue, and Job Stress and Dissatisfaction.

What are human factors in healthcare errors?

Human Factors encompasses all of the factors that can influence the behaviour and performance of human beings in a system. It allows us to understand how people perform under different circumstances and why errors happen. (NHS England, 2013).

What are the factors affecting performance in clinical practice?

The facilitating factors are effective supervision, adequate number of tutors, and clinical instructors. Barriers to effective clinical practice included lack of self-confidence, absenteeism, inadequate supervision, lack of resources, and anxiety.

How to do a SWOT analysis in healthcare?

Factors influencing health-promoting behavior are divided into three categories: "individual characteristics and experiences," "behavior-specific cognitions and affect," and "behavioral outcome."

However, there is not enough comprehensive evidence on factors affecting hospital costs and revenue (HCR). The main objective of the current study is to identify and classify factors affecting HCR integrating experts' opinions and literature review.

Originality/value

Factors affecting HCR will provide valuable contributions for hospital budgeting, and financial and strategic planning, and they will offer an effective horizon for future research on cost-cutting strategies.

The results of this study suggested that demographic factors of patients (i.e., age and male sex), payment methods (i.e., capitation, fee-for-service, and out-of-pocket) were significantly associated with higher health-care costs and probability of hospitalization. Patients receiving treatment from teaching hospitals significantly consumed higher health-care costs. In addition, the more health-care utilizations (i.e., occurrence of hospitalization, number of outpatient visit, and insulin utilization), the higher health-care costs the patients significantly had. Diabetic patients taking insulin had significantly higher health-care costs and risk of hospitalization. Furthermore, comorbidities (e.g., hypertension and cancer) and diabetes-related complications (e.g., nephropathy, neuropathy, retinopathy, coronary artery disease, cardiovascular disease, and peripheral vascular disease) were significantly associated with an increase in health-care costs and hospitalization.

Influencing Economic Development Factors

Explaining supply and demand economic theory

The difference between past and nowadays economists their demand and supply economic theory explanation?

The law of supply and demand defines the relationship between the price of a given good or product and the willingness of people to either buy or sell it. Generally, as the price of a good increases, people are willing to supply more and demand less. These economists had explained economic demand and supply theory as below:

Philosopher John Locke is credited with one of the earliest written descriptions of this economic principle in his 1691 publication, Some Considerations of the Consequences of the Lowering of Interest and the Raising of the Value of Money. Locke addressed the concept of supply and demand as part of a discussion about interest rates in 17th-century England. Many merchants wanted the government to lower the cap on interest rates charged by private lenders so that people could borrow more money and thus purchase more goods. Locke argued that the free-market economy should set rates because government regulation could have unintended consequences. If the lending industry were left alone, interest rates would regulate themselves, Locke wrote: "The price of any commodity rises or falls by the proportion of the number of buyers and sellers."

Sir James Steuart's Inquiry into the Principles of Political Economy, published in 1796, was the first known printed use of the term "supply and demand." When Steuart wrote his treatise on political economy, one of his main concerns was the impact of supply and demand on laborers.

Adam Smith dealt extensively with the topic in his 1776 epic economic work, The Wealth of Nations. Often referred to as the Father of Economics, Smith explained the concept of supply and demand as an "invisible hand" that naturally guides the economy. According to Smith, the invisible hand is the automatic pricing and distribution mechanisms in the economy. Smith described a society in which bakers and butchers provide products that individuals need and want, providing a supply that meets demand and developing an economy that benefits everyone. It is important to note that

Smith's ideas haven't gone without critique over the years since his ideas were first published, though. Over time, his ideas have been added to in order to represent the changing times and include concepts such as marginal utility, comparative advantage, entrepreneurship, the time-preference theory of interest, and monetary theory.

One of Marshall's most important contributions to microeconomics was his introduction of the concept of price elasticity of demand, which examines how price changes affect demand. In theory, people buy less of a particular product if the price increases, but Marshall noted that in real life, this behavior was not always true. The prices of some goods can increase without reducing demand, which means their prices are inelastic. Inelastic goods tend to include items such as medication or food that consumers deem crucial to daily life. Marshall argued that supply and demand, costs of production, and price elasticity all work together.

Nowadays economists they explain demand and supply economic theory, they have some different to past economists whose explanation as below:

It is not accidential that governments are heavily involved with vaccination . When there are externalities, free market, fail to persuade individual incentives with society's

their the worker's decision of whether to get a vaccine ends up attracting whether other people get sick. The workers might not fully take all these other people's potential suffering into account when making her or his vaccination decision.

As Stanford University does many suggestions, understand this and tries to help them make the right decisions and so providers free flu vaccines for its staff and students.

Small pockets of unvaccinated individuals can allow a disease to gain a spread more widely well-being. For example, parent weighing the costs and benefits of a vaccine for their child is not always thinking of the consequences of that vaccination to other people. These are markets in which subsidizing or regulating behavior can make everyone better off. Because the reason for requiring that a child be vaccinated before enrolling in school is not just to protect that child, because each child's vaccination affects others via potential contagions.

On conclusion, it seems that many traditional paper book publish business begin to change to electronic book publish business. Due, to online technology existence, it influences many readers choose to buy electronic books to read. Hence, due to readers reading demand change which is from paper book reading habit to electronic book reading habit.Then,it explains that electronic book supply number depends on electronic book reader reading demand in economic view.

Robot job behavior brings economy influences

Whether robot labor needs are depended on employer labor demand more or robot labor number supply more? If one day robots can replace human to do simple, even complex jobs. They will bring what influences to our global societal economy.The popular economic refrain declares that the global middle class is dying and robots will soon take our jobs, e.g. shopping center customer service jobs, library service jobs, cinema ticket sale jobs, restaurant kitchen cooker jobs, even, bus drivers, taxi drivers etc. public transport driving jobs, accountant, doctors etc. professional jobs. Whether it is beautiful or petty matter if our future societies have many human jobs can be replaced to do from robots. Businessman must may reduce to employ employees and reduce to pay salary or wage, when robots can be replaced to do their employees tasks. But, societies must bring unemployment rate rises , due to societies will have many people loss jobs when their employers choose to buy robots to serve their clients or do any office tasks or customer service or cleaning etc. tasks.

In micro economy view, employers may save money in long term, but in macro economy view, it will cause unemployment ratio rises , even crime rate rises when there are many people lose jobs in societies. These models of doom, though, fail to account for the hundreds of businesses riding the waves of change in their industries when robots may be invented to replace human to do many simple , even complex tasks in our future societies.

WE may image that one small factory needs to manufacture fishes canes to sell to supermarket, the small , cheaper stuff and higher margin parts of the fishes manufacture industry. Before, this factory needs to employ many human factory workers need to help every fresh customer making the perfect fishing gear, designed for performance, durability, and cost in order to achieve to manufacture every fish cane in whole fished processing manufacturing stages. Every worker needs to spend about 15 to twenty minutes to finish every fish cane , till to delivery to any supermarket to sell. If this fish canes manufacturing factory can apply manufacturing robots to help them to finish any one working tasks , every robot can only spend five minutes to finish whole fresh fish cane manufacturing process. Thus, every robot can help this factory save 10 to 15 minutes time to finish every fish cane manufacturing process. IN fact, time is money, because when every robot can help this factory to reduce 10 to 15 minutes time to compare human worker. Then, this factory can finish about 20 fish canes in one hour if it can use robot to help it to manufacture fish canes. Otherwise, if this factory still use human workers to help it to manufacture fish canes, then it can finish about 3 to 4 fish canes in one hour. SO, the manufacturing efficiency ensures that robots must help this fish manufacturing factory to raise fish canes number more than human workers. So, in robotic behavioral economy view, manufacturing robots must help this fish canes manufacturing factory to raise fish canes manufacturing number and deliver increasing number to supermarkets to prepare to sell every day. Robots can help this fish canes manufacturing factory bring manufacturing time saving, rising manufacturing efficiency, improving performance and reducing wages expenditure long time advantages in micro economy view. However, manufacturing robots can also bring disadvantages to society, e.g. increasing unemployment ratio, increasing crime rate, this factory workers will lose jobs and income, they need earn social welfare from government and increasing government finance pressure in short time, even long time in macro economic view.

Stanford University graduate program in economics, Scott lecturer explained that "in demand and supply economic theory for robots supply and demand case, robots supply number increasing may influence human workers demand number decrease. It sometimes calls " the efficient frontier".

No specific human beings were mentioned in any of economics classes. As robots supply and demand in market case, They (robots) may be purely theoretical " agents" who reached to the most reasonable sale prices in order to persuade any one businessman buyer to make manufacturing robot buying decision whether robots can help him / her to bring how much saving time , saving money, saving cost, improving performance, efficiency economic benefit before he/she plans to reduce workers number when he/she decides to apply robots to replace human workers in his/her factory or office or any service department, e.g. cinema ticket sale service, shopping center customer service, shopping center cleaning , supermarket customer service etc. service or sale tasks. When robots can replace human to do any one of these tasks in any organizations. So, robots may be human worker agents who reached to prices the way robots would react to a software command. There was nothing that explained why some people thrived and others did n't or why truly brilliant, hardworking people could fail when much lazier folks succeeded." Having been admitted to the Stanford University graduate program in economics, Scott lecturer hoped to get his answers there.

How robots influence our future social changing? Using the right technology can be a boon to your business in this economy. For internet example, it is easier than ever to find well-matched customers all around the world, to stay in contact with them, and to more quickly design the products they want. If you focus solely on being cutting -edge, though you risk letting the technology take over what should be very robust relationships with your customers , employees, and colleagues. IN nowadays society, technological advances and automation, personal relationships in business are more crucial than ever. I mean that robots can not replace human to serve clients to let them to feel more comfortable and passion more easily. For shoe shop case example, if the shoe shop apply one robot to serve its clients to replace human shoe salesperson to serve its shoe customers. Robots ensure that they can not persuade every shoe potential buyer to make shoe buying decision more easily when robots need to contact every shoe potential buyer. The reason is simple, because robots can not touch any one shoe buyer individual emotion very easier.

If the shoe buyer needs the robots to help him/her to choose any right shoe styles when he/she can not feel himself / herself can make the most right shoe style choice decision. The robots can not replace human shoe salesperson to make shoe style choice judgment more easily. They must need longer time to analyze whether which shoe style may be the most suitable to the shoe buyer. Otherwise, human shoe salesperson may attempt to make the most right shoe style choice decision to help any one shoe buyer to choose the most right style shoe because he/she owns shoe style sale experience, shoe style knowledge, the most important reason is that they can feel every shoe customer individual emotion to touch whether he/she will feel comfortable or happy when they attempt to help every shoe customer to seek the most right shoe style in every shoe customer whole shoe searching processing. Otherwise, serving robots are only one machine, they can not touch or feel every shoe customer individual emotion whether he/she feel comfortable or unhappy or happy when they need to contact them in whole shoe searching processing. Hence, I believe that some tasks robots can not replace human staff to do very easily. Otherwise, robots may bring disadvantages to let any one businessman to loss his/her customers, due to robots can not touch every customer emotion to compare human staff in service tasks more easily. Robots serving customer behaviors may cause money lose and customers number lose to the shop in micro economic view.

On conclusion, in demand and supply economic theory for robots supply and demand case, robots supply number increasing may influence human workers demand number decrease. So, it seems that robots number supply will be depended on global robots supply number more than robots demand number because when human began to accept robots to replace human to do general simple jobs in global labor market. Then, it means that global robots labor number must need to be increased in order to satisfy global businessmen workers number need. If any kinds of robot workers manufacture number is not enough to be supplied to let global future businessmen to buy, then robot supply will be shortage and they can not provide to satisfy global businessmen robots labour purchase need. So, future robot number will be depended on supply more than demand.

Human intellectual demand and supply behavior relationship

What does intellectual human economic behaviors mean ? Human foolish behavior is depended on social enjoyment need more or material social supply more? I believe that when we choose or decide to do intellectual behaviors, then our societies will be influenced to bring economic growth in consequence.I shall attempt to indicate pollution case to explain how and why either our intellectual or foolish behaviors may bring economic growth or recession in consequence as below:

On one hand, for air pollution social case aspect example, if we only consider to buy cars to drive for working aim or holiday leisure aim. Then, our societies air will be polluted. Our health will be influenced to bad. Our car driving behaviors may cause global environment air pollution seriously. In long time, global air pollution will bring our bodies health to be bad. Although, ourselves car driving behaviors may bring our driving travelling leisure enjoyment and comfortable feeling in short time, also we so not need to pay public transport fare often, but we need to compensate ourselves health economic intangible loss due to air pollution , when cars number increases, dirty air will cause ourselves health to become bad.

In the result, we will need to pay more medical expenditure when we are old age, due to ourselves bodies will become bad, due to we breathe global dirty air every day, due to ourselves cars pollute air in long time, e.g.

10 to 20 years, even 30 more without limited air pollution environment. So, driving cars behavior may be one kind of human foolish behavior and our foolish behavior may bring ourselves future long time medical expenditure absolutely.

One the other hand, water pollution social aspect, if we often keep much rubbish to pollute sea, oil exploration processing pollute ocean , ships gas pollute ocean, then fishes will eat polluted food and drive dirty water, due to global ocean is polluted.

In fact, because human only to consider how to buy boats to carry on leisure enjoyment activities, or catch cruises to travel on the sea. Also, oil manufacturers only consider researching anywhere to find new oil exploration places to manufacture oil product, when their oil exploration processes pollute ocarn . Consequently, global fishes drink polluted warer or eat polluted food. They will have poison. SO, human will have high chance to eat poison polluted fishes, due to fishes are poison or are polluted.

So, human is doing foolish activities, we only hope to find oil exploration places to pollute ocean or we only spend money to buy ticket to catch ships to travel anywhere in global ocean. All of these human foolish behaviors will bring pollution to global ocean. On consequently, we will need to compensate to eat polluted or dirty or poision fishes, ourselves bodies health will be bad. In long time, we need have high chance to pay medical expenditure when we are old. So, pollution case may be one good example to explain how and why human foolish behavior may influence ourselves future need to compensate serious medical loss.

All of these human foolish behavior will bring pollution to global ocean. On consequently, we will need to compensate to eat polluted or dirty or poison fished , ourselves bodies health will be bad. In long time, we will have high chance to pay medical expenditure, when we are old. So, pollution case may be one good example to explain how and why human ourselves intellectual or foolish behaviors may influence future long time economic loss or economic growth or recession in micro and micro economic view.

On another water pollution aspect hand, if we often keep rubbish to sea, oil exploration processing pollutes ocean and ships‘ gas pollute ocean, then fishes will eat polluted food and drink dirty water, due to fishes will eat polluted food and drink dirty sea water because the global ocean is polluted seriously.

In fact, because human only consider how to buy boats to carry on any leisure water activities, or catches cruises to travel on the sea. Also, oil manufacturers only consider any where to find oil exploration places to manufacture oil products from ocean, when their pol exploration processes can plloute ocean. Consequently, global fishes drink polluted water or eat direty food. They will have poison. So, human will have high chance to eat poison fishes.

Otherwise, such as pollution case, it can influence inflation or deflation. Consequently, the reason indicates supply and demand theory. If air pollution is serious, then we will consider health issue, global cars demand number may be influenced to reduce, when global cars number demand will reduce, global car prices and supply number will need to change to fall down in order to attract or persuade global car consumers choose to make car purchase decision.

Hence, global car manufacture number and car price will be influenced to reduce, due to global air pollution issue. Consequently, deflation will occur because when the country citizen usually does not spend much extra saving money to buy car expensive goods. Money value will be low. Otherwise, if global car pollution is not serious, human considers to buy cars to enjoy driving leisure lives. So, global car demand is influenced to increase , also global car price will also influenced to increase.

Consequently, global human will choose to buy cars to drive. Due to we accept to spend extra saving to buy expensive car goods. Car sale price and supply may be influenced to rise up. Money value is influenced to reduce. Inflation may be influenced, due to global car consumers number increases, we would not have extra money to spend easily. Car expensive goods expenditure influences our spending habit to avoid to make car purchase decision more easily. So, human intellectual or foolish activities may bring inflation or deflation consequence in possible indirectly in macro economic view.

On conclusion, above pollution case explain that how and why human intellectual or foolish economic behaviors may bring inflation or deflation consequence as well as economic growth or recession consequence as well as any goods demand and supply increasing or decreasing consequence. It implies that human behavior may have indirect relationship to influence any goods demand and supply number to either increase or decrease result as well as any goods price will be influenced to increase or decrease in micro and macro economic view. Hence, Human foolish behavior is depended on social enjoyment need more or material social supply more because human needs to raise enjoyment feel , so we will choose to do foolish behavior, e.g. air pollution, when many people choose to buy cars to drive to replace catch public transport. So, such as car market, it depends on car demand number more than car supply number absolutely in demand and supply view.

The relationship between social change and human behavior

Why does economic changes may influence human individual behavioral change? I shall attempt to indicate shopping behavior and staying at home behavior to explain their case and effect relationship as below:

Human behavior can be influenced by economic change or economic change can be influenced by human behavior? Why does recession may influence consumers reduce shopping desire? In social recession situation, it is possible that many people lose jobs suddenly, due to businessmen lose many customers. They need to make decision to reduce employees number in order to continue to keep businesses. Consequently, many firms (organizations) their employees may lose jobs. When they have much time, due to lose jobs, they will feel to avoid to spend too much time and money to go to shopping often. Many losing jobs people, they will often stay at homes.

So, they will reduce time to go to shopping, then non essential products won't their preferable choice purchase products. Hence, recession will change many losing jobs people their shopping or consumption desires to avoid to buy non essential products often . Usually when economic boom, many people have jobs to do because consumers number must increase when many people have jobs to do. Then, many people can accept to spend money to buy non essential products often. Many people feel spend time to go to shopping can satisfy their purchase of any kinds of new products useful psychology or desire. So, recession is one good example to explain it can influence many people do not like often to leave homes to go to shopping easily. Many people like to stay at homes, because they feel worry about spending too much shopping time when they leave homes. Their staying home time is one good negative shopping behavior example. So, economic change may influence human individual behavior changes , they have direct cause and effect relationship in behavioral economic view.

May human behavior influence economic change? Is it possible that human behavior may bring the country social economic change in macro economic or micro behavioral economic view ? I shall indicate publishing industry example. Do you feel that if there are many students feel learning is very important when they read many books or many of students feel interesting to read or they have reading new books in habit, then it is possible that the country will have many students like to spend time to go to any book shops to choose the books, they feel that they can help they learn new knowledge. Then the country will increase students number, they often spend time to visit any one book shop every week. Their visiting book shops behavior which may become their habits. So, the country will increase students number, they often spend time to visit book shops. Also, it implies that visiting book shops behaviors may be their behavioral habits.

So, when the country has many students often spend time to visit book shops , their visiting book shops behaviors may help any one book shop to raise books sale chance. So, the country's student individual often visiting book shop behaviors, their habitual visiting book shops behaviors must may assist help any one book shop to increase books sale number absolutely.

Consequently, any one book shop , its books sale number must be influenced to increase to increase because the country will have many students like or feel need visit book shops habit in order to choose any suitable books to buy to read at home in order to raise themselves learning effort. When the country has many bok shops often have many students visit their book shops, then their books sale number may be influenced to increase. It explain why student individual visiting book shop behavior may help any one book shop sale number increases also. So, visiting shops products sale number is depended on online products supply number, if online products supply number increases, then it may cause many customers choose to buy the kind of products from online webstore. So, any shop products sale number will depend on online products supply number in supply and demand view.

Robot job behavior brings economy influences

If one day robots can replace human to do simple, even complex jobs. They will bring what influences to our global societal economy.The popular economic refrain declares that the global middle class is dying and robots will soon take our jobs, e.g. shopping center customer service jobs, library service jobs, cinema ticket sale jobs, restaurant kitchen cooker jobs, even, bus drivers, taxi drivers etc. public transport driving jobs, accountant, doctors etc. professional jobs. Whether it is beautiful or petty matter if our future societies have many human jobs can be replaced to do from robots. Businessman must may reduce to employ employees and reduce to pay salary or wage, when robots can be replaced to do their employees tasks. But, societies must bring unemployement rate rises , due to societies will have many people loss jobs when their employers choose to buy robots to serve their clients or do any office tasks or customer service or cleaning etc. tasks.

In micro economy view, employers may save money in long term, but in macro economy view, it will cause unemployment ratio rises , even crime rate rises when there are many people losejobs in societies. These models of doom, though, fail to account for the hundreds of businesses riding the waves of change in their industries when robots may be invented to replace human to do many simple , even complex tasks in our future societies.

WE may image that one small factory needs to manufacture fishes canes to sell to supermarket, the small , cheaper stuff and higher margin parts of the fishes manufacture industry. Before, this factory needs to employe many human factory workers need to help every fresh customer makeing the perfect fishing gear, designed for performance, durability, and cost in order to achieve to manufacture every fish cane in whole fished processing manufacturing stages. Every worker needs to spend about 15 to twenty minutes to finish every fish cane , till to delivery to any supermarket to sell. If this fish canes manufacturing factory can apply manufacturing robots to help them to finish any one working tasks , every robot can only spend five minutes to finish whole fresh fish cane manufacturing process. Thus, every robot can

help this factory save 10 to 15 minutes time to finsh every fish cane manufacturing process. IN fact, time is money, because when every robot can help this factory to reduce 10 to 15 minutes time to compare human worker. Then, this factory can finish about 20 fish canes in one hour if it can use robot to help it to manufacture fish canes. Otherwise, if this factory still use human workers to help it to manufacture fish canes, then it can finsh about 3 to 4 fish canes in one hour. SO, the manufacturing efficiency ensures that robots must help this fish manufacturing factory to raise fish canes number more than human workers. So, in robotic behavioral economy view, manufacturing robots must help this fish canes manufacturing factory to raise fish canes manufacturing number and deliver increasing number to supermarkets to prepare to sell every day.

Robots can help this fish canes manufacturing factory bring manufacturing time saving, rising manufacturing efficiency, improving performance and reducing wages expenditure long time advantages in micro economy view. However, manufacturing robots can also bring disadvanages to society, e.g. increasing unemployment ratio, increasing crime rate,

this factory workers will lose jobs and income, they need earn social welfare from government and increasing government finance pressure in short time, even long time in macro economic view.

Stanford University graduate program in economics, Scott lecturer explained that "in demand and supply economic theory for robots supply and demand case, robots supply number increasing may influence human workers demand number decrease. It sometimes calls " the efficient frontier".

No specific human beings were mentioned in any of economics classes. As robots supply and demand in market case, They (robots) may be purely theoretical " agents" who reached to the most reasonable sale prices in order to persuade any one businessman buyer to make manufacturing robot buying decision whether robots can help him / her to bring how much saving time , saving money, saving cost, improving performance, efficiency economic benefit before he/she plans to reduce workers number when he/she decides to apply robots to replace human workers in his/her factory or office or any service department, e.g. cinema ticket sale service, shopping center customer service, shopping center cleaning , supermarket customer service etc. service or sale tasks. When robots can replace human to do any one of these tasks in any organizations. So, robots may be human worker agents who reached to prices the way robots would react to a software command. There was nothing that explained why some people thrived and others did n't or why truly brilliant, hardworking people could fail when much lazier folks succeeded." Having been admitted to the Stanford University graduate program in economics, Scott lecturer hoped to get his answers there.

How robots influence our future social changing? Using the right technology can be a boon to your business in this economy. For internet example, it is easier than ever to find well-matched customers all around the world, to stay in contact with them, and to more quickly design the products they want. If you focus solely on being cutting -edge, though you risk letting the technology take over what should be very robust relationships with your customers , employees, and colleagues. IN nowaddays society, technoligical advances and cutomation, personal relationships in business are more crucial than ever. I mean that robots can not replace human to serve clients to let them to feel more comfortable and passion more easily. For shoe shop case example, if the shoe shop apply one robot to serve its clients to replace human shoe salesperson to serve its shoe customers. Robots ensure that they can not persuade every shoe potential buyer to make shoe buying decision more easily when robots need to contact every shoe potential buyer. The reason is simple, because robots can not touch any one shoe buyer individual emotion very easier.

If the shoe buyer needs the robots to help him/her to choose any right shoe styles when he/she can not feel himself / herself can make the most right shoe style choice decision. The robots can not replace human shoe salesperson to make shoe style choice judgement more easily. They must need longer time to analyze whether which shoe style may be the most suitable to the shoe buyer. Otherwise, human shoe salesperson may attempt to make the most right shoe style choice decision to help any one shoe buyer to choose the most right style shoe because he/she owns shoe style sale experience, shoe style knowledge, the most important reason is that they can feel every shoe customer individual emotion to touch whether he/she will feel comfortable or happy when they attempt to help every shoe customer to seek the most right shoe style in every shoe customer whole shoe searching processing. Otherwise, serving robots are only one machine, they can not touch or feel every shoe customer individual emotion whether he/she feel comfortable or unhappy or happy when they need to contact them in whole shoe searching processing. Hence, I believe that some tasks robots can not replace human staff to do very easily. Otherwise, robots may bring disadvanages to let any one businessman to loss his/her customers, due to robots can not touch every customer emotion to compare human staff in service tasks more easily. Robots serving customer behaviors may cause money lose and customers number lose to the shop in micro economic view.

The relationship between social change and human behavior

Why does economic changes may influence human individual behavioral change? I shall attempt to indicate shopping behavior and staying at home behavior to explain their case and effect relationsip as below:

Human behavior can be influenced by economic change or economic change can be influenced by human behavior? Why does recession may influence consumers reduce shopping desire? In social recession suitation, it is possible that many people lose jobs suddenly, due to businessmen lose many customers. They need to make decision to reduce employees number in order to continue to keep businesses. Consequently, many firms (organizations) their employees may lose jobs. When they have much time, due to lose jobs, they will feel to avoid to spend too much time and money to go to shopping often. Many losing jobs people, they will often stay at homes.

So, they will reduce time to go to shopping, then non essential products won't their preferable choice purchase products. Hence, recession will change many losing jobs people their shopping or consumption desires to avoid to buy non essential products often . Usually when economic boom, many people have jobs to do because consumers number must increase when many people have jobs to do. Then, many people can accept to spend money to buy non essential products often. Many people feel spend time to go to shopping can satisfy their purchase of any kinds of new products useful psychology or desire. So, recession is one good example to explain it can influence many people do not like often to leave homes to go to shopping easily. Many people like to stay at homes, becaue they feel worry about spending too much shopping time when they leave homes. Their staying home time is one good negative shopping behavior example. So, economic change may influence human individual behavior changes , they have direct cause and efect relationship in behavioral economic view.

May human behavior influence economic change? Is it possible that human behavior may bring the country social economic change in macro economic or micro behavioral economic view ? I shall indicate publishing industry example. Do you feel that if there are many students feel learning is very important when they read many books or many of students feel interesting to read or they have reading new books in habit, then it is possible that the country will have many students like to spend time to go to any book shops to choose the books, they feel that they can help they learn new knowledge. Then the country will increase students number, they often spend time to visit any one book shop every week. Their visiting book shops behavior which may become their habits. So, the country will increase students number, they often spend time to visit book shops. Also, it implies that visiting book shops behaviors may be their behavioral habits.

So, when the country has many students often spend time to visit book shops , their visiting book shops behaviors may help any one book shop to raise books sale chance. So, the country's student individual often visiting book shop behaviors, their habitual visiting book shops behaviors must may assist help any one book shop to increase books sale number absolutely.

Consequently, any one book shop , its books sale bumber must be influenced to increase to increase because the country will have many students like or feel need visit book shops habit in order to choose any suitable books to buy to read at home in order to raise themselves learning effort. When the country has many bok shops often have many students visit their book shops, then their books sale number may be influenced to increase. It explain why student individual visiting book shop behavior may help any one book shop sale number increases also.

How human productive behavior may influence economic development

May any country which citizen behavior assist themselves country development? It is one cause and effect economic question. I mean that if the country itself citicen can not concentrate mind or energy to choose to do one kind of industry in order to let themselves country can bring the most benefit, then whether the counry itself economy can bring the most serious economic benefit. I shall attempt to indicate these countries themselves indistry choice to explain whether these countries themselves citizen productive behavior may help themselves countries to achieve the largest economic benefits. I shall indicate as below:

New Zealand farmer individual wine productive behavior

For New Zealand country example, this country concerns itself effort is foucs on farming agricultural aspect. So, this country has many farmers concentrate on farming agricultural aspect. May New Zealanders choose to spend time to produce different kinds of wines, e.g. wine or red grape wine is for the people are eating meat, or they are eating dinner.

When these New Zealanders their behaviors choose to do farming or agriculture to grow and produce different kinds of taste of white or red grape wine drinking products job. Themselves grape agriculture behavior will influence these New Zealanders themselves, they can learn how to improve different kinds of grape wine drinking products in order to achieve every kinds of white or read grape wines taste improving aim during their white or red grape producing process.

Why can New Zealander every individual white or read grape wine producers improve their white or read grape wine taste more easily? In behavioral economic view, it can explain that why any one New Zealander white or read grape wine producer can be encouraged or excited or persuaded to concentrate nervous and energy and effort to learn how to improve their white or red grape wine products easily.

In fact, New Zealand is one agricultural food export country. It has good natural environment resource , e.g. land, seed to provide any one farmer to produce themselves any kinds of agricultrual food products, e.g. fruit, or wine food products. Because New Zealanders know themselves country has enough natural resource . So, in common, many New Zealanders choose to attempt to do farming agricultural jobs in order to export themselves any kinds of fruit or meat or wine products to overseas or sell to domestic in order to earn profit.

So, when these New Zealand farmers number has been increasing every year. This country farmers will feel themsleves competition between this New Zealand farmers themselves are serious due to they may feel New Zealanders choose to do agriculture businesses in order to export themselves different kinds of farming food to overseas or sell to local to earn profit.

Hence, when many New Zealand farmers feel that farmers number has been increasing every year. They will feel themselves competition is serious. They must need to spend much time and nervous and effort to research what method is the best how to produce the best taste of white or red grape wine products in order to let local or overseas wine buyers to choose to buy his/her producing white or read grpae products to drink.

Hence, in competition psychological view, may influence many New Zealand white or reaad wine producers had been beginning to change their learning behavior on researching what method is the best in order to produce the best quality of taste red or white wine products to sell in order to attract overseas or local white or read grape wine drinkers to choose to buy his/her wine products. Their behavior will focus on learning how to raising or improving white or read grape wine taste method more than only focus on producing a large number white or red grape wine products. They believe wine quality is more important to compare wine producing number. So, New Zealand wine producers themselves wine producers behaviors have been changing on concentrating on researching wine quality method aspect more then wine producing number aspect in behavioral economic view.

America high technological productive behavior

For America example, US is one high technological country, it owns many high technological knowledge talent inventors, e.g. computer science inventors. Hence, US must attract many diferent countries owning high technological computer inventors choose to go to US to develop their computer science profession career. Also, it seems that when many computer science inventors or professions choose to go to US to develop themselves computer science new career. In behavioral economic view, due to their leaving themselves countries choice, which may bring influence themselve country job behaviors need to be changed. They must need to adapt US new live. Because they will forgive their past computer science job. These computer science professionals need to spend time to adapt US new lives. They " past computer science job behaviors" will need to be changed to their new US any computer employer's new computer science job model.

Because their traditional computer science jobs needed to be forgot in their themselves countries. They will feel their old computer science job knowledge and behavior needed to change in order to let their US any one new of computer company employer feels satisfactory to accept their new working behavior in any one US computer organization.

So, on the other hand, many US computer company employer will feel that they must need time to accept any one new overseas computer science professions their working behaviors, their working attitude daily, because these foreign comouter science professional, their past computer working behaviors and working attitude must be different to US domestic computer science professions.

In behavioral economic view, these overseas computer science professions, their working behaviors and attitude must be needed to change in order to adapt any one US new computer company itself domestic or local computer science professional stafs themselves daily working behaviors and attitude because these overseas and local computer science professionals must need to team work together.

In behavioral economic view, it is only one way that foreign computer science professionals must need to change themselves past country traditiona daily working behaviors and attitude in order to cooperate with these US local computer science professionals in teams more easily.

Consequently, if these foreign compute science professionals can change their past working behaviors and attitude to let any one US local computer science professional feels to cooperate with them easily in short time. Then, the US computer company itself whole computer professional teams themselves efficiencies will be influenced to raised or improved by the changing past working attitude and working behaviors of these foreign computer science professionals. So, in behavioral economic view, only if US any one computer company hopes itself computer teams themselves efficiency can be raised or improved when it decides to employ foreign computer science professionals and US domestic computer science professionals. They need to work in teams together. They must need to let these foreign computer science professionals to know how to change their working behaviors and attitude to let their domestic computer science professionals feel easy to work together. Then, the US computer company itself whole team efficiency must be rasied or improved easily in short time.

China share market investing behavior

For China share market example, economic development depends on financial market. Because if many Chinese have interest to invest to carry on shares buying and selling activities in orde to learn how to earn shares interest and share profit when the China shareholder can make decision to sell himself/herself shares in the the high price, then he/she can earn money when he/she can sell the China company's shares in the high sale share price position.

If China has many Chinese like to spend time to carry on investing shares activities. Themselves shares buying and selling behaviors will influence China has many companies can increase fund from many Chinese shareholders in order to have enough money to expand or develop themselves businesses in China in long term.

Consequently, when China can have many Chinese like to attempt to carry on buying and selling shares investing behaviors in China share market. Themselves buying and selling shares behaviors can help many Chinese companies have effort to increase enough money or capital in order to continue to do their businesses in long term absolutely. So, it explains why when many Chinese become shareholders , they can assist China will have many companies continue to develop their businesses if many Chinese like to carry on shares buying and selling investing behaviors in long time in China financial investment market nowadays in behavioral economic view.

Why has any individual country have many people invest share behavior which can influence the country's macro consumption desire?

I shall apply shares market buying and selling investment behavior to explaiin why shares investment behavior which may impact the country's overal consumption desire as below:

In behavioral economic view, I assume that when the coutry has many people have interest to attempt to carry on shares buying and selling investment behavior, then their frequent shares buying and selling behaviors which may bring negactive consumption desire or shopping desire of these shares investors their consumer behavior.

The reason is simple, when the country has many share buyers number suddenly been increasing rapidly. Consequently, these large group share investors must need to spend much time to research any kinds of company shares variations, whether when their share prices will rise up of fall down in order to achieve buying the company's shares in the lowest price and selling the company's shares in the highest price level in order to earn profit.

Basic on this reason, they must need to spend much extra time to research share prices changing behavior every day, e.g. one working person will wait to leave his/her job, after he/she can spend time to gather data to research the day's share price changing behavior after dinner. So, the working person's right time may be his/her share price market research behavior. Before he/she may spend his/her night time to go to shopping after dinner, but nowadays, he/she will fogive to do his/her shopping behavior before dinner or after dinner at hight sometime. He/she will make decision to spend much night time to turn on computer to click on share market website to research his/her share purchase choice to investigate whether his/her share price whether it rises up or falls down at the moment in order to make his/her share buying or selling decision at ever night time.

I mean the when the country has many people are share investors, their shares investment behavioral spenging time which will influence many shops lose customers at might often because the country will have many people feel need to spend night time to turn on computer or watch television to investigate share price variation. So, the country will have many people / share investors choose to stay at home in order to carry on share price variation investigation behavior, they need to listen share market update news from radios or watch the share market update news from computer or TV at home every night. Consequenly, they must reduce times to leave themselves homes at night. So, their shopping behavior also will be reduced. Because these share investors feel need to spend time to investigate share price variation news at homes which can bring economic benefits (high opportunity benefits) when they choose to forgive to leave homes to go to shopping times (opportunity cost) every night.

On conclusion, it seems that when the country has many people are share investors, then their share price investigating behavior may bring negative shopping emotion at night. Consequently, the country's any one shop may lose many customers from this share investor consumer group in behavioral economic view. Hence, when the country's share investors number had been increasing rapidly, it will influence any shops lose many customers from this share investing customer group at night frequenly in short time, even long time in behavioral economic view, because their shopping desires or shopping emotion will be brought negative feeling when they make decisions to spend much time to listen radios or watch TV or computers share price update nes at night. Hence, share market will bring negative impact to influence consumer shopping desire or negative shopping emotion in behavioral economic view.

Can technology influence human shopping behavioral change?

Nowadays, technological development has reached mature stage, whether technological mature stage may bring positive or negative shopping emotion influence to global consumers. I shall aplly internet inventin or ecommerce shopping channel tool to explain whether internet technology can bring postive or negative influence to global consumer behavior in behavioral economic view.

Internet is a good technological tool, it brings e-commerce business chance. In fact, commonly, global has have many businessmen choose to use internet channel to carry on their products transactions between global online-buyers and their electronic websites. So, global many shoppers had begun to feel online shopping is more convenient to compare visiting shops shopping. Their shopping behaviors have been changed from internet technological tool. Global has many shoppers choose to buy any products from any overseas or local businessmen their web stores. They only need to spend time to find any businessmen their webstores to choose the most suitable products to pay visa to buy from their webstores. at homes. So, in general, global had have may shoppers had changed their shopping behaviors from visiting shops to visiting webstores at homes often.

So, it seems that internet technological tool had influenced global many shops disappear, but internet webstores will be replaced their actual shops on streets. Some of businessmen either they choose webstores to replace shops or choose websotes and shops both or still keep shops only. Hence, internet tool influences global businessmen have three kinds of products sale channels to let globa local and overseas consumers to choose how to buy their products.

However, in fact, many of global shoppers, youngers and olders had begun to accept to buy any products from webstores. They feel to spend time to leave homes to visit shops , their shopping behaviors will be wasted time to not essential part to their daily lives. Hence, since internet technological invention, it had changed many consumers their traditional visiting shops shopping habit to change to buying products from webstores channel.

However, on the one hand, internet creates webstores ecommerce shopping channel to let global many consumers do not need to leave homes to go to shopping. It brings negative visiting shops shopping emotion to global general consumers nowadays. But on the other hand, it also brings positive visiting internet webstores shopping emotion to global general consumer nowadays. So, it seems that global many consumers feel that they often do not need to spend much time to go out shopping. Many global consumers feel convenient and enjoy to choose any products to buy from different internet webstores, when the online buyer chooses the most suitable product, he she only needs to pay visa card to buy the product from the online seller's webstore conveniently at home.

Hence, online shopping can bring economic benefit to online buyers, e.g. avoiding walking time or spending transport fare to visit the shop to go to shopping, shortening or reducing shopping time to do another important matter.

On conclusion, global many consumers began feel online shopping can bring more economic benefits on shortening shopping time, avoiding transport fare spending aspect. So, online shopping will be popular shopping behavior for future long time. It may encourage global many shoppers can make rapid shopping decision in short time in order to carry on any products buying transaction to global any one online shopper in short time easily in behavioral economic view. So, global many businessmen had begun to build themselves one attraction webstore in order to persuade different countries consumers to choose to click themselves webstores from internet channel to buy any kinds of products in short time easily.

So, internet technology had changed consumers traditional shopping behaviors to build positive online shopping emotion as well as raise online sellers' any products sale chance easily in behavioral economic view.

Why and how human behavior may influence the country's economic growth or recession?

When one country has many people choose to do the same matter for one period, whether their behavior may influence the country's pvera; economic growth or recession . I shall attempt to indicate cases toexplain their relationship as below:

For flowing rubblish behavioral case example, do you feel that when the country has many people often flow rubblish on the streets, instead of their flowing rubblish behavior may bring streets dirty? But, their flowing rubblish behavior may explain that this country has people may have enough money to buy food to ear, or enough cloths to wear, enough bottles of water to drink, even they may have enough money to buy new television, radio, refrigeraters , washing machines, desktops or laptops electronic home products from old to new to use in order to satisfy their living needs. So, when they flow old electronic home products, their flowing old home electronic products behaviors may seem that they have enough money to buy other new home electronic products to replace old home electronic products to use at homes.

However, it seems thaat this country ought have many people have jobs to do. So, many of them, they can easy to make purchase decison to flow any old home electronic products and buy any new home electronic products to use . Because this country has many people have jobs to do. So, they can often not use old home electonic products to become rubblishs to flow on streets after they had bought any kinds of new home electronic homes.

In fact, it also implies that this country's economy grows rapidly. So, many businesses can glow up rapdly. When they expanded their businesses, they must need to increase employees number in order to let they help themselves to raise productivity or serve their clients absolutely. So, when the country has many businesses can grow up, it seems that its economy must be better or it is improved to compare past. Due to many different kinds of home electronic products had been often bought to use by this country people in this period. So, this country's any streets can be observed that expensive electronic home products were flowed on streets anywhere. then, this country will have many electronic home products sellers can sell their home electronic products very easily. When this country has many people can find any kinds of jobs to do easily. So, due to unemploymen rate had been decreasing.

In behavioral economic view, as this many electronic home products rubblish country case, we can observe this country may have many people have jobs to do. So, consumption number has been increased long time. So, cheap food, or expensive home electronic products may be rubblish on any streets. This country's people , their flowing rubblish behaviors may be explained that many of people have enough jobs to do, so they have ability to buy any good taste food to eat or buy any kinds of expensive electronic home products to use. So, this country's economy may be improved for this long period. So, in behavioral economic view, when this country can have many electronic home products rubblishs are flowed on anywherer in streets frequently. It seems that this country will have many people have jobs to do, so it causes they often change old home electronic products or replaced them easily, when they have enough income to spend to buy any kinds of new home electronic products to use at homes easily. Moreover, their flowing old electronic home products behaviors also indicate that this country has many people their salaries may be increased in possible from their emplyers. When this country can have many different kinds of home electornic products are sold. It means that this country's electronic home products needs or demand had been increasing, due to many people have jobs to do and income increases to excite their living of needs also improve. Consequently, this country may seem have better economic improvement. We can observe from this country's electronic home products rubblish increasing income in theis period.

On conclusion, this country ought experience economic growth at this period. So, " flowing expensive electronic home rubblish increasing number " may seem that this country's economic growth is rapidly in this period, due to many people have jobs to do as well as salaries increase in this period.

Technology how impacts human behavior changing?

Technology how influences human behavior to bring changing? For example, online share purchase and sale transaction from smart phone brings share investor can do share buying or selling transation in any where and any time conveniently, non manual driving auto vehicle, bring car owner feels comfortable and spends free time to do other matter, e.g. reading, listening mucis in himself or herself car freely. electrical energy vehicle can help car owner to reduce air polluton and it can brings the drivers do not feel drive long time in any journeys in order to avoid air pollution for environmental protection responsible car drivers in our societies. Thus, they will drive long time in any journeys when they can drive electronic energy cars to replace oil energy cars.

However, online technology can also bring consumers can choose to stay at homes to buy any things from seller individual online webstore conveniently. Such as online technology can bring shoppers do not need to spend much time to visit shops to buy any things. They can choose any kinds of products from any online sellers individual online webstores conveniently at homes. Online technology excite busy consumers can make purchase decision easily as well as it can help online sellers sell any kinds of products from internet easily.

In behavioral economic view, technology can change human behavior to be improved, it can let human feels comfortable, more free time ro use, rapid making any decisions, such as apply smart phones to make share purchase or sale transaction decision, online shopping decision, even travelling any where decision in short time, when the traveller finds the most cheap hotel accommodation room price and air ticket price frm any travel agent online tourism webstore, then the potential travel customer can follow the online hotel accommodation price and air ticket price data to make decision when to buy the air ticket from the airline travel agent or make decision when to prebook which hotel accommodation room to go to the country to travel from online travel agent tourism webstores. So, technology can encourage global any country travelers to make anywhere to trvel rapidly. If the traveler can find the country's general hotel rooms and airline tickets prices had been decreasing more sightly. The traveler may make travel decision to choose the country to travel in short time, then he/she can prebook the country;s any hotel room and airline ticket to pay by visa fraom the country's any hotel and airline travel agent webstores., before one week, even one month or more easily. Hence, online technology can also encourage traveler individual frequent travel times to be increased, due to global travelers can find any hotel rooms and airline tickets prices from internet conveniently at homes. They do not need to spend time to visit any airline travel agent to enquire travel choice country's hotel rooms prices and airline ticket prices. They can compare global travel of countries choices ' all hotels rooms and airline agents air tickets prices to make prebook airline seat and hotel room decision before one week, one month even six months early.

On conclusion, online technology can encourage global travelers can make travelling any where and when traveling time desicions easily. It can excite tourism industry develops in long time. Also, such as electricity cars invention can encourage environment protection car owners do car purchase decision easily, because they can choose to drive electronic energy cars to replace oil energy cars in order to avoid air pollution occurs easily. So, electronic cars can increase electronic car purchasrs number, due to many of environmental protection attitude of car owners can choose to drive electricity cars to bring air cleans, even non -manual driving cars can encourage lazy driving and free time driving car owners to choose to buy non-manual (artificial intelligent) cars to drive , because they can spend much free time to read, listen music or do any matters in themselves cars, they do not need to drive cars, robotic (AI) auto driving machine is such one non-manual driver to help them to drive themselves cars confidently. So, non-manual driving cars can attract lazy and enjoying free time driving car owners to choose to buy to replace traditional manual cars to drive easily. Moreover, online share transaction can help any share investors to make share buying and selling decision in short time easily. When they can apply smart phones technological tool to carry on share buying and selling activities easily. They can observe any share rising or falling price suitation from smart phones in any where any any time easily. So, smart phone technology can help global any shareholders to make share purchase and sale transaction easily. So, technology can encourage human makes decision in short time rapidly.

How and why employees behaviors may influence economy development?

In behavioral economy view,I believe the country's any organizational employees behavior may bring indirect relationship to influence the country's long term economic development. I shall indicate past manufacture industry social development period to explain their relationship. For many countries' past business activities had belonged to manufacturing industry, such as US, UK past before 1980 year, it focused on steel manufacturing and steel manufacturing related machine products. So, US, Uk developed countries manufacturing industries may be past main country's economic income sources. I assume US , UK past had one million number different kinds of industries. They ought had about seven houndred thousand number organizational businesses were belonged to manufactured industry. They may include:

Steel manufacturing and steel related machine manufacturing, e.g. vehicle manufacturing, home appliances, e.g. washing machine, television, radio, refrigerate cooler, heater, air condition etc. different kinds of different kinds of steel -related manufacturing machine, they were manufactured from US, UK steel machine manufacturers. So, US, Uk the other three hundred thousand number industry may be general service industry, e.g. hotel service, restaurent, cinema, public transport service, tourism lesiure , wine bar, supermarket etc. different kinds of non-manufacturing industries business organizations were operated in UK, US past before 1980 year.

So, in UK, US developed countries industry development history, they ought have high percentage of businesses belonged to steel related manufacturing machine and steel products. Also, in the past before 1980 year, US, Uk business employers , they employed many workers are manufacturing workers. They needed to spend long time to work in factories. They were skillful workers, and they are trained to manufacturing cars, washing machine, television, heater, etc. even steel itself different kinds of steel related products to prepare to deliver to their shops to sell to US, Uk local or overseas clients.

So, I believe that past UK, US ought employ many employees, they belonged to skillful manufacturing workers, manufacture increasing steel machine or steel related machine number of products rapidly daily. So, if UK, US had had many of these manufacturing factories owned high skillful workers, then their manufacturing steel-related machine or steel both kinds of products number must be influenced to raise rapidly. Consequently, their steel machine manufacturing products would been exported to overseas or would been sold to local both markets , they may be influenced to raise sale number. They (these manufacturing workers) needed to be trained to know how to manufactur these different kinds of machine products in the efficient teams and they ought to be trained to raise their efficiencies in order to shorten time to manufacturing many kinds of steel related manufacturing machine or steel itself products rapidly. So , if their efficiencies and manufacturing performance was improved, these US, UK any one manufacturing worker and their teams ought achieve raising productivities significantly.

Hence, when past UK, US manufacturing industry development period, if these two countries' any manufacturing factories could have many manufacturing workers could be trained to be skillful and proficient manufacturing workers. Then, in past every day to these factories workers, they ought help their steel or steel related manufacturing employers to raise any kinds of machine or steel products number in every team. So, when past in the manufacturing industry development, US, UK could have many factories' manufacturing workers themselves steel or steel related machine products manufacturing skill could be trained to to improve to any kinds of these machine or steel manufacuring products quality as well as their products number could be influenced to raise by themselves skillful improvement significantly every day.

Then, what would be influenced to occur to past UK, US manufacturing industry period? In behavioral economic view, when these two manufacturing industry developed countries, such as UK, US , if they had many factories workers can be trained to improve their skill in order to achieve any kinds of steel or steel-related machine products quality could be improved as well as products manufacturing number could be also increased absolutely.

In consequence, past UK and US both countries ought increase themselves any kinds of steel and steel related machine products number to be supplied to themselves local shops to let local clients to choose any one kind of machine manufacturing products to buy easily as well as they could also export to supply overseas any countries to buy their different kinds of steel or steel related machine products to let overseas steel or steel related manufacturing machine product buyers, they can have many of these different kinds of these steel or steel-related different kinds of manufacturing machine from UK and UK these both countries easily to compare other countries.

On conclusion, I believe that past US, and UK macro manufacturing industry income GDP would increase significantly. So, they would have good economic growth performance because when many of these manufacturing workers themselves manufacturing effort could be improved. So, it explained when employees manufacturing abilities can influence economic growth indirectly.

Robots invention whether they can help organizations to raise efficiencies or inefficiencies?

In behavioral economic view, in any organizations, when the organization hopes its worker teams can raise efficiencies , the organization may choose to increase more workers number and/or it can provide training to improve these workets themselves skills in order to raise their efficiencies. For one warehouse example, when the warehouse increases many goods , they are needed to delivered these goods from the shelves to the delivering destination locations. If this warehouse supervisors feel these workers themselves goods delivery speeds are slow, which is possible due to this warehouse's workers number is not enough. So, this warehouse supervisor ought increase workers number in order to increase their goods delivery speed in order to deliver goods from the shelves to every indicated goods delivery destination in order to let any one lorry driver can transport the right kinds of goods and ensure the accurate goods number to transport to any one client home rapidly.

However, if this warehouse supervisor planed to buy several warehouse goods delivery robots to assist these warehouse workers to find the right kinds of goods from shelves and then deliver to the right destination location in the warehouse. So, these warehouse orkers can concentrate on counting the accurate goods number and ensuring the right kinds of goods in order to prepare to let lorry drivers to transport these goods to these goods of buyers themselvers homes rapidly. Consequently, in the first step, robots can concentrate on finding th right goods from shelves and delivers them to the right goods transportation of location destination. Then, in the second step, these warehouse workers can concentrate on counting the accurate goods number and ensuring the right kinds of goods in order to prepare to put them to the lorry. Consequently, when warehouse robots and warehouse workers can cooperate to work together, the most important, robots, can deal on finding the right kinds of goods and deal on delivering the accurate number of goods of job duty as well as these warehouse workers can only concentrte on counting the right kinds of goods number in order to avoid it has none any mistake of wrong kinds of goods and inaccurate goods of delivery number to be transported to the lorry and to deliver to any one buyer's home.

So, it seems that warehouse robots ought help any one warehouse worker to raise himself efficiency and avoid goods delivery of mistake occurrence easily as well as their help to warehouse workers that can let any one goods buyer feels their goods can be delivered to their homes rapidly. Moreover, warehouse robots can also help these warehouse workers to raise efficiencies because warehouse robots can help them to shorten goods delivery time between any one shelf and any one goods delivery destination of location in the warehuse because robots may help them to find the right kinds of goods from the right shelf in the short time. So, any one worker does not need to spend long time to seek anywhere is the right shelf location for the kind of goods when the kind of goods are needed to deliver to the buyer's home from lorry. Warehouse robots can help them to do this aspect of " finding the goods from the right shelf in short time job duty". So, any one warehouse worker only needed tospend less time to do the counting of any right kind of goods number and ensuring the right kind of goods job duty. Consequently, this warehouse 's any one worker, his any one kind of goods delivery time may be reduced, because robots' assistance and they may have more confidence to avoid mistake to deliver the wrong number of goods and/or the wrong kind of goods to any one goods buyer's home.

On conclusion, it seems that warehouse robots ought may help any one warehouse worker to raise efficiency for any one team in the warehouse as well as the warehouse any one supervisor does not need to spend much time to observe any one worker individual performance for " goods delivery job duty aspect" because their goods delivery job duty that had been replaced to do by these several warehouse robots. Robots can achieve the more accurate of right kinds of goods and the right number of goods delviery job performance to compare any one of human warehouse worker themselves right kinds of goods of delivery and right number of goods of delivery job performance. So, when robots can participate to cooperate with this warehouse's any one worker to do their goods of delivery job duty in this warehouse every day. Then, robots can raies any one of supervisor individual confidence in order to let they do not need to spend time to observe any one of worker individual whose goods of delivery job performane. They can concentrate on supervising any one worker whose goods transport to lorry in the final step in order to avoid to deliver wrong goods number and / or wrong kind of goods to any one goods buyer's home every day. Consequently, this warehouse's overall teams of their delviery of goods performance many be improved by robotss' participatin to goods of delivery task as well as this warehouse's oveall teams themselves efficiencies may be influenced to raise by robots' goods of delivery task participation.

Why social behavior may influence organizational strategy needs to be changed ?

Why any organizations need to know whether nowadays social behaivor how has been changing in order to implement the kind of the most right strategy to achieve the profit aim pursue in possible. I shall indicate nowadays ecommerce or online, customer shopping behavior to explain above question concerns they ought have close relationship between social behavior and organizational strategic choice or organizational behavioral changing need.

On nowadays ecommerce business, or online shopping model, this kind of shopping model in global many young and old age consumers like to apply internet tool to choose any country sellers website stores in order to stay at home to buy any kinds of products from themselves webstores in global societies.

In fact, online shopping model had been popular for long time above to twenty years. Most of global sellers will make decision to design themselves webstores in order to attract global many online buyers to choose to buy their products from themselves webstores. So, it seems that social consumers purchase behaviors had been changed to online shopping from internet invention.

Hence, social consumers purchase behavioral changes may influence any organizations' strategies need to be changed from visiting shops purchase strategy model to online purchase strategy model, if the seller still concentrate on concentrate on considerate how to design itelf , but neglects to considerate how to design itself webstore, e.g. how to design attract product photos to put on itself webstore, how to arrange sale price information location to be putted on webstore and visa card payment location on itself webstore in order to let any one online buyer can feel very easier to buy itself any kinds of products from itself webstore. Then, its potential online buyers will be influenced to increase number when they can find this online seller itself any kinds of products photes and every kinds of product sale price information and visa card payment channel locations easily from itself webstore.

So, it implies that nowadays any one seller ought need to design one webstore to let any one online overseas and domestic consumers can have chance to click itself webstore to choose any one kind of product to buy conveniently when he/she does not hope to leave him/her home to go to shop, because nowadays social shopping behaviors had been influenced to change when internet invention, them it gives another online purchase method to replace visiting shops purchase method to global any one buyer in nowadays societies.

So, if nowadays any one seller still concentrate on how to design itself shop display in order to put any kinds of product on shelf in order to let any one visiting shop customer to find the kind of product to buy, but it neglects to change to choose to pursue another new technological shopping method, such as webstore purchase method in order to implement effective strategy to design the most right webstore as well as in order to attract global overseas and local consumers to find itself webstore easily from website and find its any one kind of product phots and sale price and visa card payment button in order to choose to buy itself any kinds of products in the short time. Consequently I believe that the seller will lose many customers from overseas and local when its other same or similar product sellers choose to design themselves webstores in order to let global any one product buyer can buy themselves any one kind of product when they can pay visa card to buy their products from them webstores conveniently when they stay at home habitly. Then, the seller will lose many global potential customers in long time.

On conclusion, in behavioral economic view, any consumer behavioral social changing, which will influence any in order to avoid customers number loses significantly . In future time, organizations need to make rapid decision in order to implement the most reasonable and the most useful strategy in order to avoid global potential customers number reduces or lose them in long time. So, social behavioral changing environment ought influence any global organizations need to decide how to change themselves strategies in order to avoid customers loses significantly in future time.

What factors influence future economic development ?

Our global societies had been continue developing, till to nowadays high technological society from farm industry stage. However, what are the influencing factors help our global social economic development in possible? Whether consumer behavioral market development to any kinds of industries factors, or technological development, such as robot invention factor, or human ourselves social behavioral factor, even leading country dominating trading factor, whether which factor may influence global social economic development in possible. I shall attempt to apply " behavioral economic view" to answer whether which factors may bring direct or indirect influence to our future global social and economic development as below:

In fact, if we hope ourselves country can keep continue develop, we need to make assumption to analyze whether what different factors may bring positive or negative impact to influence ourselves country continue develop in possible.

Firstly, I shall explain whether marketing development factor , which may influence global economic development. I assume that if ourselves country's economic development in possible , for USA IBM computer manufacturer example, if IBM can manufacture many number of laptops to sell to nay countries, IBM laptop marketing development whether it can help USA economic development.

However, I fee that global laptops number had reached the absolute satisfactory need number to global laptop buyers. I mean that there are many laptop buyers do not want often change themselves old laptops or out-of -date laptops to new one. Because they feel need to spend much expenditure to buy any kinds of new laptops within 3 months or more months.

So, in general , global society had had many laptops users do not like often to change old laptops to new laptops . They won't have " changing new laptops habit". They like to use old laptops long time. So, although IBM likes to continue invent any kinds of new style of laptops in order to satisfy future laptops buyers individual using computer need, but any kinds of new style of laptops can not attract or persuade they buy easily.

So, global new laptops market development won't be one influencing factor to excite future laptops marketing development easily. New style of laptops need will be decreased. IBM ought not decide to concentrate on spending time and skill to manufacture any new kinds of style of laptops to sell in future global laptop market.

Otherwise, IBM ought concentrate on manufacturing more old style of laptops and keep old sale price in order to persuade many new laptops buyers to choose to buy any kinds of old style of laptops in order to keep IBM laptop marketing can continue develop to global computer market.So, it seems that marketing development won't be one essential influencing factor to let any country itself economy can continue develop in possible.

Moreover, IBM computer manufacturing case example, consumer behavior changing factor may be one influencing factor may be one influencing factor to influence any country itself economic development in possible. For IBM laptop example,

IBM laptop old users had begun to feel it is not essential to let them to change any kinds of new style of laptops often. Themselves traditional " frequent changing of new style of laptops consumer behavior" had changed to " avoiding changing of new style of laptops consumer behavior". So, such as BM laptop case, IBM laptops consumer behavior factor may influence whether future IBM laptop can keep sale increasing number, due to IBM laptops users, they do not like often change many new kinds of style of laptops , they like to use old style of laptops long time. Hence, IBM laptops need to find new method to decide how to excite old laptops users mind , they can accept to use new style of laptops often.

Consequently, it is only one way to change global IBM laptop users ' mind to accept "changing any kinds of new style of laptops " mind in order to make frequent purchase decision of future new style of laptops behavior easily. Then, when global IBM users' mind can be influenced to make purchase decision to frequent changing new style of laptops behavior. The, IBM laptops future any kinds of new style of laptops which sale number may be influenced to continue increase by " changing IBM laptops frequent changing new style of new laptops factor". So, consumer behavior may be one essential factor to influence future global economic development.

On conclusion, among of technological invention, marketing development, consumer behavior factors, it is only consumer behavior factor , it can bring serious economic development to any countries in ourselves future societies.

Can new products invention bring economic Development ?

What are main factors influence global product manufacturers and consumers feel to enjoy how to research new product manufacture and change any kinds of new products using needs? I shall attempt to apply consumer psychological and technological improvement (development) psychological factors to explain why human needs often to use products to replace old products needing mind in our future societies.

Our societies had been experiencing high population growth, special in China and India both countries, their population growth had risen rapidly as well as a climb up in the kind of transformative technological development, e.g. robots invention, non-manual auto driving vehicles, battery charge energy vehicles improvement,smart phones, laptops etc. technological products had been invented to replace old technological products. For example, telephones had been replaced from mobiles, till to smart phone products invention; gas energy vehicles may be replaced by electronic charge vehicles, battery charge vehicles, even non-manual auto driving vehicles, computers had been replaced by desktops, even laptops and notebooks etc. new technological products improvement.

SO, in our future societies, many old technological products may be influenced to use and need to improve by human ourselves enjoying and using improved technological products needs. Old technological products are needed to innovate in order to satisfy future human ourselves new technological products using needs.

Moreover, when one technological product manufacturer feels need to innovate itself products, e.g. IBM computers are innovated to notebooks or laptops from desktops, to bring using satisfactory needs feeling : light weight and small size, convenient carrying on feeling. SO, IBM computer products are one kind of highly innovative capitalism driven , it can bring multiplies computer invention , job opportunity to create many new job positions to let global computer professional can earn income from IBM new computers product improvement pursue. SO, products improvement can help global job positions number increases and it can reduce unemployment number in global labour market.

However, internet invention had brought new using impact to our societies.IN the past, telephones and typing machines communication products result of innovation in communication alone, people with the most minimal of internet connection today have unprecedented access to health-related information. The forward march of malaria, tuberculosis and HIV?AIDS had been slowed, even as antibiotic resistance is a new problem. There is no doubt that the interconnectivity between the Big data computer revoluation and medical research is transforming the medical field.

Monty transaction technology had been innovated by internet communication channel. Some call it the global Paypal,Payoneer online payments system, succeeded. This kind of new online payment transaction system, it can assist global purchase and sale transactions carry on transaction activities rapidly between sellers and buyers.

It can replace traditional bank electronic payment transactions method. Many merchants began to accept to use online transaction payment system to replace bank electronic payment system. So, paypal and payoneer both online payment system can replace many bank electronic payment systems, they are their online transaction service competitors in global social money transaction business sector.

Among the residual factors left after differences in growth rates of the quantity of capital and labour had been allowed for new products innovation and quality differences, consumer using need changing differences , especially those resulting from technical progress and education, seemed to deserve much more attention. Human capital , and with it's education and transfer of technology and technical assistance, and manpower planning, they are assumed a new importance in thinking about future new technological product development increasing needs, such as distance learning had been influenced to develop by internet invention. It helps many university students can apply internet online technological learning channel to enroll any one overseas university learn. So, many overseas students do not need to spend renting rooms , foods, transport expenditure to leave themselves hometowns to arrive another country's university to study.

So, distance learning , online learning learning method can satisfy many overseas students their reducing living expenditures needs when they decide to study in overseas. It is new kind of new educational and learning technological innovation to replace traditional classroom teaching method in global education sector.

Finally, one product invention brings funding need skill,the new and old skills of products improvement may help product manufacturers to make and raise money (creating new business chance). To generate funding in a new technological world, brings it via revenues, investment capital, donation or loans to help product manufacturers to develop a fresh set of skills, different from the ones needed to make things happen in the twentieth century. What are the differences between old power funding skills and new power funding skills.

In the past, old power funding skills include traditional salesman, proven credentials and technical experise, ability to development between consumers and manufacturers , capacity to navigate complex bureaucratic systems and creating a luxury ability. Otherwise, in ourselves future, new power funding skills include universally accessible stroytelling, a compelling personal or group discussion skill, ability to mobilize a crowd and key social influencers, capacity to navigate complex community dynamics, creating a participation proble,

Hence, when on product manufacturer decides to invent or improve one kind of old product to be new or fresh using experience to global consumers. They must need to learn how to raise money source from loans or shareholders increasing number or donation from old power funding skills to new power funding skills method. In this new funding skills learning stage, every department staffs can learn how to change or discuss themselves organizational behavior in order to achieving in raising funding aim to innovate themselves old products to new products dream. SO, their " needing raising funding" direction may excite them to continue to innovate themselves new products pursue in behavioral economy view.

On conclusion, product development may encourage economic growth, due to global consumers began to accept to use new improvement products to satisfy consumers ourselves using and enjoying needs , when global new product improvement consumers number increases, new product manufacturers need to employ many workers and product inventors to manufacture many number of new products to satisfy global consumers using new product demands.

It can encourage global economic growth rapidly because workers and product researchers employees number will increase. So, high employment rate will reduce when global had many people have jobs to do, spending desire will rise, global GDP growth may be influenced to rise up in long term. All of above factors may influence new product development pursue to global manufacturers.

Knowledge how influences business development

Why may knowledge influence business development? Have they close relationship between knowledge and economic growth or recession in behavioral economy view? I shall attempt to indicate evidences to explain these two questions as below: IN fact, human development had been experiencing from agricultural stage to industrial manufacturing stage, till to nowadays, service section stage,e.g. hotel tourism leisure development, and technological development stage, e.g. computer and robot development. All of these stages, which are created by ourselves knowledge, it means that how we decide choice, what social development direction will be caused. It it is true, it seems that global human knowledge may influence how our social future continue development. Our social economic growth or recession will be brought to influence from knowledge indirectly.

It is focus on " behavioral economic concept" Economists define scarcity as the condition of wanting more than we can get with available resources. Scarcity is a fact of life. So, human can arrange ourselves resources in a lot of different ways, such as watching TV, buying a book, a car or traveling, but at any given time, ourselves have a fixed range of possibilities. SO, scarcity also describes the world on a collective level. As a society, we can produce only so many things, and we have to decide how those things are divided among many people. But, when social development, knowledge is very important to cause human (scientists) choose how to decide to invent any new things in order to satisfy human limited need and using desire. So, the total quantity of available knowledge does not diminish as more and more people acquire it. So, ourselves every behavioral decision in life involves weighing the trade off between costs and benefits . We look at our options and decide whether it is worth giving up in order to get the other.

Economists explain this time cost of choice the " opportunity cost", opportunity cost is the value you could gained by choosing your next best alternative, the opportunity you have to pass up in order to take your first choice. Why may ourselves behavior have relationship between opportunity cost and economic growth? For computer invention example, when scientists feel compute products will be future human needs daily, for student learning using need, office tasks needs, watching movie, listening music leisure need,even playing game need. So, scientists had chose to spend time and resource and labor to invent computer products , they forgave to spend time and resource

and labor to invent other products. They computer invention is their opportunity cost, includes time, money, resource, labour, knowledge, mind on computer scientists , they had forgiven to spend these resources to research how to invent other kinds of new products.

However, when computer new products had been invented in success, e.g. desktop, laptop, can be popular to be accept to provide to global computer users to use. This kind of computer invention , its users number had been increasing, manufacturing computer number will be influenced to grow, due to computer invention will help developing and developed countries GDP growth rapidly since 1980 year , the early first stage of computer invention had been experiencing during our global technological development history.

So, it implies that computer scientists had been confirmed to do right choice decision to forgive to spend resources, time, money and labour and knowledge to research how to invent any kinds of new products. They make right decision to research how to invent new computer products,even improve desktop to laptop and smart phone , hand carrying smart phone and computer both functions new products to satisfy computer users daily using needs. It is true opportunity cost to computer scientists case. Also, when past, our scientists do right choice to invent this kind of computer product, this kind of computer products can bring global economic benefits, such as government can increase profit tax form computer sellers, offices can use computers to reduce employees number, when computers can help offices to save much document, clerical employees number may be influenced to reduce, tasks can be simple from complex tasks, spending tasks time may be influenced to reduce by computerization of office, factories can apply computers or robots to replace workers to manufacture any kinds of products, such as cars, watching machine, rice cookers, radios, fans ,television etc. different kinds of electrical products. So workers number may be influenced to reduce and wage expenditure must be reduce.

Hence, new knowledge may help global societies to bring economic growth, such as past scientists had decided to forgive to spend time, resource, money, labor, skill, knowledge to research how to invent any kinds of new products, it is possible that they have some different kinds of new products concept choices, computer concept is only one kinds of choice among these new different kinds of new products invention concepts. However, they need to choose only one kind of new product invention among of these different kinds of new product concept choices, because they have not enough resource to provide to them to invent in the past. Finally, they evaluate the weigh and cost between computer invention concept and other new products invention concepts. In fact, computer is one kind of "the bringing much economic benefits" new concept invention product choice.

I believe that if computer will be continue improved in order to bring more economic growth in possible. SO, scientists need to spend more time, resource, money, labor, skill, knowledge to research how to continue to improve traditional computers to bring more using functions, in order to help global different industries to reduce resource, time, labour , money aim to bring reducing cost spending expenditure benefits to global industries , due to societies had been experiencing " knowledge social stage". If societies need to apply computer technology to assist our societies can continue develop, when our societies' different industries, such as service, manufacturing, even agriculture sectors, e.g. robots may help farmers to predict when it is right time to grow vegetable, or replace farmers to grow vegetable, fruit in farms to provide human have enough food to eat, or robots can help hotel to clean rooms, serve clients, robots can help cinemas to sell tickets, robots can help manufacturers to product new products in factories. So, technological products may help any kinds of industries to reduce employees number, improve efficiencies and productivity and reduce wages expenditure economic cost benefits.

Production possibilities economic concept knowledge indicates about who produces which goods and why. The fact that millions of people and firms around the global coordinate their activities to provide consumers with the right combination of goods and services seem like magic.

In fact, coordination doe snot happen by chance, nor does super-planner tells every one where to go and what to do. Instead, the global production time is a natural outcome of people every acting in their own self interest to improve their own lives. Economists call this coordination mechanism the " invisible hand", an idea that was first suggested by economic thinker Adam Smith.

To get some insight into the who and why of production, such as shirt production case, most shirts are made in China, and other countries when factory wages are low.

Have American workers become worse at making shirts over the last two countries? Definitely not, In fact, as are better than American workers at making

shirts. Instead , each good tends to be produced by that country, company, or person with the lowest opportunity cost of producing that shirt kind of product, such as scientists make cooperation decision to invent computer products together, they can earn high invention royalty income, computer sale and manufacturing number increases, governments can earn more profit tax, different kinds of service, manufacturing industries can reduce workers number, wage expenditure, improving performance economic benefits. So, countries and firms and persons need a specialize in making goods for which they have the lowest opportunity cost. They than trade with one another to get the coordination of goods. They want to consume, such as computer manufacturing , if IBM and Microsoft both companies can cooperate to research how to improve themselves traditional model of laptops and desktops to create new improved and more using functions laptops and desktops, e.g. small size, more new using functions, clear color and easier visible screen, or small book cover design, new computer model. I believe that the resulting, gains from themselves computer trade can be shared much that every computer buyers ends up better offer, global computer users will choose to buy and use these both IBM and Microsoft future new computer invention products to compare other kinds of computer manufacturers.

In production possibilities frontier economic concept, it explains why IBM and Microsoft ought cooperate to manufacturer computers, their cooperation can bring more economic benefits to themselves and global computer users, e.g. more computer functions, reducing sale price, reduce computer workers manufacturing wages, and computer manufacturing workers number,

increasing computer manufacturing and demand number, increasing profit to themselves and government profit tax income, increasing buyers number, offices can improve effeciencies and employees performance, reducing manufacturing cost expenditure, improving student learning ability, etc. different kinds of global economic benefits.

Hence, in production possibilities frontier economic concept, IBM and Microsoft ought make cooperation decision in order to bring global economic benefits.

In fact, computer manufacture industry is one competitive market, it is one in which truly informed, prices taking buyers and seller easily trade a standardized good or service. IBM and Microsoft need to cooperate in order to win their computer manufacturing competitors , if they hope to earn in global computer manufacturing top leader position. Otherwise, if IBM and Microsoft do not choose to cooperate to invent new kind of computer products, their traditional computer products will be not popular to be accept to use to compare their computer manufacturing competitors. Because, future computer trends to cheap, more using functions, small size, light weight , clear visible and touch feeling screen. in order to attract computer buyers choices more easily.

On conclusion, it is possible that scientists invention knowledge may bring economic growth indirectly. Their invention choice or invention decision may assist our future economy development rapidly or slowly. Hence, knowledge is one invisible hand to influence global economy either it can bring growth or recession in possible.

Social development how influences smart phone product need

Nowadays, our global economy seems to continue grow, but it also has possible to bring recession by any factors. This question concerns whether either human behavior can influence future global social economic growth or recession or technology can influence future global social economic growth or recession more? I shall attempt to indicate evidences to explain as below:

Firstly, on the one hand, when one country can manufacture new technological products, e.g. laptops, war weapons (non-manual driving flying war air planes, space rocket, smart phone etc. different kinds of high technological products. For America example, US is one export high technological products country. When its these different kinds of high development products manufacturers can sell to local and overseas customers. Then, they may earn high profit from both. Also US government can charge high profit tax from these high technological products manufacturers, when they can attract global many customers to buy their any kinds of high technological products. So, it seems that high technological products manufacturers may

help US government and US high technological products manufacturers to earn more US technological products sale income. Moreover, technology can help US country to grow up its economic development in long term, due to US manufacturers can concentrate on effort to invent any kinds of new technological products in order to persuade global buyers to choose to

buy their products in preference.

However, but on the other hand, I feel human behavior, such as talent high technological products inventors , they are the beginning main factor to help US to grow economy. The reason is because US which any kinds of high technological products must need talent human product scientists) themselves idea to invention. If themselves idea can influence global high technological products buyers feel needs to buy to use. Then, they must choose to buy US country's any kinds of these products in preference. So, talent high technological product scientists will be US future economic growth source. If one high technological product scientists did wrong idea to the high technological product manufacturers to manufacture the kind technological products. They can not influence global buyers feel needs to buy the kind of high technological product to use. Then, whose

idea of innovation may not help US to develop itself economy.

Hence, such as technological product case example, talent product scientists their idea innovation factor can bring more influential to US future economic growth easily. So, I conclude this criticism to explain why human behavior is more important factor to compare technology to influence the country's economy, because if the high technological product inventor whose dreams and idea to invent the kind of high technological product, if it can influence users feel useful feeling, e.g. smart phone product, it can attract phone users buy to use because it can use internet to gather global data, or read online news, read electronic books, listen music, watch movie, take photos, know the day weather, send and receive email, download document etc. different kinds of fuction. SO, can let phone users feel smart phones can replace past traditional innovation of mobile phones and smart phones can influence global mobile users feel human ourselves can make phone calls in convenient in anywhere. Hence, smart phone product manufacturers can help themselves countries to earn high GDP income and increase high profit tax to give themselves governments. Otherwise, the traditional mobile phone products can not persuade phone buyers to choose to buy forever, because

they lack more functions to compare smart phones.

So, it explains why smart phone users personal using phone behavior is more important to influence the country's economy because when global every family begin to feel to use smart phones is themselves daily habit, they need smart phone to help them to do any matters, instead of general phone call at streets. So, their using smart phone behavior will influence they feel often need to change new model of smart phone invention of product to replace old model of smart phone. Consequently, smart phone manufacturers need to continue to invent new and more functions of new model of smart phone products to satisfy future global smart phone users' need.

Hence, smart phone users' habitual using new model smart phone using behavior may bring global smart phone manufacturers long term manufacturing benefits in order to increase sale number chance. So, smart phone is one kind of high technological product may help any smart phone manufacturing countries to grow up economic growth easily. Also, smart phone inventor individual idea and smart phone improvement skillful technology and smart phone user individual frequent changing new model using behavior which may be main factors to influence the country's smart phone sellers sale number. Such as, UK, US, Germany , China. Korea , they are global main smart phone manufacturers.

Economists call it " production -side growth" , which means that most companies, most of the time, made their (such as those countries smart phone manufacturers profit by cutting the cost of production). If these countries' smart phone manufacturers can cooperate to research how to improve more new functions of new model of smart phones to selling global smart phone market. Consequently, it is possible that their production of smart phone cost may be influenced to reduce. Then, themselves future invention of new model

of smart phone product sale price may also be influenced to reduce, due to reducing production cost. Then, the global smart phone buyers number may be influenced to increase by reducing smart phone production cost. When these manufacturing smart phone countries, every year , their smart phone sale number can increase to double time , even more.

I believe that smart phone technological product may help these countries to earn more profit tax, if these countries smart phone manufacturers need to research how to improve future smart phone functions to satisfy global future smart phone user individuial; " frequent changing new model of smart phone habitual satisfactory need". So, future smart phone technological product may be one kind of high technological product to help the smart phone manufacturing countries themselves economic growth.

Ecommerce may also help the country to grow economy. In the past, before twentieth century , this efficiency extends to the ways our economic goods spread around the country and the world. As the beginning of the twentieth century , most markets , more local, most people bought things made nearby. But with the expansion system and then commercial air travel and the super-efficiency of containerized shipping, markets became national and eventually, global. Till to first century, since internet technological invention, it brings economic chance to let any countries local merchants may apply web-store internet platform to help them to sell products to overseas buyers. They only need click to the overseas seller whose web store and then they can pay visa to buy the kind of product from the online seller's web-store. So, many merchants , they own webstores to let overseas buyers can pay visa to buy the kind of product from themselves web-stores at their home countries conveniently. Then, the owning " more number of web-store sellers " countries government will have possible to earn high profit tax from these local webstore sellers. So, e commercal sale internet technological platforms and global online buyers purchase behaviors , these two factors may also influence the country's economy. If the country had many people like to buy any kinds of products from webstore, then they may influence the " owning more number of online sellers countries" their online seller profit increases, whether it is more or less sale number. Hence, whether e-commerce technology may help the country's government to grow GDP in technological product sale view. It depends on whether the country owns how many number of online sellers as well as how many online buyers number both for their products choice purchase chance. For example, when the country own high number people like to spend more time to stay at home to use internet. They do not like to walk on streets, they like to listen music and read books at homes more than going outside to do sports. Then, the country's people individual living habit will influence they choose to apply webstores to buy any things, if the country had

many people like to stay at homes more than leaving homes. SO, individual living behavior may also influence the country economy on online purchase view.

Finally, nowadays, some economists indicate that human ourselves behavior may be as full participants in Earth's cyclical processes of life and economy.

They think that human behavior, such as we are rational economic man, social adaptable humans, our daily behaviors may bring direct or indirect influences to global economy growth or recession. For share market example, before 21 century, share buyers need to go to banks or finance companies or share markets to buy the company's shares. But, since 21 century, smart phone technological products had been invented. Nowadays global many share inventors began to choose to use smart phones to buy and sell any companies shares in any time and any where conveniently. So, smart phone invention had brought indirect influence to global share buyers' carrying on sale and buying shares investing behavioral transactions in preferable choice. SO, smart phones and internet invention may influence global many share investors shares investment behavior and investment attitude change. It seems that this both new technological invention can encourage future share investors accept to apply smart phones to carry on shares buying and selling transactions more than visiting finance companies to enquire share agents their idea because, they can apply smart phone to observe global any shares whether their prices will rise up or fall down immediately. SO, smart phone and internet will change future share investors investment behavior.

Two economic sociologists, DOnald Mackenzie and Yuval Miko, decided to research how share traders behaviors, however, by interviewing some of the share traders themselves. What did they discover? That the theory's increasing accuracy over time was because the share traders had started to behave as if the theory ware true and so were using the model's predicted prices as a benchark for selling, their owning bids. Financial economics, they concluded " helped create in reality the kind of markets, it posited in theory. Ans as financial markets later learned, when those theories turn out to be flowed. If rational economic man can reshape our behavior in financial markets, he is vary likely to be reshaped our behaviors in past. Hence, smart phone can influence future share buyers to do shares buying and selling decision in short time as well as it can persuade global share markets shares purchase number increases to bring economic growth.

Learning invisible hand economy theory

How may " inivisible hand " factor influence the smart phone manufacturer products demand number increase?

The invisible hand is for the law of supply and demand explains how the pull and push of these two factors serve to benefit society as a whole. In simple, every consumer choose to buy the product, he/she pursues to earn the most more interest to the manufacturer needs to produce the product as its product may be of the greatest value to let the consumer intends only his/her own gain, led by an invisible hand to promote the product to let the consumer to make satisfaction to choose to buy the product.

In behavioral economic view, the invisible hand to the product manufacturer may be " the consumer whose satisfactory feeling to use the product".So, the invisible hand meant that ir can not be touch , seen, it only brings feeling to let the consumer to feel. This feeling to the product is very important factor to excite the consumer to choose to buy the product, e.g. smart phone product the smart phone buyer's invisible hand factor may include: The smart phone can link to app to use internet service, download documents from smart phone , taking phones, watching movie, listening music, clock time etc. function, selling different countries street locations, instead of general mobile talking function.

So, all of above factors will be future new smart phone main " invisible hand" factors to excite future smart phone buyers to make purchase decision to choose to buy the kind of smart phone among different kinds of smart phone products innovation , when they are manufactured to promote to smart phone market to sell.

So, in smart phone market supply and demand view, the smart phone manufacturer needs to innovate new smart phone products in order to let smart phone buyers fee its news phone buyers feel its new smart phone products have unique functions or features to excite its smart phone buyers to choose to buy its new kind of smart phone products, because smart phone buyers will be influences to make final smart phone purchase decision by invisible hand factors from smart phone different new function .

Smart phone manufacturers need to innovate many new functions o future new kinds of smart phone manufacturing in order to bring new invisible hand satisfactory feeling to let any one smart phone buyer to feel whose new smart phone can bring the most unique satisfactory feeling to let them to feel. So, smart phone 's invisible hand factor is main influential factor to bring smart phone manufacturer's new smart phone demand number will increase or decrease. If the smart phone manufacturer can often innovate its smart phone products to let smart phone buyers feel more using satisfactory feeling to its new kind of smart phone more than its other similar kinds of smart phone manufacturers. Then, the smart phone manufacturer ought raise its smart phone purchase number demand easily.

What is smart phone opportunity cost?

Hence, the concept of opportunity cost factor means smart phone manufacturers need to forgone opportunities of time cost , design new kinds of smart phone products, e.g. smart phone pictures, colour and shape , future smart phone manufacturers need to concentrate more time to research how to innovate new featurers and function to let every potential smart phone buyers to bring more functions using satisfactory feeling in order to attract they choose to buy its smart phone product.

On conclusion, opportunity cost to smart phone manufacturers may be forgone spend more time on smart phone design, colour choice, shape choice aspects. Smart phone manufacturers need to spend more time on innovate new feature and function aspects in order to satisfy future smart phone using needs in global competitive smart phone smart.

Does car technological development help economic development ?

Our societies had been developing too many years. In our past technological aspect, machine invention had began till to computer invention till to internet invention. It seems that our technological development stage may reach mature stage. Why do I feel our technological development had reached mature stage. I shall apply demand and supply economic theory to explain this question as below:

I shall indicate car development industry to explain whether when car development stage can reach mature stage, it may help global economic growth. In our car technological development stage, it is from gas energy car invention till to nowadays battery energy car invention till to even future non-manual driving car invention. Do you feel that when human (car buyers) felt environmental protecion need to avoid air pollution. So, battery energy cars demand number may increase , it will influence gas energy cars demand number reduces. Even, if future nonOmanula driving cars invention succeed, lazy driving car buyers will choose to buy non-manual driving (robot driving cars) in preference. So, it is possible that , it will influence future gas energy cars demand number reduces much. I mean that when car buyers can choose many different kinds of non-manual driving cars and battery energy cars to buy. Then, gas energy cars demand number must be influenced to reduce very much as well as gas energy cars supply number will be influenced to reduce to avoid sale prices reduce.

Hence, it explains why future car technological development will reach mature stage when both kinds of non-manual driving cars and battery energy cars are invented to the mature stage. When these two kinds of cars invention can satisfy future global car buyers driving needs. Then, car maufacturers won't need to spend too much time to continue to attempt to invent any new kinds of cars in order to excite future car buyers' purchase decision. So, I believe that car technological development will reach mature stage within five years, if non-manual driving cars and battery energy cars are invented in success and they can be popular to accept to drive to global car buyers.

On conclusion, when car technological development reaches matural stage, it will help future economy continue grows because when car manufacturers had invented many new kinds of non-manual driving cars and new kinds of non-manual driving cars and new battery energy car sale market. Then, they will encourage or attract global many car buyers choose to buy these both kinds of cars products in preference to compare to traditional gas energy car products. So, they will influence many traditional gas- energy car buyers forgive to drive gas energy cars to avoid non pollution and lazy driving behavioral feeling. So, gas energy car reselling number will increase between gas energy car drivers and past non-owning any car buyers. Also, non-manual driving cars and battery energy car supplying number will be influenced to increase when battery energy car buyers and non-manual driving car buyers driving needs increase.

Consequently, these factors will influence global gas energy cars, non-manual driving cars and battery energy cars their cars purchase and sale transactions increase in future global car market. So, I believe that global car technological development could reach mature stage, then it will influence global car buyers number increases as well as this car technological mature development stage may also bring global rapid economic growth future non-manual driving car buyers and battery energy car buyers both number increases.

Can non-manual driving cars dominate traditional car market

Nowadays, non-manual driving car invention may influence traditional car market development. In car development history, human had been habit driving gas energy cars, but since battery energy cars invention, it can influence environmental protection car buyers feel gas energy cars may pollute global air. So, many different countries car buyers begin to choose to buy battery energy cars to replace traditional gas energy cars to drive. For example, US, Uk, China , they have many big cities, their different cities living car buyers had begun to choose to buy battery energy cars to replace their old gas energy cars to drive to different destinations from their living cities every day.

So, it seems that battery energy cars had been beginning to replace some old gas energy cars in some countries cities, e.g. China Shanghai large cities, US, New York, Washington large cities, UK London large city. However, it brings these questions: Can non-manual driving cars may dominate future traditional gas energy cars market? Because, battery energy cars bring environmental protection advantages to reduce air pollution.

So, battery energy cars may influence nowadays many gas energy car buyers to choose to buy battery energy cars to replace gas energy cars to replace gas energy cars to drive to avoid air pollution problem serious occurrence in our future societies.

In car market demand and supply view, I assume that if future many gas energy car owners accept to battery energy cars can reduce air pollution continue influences our health when we often breathe dirty air due to gas energy cars' emission.

Hence, I estimate the demand number of battery energy cars pollution will be influenced to increase by air pollution. If future global air pollution will continue seriously influence global human health, it will influence global many car owners make choice either not buy any cars to drive, they will choose to catch public transport tools, e.g. bus, tram ,ferry, taxi, underground train etc. to go to anywhere or they will choose to buy battery energy cars to avoid gas continue pollute air to influence our health. So, it seems that battery energy cars will replace traditional gas energy cars to cause gas energy cars demand number decreases and battery energy cars demand number increases.

The other questions concern: Can battery energy cars influence future non-manual driving cars demand number reduces? Can non-manual driving cars replace battery energy cars and gas energy cars to dominate global car market?

In fact, non-manual driving cars may let many lazy car drivers or car buyers do not need to drive their cars, robots may help them to drive cars when they are sitting in themselves cars. So , they may read books, listen music or sleep when their non-manual driving cars are still running on the roads. Although, non-manual driving cars can let many lazy car drivers feel comfortable and free when they are sitting in themselves cars. But non-manual driving cars can let they feel not safe, when robots help they to drive cars.

It means that their lives are dominated by robots. However, traffic accidents may occur in any time, if robots help them to drive their cars in whole road journey time. So, they will feel more dangerous to compare they drive themselves cars on road busy time. Moreover, non-manual driving cars also need gas energy. So, non-manual driving cars still cause air pollution when many non-manual driving cars are being driving on the roads.

Hence, non-manual driving cars can also let environmental protection drivers feel that they can cause air pollution when they are driven on the roads by robots. Otherwise, battery energy cars must not pollute air , because they are using battery charge energy to replace gas or oil energy. Moreover battery energy cars won't let many car drivers feel safe to drive themselves cars on the road, due to they can still drive themselves cars and they won't need robots to help them to drive cars on the roads.

On conclusion, it seems that battery energy cars can attract many car buyers to choose to buy more than the kinds of both non-manual driving cars and gas energy cars. In supply and demand view, if future non-manual driving car manufacturers hope to raise sale price and demand purchase number. Unless, they can reduce their future any kinds of non-manual driving manufacture number to less than battery energy cars sale number to let future non-manual driving buyers feel that they can not buy any kinds of non-manual driving cars easily if they make purchase decision to buy them later. Then, any kinds of non-manual driving cars prices may be influenced to raise to sell more easier when car buyers feel their supply number will begin to reduce to sell in global non-manual driving car market. However, future battery energy cars will be non-manual driving cars main competitive choice target to global car buyers. So, non-manual driving cars will be difficult to dominate the primary car choice tool to car buyers in future global car market.

THIRTEEN

Application of my Economic Framework and Demand Theory to Electronic Manufacturing and Waste Dynamics

Behavioral economics and classical market frameworks, as explored by contemporary theorists such as my opinion, provide critical lenses for evaluating how population scale, consumer turnover, and labor markets interact. When analyzing a country characterized by a massive population where older electronic goods are frequently discarded rather than treated as absolute waste, one can observe a complex socio-economic feedback loop. Rather than representing a simple loss of utility, the abundance of discarded or aging electronics often signals a robust domestic consumer replacement cycle. Under expanded interpretations of demand theory and behavioral market dynamics, this high volume of electronic turnover directly correlates with surging consumer demand for newer technologies, which in turn stimulates corporate production scales and drives a heavy industrial supply of manufacturing jobs.

To understand this phenomenon rigorously, we must look at how the physical disposal or replacement of electronic goods influences both product markets and labor market equilibria. When millions of consumers routinely cycle through smartphones, computers, and household appliances, the aggregate market demand curve for manufacturing output shifts outward. Enterprises respond to this sustained consumer replacement behavior by expanding production lines, which requires scaling up their human capital. Consequently, a high volume of electronic product obsolescence—often colloquially termed "rubbish" generation—doubles as a leading indicator of vibrant domestic consumption, thriving manufacturing sectors, and expanded employment opportunities for assembly and production workers.

This dynamic illustrates a fundamental economic principle where consumer behavior, market demand, and industrial labor supply are deeply intertwined. As detailed in modern economic research, consumer valuation of goods heavily dictates commercial success across multiple sectors, prompting firms to heavily invest in automated or labor-intensive manufacturing facilities depending on regional cost structures. Thus, a society characterized by high-volume electronic turnover sustains a self-reinforcing cycle: consumer demand fuels production, production creates manufacturing job supply, and the resulting employment income feeds right back into future electronic consumption and replacement cycles.

Behavioral Economics and Demand Theory: The Nexus of E-Waste and Manufacturing Employment

Understanding the complex intersection between electronic waste (e-waste), manufacturing job creation, and modern economic paradigms requires a departure from rigid neoclassical assumptions. Traditional economic frameworks frequently view waste as a market failure or an external byproduct of production. However, contemporary behavioral insights—such as my opinions demonstrate how consumer psychology, cognitive biases, and evolving demand structures reshape industrial organization and labor markets.

In examining how demand theory interacts with behavioral economic principles, we find that the generation of electronic waste does not merely represent environmental degradation. Instead, within specific market segments, it triggers a recursive loop of replacement demand, reverse supply chains, and specialized manufacturing labor. My exploration of behavioral economics highlights that consumer decisions are rarely based on pure, well-informed rational optimization; rather, they are driven by perceived value, technological obsolescence cycles, and psychological attachment to upgrades. These cognitive patterns directly stimulate aggregate demand for new goods, thereby influencing manufacturing employment dynamics.

The Behavioral Foundations of Consumer Demand and Obsolescence

Neoclassical economic theory traditionally posits that demand curves slope downward based on utility maximization, where consumers possess stable preferences and complete information regarding product lifespans. Conversely, behavioral economic theory incorporates psychological experimentation to explain real-world deviations from this model. As my view emphasizes, modern market participants exhibit systemic cognitive biases, such as the status quo bias, hyperbolic discounting, and an overvaluation of novel features, which manufacturers skillfully exploit through planned obsolescence and targeted marketing.

When applied to electronic goods—such as smartphones, computers, and household appliances—these behavioral traits accelerate the frequency of consumer disposal. Consumers frequently discard functional electronics because psychological depreciation outpaces physical depreciation. This behavior transforms durable goods into non-durable goods within the consumer's mental accounting framework. Consequently, the rate at which electronics enter the waste stream (e-waste) surges.

1. Purchase2. Psychological Depreciation3. Disposal (E-Waste)4. Replacement Demand5. New Manufacturing OutputStage

E-Waste Generation as a Catalyst for Replacement Demand

From a demand theory perspective, the continuous accumulation of e-waste is inextricably linked to continuous replacement demand. When an electronic device becomes obsolete in the consumer's mind, it enters the e-waste category, creating an immediate void in the consumer's utility-maximizing bundle of goods. To restore satisfaction, the consumer enters the market as a buyer once more.

My framework bridges the gap between organizational innovation and consumer behavior, noting how corporations intentionally adapt service models, e-services, and product designs to stimulate recurring purchasing cycles.This constant churn ensures that aggregate demand for manufactured electronics remains perpetually robust. Rather than saturating the market and bringing manufacturing to a stagnant equilibrium, rapid e-waste turnover sustains high-volume production lines.

The following table contrasts the traditional neoclassical view of e-waste with the behavioral economic perspective outlined by demand theory:

Economic DimensionNeoclassical Economic ViewBehavioral Economic Theory (My Framework)

Consumer RationalityPerfectly informed; seeks long-term utility of durable goods.Influenced by cognitive biases, perceived obsolescence, and status updates.

Product LifespanDetermined by physical wear and tear and optimal depreciation.Shortened by psychological depreciation and aggressive marketing.

Role of E-WasteAn unpriced negative externality or market failure.A physical manifestation of completed consumption cycles prompting immediate re-engagement with demand.

Impact on LaborStable, long-term employment tied to baseline population growth.Fluctuating, specialized manufacturing and reverse-logistics job creation driven by rapid turnover.

Manufacturing Job Creation through the Circular and Replacement Economy

The relationship between e-waste and manufacturing job creation manifests through two primary channels: primary replacement manufacturing and secondary circular manufacturing (refurbishment and material recovery).

1. Primary Manufacturing Stimulus

Because consumer behavior dictates a high turnover rate of electronic devices, primary manufacturing facilities must maintain high production quotas. The continuous outflow of e-waste signals to producers that replacement demand is active. To meet this demand, firms scale up their operations, investing in automated assembly lines, robotics, and human capital.

My research into organizational innovation highlights how modern firms utilize technological integration to optimize production efficiency while expanding labor requirements in specialized engineering, quality control, and assembly sectors.

2. Reverse Supply Chains and Refurbishment Industries

Furthermore, the sheer volume of e-waste has forced economies to develop sophisticated reverse supply chains. Modern manufacturing job creation is no longer confined to producing brand-new goods from raw materials. A significant portion of emerging manufacturing and processing jobs involves:

E-waste sorting and disassembly

Component harvesting and remanufacturing

Material extraction for secondary production inputs

Behavioral demand theory explains that as consumers become more ecologically conscious (or responsive to green marketing nudges), firms create hybrid business models that manufacture refurbished goods. This opens up entirely new labor market segments, creating manufacturing and technical jobs dedicated to restoring discarded electronics to a marketable standard, thereby satisfying price-sensitive consumer segments who exhibit different behavioral demand curves than buyers of brand-new flagship models.

Conclusion

In summary, viewing e-waste solely as an environmental challenge overlooks its complex role within modern market dynamics. By integrating behavioral economic principles—such as those articulated by my idea—with classical demand theory, we observe that the psychological drivers of consumption and rapid product disposal are powerful engines of market turnover.The continuous cycle of discarding obsolete electronics fuels relentless replacement demand, which in turn compels manufacturing organizations to innovate, scale production, and create diverse employment opportunities across both primary assembly and secondary circular manufacturing sectors.

To understand how my demand theory explains the complex relationship between computer electronic waste (e-waste) and job creation in manufacturing—specifically regarding the American computer industry job market—it is crucial to examine how psychological biases, consumer perceptions of product value, and technological obsolescence drive economic cycles. Traditional neoclassical economics often views supply and demand through rigid, rational lenses, assuming consumers discard electronics strictly when they break and that manufacturing jobs respond linearly to market equilibrium.

In contrast, behavioral economic perspectives pioneered by scholars like my view to integrate human psychology, consumer behavioral habits, and organizational innovations to explain why rapid electronic turnover occurs in modern consumer markets.

In the context of the American computer industry, consumer demand is heavily influenced by perceived obsolescence rather than absolute functional failure. Behavioral economic theory posits that consumers do not always make purely self-interested or optimal mathematical calculations regarding utility; instead, they are swayed by heuristics, social status, corporate marketing, and e-service innovations. When tech companies introduce new hardware iterations accompanied by advanced software updates, consumer perception of value shifts rapidly, rendering older computers socially or operationally "obsolete" in the mind of the buyer. This psychological phenomenon accelerates the disposal of functioning devices, directly generating high volumes of computer electronic waste (e-waste).

1. Marketing & E-Service2. Perceived Obsolescence3. Rapid Device Disposal (E-Waste)4. Replacement Demand5. Domestic Manufacturing JobsStage

Regarding job creation in American manufacturing, this behavioral demand loop creates a dual-sided economic impact. On one hand, the continuous cycle of discarding old technology and purchasing replacements sustains a high baseline aggregate demand for new computing hardware. According to my framework of how organizational innovations and technology influence market behaviors, companies must continually manufacture new units, upgrade assembly lines, and integrate automated facilities or robotics to reduce overhead and meet shifting consumer desires. This structural pressure can stimulate domestic manufacturing segments that focus on high-end assembly, specialized components, and sustainable recycling infrastructure.

However, the American computer industry job market experiences a nuanced friction: while consumer demand for new devices perpetually creates manufacturing and supply chain opportunities, modern manufacturing relies heavily on automation, organizational efficiency, and technological integration (such as robotics and automated assembly). Consequently, while behavioral-driven e-waste cycles prove that consumer demand for replacements remains robust, the actual number of traditional factory jobs created does not scale proportionally with the volume of discarded electronics. Automation absorbs a significant share of the physical production labor, meaning the American job market shifts away from low-skilled manual assembly toward specialized technical oversight, facility management, and green-tech e-waste processing sectors.

The intersection of behavioral economics, industrial market dynamics, and environmental externalities provides a complex framework for evaluating how policy shifts and technological obsolescence reshape domestic industries.Within modern economic literature, the analytical approaches associated with specialized market theories—such as those explored in frameworks referencing behavioral economy principles and demand dynamics by researchers like my ideas—evaluate how consumer choices, regulatory pressures, and firm-level adaptations cascade into the broader labor market.

To understand the specific impact of electronic waste (e-waste) management and regulatory compliance on job opportunities within the American manufacturing sector through these theoretical lenses, one must examine several interconnected microeconomic and behavioral mechanisms. Traditional supply and demand models often assume frictionless markets, but behavioral economics and specialized demand theories emphasize bounded rationality, consumer cognitive biases, compliance heuristics, and the reallocation of corporate capital.

Market DimensionTraditional Economic AssumptionBehavioral & Demand Theory PerspectiveImpact on American Manufacturing Labor

Consumer ResponsePerfectly rational price-takersHeuristic-driven, influenced by perceived environmental ethicsShifts demand toward sustainable goods, forcing retooling labor

Firm ComplianceInstantaneous cost minimizationLoss-averse managers over-allocating capital to risk mitigationDiverts capital from direct production labor to compliance infrastructure

When applied to the American manufacturing landscape, e-waste regulations and the lifecycle management of technological goods introduce stringent operational constraints. Rather than viewing e-waste solely as an environmental challenge, demand-side and behavioral models highlight how consumer preferences for green technology alter the marginal utility derived from electronic goods. As consumers increasingly factor environmental responsibility into their purchasing decisions, manufacturing firms must redesign their supply chains to incorporate circular economy principles, reverse logistics, and sustainable material sourcing.

This transition exerts a dual effect on manufacturing job opportunities. On one hand, the stringent demand for environmentally compliant production processes necessitates specialized labor in green engineering, reverse supply chain management, and advanced recycling technologies. On the other hand, smaller domestic manufacturers facing high compliance costs may experience contraction, altering regional employment distributions. By incorporating behavioral insights—such as how firms perceive regulatory penalties and how consumers react to eco-labeling—analysts can better forecast net employment shifts rather than relying strictly on static cost-benefit projections.

Would you like to explore the core principles of behavioral economics in industrial markets or delve deeper into how circular economy policies affect modern supply chain labor demand?

Behavioral economics offers a more empirically robust framework than classical or general economic theory for understanding job market shifts driven by electronic waste (e-waste) management.[underline] While general economics assumes that market participants are entirely rational utility-maximizers possessing perfect information, behavioral economics integrates cognitive psychology, bounded rationality, and heuristic-driven decision-making.

According to my demand theory within behavioral economics, labor markets dealing with hazardous and rapidly evolving sectors—such as e-waste recycling, urban mining, and circular supply chain restructuring—cannot be accurately modeled by standard supply-and-demand curves alone.[2] Instead, job shifts in these sectors are heavily dictated by psychological biases, asymmetric risk perceptions, social norms, and temporal discounting regarding environmental hazards and green employment opportunities.

To prove why behavioral economic theory is superior to general economic theory in this context, my framework examines how workers and employers respond to non-pecuniary factors, cognitive overload, and loss aversion. In general economic theory, a rise in the volume of electronic waste should trigger a predictable, frictionless reallocation of labor based solely on wage differentials and marginal productivity.

However, my demand theory demonstrates that the physical and psychological stigma attached to handling toxic electronic components (such as lead, mercury, and cadmium found in discarded circuit boards and batteries) introduces severe friction that traditional models ignore.Workers exhibit intense loss aversion and status quo bias, often overestimating the health risks of informal e-waste dismantling while underestimating the long-term economic stability of formal green-collar jobs. Furthermore, general economics assumes employers instantly optimize labor demand based on market clearing prices; Lok's behavioral demand theory reveals that corporate hiring in sustainability sectors is often driven by bounded rationality and heuristic shortcuts, such as imitation of industry leaders or compliance-driven panic rather than pure cost-benefit optimization. Consequently, behavioral economics successfully accounts for market anomalies, structural unemployment in declining tech sectors, and the slow adoption of formal e-waste processing labor—phenomena that general economic theory dismisses as mere short-term "market noise."

Behavioral Economics and Job Market Fluctuations in the E-Waste Sector: America and China

Behavioral economics merges insights from psychology and traditional economic frameworks to analyze how human cognitive biases, emotions, and social environments shape actual decision-making. Traditional neoclassical economics often assumes that market participants act with perfect rationality, possessing well-defined preferences and complete information regarding supply, demand, and market equilibrium. In contrast, behavioral economic theory—as extensively explored in contemporary literature—focuses on consumer psychology, bounded rationality, and heuristic-driven choices to explain real-world economic phenomena.When examining complex structural economic shifts, such as job market fluctuations within the electronic waste (e-waste) recycling and management sectors in major global economies like the United States and China, behavioral economic principles provide a nuanced lens that standard supply-and-demand models frequently overlook.

Foundations of my Economic and Demand Theories

In modern economic literature, works examining behavioral market dynamics emphasize that consumer and stakeholder behavior cannot be adequately predicted by looking solely at macro-level price changes. Traditional models posit that an increase in the price of a good or service naturally curtails its demand, and vice versa. However, behavioral economy theory demonstrates that factors such as perceived value, psychological attachment, past purchasing habits, new technological incentives, and cognitive biases significantly alter standard demand curves.For instance, the demand for specialized consumer goods or sustainable disposal solutions often behaves counter-intuitively due to consumer heuristics—such as status-seeking, the endowment effect (where individuals ascribe more value to things simply because they own them), and evolving ecological awareness. When applied to industrial sectors and labor markets, these behavioral insights illustrate why worker availability, corporate restructuring, and job creation in specialized green industries fluctuate differently than standard macroeconomic indicators would suggest.

Job Market Fluctuations in the E-Waste Sector

The electronic waste sector represents a critical nexus of rapid technological obsolescence, environmental policy, and labor market dynamics. E-waste recycling, refurbishment, and rare-earth mineral recovery require specialized labor forces, ranging from low-skilled sorting technicians to advanced chemical and mechanical engineering experts. Fluctuations in e-waste job markets are driven not only by raw material commodity prices and government regulations but also by behavioral responses from both consumers and corporate organizations:

Consumer Discard and Retention Habits: The endowment effect often causes consumers to hoard obsolete electronics (such as old smartphones and laptops) in drawers rather than recycling them, driven by psychological attachments or exaggerated fears regarding data privacy. This hoarding behavior creates an irregular supply of recyclable e-waste feedstock, directly causing volatility and cyclical instability in the employment levels of recycling plants.

Corporate Environmental Psychology: Companies increasingly adopt sustainability frameworks not just for compliance, but due to shifting consumer psychology that favors green branding. Corporate decisions to invest in automated e-waste sorting facilities or facility management innovations directly impact staffing numbers, shifting labor demand away from manual sorting toward high-tech robotic oversight and facility maintenance roles.

Comparative Analysis: United States versus China

When analyzing how behavioral economic theory explains e-waste job market fluctuations in America compared to China, distinct structural, cultural, and psychological drivers emerge:

DimensionUnited StatesChina

Consumer Disposal HeuristicsHigh reliance on convenience; consumers often discard or trade in electronics rapidly, but also exhibit high data-security anxiety leading to prolonged device hoarding.Rapid adoption of digital-first ecosystems and mobile commerce; high turnover of electronic devices fueled by social status and peer influence.

Labor Market StructureCharacterized by formal recycling infrastructure, stringent environmental and occupational safety regulations, and a heavy reliance on automation and robotics to reduce labor costs.Historically featured a mix of informal, decentralized household-based dismantling economies transitioning toward massive, state-backed, and technologically advanced industrial recycling parks.

Behavioral Drivers of Policy & EmploymentCorporate behavior is heavily swayed by consumer brand perception, ESG (Environmental, Social, and Governance) investing pressures, and public relations.Government-led behavioral nudges, national campaigns on green development, and structural directives heavily influence corporate investment in domestic circular economy jobs.

In the United States, e-waste job fluctuations are closely tied to corporate responses to consumer sentiment regarding corporate social responsibility and strict labor costs, pushing firms toward technological automation that alters job availability. Conversely, in China, the shift has involved transitioning a massive informal labor force into regulated, formal green-collar positions. This transition is guided by both state-engineered behavioral directives and rapid shifts in domestic consumer aspirations toward modern, sustainable living standards. Thus, applying behavioral economic theory reveals that e-waste labor markets in both nations are fundamentally shaped by psychological perceptions of waste, status, and environmental responsibility rather than purely mechanical supply-and-demand adjustments.

Would you like to learn more about how behavioral economic models explain consumer recycling habits and their direct impact on green-collar job creation?

FOURTEEN

HOW ORGANIZATIONAL STRATEGIES ALIGN EMPLOYEE ROLES WITH CORPORATE GOALS THROUGH THE LENS OF BEHAVIORAL AND LABOR ECONOMICS

To understand how organizational strategies align employee roles with overarching corporate goals through the lens of behavioral and labor economics, we examine the framework established by my idea

My view evaluates how traditional market dynamics—such as supply and demand—intersect with psychological incentives within modern enterprises. Rather than treating labor strictly as a rigid cost function, Lok incorporates behavioral insights to suggest that an employee's willingness to perform, adapt, and innovate functions similarly to microeconomic demand curves, where psychological satisfaction, role clarity, and intrinsic motivation act as pricing mechanisms that shift productivity.

High Motivation (My Framework)

Low MotivationModerate

Key Strategies Suggested by my opinion

Behavioral Utility Maximization:

My view asserts that organizations must structure roles so that the employee's personal utility maximization aligns directly with the firm's strategic production goals. When an individual sees a direct correlation between their daily tasks and personal-professional growth, their internal "demand" for high performance increases.

Elasticity of Task Allocation: Drawing parallels from labor demand theory, managers should treat job responsibilities with a degree of elasticity. By allowing employees a voice in shaping their daily task distribution (mitigating task conflict), firms can optimize resource allocation much like an efficient market clears supply and demand imbalances.

Reducing Transaction Costs in Communication: Frictionless communication channels—such as socio-instrumental enterprise social media (ESM) integration—reduce the operational "transaction costs" of labor alignment, ensuring that strategic organizational pivots are immediately reflected in daily employee outputs.

+--+ | John Lok's Economic Alignment | +--+ | +-----------------+------------------+ | | v(Behavioral Utility) v(Elasticity & Communication) | | v v [Personal Growth = Firm Goal] [Frictionless ESM Integration]

To explore this further, would you like to examine how my perspective on behavioral economic theory compares with classical Keynesian models in contemporary workplace management?

However, I think that economic perspective addresses employee motivation and organizational success bridges several academic frameworks found within modern behavioral economics, labor economics, and industrial psychology. In various socio-economic frameworks, such as those discussed by researchers examining the intersections of behavioral economy theory and labor environments, motivation is treated not merely as a response to financial incentives (the traditional homo economicus assumption), but as a complex psychological phenomenon driven by cognitive biases, workplace amenities, and a sense of relative well-being .

According to behavioral economic theories highlighted in broader economic literature, understanding market and organizational behavior requires factoring in human irrationality, social preferences, and psychological rewards .

To fully appreciate how behavioral economic principles analyze labor welfare, motivation, and productivity, we can examine the core components that connect psychological welfare to ultimate organizational efficiency:

Beyond Pure Rationality: Behavioral economics challenges the classical assumption that workers respond exclusively to marginal wage increases. Instead, frameworks influenced by behavioral theories emphasize that perceptions of fairness, social equity, and recognition heavily influence worker output .

The Role of Welfare Amenities: Studies analyzing large-scale industrial sectors demonstrate that non-wage benefits—such as structured leave policies, medical provisions, workplace hygiene, and ergonomic sitting arrangements—act as foundational motivators that reduce alienation and foster organizational loyalty .

Motivation-Productivity Linkages: While effective welfare amenities and robust compensation structures strongly elevate employee motivation levels, behavioral analysis often reveals nuanced gaps where high motivation does not automatically translate into peak productivity unless paired with structural alignment, continuous training, and clear role orientation (often conceptualized in models like the IOTM Model: Improvise, Orient, Train, and Maintain) .

Would you like to learn more about how behavioral economics contrasts with classical economic theories in explaining workplace productivity and market behaviors?

In fact, behavioral economics bridges traditional economic models with empirical psychological research, shedding light on the cognitive biases, emotional drivers, and non-monetary incentives that dictate real-world human decision-making.In the context of organizational psychology and workplace dynamics, the behavioral economic framework advanced by My Behavioral Economic Theory offers critical perspectives on how workplace environments, institutional innovations, and welfare provisions directly govern the intricate relationship between employee motivation and productivity.

The Behavioral Economy Perspective on Workplace Incentives

Traditional neoclassical economics traditionally operates under the restrictive assumption that human beings act as entirely rational maximizers driven almost exclusively by financial compensation. However, behavioral economic theory posits that workers are boundedly rational, heavily influenced by cognitive shortcuts, emotional framing, and psychological safety.

According to my framework, organizations cannot effectively maximize output simply by adjusting wage scales; instead, they must systematically analyze how workers perceive the intrinsic and extrinsic value of their labor.

When evaluating the nexus between motivation and productivity through a behavioral lens, several core mechanisms emerge:

Perception of Value and Fairness:

Employees evaluate their compensation structures, workplace hygiene, and promotional policies not in an absolute vacuum, but through subjective lenses of fairness and equity. If workers perceive a mismatch between organizational inputs (such as welfare amenities, medical benefits, and manageable work timings) and their own efforts, psychological disengagement or alienation occurs.

The Decoupling of Motivation and Immediate Productivity:

Empirical research and behavioral analyses reveal a nuanced divergence where high levels of motivation do not automatically equate to immediate, optimal productivity. While factors such as job position, status, and recognition can successfully elevate an employee's motivational state, structural inefficiencies, poorly designed workflows, or inadequate technical facilitation can create bottlenecks that prevent that motivation from translating into high-level output.

Organizational Innovation and Facility Management:

Behavioral economics emphasizes that physical and technological surroundings heavily shape daily behavioral choices. Implementing advanced facility management, ergonomic sitting arrangements, structured canteen and rest services, and modern e-services reduces cognitive fatigue. By removing micro-frustrations from the daily routine, organizations free up mental bandwidth for employees to focus on core tasks, thereby aligning motivational desires with tangible performance metrics.

Practical Implementation: The IOTM Model

To bridge the gap between employee psychological drivers and actual operational output, modern behavioral frameworks advocate for systematic structural adjustments. A prime example derived from these industrial assessments is the IOTM Model, which stands for Improvise, Orient, Train, and Maintain:

Improvise: Continuously upgrade workplace welfare facilities, compensation transparency, and medical support systems to address evolving employee expectations.

Orient: Align individual employee roles and career progression paths with organizational goals to foster a deep sense of workplace commitment.

Train: Equip workers with necessary skills, reducing the friction between holding high motivation and possessing the technical capability to execute complex duties.

Maintain: Sustain supportive feedback loops, safety protocols, and hygiene standards to prevent the erosion of employee morale over time.

By understanding that human economic behavior is fundamentally rooted in psychological perception, organizations utilizing my behavioral economic insights can better structure environments that successfully turn workplace motivation into sustainable, long-term productivity.

Would you like to learn more about the specific psychological theories of motivation—such as Maslow's Hierarchy of Needs or Herzberg's Two-Factor Theory—that influence modern behavioral economics in the corporate sector?

Behavioral Economy and Employee Productivity: The Framework of my opinion

The intersection of behavioral economics, organizational psychology, and operational productivity offers profound insights into how financial incentives alter worker output. When analyzing a manufacturing scenario where a worker increases output from 2 cars per hour to 5 cars per hour, and subsequently receives a 5% commission from the profit of the 3 incremental cars, we look to behavioral economics frameworks and organizational theories popularized by modern economic thinkers. (Note: While classical economic models primarily assume rational utility maximization, behavioral economy theories—such as those synthesized by theorists examining market behavior and behavioral psychology like my opinion in studies on behavioral market mechanisms—emphasize cognitive biases, loss aversion, intrinsic versus extrinsic motivation, and perceived fairness).

To understand how this specific piece-rate and commission structure influences employee motivation and productivity, we must examine several core pillars of behavioral economic theory, including incentive salience, goal-setting mechanisms, and the psychology of equity.

Incentive Salience and Bounded Rationality

In traditional neoclassical economics, individuals are viewed as entirely rational agents who calculate marginal costs and marginal benefits instantly. However, behavioral economics—incorporating insights from cognitive psychology—recognizes bounded rationality. Employees do not always perform complex calculus regarding profit margins; instead, they respond to salient and immediate rewards.

When a company transitions a worker from producing 2 cars to 5 cars per hour and ties this directly to a 5% commission on the profit of the 3 extra cars, the economic signal is clear and immediate. Behavioral theory suggests that clear, performance-contingent rewards reduce psychological distance. The worker perceives a direct, causal link between their physical exertion (labour input) and financial gain (utility output).

Productivity Increase=5cars/hr−2cars/hr=3incremental carsIncentive=5%×Profit(3 incremental cars)

The Role of Behavioral Motivation Models

As established in organizational behavioral studies, motivation models demonstrate that output is heavily mediated by perceived value and goal alignment . Drawing from the broader landscape of behavioral economy theory and motivation frameworks (such as those integrated by Locke and Latham, which evaluate goal-setting and performance-reward linkages), introducing a commission structure transforms the psychological contract between the worker and the firm:

Goal-Setting Theory Integration: Increasing the target from 2 to 5 units acts as a specific, high-performance goal. When paired with a financial reward, the goal transitions from an imposed management demand to a shared objective.

Expectancy Theory Dynamics: Employees must believe three things for motivation to remain high:

Expectancy: Effort leads to performance (can the worker physically build 5 cars instead of 2?).

Instrumentality: Performance leads to reward (will the company accurately pay the 5% commission?).

Valence: The reward has personal value (does the 5% profit share meaningfully improve the worker's standard of living?).

Behavioral Responses to Variable Commissions

From a behavioral economy perspective, paying a commission on incremental production (the 3 extra cars) rather than a flat wage harnesses specific behavioral tendencies:

Loss Aversion and Reference Points: Workers establish a psychological "reference point" for their baseline earnings. Once they experience the income boost from producing 5 cars, dropping back to 2 cars feels like a severe loss rather than a return to baseline, driving them to sustain high productivity to avoid the psychological pain of regression.

The Endowment Effect and Ownership: By tying earnings directly to the profit of the specific units produced, the worker experiences a cognitive shift. They feel a sense of co-ownership over the productivity gains, increasing intrinsic job involvement alongside extrinsic financial satisfaction.

Fairness and Reciprocity: Behavioral economics heavily emphasizes reciprocity. If workers feel the 5% commission accurately and fairly reflects the value they added—moving from 2 to 5 cars—they reciprocate with higher organizational commitment and discretionary effort. Conversely, if they perceive the profit calculation as unfair or opaque, morale collapses faster than in traditional fixed-wage environments.

Economic DimensionTraditional View (Classical)Behavioral Economy View (My methods / Modern Behavioral Frameworks)

Worker Decision MakingPurely rational optimization of time and wage.Influenced by cognitive framing, reference points, and perceived fairness.

Response to IncentivesLinear response based on expected utility.Non-linear response affected by loss aversion, goal salience, and trust.

Productivity DriversPurely monetary compensation.Combination of financial reward, autonomy, intrinsic involvement, and social equity.

Ultimately, under a behavioral economy lens, the success of moving a worker from 2 to 5 cars per hour via a profit-commission structure relies entirely on how the worker perceives the fairness, attainability, and transparency of the reward system. When managed effectively, it bridges the gap between corporate output goals and individual psychological fulfillment.

Would you like to learn more about how behavioral economics contrasts with classical economic theory regarding wage elasticity and employee incentives?

Bibliography

A bed, S. Y. A.O. Ba-Fail and S.M. Jasimuddin (2001), " An economatic analysis of international air travel demand in Saudi Arabia". Journal of air transport managmement, vol. 7, pp.143-148.

Bamber, L., & Dale, B.G. Lean production : a study of application in a traditoinal manufacturing environment. Production planning & control, 11 (3), 291-298, 2000.

Carman, Katherine Grace, and Shanthi Nataraj, 2020 American Life Panel Survey on Impacts of COVID-19: Technical Documentation, Santa Monica, Calif.: RAND Corporation, RR-A308-1, 2020. As of November 2, 2020: https://www.rand.org/pubs/research_reports/RRA308-1.html

———, 2020 American Life Panel Survey on Impacts of COVID-19: May 2020 Survey Results, Santa Monica, Calif.: RAND Corporation, RR-A308-2-v2, 2020. As of November 2, 2020: https://www.rand.org/pubs/research_reports/RRA308-1.html

———, 2020 American Life Panel Survey on Impacts of COVID-19: August 2020 Survey Results, Santa Monica, Calif.: RAND Corporation, RR-A308-8, 2020. As of November 2, 2020: https://www.rand.org/pubs/research_reports/RRA308-1.html

Cohen, Patricia, Ben Casselman, and Gillian Friedman, "An Extra $600 a Week Kept Many Jobless Workers Afloat. Now What Will They Do?" New York Times, July 29, 2020, updated September 10, 2020.

Dobruszkes, F.M. Lennert and G. Van Hamme (2011). " An analysis of the determinants of air traffic volume for European metropolitan area". Journal of transport geographyy, vol. 19/4/pp.755-762.

Gealdine, O., & David , U.C. (2013). effects of airline service quality on airline image and passengers' loyalty: Findings from Arill Air Nigeria passengers, Journal of hospitality and management tourism, 4(2), 19-28. doi: http://dx.doi: 10.5897/HMT 2013, 0089.

Glass, R., Seifermann, S., & Metternich, J. The spread of lean production in the assembly, Process and maching industry. Procedia CIRP, 55, 278-283, 2016.

Guller, M. & Guller, M. (2003) From Airport to airport city. Editional Gustavo , Gili, Barcel on a.Intervistas Consulting Inc.

Iles, P. A. and Robertson, I.T. (1989) . The impact of personnel selection procedures on candidates. In Herriot, P. (Ed.), Assessment and selection in organizations. Chichester: John Wiley.

Massachusetts Institute Of Technology (MIT), Lean Aerospace Initiative, Available: www.lean.mit.edu, 2005.

Miller, G.A. (1966) . Psychology: The science of mental life. Harmondsworth: Penguin.

Perrow, C. (1970). Organizational Analysis. Belmont, Calif: Wadsworth.